Lecture Notes in Computer Science   8025

Commenced Publication in 1973
Founding and Former Series Editors:
Gerhard Goos, Juris Hartmanis, and Jan van ̶̶̶̶̶̶̶en

Vincent G. Duffy (Ed.)

Digital Human Modeling and Applications in Health, Safety, Ergonomics, and Risk Management

Healthcare and Safety of the Environment and Transport

4th International Conference, DHM 2013
Held as Part of HCI International 2013
Las Vegas, NV, USA, July 21-26, 2013
Proceedings, Part I

 Springer

Volume Editor

Vincent G. Duffy
Purdue University
College of Engineering
West Lafayette, IN 47907-2045, USA
E-mail: duffy@purdue.edu

ISSN 0302-9743   e-ISSN 1611-3349
ISBN 978-3-642-39172-9   e-ISBN 978-3-642-39173-6
DOI 10.1007/978-3-642-39173-6
Springer Heidelberg Dordrecht London New York

Library of Congress Control Number: 2013941252

CR Subject Classification (1998): H.5, J.2, J.3, H.3, H.1, I.6, I.2

LNCS Sublibrary: SL 3 – Information Systems and Application, incl. Internet/Web
and HCI

Typesetting: Camera-ready by author, data conversion by Scientific Publishing Services, Chennai, India

Printed on acid-free paper

Springer is part of Springer Science+Business Media (www.springer.com)

Foreword

The 15th International Conference on Human–Computer Interaction, HCI International 2013, was held in Las Vegas, Nevada, USA, 21–26 July 2013, incorporating 12 conferences / thematic areas:

Thematic areas:

- Human–Computer Interaction
- Human Interface and the Management of Information

Affiliated conferences:

- 10th International Conference on Engineering Psychology and Cognitive Ergonomics
- 7th International Conference on Universal Access in Human–Computer Interaction
- 5th International Conference on Virtual, Augmented and Mixed Reality
- 5th International Conference on Cross-Cultural Design
- 5th International Conference on Online Communities and Social Computing
- 7th International Conference on Augmented Cognition
- 4th International Conference on Digital Human Modeling and Applications in Health, Safety, Ergonomics and Risk Management
- 2nd International Conference on Design, User Experience and Usability
- 1st International Conference on Distributed, Ambient and Pervasive Interactions
- 1st International Conference on Human Aspects of Information Security, Privacy and Trust

A total of 5210 individuals from academia, research institutes, industry and governmental agencies from 70 countries submitted contributions, and 1666 papers and 303 posters were included in the program. These papers address the latest research and development efforts and highlight the human aspects of design and use of computing systems. The papers accepted for presentation thoroughly cover the entire field of Human–Computer Interaction, addressing major advances in knowledge and effective use of computers in a variety of application areas.

This volume, edited by Vincent G. Duffy, contains papers focusing on the thematic area of Digital Human Modeling and Applications in Health, Safety, Ergonomics and Risk Management, and addressing the following major topics:

- Driving and Aviation Safety
- Human Factors and Digital Human Modeling in Healthcare
- Safety of the Human Environment

The remaining volumes of the HCI International 2013 proceedings are:

- Volume 1, LNCS 8004, Human–Computer Interaction: Human-Centred Design Approaches, Methods, Tools and Environments (Part I), edited by Masaaki Kurosu
- Volume 2, LNCS 8005, Human–Computer Interaction: Applications and Services (Part II), edited by Masaaki Kurosu
- Volume 3, LNCS 8006, Human–Computer Interaction: Users and Contexts of Use (Part III), edited by Masaaki Kurosu
- Volume 4, LNCS 8007, Human–Computer Interaction: Interaction Modalities and Techniques (Part IV), edited by Masaaki Kurosu
- Volume 5, LNCS 8008, Human–Computer Interaction: Towards Intelligent and Implicit Interaction (Part V), edited by Masaaki Kurosu
- Volume 6, LNCS 8009, Universal Access in Human–Computer Interaction: Design Methods, Tools and Interaction Techniques for eInclusion (Part I), edited by Constantine Stephanidis and Margherita Antona
- Volume 7, LNCS 8010, Universal Access in Human–Computer Interaction: User and Context Diversity (Part II), edited by Constantine Stephanidis and Margherita Antona
- Volume 8, LNCS 8011, Universal Access in Human–Computer Interaction: Applications and Services for Quality of Life (Part III), edited by Constantine Stephanidis and Margherita Antona
- Volume 9, LNCS 8012, Design, User Experience, and Usability: Design Philosophy, Methods and Tools (Part I), edited by Aaron Marcus
- Volume 10, LNCS 8013, Design, User Experience, and Usability: Health, Learning, Playing, Cultural, and Cross-Cultural User Experience (Part II), edited by Aaron Marcus
- Volume 11, LNCS 8014, Design, User Experience, and Usability: User Experience in Novel Technological Environments (Part III), edited by Aaron Marcus
- Volume 12, LNCS 8015, Design, User Experience, and Usability: Web, Mobile and Product Design (Part IV), edited by Aaron Marcus
- Volume 13, LNCS 8016, Human Interface and the Management of Information: Information and Interaction Design (Part I), edited by Sakae Yamamoto
- Volume 14, LNCS 8017, Human Interface and the Management of Information: Information and Interaction for Health, Safety, Mobility and Complex Environments (Part II), edited by Sakae Yamamoto
- Volume 15, LNCS 8018, Human Interface and the Management of Information: Information and Interaction for Learning, Culture, Collaboration and Business (Part III), edited by Sakae Yamamoto
- Volume 16, LNAI 8019, Engineering Psychology and Cognitive Ergonomics: Understanding Human Cognition (Part I), edited by Don Harris
- Volume 17, LNAI 8020, Engineering Psychology and Cognitive Ergonomics: Applications and Services (Part II), edited by Don Harris
- Volume 18, LNCS 8021, Virtual, Augmented and Mixed Reality: Designing and Developing Augmented and Virtual Environments (Part I), edited by Randall Shumaker

- Volume 19, LNCS 8022, Virtual, Augmented and Mixed Reality: Systems and Applications (Part II), edited by Randall Shumaker
- Volume 20, LNCS 8023, Cross-Cultural Design: Methods, Practice and Case Studies (Part I), edited by P.L. Patrick Rau
- Volume 21, LNCS 8024, Cross-Cultural Design: Cultural Differences in Everyday Life (Part II), edited by P.L. Patrick Rau
- Volume 23, LNCS 8026, Digital Human Modeling and Applications in Health, Safety, Ergonomics and Risk Management: Human Body Modeling and Ergonomics (Part II), edited by Vincent G. Duffy
- Volume 24, LNAI 8027, Foundations of Augmented Cognition, edited by Dylan D. Schmorrow and Cali M. Fidopiastis
- Volume 25, LNCS 8028, Distributed, Ambient and Pervasive Interactions, edited by Norbert Streitz and Constantine Stephanidis
- Volume 26, LNCS 8029, Online Communities and Social Computing, edited by A. Ant Ozok and Panayiotis Zaphiris
- Volume 27, LNCS 8030, Human Aspects of Information Security, Privacy and Trust, edited by Louis Marinos and Ioannis Askoxylakis
- Volume 28, CCIS 373, HCI International 2013 Posters Proceedings (Part I), edited by Constantine Stephanidis
- Volume 29, CCIS 374, HCI International 2013 Posters Proceedings (Part II), edited by Constantine Stephanidis

I would like to thank the Program Chairs and the members of the Program Boards of all affiliated conferences and thematic areas, listed below, for their contribution to the highest scientific quality and the overall success of the HCI International 2013 conference.

This conference could not have been possible without the continuous support and advice of the Founding Chair and Conference Scientific Advisor, Prof. Gavriel Salvendy, as well as the dedicated work and outstanding efforts of the Communications Chair and Editor of HCI International News, Abbas Moallem.

I would also like to thank for their contribution towards the smooth organization of the HCI International 2013 Conference the members of the Human–Computer Interaction Laboratory of ICS-FORTH, and in particular George Paparoulis, Maria Pitsoulaki, Stavroula Ntoa, Maria Bouhli and George Kapnas.

May 2013   Constantine Stephanidis
                                          General Chair, HCI International 2013

Organization

Human–Computer Interaction

Program Chair: Masaaki Kurosu, Japan

Jose Abdelnour-Nocera, UK
Sebastiano Bagnara, Italy
Simone Barbosa, Brazil
Tomas Berns, Sweden
Nigel Bevan, UK
Simone Borsci, UK
Apala Lahiri Chavan, India
Sherry Chen, Taiwan
Kevin Clark, USA
Torkil Clemmensen, Denmark
Xiaowen Fang, USA
Shin'ichi Fukuzumi, Japan
Vicki Hanson, UK
Ayako Hashizume, Japan
Anzai Hiroyuki, Italy
Sheue-Ling Hwang, Taiwan
Wonil Hwang, South Korea
Minna Isomursu, Finland
Yong Gu Ji, South Korea
Esther Jun, USA
Mitsuhiko Karashima, Japan

Kyungdoh Kim, South Korea
Heidi Krömker, Germany
Chen Ling, USA
Yan Liu, USA
Zhengjie Liu, P.R. China
Loïc Martínez Normand, Spain
Chang S. Nam, USA
Naoko Okuizumi, Japan
Noriko Osaka, Japan
Philippe Palanque, France
Hans Persson, Sweden
Ling Rothrock, USA
Naoki Sakakibara, Japan
Dominique Scapin, France
Guangfeng Song, USA
Sanjay Tripathi, India
Chui Yin Wong, Malaysia
Toshiki Yamaoka, Japan
Kazuhiko Yamazaki, Japan
Ryoji Yoshitake, Japan
Silvia Zimmermann, Switzerland

Human Interface and the Management of Information

Program Chair: Sakae Yamamoto, Japan

Hans-Jorg Bullinger, Germany
Alan Chan, Hong Kong
Gilsoo Cho, South Korea
Jon R. Gunderson, USA
Shin'ichi Fukuzumi, Japan
Michitaka Hirose, Japan
Jhilmil Jain, USA
Yasufumi Kume, Japan

Mark Lehto, USA
Hiroyuki Miki, Japan
Hirohiko Mori, Japan
Fiona Fui-Hoon Nah, USA
Shogo Nishida, Japan
Robert Proctor, USA
Youngho Rhee, South Korea
Katsunori Shimohara, Japan

Michale Smith, USA
Tsutomu Tabe, Japan
Hiroshi Tsuji, Japan

Kim-Phuong Vu, USA
Tomio Watanabe, Japan
Hidekazu Yoshikawa, Japan

Engineering Psychology and Cognitive Ergonomics

Program Chair: Don Harris, UK

Guy Andre Boy, USA
Joakim Dahlman, Sweden
Trevor Dobbins, UK
Mike Feary, USA
Shan Fu, P.R. China
Michaela Heese, Austria
Hung-Sying Jing, Taiwan
Wen-Chin Li, Taiwan
Mark A. Neerincx, The Netherlands
Jan M. Noyes, UK
Taezoon Park, Singapore

Paul Salmon, Australia
Axel Schulte, Germany
Siraj Shaikh, UK
Sarah C. Sharples, UK
Anthony Smoker, UK
Neville A. Stanton, UK
Alex Stedmon, UK
Xianghong Sun, P.R. China
Andrew Thatcher, South Africa
Matthew J.W. Thomas, Australia
Rolf Zon, The Netherlands

Universal Access in Human–Computer Interaction

Program Chairs: Constantine Stephanidis, Greece, and Margherita Antona, Greece

Julio Abascal, Spain
Ray Adams, UK
Gisela Susanne Bahr, USA
Margit Betke, USA
Christian Bühler, Germany
Stefan Carmien, Spain
Jerzy Charytonowicz, Poland
Carlos Duarte, Portugal
Pier Luigi Emiliani, Italy
Qin Gao, P.R. China
Andrina Granić, Croatia
Andreas Holzinger, Austria
Josette Jones, USA
Simeon Keates, UK

Georgios Kouroupetroglou, Greece
Patrick Langdon, UK
Seongil Lee, Korea
Ana Isabel B.B. Paraguay, Brazil
Helen Petrie, UK
Michael Pieper, Germany
Enrico Pontelli, USA
Jaime Sanchez, Chile
Anthony Savidis, Greece
Christian Stary, Austria
Hirotada Ueda, Japan
Gerhard Weber, Germany
Harald Weber, Germany

Virtual, Augmented and Mixed Reality

Program Chair: Randall Shumaker, USA

Waymon Armstrong, USA
Juan Cendan, USA
Rudy Darken, USA
Cali M. Fidopiastis, USA
Charles Hughes, USA
David Kaber, USA
Hirokazu Kato, Japan
Denis Laurendeau, Canada
Fotis Liarokapis, UK

Mark Livingston, USA
Michael Macedonia, USA
Gordon Mair, UK
Jose San Martin, Spain
Jacquelyn Morie, USA
Albert "Skip" Rizzo, USA
Kay Stanney, USA
Christopher Stapleton, USA
Gregory Welch, USA

Cross-Cultural Design

Program Chair: P.L. Patrick Rau, P.R. China

Pilsung Choe, P.R. China
Henry Been-Lirn Duh, Singapore
Vanessa Evers, The Netherlands
Paul Fu, USA
Zhiyong Fu, P.R. China
Fu Guo, P.R. China
Sung H. Han, Korea
Toshikazu Kato, Japan
Dyi-Yih Michael Lin, Taiwan
Rungtai Lin, Taiwan

Sheau-Farn Max Liang, Taiwan
Liang Ma, P.R. China
Alexander Mädche, Germany
Katsuhiko Ogawa, Japan
Tom Plocher, USA
Kerstin Röse, Germany
Supriya Singh, Australia
Hsiu-Ping Yueh, Taiwan
Liang (Leon) Zeng, USA
Chen Zhao, USA

Online Communities and Social Computing

Program Chairs: A. Ant Ozok, USA, and Panayiotis Zaphiris, Cyprus

Areej Al-Wabil, Saudi Arabia
Leonelo Almeida, Brazil
Bjørn Andersen, Norway
Chee Siang Ang, UK
Aneesha Bakharia, Australia
Ania Bobrowicz, UK
Paul Cairns, UK
Farzin Deravi, UK
Andri Ioannou, Cyprus
Slava Kisilevich, Germany

Niki Lambropoulos, Greece
Effie Law, Switzerland
Soo Ling Lim, UK
Fernando Loizides, Cyprus
Gabriele Meiselwitz, USA
Anthony Norcio, USA
Elaine Raybourn, USA
Panote Siriaraya, UK
David Stuart, UK
June Wei, USA

Augmented Cognition

Program Chairs: Dylan D. Schmorrow, USA, and Cali M. Fidopiastis, USA

Robert Arrabito, Canada
Richard Backs, USA
Chris Berka, USA
Joseph Cohn, USA
Martha E. Crosby, USA
Julie Drexler, USA
Ivy Estabrooke, USA
Chris Forsythe, USA
Wai Tat Fu, USA
Rodolphe Gentili, USA
Marc Grootjen, The Netherlands
Jefferson Grubb, USA
Ming Hou, Canada

Santosh Mathan, USA
Rob Matthews, Australia
Dennis McBride, USA
Jeff Morrison, USA
Mark A. Neerincx, The Netherlands
Denise Nicholson, USA
Banu Onaral, USA
Lee Sciarini, USA
Kay Stanney, USA
Roy Stripling, USA
Rob Taylor, UK
Karl van Orden, USA

Digital Human Modeling and Applications in Health, Safety, Ergonomics and Risk Management

Program Chair: Vincent G. Duffy, USA and Russia

Karim Abdel-Malek, USA
Giuseppe Andreoni, Italy
Daniel Carruth, USA
Eliza Yingzi Du, USA
Enda Fallon, Ireland
Afzal Godil, USA
Ravindra Goonetilleke, Hong Kong
Bo Hoege, Germany
Waldemar Karwowski, USA
Zhizhong Li, P.R. China

Kang Li, USA
Tim Marler, USA
Michelle Robertson, USA
Matthias Rötting, Germany
Peter Vink, The Netherlands
Mao-Jiun Wang, Taiwan
Xuguang Wang, France
Jingzhou (James) Yang, USA
Xiugan Yuan, P.R. China
Gülcin Yücel Hoge, Germany

Design, User Experience, and Usability

Program Chair: Aaron Marcus, USA

Sisira Adikari, Australia
Ronald Baecker, Canada
Arne Berger, Germany
Jamie Blustein, Canada

Ana Boa-Ventura, USA
Jan Brejcha, Czech Republic
Lorenzo Cantoni, Switzerland
Maximilian Eibl, Germany

Anthony Faiola, USA
Emilie Gould, USA
Zelda Harrison, USA
Rüdiger Heimgärtner, Germany
Brigitte Herrmann, Germany
Steffen Hess, Germany
Kaleem Khan, Canada

Jennifer McGinn, USA
Francisco Rebelo, Portugal
Michael Renner, Switzerland
Kerem Rızvanoğlu, Turkey
Marcelo Soares, Brazil
Christian Sturm, Germany
Michele Visciola, Italy

Distributed, Ambient and Pervasive Interactions

Program Chairs: Norbert Streitz, Germany, and Constantine Stephanidis, Greece

Emile Aarts, The Netherlands
Adnan Abu-Dayya, Qatar
Juan Carlos Augusto, UK
Boris de Ruyter, The Netherlands
Anind Dey, USA
Dimitris Grammenos, Greece
Nuno M. Guimaraes, Portugal
Shin'ichi Konomi, Japan
Carsten Magerkurth, Switzerland

Christian Müller-Tomfelde, Australia
Fabio Paternó, Italy
Gilles Privat, France
Harald Reiterer, Germany
Carsten Röcker, Germany
Reiner Wichert, Germany
Woontack Woo, South Korea
Xenophon Zabulis, Greece

Human Aspects of Information Security, Privacy and Trust

Program Chairs: Louis Marinos, ENISA EU, and Ioannis Askoxylakis, Greece

Claudio Agostino Ardagna, Italy
Zinaida Benenson, Germany
Daniele Catteddu, Italy
Raoul Chiesa, Italy
Bryan Cline, USA
Sadie Creese, UK
Jorge Cuellar, Germany
Marc Dacier, USA
Dieter Gollmann, Germany
Kirstie Hawkey, Canada
Jaap-Henk Hoepman, The Netherlands
Cagatay Karabat, Turkey
Angelos Keromytis, USA
Ayako Komatsu, Japan

Ronald Leenes, The Netherlands
Javier Lopez, Spain
Steve Marsh, Canada
Gregorio Martinez, Spain
Emilio Mordini, Italy
Yuko Murayama, Japan
Masakatsu Nishigaki, Japan
Aljosa Pasic, Spain
Milan Petković, The Netherlands
Joachim Posegga, Germany
Jean-Jacques Quisquater, Belgium
Damien Sauveron, France
George Spanoudakis, UK
Kerry-Lynn Thomson, South Africa

Julien Touzeau, France
Theo Tryfonas, UK
João Vilela, Portugal

Claire Vishik, UK
Melanie Volkamer, Germany

External Reviewers

Maysoon Abulkhair, Saudi Arabia
Ilia Adami, Greece
Vishal Barot, UK
Stephan Böhm, Germany
Vassilis Charissis, UK
Francisco Cipolla-Ficarra, Spain
Maria De Marsico, Italy
Marc Fabri, UK
David Fonseca, Spain
Linda Harley, USA
Yasushi Ikei, Japan
Wei Ji, USA
Nouf Khashman, Canada
John Killilea, USA
Iosif Klironomos, Greece
Ute Klotz, Switzerland
Maria Korozi, Greece
Kentaro Kotani, Japan

Vassilis Kouroumalis, Greece
Stephanie Lackey, USA
Janelle LaMarche, USA
Asterios Leonidis, Greece
Nickolas Macchiarella, USA
George Margetis, Greece
Matthew Marraffino, USA
Joseph Mercado, USA
Claudia Mont'Alvão, Brazil
Yoichi Motomura, Japan
Karsten Nebe, Germany
Stavroula Ntoa, Greece
Martin Osen, Austria
Stephen Prior, UK
Farid Shirazi, Canada
Jan Stelovsky, USA
Sarah Swierenga, USA

HCI International 2014

The 16th International Conference on Human–Computer Interaction, HCI International 2014, will be held jointly with the affiliated conferences in the summer of 2014. It will cover a broad spectrum of themes related to Human–Computer Interaction, including theoretical issues, methods, tools, processes and case studies in HCI design, as well as novel interaction techniques, interfaces and applications. The proceedings will be published by Springer. More information about the topics, as well as the venue and dates of the conference, will be announced through the HCI International Conference series website: http://www.hci-international.org/

General Chair
Professor Constantine Stephanidis
University of Crete and ICS-FORTH
Heraklion, Crete, Greece
Email: cs@ics.forth.gr

Table of Contents – Part I

Driving and Aviation Safety

Human Factors and Digital Human Modeling in Healthcare

Safety of the Human Environment

Table of Contents – Part II

Digital Human Modeling and Ergonomics in Working Environments

Ergonomics of Work with Computers

Anthropometry, Posture and Motion Modeling

Part I
Driving and Aviation Safety

Human Centered Design of a Pre-collision System

Hirofumi Aoki [1], Hiroyuki Takahashi [1], Satoshi Udaka[1], Toshinori Okita[1],
Hiroyasu Ichida [1], and Masami Aga[2]

[1] Toyota Motor Corporation, Japan
`hiro@a.tec.toyota.co.jp, ud@ka.tec.toyota.co.jp,`
`{taka,okita}@mail.tec.toyota.co.jp,`
`hiroyasu@ichida.tec.toyota.co.jp`
[2] Toyota Motor North America, USA
`Masami_Aga@toyota.com`

Abstract. Human error such as distraction and inattention while driving is one of the major causes of the rear-end collisions. In order to help reduce those accidents, a pre-collision system (PCS) has been developed and spread. A PCS basically consists of the warning, the brake-assist, and the autonomous brake functions. The total effectiveness of the system depends on not only the autonomous brake performance but also the driver's reaction to the warning and the braking maneuver. Earlier activation timing can make the system more effective in terms of collision mitigation/avoidance; however, the drivers may feel nuisance if the timing is too early. Thus, human factors issue should be considered in designing and evaluating a PCS. This paper describesthe human-centered design of a PCS from object recognition to the effectiveness estimation method.

Keywords: Pre-Collision System, Perceptual Risk Estimate, Safety Impact Methodology.

1   Introduction

Rear-end collision is one of the major accident types in many countries (Fig. 1). It was reported that more than 60% of the rear-end collisions were caused by such human errors as distraction and inattention [1]. In order to help reduce those accidents, a pre-collision system (PCS) has been developed and spread [2, 3].

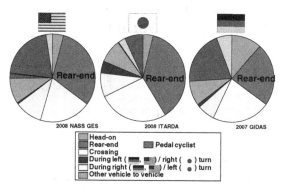

Fig. 1. Accident types in the US, Japan, and Germany

V.G. Duffy (Ed.): DHM/HCII 2013, Part I, LNCS 8025, pp. 3–10, 2013.
© Springer-Verlag Berlin Heidelberg 2013

A PCS basically consists of a forward sensing system, brake control system, and electronic control unit (ECU) to determine activation timing based on the information from the frontal sensor (Fig. 2).

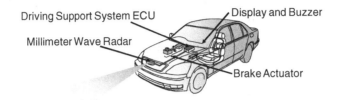

Driving Support System ECU

Millimeter Wave Radar

Display and Buzzer

Brake Actuator

Fig. 2. A basic PCS configuration

A basic PCS is defined as having three functions: 1. warning, 2. brake assist, and 3. autonomous braking (Fig. 3).

1. Warning: The warning will be provided by using a display device and buzzers when the system determines the increase of collision risk to the obstacle in front of the vehicle. The warning is expected to trigger the driver's action for collision mitigation or avoidance.
2. Pre-collision Brake Assist (PBA): A conventional Brake Assist (BA) system boosts the braking force when the brake pedal is hit rapidly, whereas the PBA is immediately activated to supplement driver's braking force to reduce the collision speed or avoid collision once the PCS determines that a collision is probable.
3. Pre-collision Brake (PB): When the system determines collision is highly possible or unavoidable, autonomous braking (PB) is activated to decelerate the vehicle regardless of driver's operation. PB can work together with PBA.

Advanced PCSs have more features and functionalities such as pedestrian detection and driver monitoring functions.

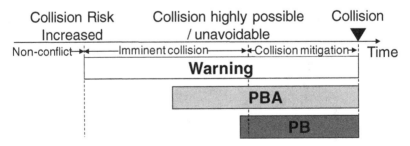

Fig. 3. Functions of a basic PCS

In the advanced driver assistance systems, one might imagine that the warning to the driver would be unnecessary if any rear-end collision was avoidable by the autonomous braking. However, due to the characteristic of the braking and steering avoidance maneuvers as described in the next chapter, the driver's steering avoidance maneuver could be intervened by the autonomous braking in a certain velocity area. Thus, human factors of the driving maneuvers should be considered in order to help mitigate/avoid rear-end collisions without intervention. The next chapter deals with the human-centered design of a PCS.

2   Human Centered Design of a PCS

2.1   The Relation between Braking and Steering Avoidance Maneuvers

The relation between braking and steering avoidance maneuver timing has been studied previously [4, 5, 6].It was found that the braking avoidance maneuver timing is later than the steering one in low relative velocity between the preceding and subject vehicles, therefore, the autonomous braking will not intervene in the driver's steering avoidance maneuver (Fig. 4). In fact, the autonomous braking system works in low velocity without any notice to the driver in advance is commercially available recently.

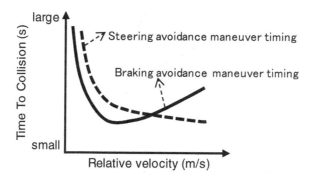

Fig. 4. Steering and braking avoidance maneuver timings

On the other hand, the avoidance maneuver timing of braking is earlier than that of steering in high relative velocity. Rear-end collisions cannot always be avoidable by the autonomous braking if you care about the intervention in the driver's steering maneuver when the relative lateral movement occurs between the preceding and subject vehicles; e.g., the faster subject vehicle overtakes the slower preceding vehicle or the subject vehicle turns whereas the preceding vehicle stops at the intersection [7]. Thus, the characteristics of steering and braking maneuvers should be considered for the object recognition, warning, PBA, and PB functions.

2.2   Object Recognition

A PCS has to determine a preceding vehicle or obstacles in front of the subject vehicle with a front-mounted sensor such as a millimeter-wave radar or a camera. As described in the previous section, it is necessary to consider the characteristic of the braking and steering avoidance maneuver for object recognition.

For a preceding vehicle, a driver usually keeps some distance; distance for reaction and deceleration, and headway offset. For obstacles outside the path (e.g., guardrails and poles), however, the driver only keeps distance to avoid them by steering maneuver. Object detection can be done by judging the subject vehicle's velocity, steering angle, yaw rate, and/or lane/object recognition.

Figure 5 shows an example of the object recognition based on the lateral acceleration (Gy). A PCS can be activate for the objects within the "keep out" zone during the normal driving.

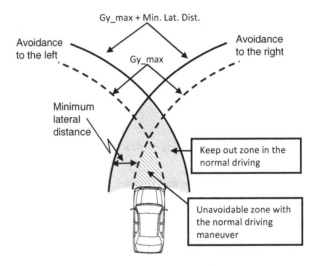

Fig. 5. Example of the object recognition by the lateral acceleration

2.3   Warning

Earlier the warning can be given, more effective the system can be. However, too early warning may cause a nuisance because the driver may not feel any avoidance maneuver is necessary at the timing. The system will be acceptable without nuisance if the system can estimate the driver's state/intention towards driving.

Hattori et al. [8] developed a warning system that utilizes driver's facial direction. The warning timing will become earlier when the system detects the driver looking aside for a certain period. Later, the system has evolved to detect the eyelid movement [9]. The system covers the situation when the driver closes their eyes due to drowsiness even though the facial direction is straight ahead.

It is assumed that drivers usually judge their braking avoidance maneuver timing based onthe perceptual proximity risk. Drivers' state can also be estimated by their braking avoidance maneuver timing if there is a useful index to show the perceptual proximity risk.

Aoki et al.[10] have developed an index of the driver's Perceptual Risk Estimate (PRE) of longitudinal direction (1).

$$\frac{Vr + \alpha Vs + \beta(Ap + Af)}{D^n} = PRE \qquad (1)$$

Where,

D: Relative distance(m)
n: Perceptual scaling of distance
Vs: Subject Vehicle speed (m/s)
Vr: Relative velocity (m/s)
Ap: Acceleration of lead vehicle (m/s2)
Af: Estimated deceleration (m/s2)
α: Sensitivity to subject vehicle speed
β: Sensitivity to deceleration (s)
PRE: Perception risk estimate

The index is formulated as "perceptual relative velocity" divided by "perceptual distance." Both elements are corrected from their physical value so as to reflect their perceptual magnitude. The model was evaluatedon the proving ground andalso on the public road. It was found that drivers' brake timings were well matched to the model; subjects braked when the proposed index reached a certain threshold. Thus, the PRE was tested asa PCS warning and found that it can distinguish nuisance alarm (false positive) and correct alarm (true positive) (Fig. 6).

It is indicated by the previous studies that the normal maneuver timing varies by the driver and the environment [11, 12].Such differences between/within the driver should also be considered for designing a receptive system. A method to predict the car-following tendency by such parameters as the throttle-pedal released timing and the braking timing is proposed to adjust the warning timing [13].

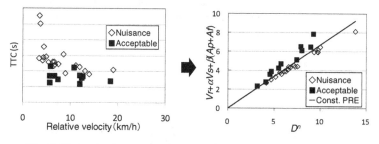

Fig. 6. Distinction between nuisance and acceptable warning by PRE

2.4   Brake Assist

Similar to the warning, the brake assist timing and the assist force should also be designed not to disturb or give incongruous brake feeling to the driver. The brake assist force can be determined by the timing after the warning is given, the speed when the brake pedal is depressed, and the time to collision (Fig. 7).

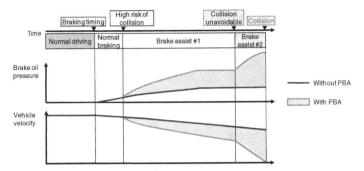

Fig. 7. Diagram of the Pre-collision Brake Assist (PBA) function

2.5   Autonomous Brake

Autonomous brake is like a double-edged sword: early correct brake will decrease much vehicle speed, i.e., collision impact or chance to avoid collision. However, the driver and even the driver in the following vehicle may be surprised if false brake is applied. Considering such a situation, autonomous brake is often initiated by the partial braking, followed by the full braking based on the proximity to the preceding vehicle. The partial braking also helps enhance the steering effort to avoid obstacles in front of the vehicle by the downward load on the front tires.

3   PCS Effectiveness Estimation

Since the benefit of each function is influenced by drivers' reaction before collision, it is difficult to estimate quantitative effectiveness of the PCS. Such drivers' reaction as the response time to the warning and the braking force by the drivers has been taken into account in the recent studies for the effectiveness estimation of a PCS [14, 15, 16].

Aoki et al. [14] proposed a safety impact methodology for the effectiveness estimation of a PCS by utilizing drivers' reaction obtained by the driving simulator (DS) test and Event Data Recorder (EDR) data.

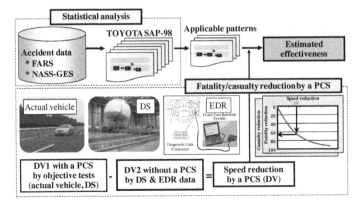

Fig. 8. Toyota-SIM for the PCS effectiveness estimation

The effectiveness can be estimated by comparing the speed reduction with and without a PCS. The speed reaction WITH a PCS was estimated by drivers' maneuvering data for rear-endcollision scenario of a DS test. A vehicle brake model measured on the proving ground and a PCS function model was numerically applied to the DS data. On the other hand, the speed reaction WITHOUT a PCS was estimated by the drivers' maneuver obtained by actual accident from EDR data. By changing the parameters of the PCS model, this method enables us to examine the influence of the system parameters on the effectiveness quantitatively.

4   Conclusion

In order to enhance the effectiveness of advanced driver assistance systems with drivers' acceptance, it is important to consider the system without disturbing their maneuvers. In this paper, we described human aspects for designing and evaluating a PCS as an example. Rear-end collision is one of the simplest form of traffic accidents. There are still a lot of human factors issues to be studied towards minimizing traffic accidents, injuries, and fatalities in the future.

References

1. Knipling, R., Mironer, D., Hendricks, D., Tijeripa, L., Everson, J., Allen, J., Wilson, A.: Assessment of IVHS Countermeasures for Collision Avoidance: Rear-End Crashes, DOT HS 807 995 (1993)
2. Yamada, Y., Tokoro, T., Fujita, Y.: Development of a 60 GHz radar for rear-end collision avoidance. In: Proc. Intelligent Vehicles Symposium 1994, pp. 207–212 (1994)
3. Tokoro, S., Kuroda, K., Kawakubo, A., Fujita, K., Fujinami, H.: Electronically scanned millimeter-wave radar for pre-crash safety and adaptive cruise control sys-tem. In: Proc. Intelligent Vehicles Symposium 2003, pp. 304–309 (2003)
4. Smith, D.L., Najm, W.G., Lam, A.H.: Analysis of Braking and Steering Performance in Car-Following Scenarios. In: SAE 2003-01-0283 (2003)
5. Kiefer, R.J., LeBlanc, D.J., Flannagan, C.A.: Developing an inverse time-to-collision crash alert timing approachbased on drivers' last-second braking and steering judgments. Accident Anal. Prev. 37, 295–303 (2005)
6. Nguyen Van, Q.H., Aoki, H., Inuzuka, Y.: A Study on Relation between Steering and Braking Timings Based on Longitudinal Collision Risk Perception. In: Proc. 18th ITS World Congress (2011)
7. Bogenrieder, R., Fehring, M., Bachmann, R.: PRE-SAFE in rear-end collision situations. In: Proc. 21st Enhanced Safety of Vehicles Conference, Paper Number 09-0129, pp. 9–129 (2011), http://www-nrd.nhtsa.dot.gov/pdf/esv/esv21/09-0129.pdf
8. Hattori, A., Tokoro, S., Miyashita, M., Tanaka, I., Ohue, K.: Development of Forward Collision Warning System using the Driver Behavioral Information. In: Proc. SAE 2006 World Congress, SAE Technical Paper 2006-01-1462 (2006)
9. Nishina, T., Moriizumi, K., Ohue, K., Uozumi, S., Kimura, K., Nakagoshi, A., Suzuki, T., Adachi, J.: Development of A New Pre-Crash Safety System. In: Proc. 15th World Congress on Intelligent Transport Systems and ITS America's 2008 Annual Meeting (2008)

10. Aoki, H., Nguyen Van, Q.H., Yasuda, H.: Perceptual risk estimate (PRE): an index of the longitudinal risk estimate. In: Proc. 22nd Enhanced Safety of Vehicles Conference, Paper Number 11-0121 (2011), http://www-nrd.nhtsa.dot.gov/pdf/esv/esv22/22ESV-000121.pdf

11. McCall, J.C., Trivedi, M.: Driver Behavior and Situation Aware Brake Assistance for Intelligent Vehicles. Proc. IEEE 95(2), 374–387 (2007)

12. Kurahashi, T., Okuwa, M., Sakaguchi, Y., Nagiri, S., Seguchi, H., Obinata, G.: Analysis of Usual Drivers' Decelerating Behavior on Public Roads. Trans. JSAE 39(2), 363–368 (2008)

13. Aoki, H., Ozaki, O.: Development of a Car-Following Tendency Prediction Method and Its Application to a Forward Collision Warning System. In: Proc. 20th World Congress (2013) (accepted for publication)

14. Aoki, H., et al.: Safety Impact Methodology (SIM) for Effectiveness Estimation of a Pre-Collision System (PCS) by Utilizing Driving Simulator Test and EDR Data Analysis. In: SAE-2010-01-1003 (2010)

15. Yasuda, H., Kozato, A., Tanaka, S., Mochida, T., Tajima, J.: A Generative Approach to Estimate Effects of Safety Systems for Rear-end Collisions Using ASSTREET. In: Proc. 22nd Enhanced Safety of Vehicles Conference, Paper Number 11-0067 (2011), http://www-nrd.nhtsa.dot.gov/pdf/esv/esv22/22ESV-000067.pdf

16. Kusano, K., Gabler, H.C.: Potential Effectiveness of Integrated Forward Collision Warning, Pre-collision Brake Assist, and Automated Pre-collision Braking Systems in Real-world, Rear-end Collisions. In: Proc. 22nd Enhanced Safety of Vehicles Conference, Paper Number 11-0364 (2011), http://www-nrd.nhtsa.dot.gov/pdf/esv/esv22/22ESV-000364.pdf

Causal Attribution and Control: Between Consciousness and Psychical Half-Shadow Application to Flight Operations

Bruno Berberian, Jean-Cristophe Sarrazin, and Laurent Chaudron

Systems Control and Flight Dynamics Department, ONERA, Salon de Provence, France
bruno.berberian@onera.fr

Abstract. The key of the development of HMI technologies lies in the acquisition of knowledge and the integration of disciplines by industrials that are in the scope of cognitive neurosciences. The purpose of this paper is to provide new models to be applied in human centered design loops for cockpit in aeronautics. Two different problems are introduced: (1) the purpose of consciousness in action control, (2) the transformation induced by automation in term of agency. For each of this problem, we detail how the problem is currently tackled by cognitive ergonomics society, and how neurosciences could help in the comprehension of the different mechanisms involved. Perspectives are proposed for each of this issue.

Keywords: Action Control, Agency, Automation, Cognition, Consciousness.

1 Introduction

In the 21st century, one of the most significant challenges with most cockpit design is human error. However, "human error" is a misleading expression that has too often been used to sweep away the real issues under the rug. It further suggests that pilots are careless, poorly trained, or otherwise unreliable, whereas in fact numerous studies in the field of human factors in aeronautics have now demonstrated that the vast majority of so-called "human errors" result from the challenges involved in understanding and in controlling poorly designed interfaces.

Why pilots have trouble coping with technology remains a crucial problem. In this paper, we defend the argument that the recent findings in neurosciences could help to resolve this problem. Indeed, the key to the development of HMI technologies lies in the acquisition of knowledge and in the integration of different disciplines such as cognitive psychology and the neurosciences by industrials. Effective technologies for Human Machine Interaction (HMI) must be informed by knowledge generated by recent advances in cognitive neuroscience in order to meet current application and industrial challenges.

In the following sections, two different problems will be introduced: (1) the purpose of consciousness in action control, (2) the transformation induced by automation in term of agency. For each of this problem, we will detail how the problem is

V.G. Duffy (Ed.): DHM/HCII 2013, Part I, LNCS 8025, pp. 11–20, 2013.

currently tackled by cognitive ergonomics society, and how neurosciences could help in the comprehension of the different mechanisms involved.

2   Consciousness and Action Control

Pilots routinely have to cope with hugely demanding complex systems, and thus continuously face both data and technology overload. Occasionally, this cognitive overload results in failure to cope. Ironically, the response to such human failures to cope has almost always resulted in the development of even more complex procedures and safeguards, which paradoxically increase the very complexity that caused the initial failure. Thus, the pilot is but the tip of a technological iceberg built from layers and layers of accumulated suboptimal solutions to problems that are the resultant of inadequate human interface designs. In this context, a first question refers to human ability to process the vast amount of data in which they are immersed so as to arrive at effective performance. Particularly, this section aims at tackling the role of consciousness in this process.

2.1   Human Factors Approach: Endsley Model

Questions about the function(s) of consciousness have long been, and are always, central to discussions. In the field of Human Factors and Ergonomics, it is admitted that consciousness plays an important role in the control of many everyday — but complex — behaviours. The recent introduction of the theory of Situation Awareness (Endsley, 1995) aims at explaining the relationship between human agents and the technologies they interact with by considering consciousness as a central determinant of controlled action. Endsley' model of reference stands situation awareness as an instantaneous state of knowledge of the world that can be splitted in several hierarchical levels where the first constitutes the core from which the following one depends. In this model, situation awareness determines, in an independent and serial way, decision making and action, and does not take into account affordances and action capabilities. This theoretical model is also the basis of a normative design and evaluation approach in which situation awareness has to be the most complete and reliable as possible considering an absolute reference. If an inadequate situation awareness is considered as one of the main factors in accidents attributed to human error, on the opposite it is assessed that a complete and accurate situation awareness is crutial when human actions are required in the control of technological complexity. Thus, situation awareness is defined as the most important factor to improve mission efficiency. For the two last decades, this theory has served as the foundation of a normative design and evaluation approach in the design of HMI.

Nowadays, and particularly thanks to some recent works in the field of neurosciences (but for all that neglecting the importance of older studies from Gestalt or Soviet psychology), this model is strongly controverted. To go back the expression from Amalberti (1996), "the serial model perception-understanding-anticipation-decision-action, that supposes a one way top-down dependency is disarmingly naïve and it exists a parallelism and interdependencies that are amplified by expertise".

2.2   Insight from Neurosciences: The Role of Implicit Processes

Consciousness is perhaps the oldest and most controversial area within experimental psychology. Quite quickly, however, observations in both the laboratory and the clinic suggested that mental life is not limited to conscious experience. Kihlstrom, Barnhardt, and Tataryn (1992) suggested that an experiment examining unconscious perception done by C.S. Peirce and Joseph Jastrow in 1884 was the first psychological experiment performed in America. Peirce and Jastrow's experiment, in which they themselves were the subjects, concerned people's ability to discriminate minute differences in the pressure placed on their fingertips. The task amounted to deciding which of two pressures was the heavier and then rating confidence in that decision. Peirce and Jastrow's results demonstrated that discrimination was at an above-chance level even when conditions were such that they considered their decisions to be pure guesses, suggesting a possible dissociation between effects in performance and awareness. There is now a body of evidence suggesting that it is indeed true. Neuroscientists have proved that the brain can represent and process some information outside the focus of attention or below the level of awareness (see for instance Debner & Jacoby, 1994; Destrebecqz & Cleeremans, 2001; Dienes & Perner, 1999; Greenwald, Abrams, Naccache, & Dehaene, 2003; Merikle, Smilek, & Eastwood, 2001). In this context, it is becoming increasingly common for scientists to argue that we 'know more than we can tell' in most of the situations of our everyday life, including language acquisition and use as well as skill learning in general, perception and memory.

The role of consciousness in action control has also been largely debated. A significant body of data emerging from cognitive neuroscience have shown that conscious experience is not involved in the control of behavior (e.g., Fourneret & Jeannerod, 1998; Goodale, Pelisson, & Prablanc, 1986). Famous examples involve pictorial illusions, particularly size-contrast illusions. Aglioti and colleagues (Aglioti, Desouza & Goodale, 1995), for example, showed that the scaling of grip aperture in flight was remarkably insensitive to the Ebbinghaus illusion, in which a target disk surrounded by smaller circles appears to be larger than the same disk surrounded by larger circles (Figure 1). Maximum grip aperture was scaled to the real not the apparent size of the target disk. According to these theorists, conscious experience serves the selection of action types, while the control of 'online' guided action proceeds via a quasi-independent non-conscious route (Milner & Goodale, 1995).

More recently, and in response to such claims, critics from an intermediate position have suggested that the image of 'zombie systems' guiding action fails to take into account the possibility that there is genuine experience occurring and controlling the actions (Jackson & Shaw, 2000). In this context, some investigators have reported that pictorial illusions affect some (but not all) aspects of motor control (e.g., Gentilucci et al., 1996; Franz, Bulthoff & Fahle, 2003), whereas others have not found any dissociation between the illusions and the scaling of grip aperture (e.g., Plodowski & Jackson, 2001). Such findings cast doubt on the dissociation between conscious experience and motor control. The complexity of this issue increases furthermore when considering that (1) time plays a central role in consciousness, at different levels and in different aspects of information processing (e.g., Cleeremans & Sarrazin, 2007); and (2) different forms of awareness arise when an unexpected event occurs versus when controlling routine actions (e.g., Block, 2005).

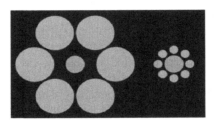

Fig. 1. Ebbinghaus illusion

In this context, it seems crucial to answer the following question: What is the role of consciousness in the control of action whether it concerns routines or some forms of adaptations to unexpected events? The next section provides our appraoch of this complex problem.

2.3   Integration of Neurosciences Issues for HMI Design

We propose a radically different model of situation awareness as it applies to human centered design loops for cockpit interaction in aeronautics. This model is rooted in the idea that the best manner through which human-machine interactions can be improved consists not in increasing situation awareness but rather in removing awareness from the dynamical loops that take place during interactions. In other words, one should strive to make such interactions as implicit, automatized, and thus self-evident as possible. In this frame, situation awareness intervenes only when an unexpected event occurs and is centered on a problem; a situation very well explained by Leroy-Gouhran (1964) with the concept of *"psychical half-shadow"* when he indicates " *it is certain that most of the chains that we unroll the whole day ask for only little consciousness... it takes place in a psychical half-shadow out of which the subject only comes when unexpected events appear in the time course of sequences. For all the movements we make successively while shaving, eating, writing, driving, the return to consciousness, even exceptional, is very important... one can neither imagine a behaviour asking for a continuous lucidity, nor a totally conditioned behaviour without any conscious intervention; the former would ask for a re-invention of every part of the smallest movement, the latter would correspond to a totally pre-conditioned brain"*.

Our (dynamical) approach considers the implicit recognition of significative patterns for action as a basic solution to the problem of the synchronization between activity and environment. In this context, modelling the frontier between conscious and non conscious processing and identifying the computational principles that govern the passage of a representation in the field of consciousness, would be particularly useful for HMI designers who needs to master when an interaction has to be cognitively controlled and when it has to be unrolled in a routine. Two basic questions has to be considered: (1) how conscious awareness enables control on our own actions, (2) how representations become conscious for or as a result of high level processing, These twin questions are crucial questions about which HMI designers need to have technological solutions. We will tackle these two questions by conducting relevant experiments, first in a simplified laboratory environment, and then in a cockpit simulation, in order to identify the computationnal principles that define the boundary between conscious and non-conscious control exerted by operators (i.e., a pilot) in a complex technological system (i.e., an aircraft).

Concerning the first question, a major motivation to integrate such considerations in human-system interaction engineering for the control of complex technological systems stems from the emerging consensus about the function of so-called access consciousness (A-consciousness). A-consciousness refers to our ability to report and act on our experiences. For a person to be in an A-conscious state entails that there is a representation in that person's brain whose content is available for high-level processes such as conscious judgment and reasoning. As there is wide agreement around the idea that conscious representations serve the function of making it possible for an agent to exert flexible, adaptive control over action, the characterization of this function is critical in the specific context of cockpit interactions design.

With regards to the conditions that determine the access to consciousness, which is connected with the second question, several findings converge to suggesting that the time available for processing is a central determinant of the extent to which a representation is conscious. Thus, consciousness takes time, as it takes time for any dynamical system to settle upon a state that best satisfies the many constraints imposed by diverse sources of such constraints, such as the environment with which the agent interacts, the goals and intentions of the agent, the properties of the action systems that it can control, and so on. But the satisfaction of these many constrains takes place at different time scales, so that the content of conscious awareness can change according to the time that a pilot has for information processing. This situation is probably exacerbated in a situation of automation supervision. Hence, a better understanding of the cognitive and sensory factors, and of the dynamical interactions which determine the contents of our conscious experience is a critical aspect for improving cockpit interactions.

3   Technology Automation and Agency

A second crucial question refers to the transformation induced by automation technology, from a human operator perspective. There is perhaps no facet of modern society in which the influence of automation technology has not been felt. ? This is especially true when one considers interactions with aeronautical systems. We have usually focused on the perceived benefits of new automated or computerized devices. This is perhaps not surprising given the sophistication and ingenuity of design of many such systems (e.g., the automatic landing of a jumbo jet, or the docking of two spacecraft). The economic benefits that automation can provide, or is perceived to offer, also tend to focus public attention on the technical capabilities of automation.

However, our fascination with the possibilities afforded by technology often obscures the fact that new computerized and automated devices also created new burdens and complexities for the individuals and teams of practitioners responsible for operating, troubleshooting, and managing high-consequences systems. Whatever the merits of any particular automation technology, it is clear that automation does not merely supplant human activity but also transforms the nature of human work. Understanding the characteristics of this transformation is vital for successful design of new automated systems.

3.1   The Classical Approach of the OOTL Performance Problem

When new automation is introduced into a system, or when there is an increase in the autonomy of automated systems, developers often assume that adding "automation" is a simple substitution of a machine activity for human activity (substitution myth, see Woods & Tinapple, 1999). Empirical data on the relationship of people and technology suggest that this is not the case and that traditional automation has many negative performance and safety consequences associated with it stemming from the human out-of-the-loop (OOTL) performance problem (see Endsley & Kiris, 1995; Kaber, Onal & Endsley, 2000).

Classically, the out-of-the-loop performance problem leaves operators of automated systems handicapped in their ability to take over manual operations in the event of automation failure (Endsley & Kiris, 1995). The OOTL performance problem has been attributed to a number of underlying factors, including human vigilance decrements (see Billings, 1991), complacency (see Parasuraman, Molloiy & Singh, 1993) and loss of operator situation awareness (SA) (see Endsley, 1996). Cognitive engineering literature has discussed at length the origins of vigilance decrements (e.g., low signal rates, lack of operator sensitivity to signals), complacency (e.g., over trust in highly reliable computer control) and the decrease in SA (use of more passive rather than active processing and the differences in the type of feedback provided) in automated system supervision and has established associations between these human information processing shortcomings and performance problems. However, though all of these undoubtedly play an important role in the out-of-the-loop performance problem, we consider that these different factors have masked a preliminary question: what is the difference between action resulting from my intention, beliefs or desires and others' action or involuntary action? What is the difference between being an agent or not? What is the difference between supervisors in control and complacent supervisors?

3.2   Insight from Neurosciences: OOTL Problem and Sense of Agency

As a matter of fact, the role of the human actors evolve from direct control to supervision with automation technology. In this sense, a crucial transformation concerns the authority sharing between the human operator and the system as claimed by Baron: *"Perhaps the major human factors concern of pilots in regard to introduction of automation is that, in some circumstances, operations with such aids*

may leave the critical question, who is in control now, the human or the machine?"
(Baron, 1988).

This problem of sense of control has been poorly investigated in the HMI context. In contrast, in recent years, this problematic has known a particular interest in the neurosciences area under the concept of agency. When we act, we usually feel ourselves controlling our own actions and causing the resulting effects. This phenomenological image of ourselves as agents is classicaly called "sense of agency" (de Vignemont & Fourneret, 2004; Gallagher, 2000), and is recognised as an important part of normal and human consciousness. How can we distinguish our actions and their effects from those of other people, how do we refer the origin of an action to its own agent, remain essential questions. Most people can readily sort many events in the world into those they have authored and those they have not. This observation suggests that each person has a system for authorship processing, a set of mental processes that monitors indications of authorship to judge whether an event, action, or thought should be ascribed to self as a causal agent (Wegner, Sparrow, & Winerman, 2004). Laboratory studies have attempted to shed more light on this mechanism and empirical data in recent psychology (e.g., Aarts, Custers, & Wegner, 2005 ; Moore, Wegner & Haggard, 2009), psychopathology (e.g., Franck & al, 2001; Frith, Blakemore & Wolpert, 2000) and neuroscience (e.g., Farrer & al., 2003; Tsakiris & Haggard, 2005) have been accumulated. Interestingly, a variety of sources of information (e.g., one's own thoughts, interoceptive sensations, external feedback, etc.) could be involved in the authorship processing. Several indicators have been already proposed, including body and environment orientation cues (e.g., Vallacher & Wegner, 1985), direct bodily feedback (e.g., Gandevia & Burke, 1992; Georgieff & Jeannerod, 1998), direct bodily feedforward (e.g., Blakemore & Frith, 2003; Blakemore, Frith & Wolpert, 1999), visual and other indirect sensory feedback (e.g., Daprati & al., 1997), social cues (e.g., Milgram, 1974), agent goal information (e.g., Langer & Roth, 1975) and own behavior relevant thought (e.g., Wegner, 2002; Wegner & Wheatley, 1999). In our opinion, research on agency opens interesting novel avenues of research.

3.3   Integration of Neurosciences Issues for HMI Design

Our belief is that the investigation of the agency mechanism may be fruitful in the comprehension of the OOTL performance problem. We assume that the introduction of the concept of agency in human factors issues open a new way to understand how automation influence operator performance. There are three central motivations to consider that the investigation of the agency mechanism may be fruitful in the comprehension of the OOTL performance problem. Firstly, causal attribution is a central mechanism in our dailylife. As famously claimed by David Hume, causality is the cement of the universe. In our daily life, perception of causality can help us under-stand how two events relate to each other and how our actions influence the world. Central to the sense of causality is the sense of agency, the experience we have of causing our own actions. Clearly, interaction with computerized and automated devices could confuse this issue of agency. Partially autonomous machine agents, increased system complexity and the use of automation technology may all contribute to transform the nature of human activity and to distance humans from many details of the ongoing operation. The interposition of more and more automation between pilot and aircraft tends to distance pilots from many details of the flying, decreasing their feeling of control. Secondly, accounts of agentive experience could have implications for conceptions of future systems. Indeed, how to design systems to allow the crew to remain "in the loop" becomes a first concern, but is also an extremely difficult problem that needs to take agentive experience seriously. Different solutions may be envisaged when designing human-machine interface. In our opinion, model of agency should help to elaborate concrete design recommendations (see for example, Berberian, et al., in press) and provide guidelines for better automatic system design. Thirdly, accounts of agentive experience should help to evaluate current/future human-machine interface in term of potentiality to remain the crew "in the loop". The ability to measure the sense of agency quantitatively is important, since it allows the sense of agency to be used as a measure in evaluating human-automation performance (see Berberian et al, 2012). For example, when we get on an airplane, we believe (and hope!) that the pilot feels in personal control of the aircraft. Accounts of agentive experience give the possibility of testing whether this is actually true. In this sense, models of agency could lead to the introduction of a new methodology for the evaluation of the potentiality for an human-machine interface to keep the operator in the loop, even online monitoring of agentive experience (i.e, neural correlates of agency).

4   Conclusion

In this paper, we have argued that neurosciences could help in the development of effective technologies for Human Machine Interaction. Insights from neurosciences could offer new way to understand some very well-known ergonomics problems, as the OOTL problem, and help IHM designers to deal with these problems. At the extreme, neurosciences could also dramatically change our apprehension of the human machine interaction (awareness and action control), IHM designers' tools and methodology. Neurosciences open interesting novel avenues of research and links between human factors teams and neurosciences laboratories has to be strengthened in order to meet current application and industrial challenges.

References

1. Aarts, H., Custers, R., Wegner, D.M.: On the inference of personal authorship: Enhancing experienced agency by priming effect information. Consciousness and Cognition 14, 439–458 (2005)
2. Aglioti, S., DeSouza, J., Goodale, M.A.: Current Biology 5, 679–685 (1995)
3. Amalberti, R.: La conduite de systemes a risques (The Control of Risky Systems). Presses Universitaires de France, Paris (1996)

4. Baron, S.: Pilot control. In: Wiener, E.L., Nagel, D.C. (eds.) Human Factors in Aviation, pp. 347–386. Academic Press, San Diego (1988)
5. Berberian, B., Sarrazin, J.C., Le Blaye, P., Haggard, P.: Automation Technology and Sense of Control: A Window on Human Agency. PLoS ONE 2012, e34075 (2012)
6. Berberian, B., Le Blaye, P., Schulte, C., Kinani, N., Sim, P.R.: Data Transmission Latency and Sense of Control. In: Proc. International Conference on Human-Computer Interaction, Las Vegas, July 21-26 (2013)
7. Billings, C.E.: Human-Centered Aircraft Automation: A Concept and Guidelines (NASA Tech. Memo. 103885). NASA-Ames Research Center, Moffet Field (April 1991)
8. Blakemore, S., Frith, C.: Self-Awareness and Action. Current Opinion in Neurobiology 13, 219–224 (2003)
9. Blakemore, S., Frith, C., Wolpert, D.: Spatiotemporal Prediction Modulates the Perception of Self Produced Stimuli. Journal of Cognitive Neuroscience 11, 551–559 (1999)
10. Block, N.: Trends in Cognitive Sciences 9, 46–52 (2005)
11. Cleeremans, A., Sarrazin, J.C.: Human Movement Science 26, 180–202 (2007)
12. Daprati, E., Franck, N., Georgieff, N., Proust, J., Pacherie, E., Dalery, J.: Looking for the Agent: An Investigation into Consciousness of Action and Self-Consciousness in Schizophrenic Patients. Cognition 65, 71–86 (1997)
13. Debner, J.A., Jacoby, L.L.: Unconscious perception: Attention, awareness and control. Journal of Experimental Psychology: Learning, Memory and Cognition 20, 304–317 (1994)
14. Destrebecqz, A., Cleeremans, A.: Can sequence learning be implicit? New evidence with the process dissociation procedure. Psychonomic Bulletin and Review 8(2), 343–350 (2001)
15. Dienes, Z., Perner, J.: A theory of implicit and explicit knowledge. Behavioral and Brain Sciences 22, 735–808 (1999)
16. De Vignemont, F., Fourneret, P.: The Sense of Agency: A Philosophical and Empirical Review of the "Who" System. Conscious Cognition 13(1), 1–19 (2004)
17. Endsley, M.: Toward a Theory of Situation Awareness in Dynamic Systems. Human Factors 37(1), 32–64 (1995)
18. Endsley, M.: Automation and situation awareness. In: Parasuraman, R., Mouloua, M. (eds.) Automation and Human Performance: Theory and Applications, pp. 163–181. Erlbaum, Mahwah (1996)
19. Endsley, M., Kiris, E.O.: The out-of-the-loop performance problem and level of control in automation. Human Factors 37, 381–394 (1995)
20. Farrer, C., Franck, N., Georgieff, N., Frith, C.D., Decety, J., Jeannerod, M.: Modulating the Experience of Agency: a Positron Emission Tomography study. Neuroimage 18(2), 324–333 (2003)
21. Fourneret, P., Jeannerod, M.: Neuropsychologia 36, 1133–1140 (1998)
22. Franck, N., Farrer, C., Georgieff, M., Marie-Cardine, N., Dalery, J., D'Amato, T., Jeannerod, M.: Defective Recognition of One's Own Actions in Patients with Schizophrenia. American Journal of Psychiatry 158, 454–459 (2001)
23. Franz, V.H., Bulthoff, H.H., Fahle, M.: Experimental Brain Research 149, 470–477 (2003)
24. Frith, C., Blakemore, S., Wolpert, D.: Explaining the Symptoms of Schizophrenia: Abnormalities in the Awareness of Action. Brain Res. Rev. 31(2-3) 357–63 (2000)
25. Gallagher, S.: Philosophical concepts of the self: implications for cognitive sciences. Trends in Cognitive Sciences 4, 14–21 (2000)
26. Gandevia, S., Burke, D.: Does the Nervous System Depend on Kinesthetic Information to Control Natural Limb Movements? Behavioral and Brain Sciences 15, 614–632 (1992)

27. Gentilucci, M., Chieffi, S., Daprati, E., Saetti, M.C., Toni, I.: Neuropsychologia 34, 369–376 (1996)

28. Georgieff, N., Jeannerod, M.: Beyond Consciousness of External Reality: A "Who" System for Consciousness of Action and Self-Consciousness. Consciousness and Cognition 7, 465–477 (1998)

29. Gilbert, D.T.: Attribution and interpersonal perception. In: Tesser, A. (ed.) Advanced Social Psychology, pp. 98–147. McGraw-Hill (1995)

30. Goodale, M.A., Pelisson, D., Prablanc, C.: Nature 320, 748–750 (1986)

31. Greenwald, A.G., Abrams, R.L., Naccache, L., Dehaene, S.: Long-term semantic memory versus contextual memory in unconscious number processing. Journal of Experimental Psychology: Learning, Memory, and Cognition 29(2), 235–247 (2003)

32. Jackson, S.R., Shaw, A.: The Ponzo illusion affects grip force but not grip aperture scaling during prehension movements. Journal of Experimental Psychology: Human Perception and Performance 26, 418–423 (2000)

33. Kaber, D., Onal, E., Endsley, M.: Design of Automation for Telerobots and the Effect on Performance, Operator Situation Awareness and Subjective Workload. Human Factors & Ergonomics in Manufacturing 10, 409–430 (2000)

34. Kihlstrom, J.F., Barnhardt, T.M., Tataryn, D.: The psychological unconscious: Found, lost, and regained. American Psychologist 47, 788–791 (1992)

35. Heads I Win, Tails it's chance: The Illusion of Control as a Function of the Sequence of Outcomes in a Pure Chance Task

36. Langer, E.J., Roth, J.: Heads I Win, Tails it's chance: The Illusion of Control as a Function of the Sequence of Outcomes in a Pure Chance Task. Journal of Personality and Social Psychology 32, 951–955 (1975)

37. Merikle, P.M., Smilek, D., Eastwood, J.D.: Perception without awareness: Perspectives from cognitive psychology. Cognition 79(1-2), 115–134 (2001)

38. Milgram, S.: Obedience to Authority. Harper & Row, New York (1974)

39. Moore, J.W., Wegner, D.M., Haggard, P.: Modulating the sense of agency with external cues. Consciousness and Cognition 18, 1056–1064 (2009)

40. Milner, A.D., Goodale, M.A.: The visual brain in action. Oxford University Press, Oxford (1998)

41. Parasuraman, R., Molloy, R., Singh, I.L.: Performance Consequences of Automation Induced Complacency. International Journal of Aviation Psychology 3, 1–23 (1993)

42. Plodowski, A., Jackson, S.R.: Current Biology 11, 304–306 (2001)

43. Tsakiris, M., Haggard, P.: Awareness of Somatic Events Associated with a Voluntary Action. Experimental Brain Research 149, 439–446 (2003)

44. Vallacher, R.R., Wegner, D.M.: A Theory of Action Identification. Lawrence Erlbaum Associates, Hillsdale (1985)

45. Wegner, D.M.: The illusion of conscious will. MIT Press (2002)

46. Wegner, D.M., Sparrow, B., Winerman, L.: Vicarious agency: Experiencing control over the movements of others. Journal of Personality and Social Psychology 86, 838–848 (2004)

47. Wegner, D.M., Wheatley, T.: Apparent mental causation: Sources of the experience of will. American Psychologist 54(7), 480–492 (1999)

48. Woods, D.D., Tinapple, D.: W3: Watching Human Factors Watch People at Work. Presidential Address, 43rd Annual Meeting of the Human Factors and Ergonomics Society (September 28, 1999)

Attentional Biases during Steering Behavior

Hans-Joachim Bieg[1], Heinrich H. Bülthoff[1,2], and Lewis L. Chuang[1,*]

[1] Department of Perception, Cognition and Action,
Max Planck Institute for Biological Cybernetics, Tübingen
{hans-joachim.bieg,heinrich.buelthoff}@tuebingen.mpg.de
[2] Department of Cognitive and Brain Engineering, Korea University

Abstract. In the current study, we examine eye movements of human operators during a combined steering and discrimination task. In this task, observers had to alternate their gaze between a central steering task and a discrimination task in the periphery. Our results show that the observer's gaze behavior is influenced by the motion direction of the steering task. Saccade reaction times (SRTs) of saccades to the discrimination target were shorter if the target appeared in the steering direction. SRTs back to the steering task were shorter when the steering target moved away from the discrimination target. These effects are likely the result of motion-related attention shifts and an interaction of the saccadic and smooth pursuit eye movement system.

Keywords: attention, eye movements, saccades, reaction time, steering.

1 Introduction

The design of human-machine interfaces in complex environments such as aircraft cockpits can benefit from approaches that model the operator's behavior in that environment [1]. One important component in such psychological models is the operator's visual attention. Attention is the process by which our perceptual system selects stimuli for further or more detailed processing [2, 3]. Understanding the factors that influence how attention is moved through the visual scene to process information is crucial for designing effective human-machine interfaces [4].

The strongest factor that influences orienting of attention are the goals of the observer. This *endogenous* influence competes with stimulus-driven or *exogenous* factors [5]. For example, an object that is very distinct in color tends to grab the attention of the observer when it suddenly appears [6]. Another stimulus property that engages exogenous orienting is object motion [7]. Objects that move through the visual field not only grab attention but also bias attentional orienting in the movement direction [8]. Such motion-induced attention shifts are particularly important in the context of machine interfaces in vehicles, which naturally deal with motion-related tasks and dynamic information. Here, attention shifts

---

* The work in this paper was supported by the Max Planck Society and the myCopter project, funded by the European Commission under the 7th Framework Program.

can result from objects that move outside the vehicle, for example, other traffic, or from on-board instruments with moving displays (e.g. augmented or synthetic vision displays [9]).

Until now, motion-induced attention shifts have been examined primarily in basic ocular pursuit tracking tasks. In these tasks, observers follow a moving spot on the computer screen with their eyes and respond to onsets of visual stimuli in the periphery either by a saccade or button press [10, 8]. The resulting behavior shows a reduction of reaction times for stimuli that appeared in the direction of pursuit – an indication for a bias of attention in this direction.

In the current study we present a more complex scenario, to test whether motion-induced attention shifts occur in the context of steering behavior. Here, the observer's eye movements are not restricted explicitly by the experimental procedure but are primarily driven by the visual needs of the ongoing steering task. We examined overt attention shifts in the form of eye movements of human operators during a manual steering task. This task resembles the control of the yaw motion of an aircraft when following a given flight trajectory [11]. We were interested in how the ongoing steering task would affect the operator's capacity to respond to and perform a secondary task that required shifts of attention to the periphery. The primary goal of the study was to establish whether motion-related attention shifts as they were observed in single-task ocular pursuit tasks [10, 8] would transfer to our steering scenario. For example, when steering to the right, shifts of attention in this direction should be facilitated.

Inferences about an observer's attention were made from measurements of saccadic eye movements. Saccades are quick eye movements that occur 3-4 times a second in normal behavior. Eye movements are closely linked to movements of visual attention. First, both movements typically coincide since eye movements are necessary to move the retinal image of an object of interest to the fovea, the area on the retina with highest acuity [12]. Second, even in the case when the regarded location does not correspond to the attended location, the properties of eye movements, for example the time required to plan and execute a saccade (saccade reaction time, SRT), can reveal which parts of the visual field received preferred processing [13, 14].

2   Method

Eight participants took part in the experiment (6 male, 2 female, age: 27-31 years). All participants had normal or corrected to normal vision. Written informed consent was obtained from all participants prior to experimentation. The procedures of the experiment had been approved by the ethical committee of the University of Tübingen. Participants were paid 8 EUR per hour for taking part in the experiment.

Participants sat in an adjustable chair in front of a TFT monitor (120 Hz refresh rate, resolution 1680×1050). A chin-rest provided support for the head at a viewing distance of 57 cm. An optical infrared head-mounted eye-tracking system was used to measure gaze at a sampling rate of 500 Hz (SR Research Eyelink II). A potentiometer joystick (0.18 ° angular accuracy, sampling rate 120

Hz) was mounted under the table within comfortable reach for the participants. With the other hand, participants pressed the cursor keys on a keyboard.

The primary *steering* task required participants to steer an on-screen cursor using a joystick (see Fig. 1 A, B). By moving the joystick to the left or right, participants controlled the horizontal velocity of the cursor. The instruction was to move the cursor "as close as possible" to a computer-controlled steering target. The steering target moved horizontally in a sinusoidal path around the center of the computer screen with an amplitude of $4.3°$ and frequency of 0.25 Hz. The steering target was a blue bar (RGB 180, 180, 255) and subtended $1.2°$ (visual angle), the cursor was an orange bar (RGB 255, 255, 100) and subtended $0.9°$. The steering task was performed continuously in blocks, each block lasting 128 s.

The secondary *object discrimination* task required participants to look at and identify an object that appeared in the periphery. This object consisted of a small square ($0.2°$) of white color (RGB 200, 200, 200). A small gap was present at one of the four sides of the square (size $0.03°$, 1.8 minutes of arc). A white border was drawn around the target to make it discernible in the visual periphery. Participants were instructed to discern the side of the target where the gap was located (top, bottom, left, right). Due to the small size of the gap, a saccade to the target was necessary in order to achieve this. After participants looked at the target to determine the gap they responded with one of the four corresponding arrow keys on the keyboard.

Each steering block was subdivided into trial epochs of 8 s. During each epoch a discrimination object appeared randomly 400 ms before the zero-crossing of the steering target either 2 or 4 s from the start of the epoch, i.e., 1.3 or 3.6 s into an epoch. Targets appeared semi-randomly either on the left or right side of the screen at an eccentricity of $13°$. The discrimination task was scheduled such that discrimination objects appeared either in the same direction as the movement (to condition) of the steering target or in the opposite direction (away condition).

Data from the following trials were removed prior to saccade analysis: Trials with blinks during the critical time period shortly before or after the target onset, missed trials (no saccade or RT greater than 800 ms), and anticipatory saccades (RT smaller than 50 ms). Based on this method, 29 data points of 720 were removed (4%). The median number of data points remaining per participant and condition was 39 (min. 36).

3   Results

Two-tailed t-tests for paired samples were employed for the comparison of mean differences ($\alpha = 0.05$). Mean-centering was performed for the computation of confidence intervals (CI) [15]. The effect size measure reported is Glass's Δ [16].

Saccades to the discrimination object (outward) commenced after 234.0 ms on average. Saccades that were initiated while the steering target moved to the discrimination object exhibited shorter RTs (225.8 ms) compared to saccades that started when the steering target moved away (242.1 ms, $t(7) = 2.48$, $p <$ 0.05, 95% CI of difference 4.3–30 ms, $\Delta = 0.27$, see also Fig. 1, C).

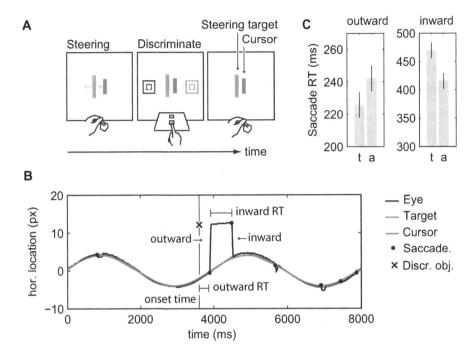

Fig. 1. A. Schematic of the experimental task. Participants controlled the horizontal velocity of an on-screen cursor by moving the joystick to the left or right. They were instructed to follow the sinusoidal motion of the steering target as closely as possible. The steering task was interrupted by a secondary task. This was an object discrimination task in which participants had to recognized the opening of a square symbol. B. The steering target performed two full cycles every 8 seconds (one epoch). During each epoch the discrimination object was presented randomly either 1.6 or 3.6 s into the epoch on the left or right side of the screen. The time and location defined whether the discrimination object was presented while the steering target was moving *to* the location of the discrimination object or while it was moving *away*. The plot shows the time course of stimulus presentation and a participant's response for a representative trial. The gaze movements during the same trial show periods of smooth pursuit eye movements, small catch-up saccades, and large saccades to the discrimination object (outward saccade, ca. at 4000 ms) and back to the steering target shortly afterward (inward saccade). C. Saccade reaction time (RT) results: Saccades to the discrimination object were initiated earlier when participants steered toward the location of that object (t = toward, a = away). Inward saccades were initiated earlier when the steering target moved away from the current fixation location. Error bars show 95% confidence intervals.

Saccades back to the steering target from the discrimination object (inward) took much longer than outward saccades (overall mean SRT: 442.3 ms). It is important to note that this time was measured from fixation onset on the discrimination object and therefore also comprised the time required to perform the discrimination task. Comparison of RTs between the two motion conditions showed that SRTs were shorter when the steering target moved away from the discrimination object (415.0 ms) and longer when the steering target moved to the discrimination object (469.75 ms, $t(7) = 4.6$, $p < 0.01$, 95% CI of difference 33–77 ms, $\Delta = 0.57$).

Other experiments on SRTs have reported a correlation between saccade amplitude and SRT [17]. A comparison of amplitudes in the current experiment revealed differences for both outward and inward saccades. Outward saccades were larger when the steering target moved to the discrimination object (13.0°) and smaller when it moved away (11.4°, $t(7) = 6.8$, $p < 0.01$, 95% CI of difference 1.2–2.1°, $\Delta = 1.9$). Inward saccades were larger when the target moved away from the discrimination object (14.8°) and smaller when it moved toward it (12.7°, $t(7) = 5.6$, $p < 0.01$, 95% CI of difference 1.6–3.1°, $\Delta = 1.3$).

4   Discussion

In the current study we examined visual attention shifts during steering behavior. Participants alternated their gaze between a continuous steering and a discrete object discrimination task.

Our study shows asymmetries in the observer's ability to react to the discrimination stimulus in the periphery. Reaction times of saccades (SRTs) to the discrimination stimulus (outward) were shorter when the stimulus appeared in the motion direction and longer when it appeared in the opposite location. We relate this result to earlier work on motion-induced attention shifts in basic ocular pursuit tasks [10, 8]. When pursuing a moving object with the eyes, attention is exogenously oriented ahead of pursuit, which could improve the observer's ability to respond to upcoming, pursuit-related stimuli (e.g., obstacles [8]). Our results show that this effect is robust: It is not only present when pursuit is the sole task but also in a more complex steering scenario.

Our results also show a second kind of asymmetry, namely in the timing of saccades back to the steering task (inward). These saccades occurred after the participants performed the discrimination task. The SRTs of these saccades were shorter when the target moved away from the current fixation location (the location of the discrimination target) and longer when it moved toward it. This difference may reflect the additional time that is required for basic oculomotor processing when the steering target moves toward the current fixation location. In this case, the oculomotor system must decide whether a fixation of the new target should be obtained by a saccadic or a smooth eye movement [18–20] (see Fig. 2). This decision process may in turn prolong the movement of attention toward the new target for the sake of accuracy.

An alternative explanation for both outward and inward SRT effects could be the noted differences in saccade amplitudes. These differences were primarily due to the timing of the discrimination target onsets 400 ms prior to crossing the center of the display and the average saccadic latencies of around 200 ms. Consequently, saccades to targets in the direction of the steering motion started farther away from the target than saccades to targets that appeared at the opposite location. Previous work has shown that SRTs depend on the amplitude of the saccade [17]. However, the differences in SRTs between the motion conditions of the current study are not in accord with what would be predicted based on differences in saccade amplitudes. For example, outward saccades were larger and SRTs of these saccades were shorter when the steering target moved to the discrimination target. According to [17], larger saccades should result in longer and not shorter SRTs. Similarly, inward saccades were larger and their SRTs were shorter when the steering target moved away from the discrimination target. Again, the opposite effect would be predicted purely based on amplitude differences.

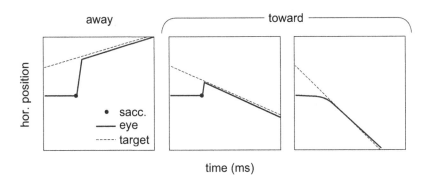

Fig. 2. Example for different eye movements when following a target that either moves away from the current fixation location or toward it at constant velocity. Left: When the target moves away, a catch-up saccade is performed to fixate the target. Right: When the target moves toward the current fixation location the oculomotor system has to make a decision whether a saccade would be useful or whether the motion of the target is such that it would move into focus by itself.

5   Conclusion

The current findings highlight the allocation of visual attention during a steering task. This is relevant to any system that requires its operator to process visual information during control itself, not just the control of a vehicle. Operator models can be developed to consider motion-induced effects on visual attention, for example, due to the motion of control instrument displays. This is useful in cases where the model should predict the operator's capacity to respond to critical situations that are indicated by peripheral visual cues (e.g., warning systems).

References

1. Gluck, K., Ball, J., Krusmark, M.: Cognitive Control in a Computational Model of the Predator Pilot. In: Gray, W.D. (ed.) Integrated Models of Cognitive Systems. Oxford University Press, New York (2007)

2. Fecteau, J.H., Munoz, D.P.: Salience, relevance, and firing: a priority map for target selection. Trends in Cognitive Sciences 10(8), 382–390 (2006)

3. Posner, M.I.: Orienting of attention. The Quarterly Journal of Experimental Psychology 32(1), 3–25 (1980)

4. Proctor, R.W., Vu, K.P.L.: Human Information Processing: An Overview for Human-Computer Interaction. In: Jacko, J.A., Sears, A. (eds.) The Human-Computer Interaction Handbook, 2nd edn. Lawrence Erlbaum Associates, Mahwah (2003)

5. Godijn, R., Theeuwes, J.: The Relationship Between Exogenous and Endogenous Saccades and Attention. In: Radach, R., Hyona, J., Deubel, H. (eds.) The Mind's Eye: Cognitive and Applied Aspects of Eye Movement Research. North-Holland, Amsterdam (2003)

6. Theeuwes, J., Olivers, C.N.L., Belopolsky, A.: Stimulus-driven capture and contingent capture. Wiley Interdisciplinary Reviews: Cognitive Science 1(6), 872–881 (2010)

7. Nothdurft, H.C.: The role of features in preattentive vision: comparison of orientation, motion and color cues. Vision Research 33(14), 1937–1958 (1993)

8. Khan, A., Lefèvre, P., Heinen, S., Blohm, G.: The default allocation of attention is broadly ahead of smooth pursuit. Journal of Vision 10(13), 1–17 (2010)

9. Merchant, S., Kwon, Y., Schnell, T., Etherington, T., Vogl, T., Collins, R.: Evaluation of synthetic vision information system (SVIS) displays based on pilot performance. In: Digital Avionics Systems Conference (DASC), pp. 1–12 (2001)

10. Tanaka, M., Yoshida, T., Fukushima, K.: Latency of saccades during smooth-pursuit eye movement in man. Directional asymmetries. Experimental Brain Research 121(1), 92–98 (1998)

11. Hess, R.A.: Pursuit Tracking and Higher Levels of Development in the Human Pilot. IEEE Transactions on Systems, Man and Cybernetics 11(4), 262–273 (1981)

12. Findlay, J.M., Gilchrist, I.D.: Active Vision: The psychology of looking and seeing. Oxford University Press, Oxford (2003)

13. Rizzolatti, G., Riggio, L., Dascola, I., Umiltá, C.: Reorienting attention across the horizontal and vertical meridians: evidence in favor of a premotor theory of attention. Neuropsychologia 25(1A), 31–40 (1987)

14. Kowler, E., Anderson, E., Dosher, B., Blaser, E.: The role of attention in the programming of saccades. Vision Research 35(13), 1897–1916 (1995)

15. Baguley, T.: Calculating and graphing within-subject confidence intervals for ANOVA. Behavior Research Methods 44(1), 158–175 (2012)

16. Kline, R.B.: American Psychological Association. American Psychological Association, Washington, DC (2005)

17. Kalesnykas, R., Hallett, P.E.: Retinal eccentricity and the latency of eye saccades. Vision Research 34(4), 517–531 (1994)

18. Gellman, R.S., Carl, J.R.: Motion procssing for saccadic eye movements in humans. Experimental Brain Research 84(3), 660–667 (1991)

19. De Brouwer, S., Yuksel, D., Blohm, G., Missal, M.: What Triggers Catch-Up Saccades During Visual Tracking. Journal of Neurophysiology 87, 1646–1650 (2002)

20. Guan, Y., Eggert, T., Bayer, O., Büttner, U.: Saccades to stationary and moving targets differ in the monkey. Experimental Brain Research 161(2), 220–232 (2005)

A Validation Approach for Complex NextGen Air Traffic Control Human Performance Models

Brian F. Gore[1] and Paul Milgram[2]

[1] San Jose State University/NASA Ames, MS 262-4, PO Box 1, Moffett Field, CA, USA
Brian.F.Gore@nasa.gov
[2] Department of Mechanical & Industrial Engineering, University of Toronto, Toronto, Canada
milgram@mie.utoronto.ca

Abstract. Validation is critically important when human performance models are used to predict the effect of future system designs on human performance. A model of air traffic control (ATC) operations was validated using a rigorous iterative model validation process that illustrated the success of representing ATC operations in NextGen en route operations. A gold-standard model was compared to three model iterations that represented different task management and human time estimation processes when dealing with handoff operations.

Keywords: Human performance model validation, air traffic control, NextGen.

1   Introduction

Human performance modeling is the process whereby human characteristics are embedded within a computer software structure that represents a simulated human operator interacting with a simulated operating environment. Integrated human performance models (HPMs) simulate and predict emergent behavior based on multiple, interacting sub-models of human behavior, such as perception, attention, working memory, long-term memory and decision-making. This is accomplished typically by incorporating sub-models of different aspects of human performance that feed both forward and back to other constituent models within the human information processing system. The use of appropriate and validated integrated HPMs can support the basic human factors principle of predicting the impact of alternative design options early in the system design process. Such HPMs may also be used synergistically with human-in-the-loop (HITL) studies, especially during the development of complex systems, a time when events cannot be studied fully with HITL subjects due to safety concerns, cost considerations, or practical difficulties associated with simulating very rare events.

Complex systems are those that include human operators interacting with actual technology and automation, to carry out multiple interacting, and often conflicting, tasks. These systems often involve time-critical tasks, that is, tasks that typically have a specific onset time and a specific time by which the task needs to be completed. Together these define a window of opportunity for the action to take place. For such systems, the dynamic interactions among system elements often form critical couplings for control of the system by the human.

V.G. Duffy (Ed.): DHM/HCII 2013, Part I, LNCS 8025, pp. 28–37, 2013.

One of the most significant hurdles facing modelers is the challenge of validating these integrated HPMs, a goal without which the credibility of any model predictions will clearly be greatly reduced [1]. Most validation efforts to date have been in the area of simpler engineering models and cognitive architectures [2], with only a small number of attempts to validate integrated HPMs. Furthermore, of the validation efforts that have been conducted for integrated models, there is little agreement as to what constitutes appropriate validation techniques and measures [1]. The development of these integrated HPMs is in its infancy, and so too are the validation techniques. There is thus a real need for the advancement of techniques and approaches for validating complex models.

2   Validating Complex Models

Modeling human behavior in complex systems such as air traffic control is very complicated, particularly when the human's tasks are highly cognitive in nature and they interact in a closed-loop fashion with other operators and environmental factors. Since cognitive tasks are not directly observable, it is very difficult to objectively validate such complex models. As a field, our ability to model these complex tasks and demonstrate that such models of human behavior validly represent actual human behavior is in its infancy. Many HPM validation efforts often rely only on subjective or qualitative measures, as opposed to objective, quantitative measures. Thus, one major objective of our work is to focus on quantitative validation techniques that can be used to demonstrate that a particular model represents human cognitive processes. The present research highlights a method that was followed to develop valid HPMs of time management in a complex operational environment exemplified in an air traffic control domain.

3   Defining Model Verification and Validation

Model verification and validation are essential elements of any modeling effort. *Model verification* is the process of determining whether a simulation model and its associated data behave as intended by the model developer / analyst. *Model validation* is the process of determining the degree to which a model or simulation and its associated predictions are an accurate representation of the real world, from the perspective of the intended users of the model or simulation [3]. Both model verification and model validation must be considered when attempts are made to validate a model, particularly as models increase in complexity.

Model validation can take many forms, ranging from common qualitative approaches to quantitative approaches [4]. For the purpose of brevity, only the quantitative approach will be focused on in the current article. Obtaining a quantitative measure of the similarity between a model's behavior and empirically determined human behavior is a complement to the qualitative approach. More explicitly, a quantitative test for a model's validity is the degree to which the model's output resembles the behavior that would be expected from the real world. Quantitative approaches are traditionally statistical in nature and attempt to measure the degree to which a model's data are similar to an empirically collected set of data. The recommended statistical tests used to measure the similarity between the data sets include goodness-of-fit tests (r^2) to assess trend consistency; ANOVAs to compare human and model data sets; root mean squared scaled deviations to assess the exactness of matching; and chi-square analyses to assess whether the underlying distributions of the two data sets (model, real world) can be regarded as coming from the same population [4].

Graphical comparisons are also an effective model validation approach, particularly as a first validation phase for initial testing of model performance [3]. Using that approach, the graphs of values of model variables over time are compared with the graphs of values of system variables, to investigate, for example, similarities in periodicities, skewness, number and location of inflection points, logarithmic rise and linearity, phase shift, trend lines, or exponential growth constants. The histogram is an estimate of the density function and is another effective graphical technique, for examining data symmetry, skewness and kurtosis.

4   Simulated Environment and Validation Approach

A complex, time-critical environment, namely the ATC environment, was used as a test-bed to develop and exercise validation techniques that concentrate on validating the time-relevant aspects of the model. Using an iterative develop-validate process, the test-bed model was augmented with sub-models (embedded models) that represent the processes required to execute a series of procedures [2], in this case, time management procedures.

Three human behavioral components occur in a time management environment; i) task management, ii) time estimation, and iii) time management. (Because the sub-models can be modified individually, any differences in model output can be attributed to the sub-model under investigation.) The particular sub-models used were based on a synthesis of existing literature on the manner in which humans' time management (task management and time estimation) changes in the face of dynamics of the operational environment, as a function of time pressure, and thus of perceived workload.

Validating the time management model required three steps. Starting with an appropriate baseline model, the first step is to assess the *task management* portion of the model. The second step is to assess the *time estimation* aspect of the model. The third step is to assess the *time management* aspect of the model. (Such an approach can be extended to any complex domain.)

The domain that was chosen was from a FAA HITL simulation of the Future En-route Workstation Study (FEWS) [5]. This dataset included three workload levels: low, medium, and high, as defined by the number of aircraft travelling in a generic airspace and the presence of assistive technologies (datalink - DL). Air Traffic Controllers (ATCos) were required to schedule tasks that differed in priority, including conflict resolution, aircraft hand-offs between sectors, and routine communications.

The baseline (BL) HPM of the ATCo, programmed in Micro Saint Sharp was used as the *gold-standard,* against which further model augmentations would be compared, as this model had been deemed by others to validly represent the FEWS performance [6]. The baseline model, depicted in Figure 1, assumed that ATCos implement nominally optimal strategic task scheduling, and that the ATCos' estimate of time passage is perfect and with no effect on workload.

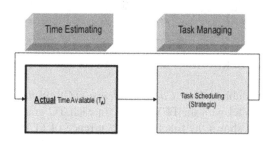

Fig. 1. Baseline Model of Task Management Behavior

To verify and validate this BL model, performance on several output variables from the model was compared to the human ATCo performance collected during the FEWS simulation. The non-human portion of the model was verified in terms of environmental performance (the number of aircraft travelling in the airspace, the flight plans, etc.). Modeled ATCo workload and queue length were assessed to verify that the model behaved as expected – that is that ATCo workload and the number of items in the queue increased as a function of task load, in the same manner as occurred in the FEWS HITL data.

A large contribution of the present work extends the validated environmental model to the modeled operator behaviors. The ATCos' Receive Handoff Duration (RHD) data – the elapsed time between the first moment at which a particular aircraft could have been handed off and the moment at which it actually was handed off – were used as the main validation measure.

The RHD was first explored at an aggregate mean level and compared by both t-tests and chi-square analysis to the FEWS RHD data. Figure 2 illustrates that no significant difference was found in the mean RHD times for the low workload between the FEWS and the baseline model, $p > .05$. A significant difference did exist, however, for the medium workload between the FEWS data and the baseline model predictions, $t(99) = 2.07$, $p < .05$. The same was true for the high workload, $t(80) = 5.51$, $p < .001$. Using these measures, validation of the BL model was supported in the low workload conditions, on the basis of not having detected a significant difference between model and FEWS data ($p > .05$). Validation was not supported in the medium and high workload condition, however ($p > .05$).

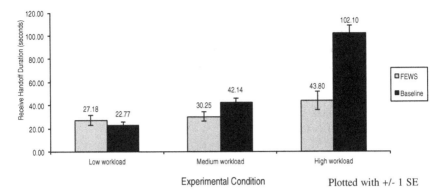

Fig. 2. Average RHD Times from the FEWS data and Baseline Model

A novel approach, dubbed *Time Correspondence (TC) graphs*, was implemented, to compare the BL model with the FEWS data. In each TC graph, such as Figure 3, the top horizontal axis shows the timeline of occurrence of FEWS events, while the lower axis shows events modeled by the HPM. The lines joining corresponding events are perfectly vertical when the times were the same in both FEWS and model. Lines that slant down to the right indicate that model times occurred later than corresponding FEWS times, and lines slanting down to the left indicate that model times preceded corresponding FEWS times. The ensemble of all lines resulting from a simulation thus form a holistic visual indication of the goodness of model fit.

The BL model results in Figure 3 show the window open times on the left and the window close times on the right, since it is necessary to look at both in order to correctly attribute the reason for any difference in the RHD times. In the figure we see that the BL model was operating too liberally, allowing the possibility of 'too many' tasks to enter into a queue - which produced delayed processing of some tasks and thus later task onset predictions than those of the real operators. The TC graphs, supported by Spearman correlation coefficients, also showed that the order in which tasks were conducted differed between the model and the FEWS simulation.

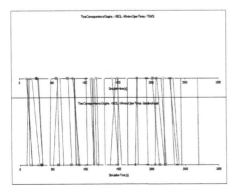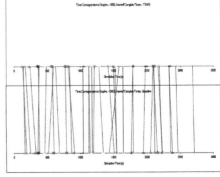

Fig. 3. TC Graphs - Window Open and Close Times (Baseline Model)

Two explanations for the breakdown in the BL model performance are offered. First, the strategy that the ATCo used to process the handoff tasks differed between the FEWS and the BL model. Second, it could be that the human operators simply failed to estimate the passage of time accurately due to excessive workload [7], as the model assumed that the operator always has "perfect" awareness of available time to complete a task and, furthermore, it assumes that tasks are completed quickly, in the right order and at the right time. Underestimating time available results in tasks being scheduled for completion early within the window resulting in a burst of early responses. That model modification is described after the task management section.

5   Development of a Framework of Time Management

The Time Management framework that follows was used to guide the development of two time management information processing models – time estimation and task management [8] - which are to be called whenever the human operator engages in a time sensitive task. As shown in Figure 4, the time management framework includes a workload projecting component, a time estimating component, and a task-managing component.

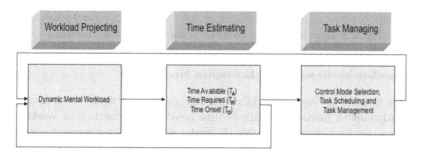

Fig. 4. Workload Projecting, Time Estimating and Task Management framework

5.1   Baseline (BL) Model with Task Management Modification

The BL model was augmented to account for the change from *strategic* to *opportunistic* control that occurs in high-workload tasks, as indicated in the literature [9]. The *task management (TM)* model utilized a 'conservative bias' paradigm, where the human operators are expected to complete all tasks in the order in which they are encountered, thereby shifting performance times towards "early" responses within the window of opportunity for certain high priority tasks. The right-most box in Figure 4 has been provided with a feedback loop around itself. This serves to impact the task ordering and onset times using the *opportunistic* control mode in the high workload condition. This new model does not allow multiple tasks to collect in the task queue; it forces the operator to manage tasks *opportunistically*, rather that strategically. That is, planning is limited and the environment drives decisions.

Using the same validation measures as for the BL model, it was apparent that limiting the queue length to zero made the model perform more "conservatively" and succeeded in bringing the modeled RHD times closer to the FEWS RHD times, with no significant difference between the FEWS and the low and medium workload conditions (see Fig 5; p>.05). Similar to the BL model, the RHD times in this TM model were significantly shorter than in the original baseline model in the high workload condition (although still significantly delayed relative to FEWS (t(80)=3.30, p<.05).

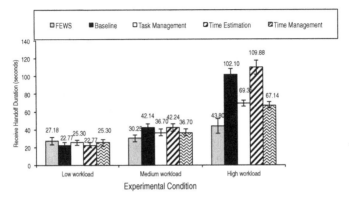

Plotted with +/- 1 SE

Fig. 5. Average RHD Times from FEWS and the Four Model Iterations

5.2   Baseline Model with Time Estimation Modification

The Time Estimating Box (TE; center box) in Figure 4 was modified to account for the degradations of human estimates of time passage as a function of workload. A quantitative verification effort of the TE model was conducted using a simple but non-trivial ATC task network model. This "generic computational model" was run 10000 times in two scenarios (baseline and TE model) at each of 5 workload levels (low, low-medium, medium, medium-high, and high) to verify the impact of time misestimates (time error) on task scheduling within the model. This verification phase revealed that the baseline model performs very close to zero mean error, as expected (Figure 5). The time estimation model time error output, on the other hand, revealed that the aircraft are being descended at increasingly late times as workload increased.

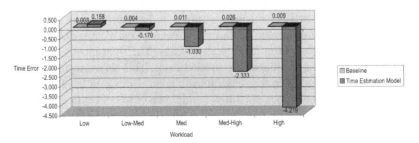

Fig. 6. Mean Time Error of 10000 Generic Model Runs to Verify TE Model Performance

As illustrated in Figure 6, the baseline model performed very close to optimally, with all of the time error values in the positive direction, meaning that the aircraft were descended early. It also illustrates the non-linear relationship that exists between workload and TE as measured by the time error in ATCo descending an aircraft.

As a result, a formal validation effort of the TE model in a specific ATCo environmental context was conducted to determine the generalizability of the TE model. The BL model's strategic task scheduling was combined with the TE underestimates of time passage as a function of increasing workload. The same validation approach that was applied to the BL model development iterations was applied to the TE model iteration. As can be seen in Figure 5, the TE model did not improve RHD predictions as compared to the baseline model. Relative to the FEWS data, the RHD times produced by the TE model were not significantly different from those produced from FEWS in the low workload condition (p>.05), but they were significantly higher in the medium (t(99)=2.08, p<.05) and high workload conditions (t(80)=5.85, p<.05).

5.3   Baseline Model with Time Management (TM+TE) Modification

To perform the *Time Management* (TM+TE) augmentation, the Time Estimating (center) and the Task Management (right most) boxes in Figure 4 were modified to account for the task management and the human estimates of time passage degradations that occur as a function of workload. Using the validation approach developed in this effort, it was apparent that limiting the queue length to zero in the TM model made it perform more "conservatively" and including a time estimation model succeeded in bringing the modeled RHD times closer to the FEWS RHD times than any of the other models alone. Relative to the FEWS data, the RHD times produced by the *Time Management* model were not significantly different from those produced from FEWS in the low (p>.05), and the medium workload conditions (p>.05) but they were significantly greater in the high workload conditions (t(80)=2.28, p<.05) (Figure 5).

The TC graphs also show that the order in which tasks were conducted in the *Time Management* model differed between the model and the FEWS simulation as illustrated in Figure 7 for the window open (left) and window close times (right).

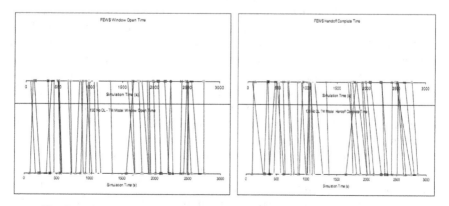

Fig. 7. TC Graphs - Window Open and Close Times (High Workload Model)

The TC window open time graphs illustrate that the order and the onset times are not precisely the same. While the overall data suggest that the high workload condition produced the greatest difference in RHD times, this effect can not be attributed primarily to the time that the window opened, since the present analysis suggests that the number of window open times that differed in order from the modeled and actual aircraft were fairly consistent across traffic conditions. The same holds true for the window close times.

It appears that the *Time Management* model did not succeed in bringing the model's RHD performance closer to the FEWS than the baseline model alone. Both the baseline and the *Time Management* model predictions of RHD remain significantly different than those produced by the ATCos in the FEWS experiment for the high workload condition. There did not appear to be any added benefit to the RHD prediction by both TM and TE together, although the *Time Management* manipulation did bring the mean RHD times closer than any of the other model manipulations alone.

6   Discussion

The recent proliferation of human-system models has resulted in highly complex human behavior models being used to generate predictions of operator performance within increasingly complex operational domains (e.g. process control, aircraft, and ATC operations, etc.). This proliferation is certain to continue along its growth path in the foreseeable future as computer technologies increase and the software implements more accurate representations of the human-system relationship. Many of the models that have been developed for system predictions have undergone some degree of verification and validation. However, creating valid behavioral models of a human is a challenging endeavor, particularly because of the complexity of human behaviors, which are further heightened when integrating multiple models that comprise the system. Assumptions made for one sub-model may interact with other sub-models and may invalidate the system prediction. As a result, it is vital that the complex human models that are used to generate predictions of human-system performance be designed and validated in accordance with a principled approach.

Validating the model using a limited number of validation measures (often only one measure) allows model developers flexibility with respect to the manipulation that will be made to the model to get it to perform consistently with the input data. It is often quite easy to tweak a model to perform well on one measure, while sacrificing the validity of other measures. When model analysts change a model's parameters, they typically do not examine the performance of the integrated representation of the model; rather they look at the effect of the individual parameter that they tweaked. While this is arguably an appropriate validation process for some small, non-integrated models, it is advisable that the more integrated and closed-loop HPMs conduct validation efforts use multiple human performance measures.

In summary, this research has introduced and demonstrated a comprehensive iterative develop-validate *approach* for validating a complex, closed-loop model of air traffic control using multiple measures at varying levels of fidelity designed to provide a validation approach for *time-sensitive* tasks. A series of objective and quantitative validation measures were applied to assess the validity of a baseline model that was then carried through as model iterations were completed. The iterative approach enabled the assessment of the impact of each model manipulation to determine whether the model developed operated verifiably and validly. It is only with such a rigorous approach that the models that are developed for complex human-system operations can be deemed credible representations of actual human performance.

Acknowledgments. We would like to express our sincere appreciation to Professors Daniel Frances, Mark Chignell, Baris Balcioglu, to Dr. Ronald Laughery, and to Mr. Ken Leiden for their input and guidance throughout this research project. This research was conducted as part of the first author's doctoral dissertation at the University of Toronto in the Department of Mechanical and Industrial Engineering.

References

1. DMSO 2001 Defense Modeling & Simulation Office (DMSO): Verification, Validation, And Accreditation (VV&A) Recommended Practices Guide (RPG): Special Topic - Validation of Human Behavior Representations (Website) (September 25, 2001), http://www.msiac.dmso.mil/vva/Special_topics/hbr-Validation/default.htm
2. Baron, S., Kruser, D.S., Huey, B.M.: Quantitative modeling of human performance in complex, dynamic systems. National Research Council Washington DC Panel on Human Performance Modeling, Washington (1990)
3. Balci, O.: Verification, Validation, and Testing Techniques. In: Banks, J. (ed.) Handbook of Simulation: Principles, Methodology, Advances, Applications, And Practice, pp. 335–427. Wiley & Sons, Inc., N.Y. (1998)
4. Campbell, G.E., Bolton, A.E.: HBR Validation: Interpreting Lessons Learned From Multiple Academic Disciplines, Applied Communities, And The AMBR Project. In: Gluck, K.A., Pew, R.W. (eds.) Modeling Human Behavior With Integrated Cognitive Architectures: Comparison, Evaluation And Validation, pp. 365–395. Lawrence Erlbaum & Associates, New Jersey (2005)
5. Willems, B.: Future En Route Workstation (FEWS) Study. FAA William Hughes Technical Center Atlantic City International Airport, New Jersey (2005)
6. Leiden, K., Kamienski, J.: DAG CE-6 Modeling and Simulation Studies. DAC Program Review Presentation. NASA Ames Research Center, Moffett Field (2006)
7. Hart, S.G.: The Prediction And Measurement Of Mental Workload During Space Operations. In: NASA Space Life Sciences Symposium, National Aeronautics and Space Administration, Washington, DC (1987)
8. Gore, B.F., Milgram, P.: The Conceptual Development Of A Time Estimation Model To Predict Human Performance In Complex Environments. In: Ninth Proceedings of the Annual SAE International Conference and Exposition - Digital Human Modeling for Design and Engineering Conference, SAE Paper # 2006-01-2344. SAE, Inc., Warrendale (2006)
9. Hollnagel, E.: Cognitive reliability and error analysis method (CREAM). The Alden Group, Elsevier Science, Oxford, UK (1998)

Personality and Attitudes as Predictors of Risky Driving Behavior: Evidence from Beijing Drivers

Jun Kong[1,2], Kan Zhang[1,*], and Xuefeng Chen[1]

[1] Institute of Psychology, Chinese Academy of Sciences
[2] University of Chinese Academy of Sciences
zhangk@psych.ac.cn

Abstract. The main aim of this study is to explore the relationships between personality traits, attitudes and risky driving behavior, in order to build a model of risky driving behavior that integrates the personality and social cognition approach. The study was based on a self-completion questionnaire survey carried out among 233 drivers in Beijing. The self-completion questionnaire consisted three sections: personality, attitudes towards traffic safety, and risky driving behavior. The results suggest that personality traits are valuable predictors of attitudes and risky driving behavior, and attitudes mediated the relation between the personality traits and risky driving behavior. Implications for road safety strategies are also discussed.

Keywords: personality, attitudes towards traffic safety, risky driving behavior, drivers.

1 Introduction

With the booming of the motor vehicle, risky driving behavior and traffic accidents have aroused wide public concern, and risky driving has been identified as an important contributor to road crashes [1]. Taking environmental and human factors in consideration, it is commonly believed that human factors contributed a larger proportion to risky driving behavior [2]. Within psychology, these perspectives of social cognition and personality psychology have been attempted to explain individual differences in risky driving behavior [3]. Social cognition research based on Theory of Reasoned Action [4], emphasizes central behavioral determinants such as attitudes, perceived risk, social norms [5]. Personality perspective focuses on the predictive power of personality traits, such as sensation-seeking, anger, and altruism [5,6].

Despite abundant studies within these psychology areas to identify variables which may influence risky driving behavior, few research has attempted to combine different approaches to build a general model of risky driving behavior and influences factors in the Chinese context.

---

[*] Corresponding author.

V.G. Duffy (Ed.): DHM/HCII 2013, Part I, LNCS 8025, pp. 38–44, 2013.

The present study attempts to establish a model of risky driving behavior that integrates the personality approach and the social cognition approach, in order to understand the formation of various risky driving behavior in traffic. More specifically, the aim of this present study is to explore the relationship between personality traits, attitudes towards traffic safety, and risky driving behavior among drivers. And the study is expected to provide useful information for road safety strategies and the development of driver education and training programs.

2   Method

2.1   Sample

The study was based on a self-completion questionnaire survey carried out among 233 drivers with license in Beijing. Of these, 37.8% were men and 72.2% were women. The respondents' other demographic information and driving behavioral information were listed in Appendix Table A with four items: age, education level, total kilometrage, and license tenure.

2.2   Measurement

The self-completion questionnaire consisted three sections: personality, attitudes towards traffic safety, and risky driving behavior.

Through literature review, five personality traits were selected as significant predictors of risky driving behavior in traffic [5-7]. They contained five questionnaires which measured anger (the tendency to experience anger and frustration), sensation-seeking (i.e., the need for excitement and stimulation), altruism (characterized by active concern for others), normlessness (i.e., the belief that socially unapproved behavior are required to achieve certain goals) and self-control (i.e., the tendency to control over one's thought and behavior), respectively. Anger, sensation-seeking and altruism were assessed using facets of the NEO-Personality Inventory-Revised [8], and each facet consisted of ten items. Normlessness was measured using Kohn and Schooler's [9] normlessness scale, which consists of four items. Tangney's short term self-control scale [10] was adopted to assess self-control, including 11 items. All of items were answered on five-point Likert scales ranging from "strongly disagree" (1) to "strongly agree" (5). The alpha coefficients were 0.62, 0.71, 0.66, 0.64, and 0.61, respectively.

Attitudes towards traffic safety consisted of five dimensions: traffic flow vs. rule obedience (4 items), speeding (7 items), drinking and driving (4 items), funriding (3 items), and showing off driving skills to others (3 items). These items were extracted from the studies of Ulleberge and Rundmo [5], Iversen [10], and Yilmaz and Celik [11]. All of items were answered on five-point Likert scales ranging from "strongly disagree" (1) to "strong agree" (5).The confirmatory factor analysis of the five-factor model indicated a satisfactory fit of the data: $\chi2/df= 1.334$, GFI=0.912, AGFI=0.887, CFI=0.953, RSMEA=0.038. The alpha coefficients were 0.65, 0.85, 0.72, 0.65, and 0.68, respectively.

Risky driving behavior were measured with Driver Behavior Questionnaire (DBQ), a 28-item version of the scale which consists of aggressive violation (4 items), ordinary violation (8 items), errors (8 items) and lapses (8 items), developed by Lawton et al. [12]. Respondents were required to answer on a five-point Likert scale from "never" (1) to "all the time" (5), which indicated how often in the past year they committed specific risky driving behavior. The alpha coefficients were 0.75, 0.74, 0.80, and 0.69, respectively.

3   Results

As correlation analysis shown in table 1, all the five personality traits were significantly correlated with attitudes towards safety driving and risky driving behavior. Those who got high scores on altruism and self-control tended to have a positive attitude towards traffic safety, as well as they reported less risky driving behavior. By contrast, those scoring high on sensation seeking, anger and normlessness demonstrated a negative attitude towards traffic safety, and reported more risky driving behavior. In addition, attitudes towards traffic safety were negatively related to risky driving behavior, indicating that drivers with a positive attitude towards traffic safety were less likely to report risky driving behavior.

Table 1. Correlations between personality traits, attitudes towards traffic safety and self-reported risky driving behavior

	1	2	3	4	5	6
1normlessness						
2angry	.227**					
3sensationseeking	.246**	.106				
4self-control	-.305**	-.378**	-.207**			
5altruism	-.223**	-.303**	-.031	.333**		
6attitudes towards traffic safety	-.483**	-.174**	-.270**	.339**	.146*	
7risky driving behavior	.354**	.330**	.278**	-.347**	-.348**	-.497**

$*p<0.05$ $**p<0.01$ $***p<0.001$.

A structural modeling analysis was performed to investigate the inter-relationships between personalities, attitudes toward traffic safety, and risky driving behavior. The estimated model was shown as Fig.1 with standardized path coefficients. The fit indices indicated that the correction model fitted the data well: $\chi2/df$ (57, n=233) =1.892, GFI=0.938, AGFI=0.897, CFI=0.935, RSMEA=0.062. The path model explained 59% of the total variance in risky driving behavior.

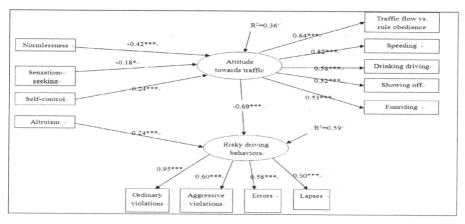

Fig. 1. Path diagram of the relationship between personality traits, attitudes, risky driving behavior

The effect of attitudes towards traffic safety on risky driving behavior was significantly negative (β=0.69, p<0.001), indicating that individuals with a positive attitude towards traffic safety were likely to engage less risky driving behavior compared to those with a negative attitude towards traffic safety.

When it came to the effects of personality on attitudes toward traffic safety, all personality traits except for altruism demonstrated their significant, direct influences on driver's safety attitudes. Specifically, self-control had a positive effect on driver's safety attitudes (β=0.24, p<0.001), while normlessness (β=0.42, p<0.001) and sensation-seeking (β=–0.18, p<0.05) had negative effects on attitudes. Those who got high scores on self-control tended to report less risky driving behavior. By contrast, those scoring high on sensation seeking, and normlessness demonstrated a negative attitude towards traffic safety, and reported more risky driving behavior.

Regarding the direct effects of personality traits on risky driving behavior, only altruism was found to have significant coefficients. Turning to the other three personality traits, all of normlessness, sensation-seeking and self-control had no direct but indirect effects on risky driving behavior mediated by attitudes towards to traffic safety. As the direct, indirect and total effect of personality traits on risky driving behavior shown in Table 2, the findings indicated that individuals scoring high on altruism and self-control were less likely to exhibit risky driving behavior. On the contrary, the higher the scores for sensation-seeking and normlessness, the more likely those individuals engaged in risky driving behavior.

Table 2. Direct, indirect and total effect of personality traits on risky driving behavior

	Altruism	Normlessness	Self-control	Sensation-seeking
Direct effect	-0.242			
Indirect effect		0.277	-0.168	0.122
Total effect	-0.242	0.277	-0.168	0.122

Furthermore, as shown in the path model, a total of 36% of the variance in attitude towards traffic safety were explained by the three different personality traits, implying that attitude towards traffic safety has incremental validity in predicting risky driving behavior beyond personality traits.

4   Discussion and Conclusion

The present study attempts to explore the relationship between personality traits, attitudes towards traffic safety, and risky driving behavior among drivers and to establish a model of risky driving behavior that integrate the personality approach and the social cognition approach, in order to understand the mechanisms underlying risky driving behavior in Chinese context.

The effect of attitudes towards traffic safety on risky driving behavior is significantly negative, indicating that individuals with a positive attitude towards traffic safety are likely to engage less risky driving behavior compared to those with a negative attitude towards traffic safety, in accordance with previous studies [6,10]. As the Theory of Reasoned Action [4] sated, attitudes are central determinants of behavior. Therefore, attitudes towards traffic safety serve as central determinants of risky driving behavior in traffic. As a result, strategies of promoting road safety can be aimed at changing individuals' attitudes related to risky driving.

When it comes to the effects of personality on attitudes toward traffic safety, all personality traits except for altruism demonstrate their significant, direct influences on driver's safety attitudes. Specifically, self-control has a positive effect on driver's safety attitudes, while normlessness and sensation-seeking have negative effects on attitudes. Those who get high scores on self-control tend to report less risky driving behavior. By contrast, those scoring high on sensation seeking, and normlessness demonstrate a negative attitude towards traffic safety, and report more risky driving behavior. The findings are consistent with previous studies [7,12]. For example, drivers scoring high on self-control are good at controlling over their thoughts and interrupting undesired behavioral tendencies, and this mirrors itself in risky attitudes towards drinking driving, speeding, and rule violation in traffic. Sensation-seekers tend to seek stimulation and excitement in driving, probably leading to risky driving behavior. Referring to normlessness, individuals scoring high on this trait are likely to have low barriers towards socially unapproved behavior, which reflect in risky attitudes towards speeding, rule violation, and funriding, and risky driving behavior in traffic.

Regarding the direct effects of personality traits on risky driving behavior, only altruism is found to have a significant coefficient, consistent with previous study [6]. In other words, individuals with high scores on altruism are less likely to exhibit risky driving behavior. A possible explanation is that drivers scoring higher on altruism are expected to consider the interests of others and show more active concern for others in traffic and thus reduce risky driving behavior.

Turning to the other three personality traits, all of normlessness, sensation-seeking and self-control have no direct but indirect effects on risky driving behavior mediated by attitudes towards to traffic safety. The lack of direct effects of the three personality traits suggests that personalities primarily influenced risky driving behavior through attitudes towards traffic safety. The findings indicate that individuals scoring high on altruism and self-control are less likely to exhibit risky driving behavior. On the contrary, the higher the scores for sensation-seeking and normlessness, the higher the likelihood individuals engage in risky driving behavior. Therefore, personality traits should be taken into account when designing road safety programs.

To sum up, personality traits primarily influence risky driving behaviors through attitudes towards traffic safety. Taking personality and attitudes into account, the integration of both personality and social cognition approaches provides a comprehensive model to understand the mechanisms underlying drivers' risky driving behaviors in traffic. This study's findings provide useful information for road safety interventions and the development of driver education and training programs [6]. For example, road safety interventions could target drivers' attitudes towards traffic safety to reduce risky driving behavior and traffic accidents. Moreover, as those who possess certain personality traits with negative attitudes towards traffic safety are more likely to commit risky driving behaviors, road safety program and driver training should be tailored to certain personality traits of drivers [6].

Appendix:

Table 3. A Demographic distribution of respondents in the sample

Variable	Category	n	%	Variable	Category	n	%
Age	21-25	27	11.6	Total kilometrage	<10,000 km	63	27.0
	26-30	58	24.9		10,000-50,000 km	75	32.2
	31-35	67	28.8		50,000-100,000 km	38	16.3
	36-40	37	15.9		100,000-300,000 km	40	17.2
	41-45	26	11.1		>300,000 km	10	4.3
	>46	18	7.7	License tenure	0-1 year	40	17.2
Education level	High school	17	7.3		2-3 years	65	27.9
	College	38	16.3		3-5 years	31	13.3
	University	146	62.7		5-15 years	72	30.9
	Master's degree/ doctorate	32	13.7		15-20 years	17	7.3
					>20years	4	1.7

References

1. Jonah, B.A.: Accident risk and risk-taking behavior among young driver. Accident Analysis & Prevention 18, 255–271 (1986)
2. Mckema, F.P.: Accident proneness: A conceptual analysis. Accident Analysis & Prevention 15, 65–71 (1983)

3. Parker, D., Manstead, A.: The social psychology of driver behaviour. Applied Social Psychology, 198–224 (1996)
4. Ajzen, I., Fishbein, M.: Understanding attitudes and predicting social behavior. Prentice-Hall, New York (1980)
5. Ulleberg, P., Rundmo, T.: Personality, attitudes and risk perception as predictors of risky driving behaviour among young drivers. Safety Science 41, 427–443 (2003)
6. Chen, C.F.: Personality, safety attitudes and risky driving behavior—Evidence from young Taiwanese motorcyclists. Accident Analysis & Prevention 41, 963–968 (2009)
7. Dahlen, E.R., Martin, R.C., et al.: Driving anger, sensation seeking, impulsiveness, and boredom proneness in the prediction of unsafe driving. Accident Analysis & Prevention 37, 341–348 (2005)
8. Costa, P.T., McCrae, R.R.: Revised neo personality inventory (neo pi-r) and neo five-factor inventory (neo-ffi). Psychological Assessment Resources, Florida (1992)
9. Kohn, M.L., Schooler, C.: Work and personality: An inquiry into the impact of social stratification, pp. 345–369. Ablex Norwood, New York (1983)
10. Tangney, J.P., Baumeister, R.F.: High self-control predicts good adjustment, less pathology, better grades, and interpersonal success. Journal of Personality 72, 271–324 (2004)
11. Yilmaz, V., Celik, H.E.: A model for risky driving attitudes in Turkey. Social Behavior and Personality: an International Journal 32, 791–796 (2004)
12. Lawton, R., Parker, D., et al.: The role of affect in predicting social behavior: the case of road traffic violations. Journal of Applied Social Psychology 27, 1258–1276 (1997)
13. Yllmaz, V., Çelik, H.E.: A model for explanation of personal attitudes toward traffic of candidate drivers attending drivers' courses: Risky candidate driver's attitude model. Transportation Research Part F: Traffic Psychology and Behaviour 11, 233–241 (2008)

Effects of Sleep Deprivation on Pilot's Cognitive Behavior in Flight Simulation

Zhong-Qi Liu[1], Qian-Xiang Zhou[1,*], and Fang Xie[2]

[1] School of Biological Science and Medical Engineering,
Beihang University, Beijing 100191, China
[2] General Technology Department,
China North Vehicle Research Institute, Beijing 100072, China
liuzhongqi@buaa.edu.cn, zqxg@sjtu.edu.cn,
christie_xie@163.com

Abstract. This study examined the effects of 32 h of continuous SD(Sleep Deprivation) on cognitive behavior in simulated flight. Four subjects who were skilled in flight simulator took part in the experiment. Eye movement and flight parameters were measured in the following 5 time periods: 1100 on DAY 1, 1500, 0400 on DAY 2, 1100, and 1500. Subject's cognitive workload and fatigue were assessed with method of NASA-TLX (national aeronautics and space administration-task load index) and RPE (rating of perceived exertion). Eye movement indices of average pupil area, average saccade amplitude and average saccade velocity decreased during the 32 h SD and they all showed significantly changes in the final SD while the index of average fixation time increased in the final SD. Flight performance that evaluated by four flight parameters of the deviation of height, pitch angle, yaw angle and tilt angle deteriorated during the 32 h SD, but not significantly. The feeling of fatigue and workload reported by subjects both increased during the 32 h SD. Effects of daily rhythm were also found, there were a obviously change at the hour of 0400. 32 h of SD has obvious effects on eye movement behaviors which have close relations to fatigue because of SD. The eye movement measurement can be served as a tool to continually monitor fatigue online.

Keywords: sleep deprivation, cognition, eye movement, flight performance.

1 Introduction

Flight is complex tasks that need high mental work. Adequate sleep is necessary for pilots' normal flights. Long-haul flights across time zones, night flights, night combat duty, repeated flights over the short term, irregular working hours will lead to pilots' SD. It is especially prevalent in the past air combat and will be more common in high-tech war in the future.

SD is a major reason contributed to the flight accident and fatigue that played a role in over 12% of all US Air Force mishaps and is a recurring concern throughout

---

* Corresponding author.

V.G. Duffy (Ed.): DHM/HCII 2013, Part I, LNCS 8025, pp. 45–54, 2013.

the aviation industry[1]. Insufficient sleep leads to a general slowing of response speed and increased variability in performance, particularly for simple measures of alertness, attention and vigilance[2-5], and aircrews are more likely to lower their standards of performance, suffer impairments in the ability to integrate information, and experience a reduced attention span that may lead to forgetting or ignoring important aspects of flying[6].There are mainly four kinds of methods of studying SD: subjective assessment method[7], physiological and biochemical measurements[8-10], performance measurement[11][12], psychology and behavioral method[13][14]. Subjective evaluation method of the data with a strong subjective component, and sometimes make people doubt its authenticity and reliability; physiological measurements and biochemical measurement usually need place device on the human body that make the subjects feel unwell and interfere the experimental task; in addition, various methods are generally measured in advance or post measurement and can't measure the actual flight task, so there was some deviation between the measurement data and the actual value.

The eyes are the windows of the soul; the information obtainment in the flight mission mainly depends on vision. In the SD process, the function of the visual system is bound to be affected. Researchers found that some eye movement parameters will change with fatigue[15]: blink rate generally increases with sleep deprivation and fatigue; pupil diameter typically decreases with sleep deprivation; saccadic velocity has been shown to decrease with sleep deprivation; mean saccade length increases with time-on-task; dwell time was shown to decrease with time-on-task.

Eye movement measures provide valuable information of not only fatigue and workload but also operators' attention, behavior performance and cognitive function that they all will be impaired during SD. The chief purpose of this study was to investigate changes in flight performance during extended wakefulness of over 30 hr and to determine the relationship of eye movement behavior and fatigue and workload during SD.

2   Method

2.1   Apparatus

This study was conducted in the fixed base flight simulators which the prototype was a military aircraft of a high validity. IT was made up of the real cockpit, joystick, throttle lever, rudder, and true flight dynamics system and the simulator can complete the aircraft's acceleration, deceleration, pitch, yaw, tilt and all the basic fights. Flight performance measurements were collected in the flight simulator.

Eye movements were recorded by means of Eyelink II measuring system manufactured by Canada's SR Research CORP. Eyelink II system is a high-bandwidth eye tracking system. Its spatial resolution is up to $0.01°$ of view; its gaze error is less than $0.05°$; the sampling frequency is 250 Hz with corneal reflection and pupil tracking mode.

2.2   Subjects

Four young healthy male adults who were university students participated in this study (age range 18–22 years, mean age=20). They have been trained expertly for all kinds of basic flight tasks in above flight simulator. Screening excluded those having sleep difficulties who napped regularly in the daytime, and were on medication that affected sleep or sleepiness. Other requisites for inclusion were: no excessive daytime sleepiness; no smoking, drinking and gambling habits; no coffee and tea drinking habits; no neurological and psychiatric history; no other eye diseases. All had normal, or corrected normal vision. They had the procedures explained, signed consent forms, and were paid to participate.

2.3   Task

Subjects were asked to accomplish 1 minute level fight above the runway and with VFR（Visual Flight Rule） in a fine and no wind day. At the beginning of the fight, aircraft faced right the runway, the vertical height from the ground was 400m, and the level distance from the centre of the runway was 5400m (Fig.1). The subject must keep the height of 400m and the heading angle of 90°. Schedule of test flights for all four subjects is as follows: 1100 on Day 1, 1500, 0400 on Day 2, 1100 and 1500 so there were five test segments.

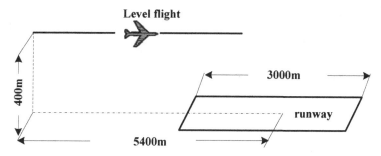

Fig. 1. Flight task schematic diagram

2.4   Procedure

Subjects were called to get up at 0700 and the SD began. Subjects were asked to keep wakeful after the entire test segment finished and it lasted almost 32 h. After breakfast, they arrived at laboratory at about 0800. An informed consent agreement was signed by subjects and all upcoming experiment procedures were briefed to them.

After the calibrations of the eye movement measuring system, the subjects exercised the flight task several times to adapt the simulator. When the subjects said ok, the formal test began. Subjects were asked to complete four times fight on each segment. Flight parameters data for flight performance and eye movement data were recorded during the test.

The feeling of drowsiness and fatigue were respectively measured with the SSS (Stanford Sleepiness Scale) and RPE (Rating of Perceived Exertion) scale before each formal test[16]. Cognitive workload was measured to investigate the subjects' state of workload with NASA-TLX (National Aeronautics and Space Administration-Task Load Index) scale after each formal test[5].

3   Results

In this study, the data of the time of 1100 on DAY 1 was the reference value and the other four segments' data were compared to it with paired t-test.

3.1   Flight Performance

Flight performance was evaluated by recording the four flight parameters which they were the deviation of height, pitch angle, yaw angle and tilt angle. The four parameters showed consistent change trend that they all got worse through the five SD segments, but the change didn't get significant level($p<0.05$) except that the deviation of height(Fig.2). All the subjects' flight performance showed a similar pattern that the value of the flight parameters got worse at the time of 0400 than the former and latter of the performance. It may be the effect of the daily rhythm. It must be mentioned that it showed some individual difference of the performance between subjects. For instance: tilt angle tended to increase through 32hs SD and only the subject of NO 2 reached significant level($p<0.05$) at 0400 while the others had not obvious change($p>0.05$); At the final time, yaw angle of two subjects is obviously greater t($p<0.05$) than baseline values of 1100 on DAY 1. It perhaps due to the difference of "SD resistance".

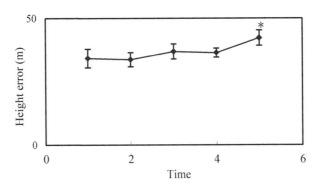

Note: * significantly different from the initial trial of 1100 on DAY 1($p<.05$).
1$-$1100 on DAY 1; 2$-$1500; 3$-$0400 on DAY 2; 4$-$1100; 5$-$1500

Fig. 2. Height deviation through 32 h SD

3.2   SSS and RPE

Subjective feeling of sleeping in SSS (Fig.3) score and fatigue in RPE (Fig.4) score were of similar trends which they were significantly increasing along with the SD time. SSS score and RPE score both reached a significant level (p<0.05) at 0400. Seen form the figures of SSS and RPE, curves slope around the time of 0400 is obviously different. It may also the effect of daily rhythm.

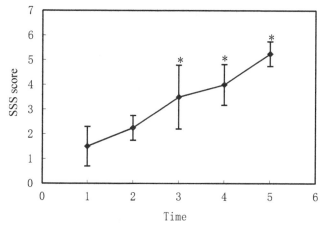

Note: * significantly different from the initial trial of 1100 on DAY 1(p<.05).
1−1100 on DAY 1; 2−1500; 3−0400 on DAY 2; 4−1100; 5−1500

Fig. 3. SSS change through 32 h SD

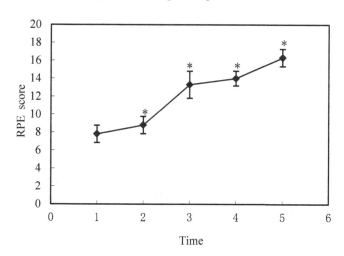

Note: * significantly different from the initial trial of 1100 on DAY 1(p<.05).
1−1100 on DAY 1; 2−1500; 3−0400 on DAY 2; 4−1100; 5−1500

Fig. 4. RPE change through 32 hs SD

3.3   Cognitive Workload

The workload of the subjects through the five test segments is assessed by the NASA-TLX score. The NASA-TLX was carried out based six parameters: mental demand (MD), physical demand (PD), temporal demand (TD), performance (Per), effort (E) and frustration level(FL). To clearly survey the change of the workload, six dimensions of the NASA-TLX were separately scored(Fig.5). They all increased with different degree through the whole SD, while MD changed most, followed by E and Per, FL changed least. Six dimensions all reached significant level (p<0.05) at the time of 0400.

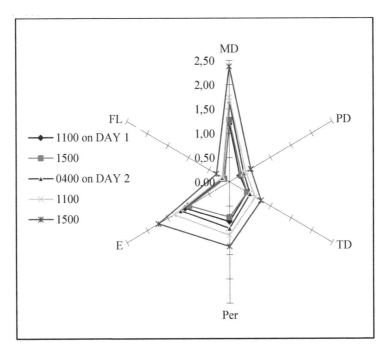

Fig. 5. NASA-TLX change through 32 hs SD

3.4   Eye Movement Parameters

As can be seen from Fig. 6, the pupil area of the four subjects showed a more consistent narrowing trend and their pupil change all reached significant level at different time that two subjects were of 0400 while one subject closed to the edge significant level at 1100 on DAY 2 and then reached significant level (p<0.05) at final time. Only one subject was some of different from the others, his pupil area increased at 1500 on DAY 1am and then decreased the following time and reached significant level.

Average saccade amplitude of four subjects decreased during 32 h SD and reached significant level (p<0.05) in different time that two subjects were at the final time of SD and the other two were at 1100 on DAY 2.

Four subjects show a consistent decreasing trend of the index of the average saccade velocity. Three subjects reached significant level (p<0.05)at 11:00 on DAY 2 while one subject was at the final time of SD.

The indicator of average fixation time increased through the 32 h SD. Four subjects all reached significant level at the final time of SD.

Indicators of fixation frequency, peak saccade velocity and vengeance did not make any obvious and regular changes in this study.

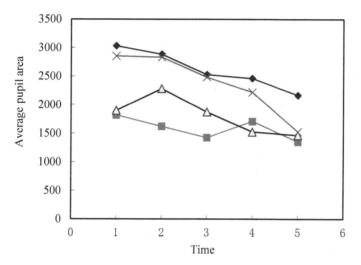

1—1100 on DAY 1 ; 2—1500; 3—0:00 on DAY 2; 4—1100; 5—1500

Fig. 6. Pupil change through 32 hs SD

4   Discussion

The direct effect of SD was enhanced fatigue and increased sleepiness. The correlation analysis between RPE and SSS showed a high degree of correlation(r= 0.987). They changed eye movement behavior and result in the pupil's miosis, decreasing saccade amplitude and saccade velocity while the average fixation time became longer. These changes might have two reasons. First, Sustained wakefulness leads to the physical fatigue of eye muscle. Eye movement load is a function of time, the longer of the watching time the greater accumulation of visual load and so as to the accumulation and generation of eye muscle fatigue. Second, sustained wakefulness leads to mental fatigue. Brain made various basic mental activities in waking state which they include exchanges with other persons, individual psychological activity, carrying out the experimental tasks and other activities. With the continued awake time, mental fatigue gradually accumulated and resulted in the alteration of person's eye movement behavior.

Fatigue is an important factor affecting pupil size. Lowenstein pointed out that pupil diameter was the largest after a good rest and narrowed with the people's fatigue[17]. Russo studied the effects of SD on human eye movement behavior and founded that the average saccade velocity decreased significantly [18]. He pointed out that saccade velocity index can be a good indicator for the alert degree in operating environment and lowered saccade velocity means that the operator was in fewer alerts that increased the probability of the accident. Gennaro studied the scan behavior during 40 hours SD. The results showed that the scan velocity and saccade amplitude reduced [19]. It can be seen that the results of this study is consistent with that of some researchers.

Average fixation time did not change in Schleicher study [20]. It might be relate to the monotonous and dull tasks because the fixation point of 150ms and 900ms increased and the fixation point less than 150ms didn't relate to cognitive processing while the fixation point more than 900ms were relation to the gradually decreasing interesting due to the monotony tasks, so the average fixation time almost had no change. In this study, flight simulation operation was a complex task. Subjects have been trying to operate, but because of the accumulating fatigue, their ability of information processing speed gradually slowed down led to the longer dwell time. NASA-TLX score of mental demand also showed that flight simulation has a higher demand to the people's mental activity.

In this study, flight performance showed decreasing trend, but it didn't reach significant level ($p < 0.05$) which may be relate to the not long enough time of SD. Some eye movement indicators have shown a significant change which illuminate that eye movement parameters were more sensitive to SD than flight performance. This may be more meaningful for fatigue monitoring and early warning because of SD. In real flight, pilots can be continuously measured in real time with modern advanced eye movements tracking technology. An early warning can be made for the pilot's fatigue or sleepiness and ensure safety driving.

In this study, almost all the experiment results were influenced by people's circadian rhythms which it have been founded in others studies[1][15]. It suggests that people who need night operations, such as various drivers and various monitoring staff, must take some action to keep alert at Time of 0400. To do that, one can make themselves have a rest or nap in the afternoon or ask the operations staff to remind themselves or remind them by communication in their physical low point.

5 Conclusion

In conclusion, the results of this study provide an important glimpse of pilot's cognitive behavior during about 32 hr of extended wakefulness. It can be seen that subjects' flight performance and eye movement performance were affected by the increasing of the subjects' fatigue and cognitive workload. Eye movement behavior is more easily suffered than that of flight performance during SD. The characteristic of the sensitiveness of the eye movement behavior to SD can be utilized to monitor pilot in real time who are operating which can forecast and warn early of pilot's fatigue and sleepiness. With that characteristic, flight performance predication and evaluation can also be made and it is the issue of further study.

Acknowledgement. This work is supported by the Technology Foundation of National Science (A0920132003) and the Natural Science Foundation of China (31170895).

References

1. Lopez, N., Previc, F.H., Fischer, G., et al.: Effects of sleep deprivation on cognitive performance by United States Air Force pilots. Journal of Applied Research in Memory and Cognition 1, 27–73 (2012)
2. Killgore, W.D.: Effects of sleep deprivation on cognition. Progress in Brain Research 185, 105–129 (2010)
3. Whitney, P., Hinson, J.M.: Measurement of cognition in studies of sleep deprivation. Progress in Brain Research 185, 37–48 (2010)
4. Kim, H.J., Kim, H., Park, K.D., Choi, K.G., Lee, H.W.: A survey of sleep deprivation patterns and their effects on cognitive functions of residents and interns in Korea. Sleep Medicine 12, 390–396 (2011)
5. Tomasko, J.M., Pauli, E.M., Kunselman, A.R., Haluck, R.S.: Sleep deprivation increases cognitive workload during simulated surgical tasks. The American Journal of Surgery 203, 37–43 (2012)
6. Perry, I.C.: Helicopter aircrew fatigue. AGARD Advisory Report No. 69
7. Cao, X.L.: Experimental Study of the Attention Character and Subjective Assessment Methods on Mental Fatigue. PhD thesis of the Fourth Military University (2003) (in Chinese)
8. Belyavin, A., Wright, N.A.: Changes in electrical activity of the brain with vigilance. Electroencephalograph. Clin. Neurophysiology 66(2), 137–144 (1987)
9. Fernstrom, J.D., Fernstrom, M.H.: Exercise, serum free tryptophan, and central fatigue. The Journal of Nutrition 136(2), 553–559 (2006)
10. Ohta, M., Hirai, N., Ono, Y., et al.: Clinical biochemical evaluation of central fatigue with 24-hour continuous exercise. The Japanese Journal of Clinical Pathology 53(9), 802–809 (2005)
11. Zhang, Q., Cheng, J.N., Yang, P.J., et al.: Preliminary Study on Balance Function Quantitative Assessment in Human. Chinese Journal of Rehabilitation 13(2), 49–52 (1998) (in Chinese)
12. Wang, S.Y., Zhang, L.F., Cheng, J.H., Wang, X.B.: Time-frequency analysis of heart rate variability during head up tilt. Journal of the Fourth Military Medical University 22(4), 301–305 (2001) (in Chinese)
13. Ji, H.G., Zhang, L., Wang, H.M.: Functional change after 24 hour sleep deprivation. Chinese Journal of Behavioral Medical Science 7(4), 258–259 (1998)
14. Yue, P., Miao, D.M., Huang, P.E., et al.: Influence of 32-hour sleep deprivation on selective attention. Journal of Fourth Military Medical University 25(4), 378–381 (2004)
15. Previc, F.H., Lopez, N., Ercoline, W.R., et al.: The Effects of Sleep Deprivation on Flight Performance, Instrument Scanning, and Physiological Arousal in Pilots. The International Journal of Aviation Psychology 19(4), 326–346 (2009)

16. Bailes, S., Libman, E., Baltzan, M., et al.: Brief and distinct empirical sleepiness and fatigue scales. Journal of Psychosomatic Research 60, 605–613 (2006)
17. Lowenstein, O., Locwenficld, I.E.: The sleep-waking cycle and pupillary activity. Animals of the New York Academy of Sciences 117, 142–156 (1964)
18. Russo, M., Thomas, M., Sing, H., et al.: Saccadic velocity and pupil constriction latency changes in partial sleep deprivation, and correlations with simulated motor vehicle crashes. Sleep 22(1), 297–298 (1999)
19. Gennaro, L.D., Ferrara, M., Urbani, L., et al.: Oculomotor impairment after 1 night of total sleep deprivation: a dissociation between measures of speed and accuracy. Clinical Neurophysiology 111(10), 1771–1778 (2000)
20. Schleicher, R., Galley, N.: Blinks and saccades as indicators of fatigue in sleepiness warners: looking tired? Ergonomics 51(7), 982–1010 (2008)

Towards Early Status Warning for Driver's Fatigue Based on Cognitive Behavior Models[*]

Yanfei Liu, Yu Zhang, Junsong Li, Jing Sun, Feng Fu, and Jiangsheng Gui

Department of Computer Science and Technology, Zhejiang Sci-Tech University,
Xiasha, Hangzhou, Zhejiang 310018, China
yliu@zju.edu.cn, {yzh,fufeng}@zstu.edu.cn, ljscg@sina.com,
sunjing531@163.com, dewgjs@126.com

Abstract. Based on ACT-R (Adaptive Control of Thought-Rational) cognitive architecture this paper implements researches on a status warning system for driver's fatigue, its goal is applying vehicle performance output and cognitive science to build driver behavior model, using non-invasive detection method that retrospect driver behavior based on model to monitor driving status, and to reach the aims of driver status monitor and early warning. First, based on the different detection methods' analysis of driving fatigue, the predominance of cognitive science, and the inherent relationship between driver behavior and cognitive science, the advantages of applying cognitive theory to researches on driver fatigue are clarified. Then, based on the analysis of the factors contribute to fatigue related accidents and observations of drowsy driving cases, the viewpoint that the fatigue driving is consist of three stage and corresponding to three status is proposed; accordingly, the declarative and procedure knowledge for ACT-R architecture is extracted, and driver fatigue behavioral model is implemented on the ACT-R software platform. Finally, the simulation methods are applied to verify the model's validity and a framework of driver status monitor and early warning system that contains the cognitive fatigue driver behavior models is put forward. The research results indicate that the fatigue driver behavior model has a strong advantage in the researches of driver status monitor and early warning.

Keywords: Cognitive driver behavior, driver status warning, ACT-R.

1   Introduction

Driver fatigue is serious potential threats of traffic crash for its high rate accidents and serious consequences. The experts pointed out that the risk of driver fatigue is as dangerous as drunk driving. An 18-hour without sleep is equivalent to half drunk, and a 24-hour without sleep is equivalent to drunk. A 1991 report by the National

---

[*] This work is supported by Zhejiang Provincial Natural Science Foundation under Grant No. LY12C09005, Y1110477, National Natural Science Foundation of China under Grant No.61100183, 6110503 and 973 Program of China under Grant No. 2011CB711000.

V.G. Duffy (Ed.): DHM/HCII 2013, Part I, LNCS 8025, pp. 55–60, 2013.

Highway Traffic Safety Administration indicates that driver drowsiness as one of the leading causes of single and multiple car accidents [1].

1.1 Research on Fatigue Driving

Various methods have been taken to detect driving fatigue and give early warning in the early days and some mechanical devices are used in the mid-1960s and early 1970s. Nowadays, driver fatigue research focus on developing algorithms for the detection of drowsiness. During Driving fatigue studies, the researchers used different techniques to solve the problem of driver fatigue detection. Due lots of advantages especially the characteristics of non-intrusive, the detection of driver fatigue by using vehicle performance's output is more acceptable to the driver [2].

1.2 Research on Cognitive Driver Behavior Modeling and ACT-R

Driver cognitive behavior modeling method gradually developed into a field of intelligent transportation system and become one of the hottest research topics recently. Truls VAA (2001) noted that cognition and emotion are a good tool for prediction, avoidance and evaluation of dangerous during driving task. After that, Salvucci DD (2002), Daiel Krajzewicz (2002) and Delphine Delorme (2001) etc. launched research work on the driver behavior in cognitive architecture. Liu (2006) is also conducted driving behavior modeling studies on the basis of cognitive tools CogTool[4].

ACT-R is one of the most typical and widely used cognitive architecture. It aims at using software to simulate a full range of cognitive tasks. Its constructs reflect assumptions about human cognition. These assumptions are based on numerous facts derived from psychology experiments. Research on ACT-R cognitive architecture is related closely to the latest achievements of neurobiology.

2 Driver Fatigue Cognitive Model in ACT-R

2.1 Modeling Driver Cognitive Behavior Using ACT-R

Driving task is the whole process which is consist of several continuous small pieces of basic task. Driver cognitive behavior is the compound of driver's perception, cognition, manipulation, and implementation for certain anticipating task [5]. Michon (1985) groups three classes of driving task, monitor, decision-making and control. the ACT-R cognitive architecture is a production executive system, driver cognitive behavior model in ACT-R is a program running in the ACT-R platform. The model handle external input and output internal information, and execute productions such as monitor, decision-making and control which represent knowledge of driving task. The model is the realization of ACT-R production system for declarative knowledge and procedural knowledge as well as driver's operation and purpose. Sequential execution circularly for monitor, decision-making and control driving tasks in ACT-R cognitive processor forms closely connected cognitive task's stream[6]. The most important thing for ACT-R model is to extract declarative knowledge, procedural knowledge and model's parameter.

2.2   Driver Behavior Characteristics of Fatigue Related Accidents

To obtain fatigue driving knowledge, related research are investigated here firstly to find characteristic of fatigue driving. There are many researchers who focused on steering-wheel manipulation behavior to detect fatigue [7], such as Horne and Reyner (1995) propose identification criterion for fatigue-related accidents which vehicle go off the road, there is no brake evidence, there is no mechanical failure, the weather is good, and exclude over speed, and Hulbert's research (1972) found that comparing with normal drivers sleep-deprived drivers conduct low-frequency steering-wheel back (steering angle exceeds zero degree) operation. The related researches indicate that when fatigue driving the driver's steering-wheel manipulation ability reduced, even there is no steering-wheel operation as it is necessary. Lower or loss of steering-wheel control ability is main characteristics of driver fatigue driving behavior [8].

2.3   Characteristic of Fatigue Driving Behavior

To descript easily, the procedure that from driver's awareness to fatigue and finally cause accident are divided three stages and defined three status accordingly, i.e. tiredness, insensitiveness, and drowsiness. Tiredness, the in this stage the driver try to take measures (such as drinking cola, coffee and hard rubbing eyes, hard opening eyes wide, etc.) to make himself sober, the driver maintains sober, and the driver have necessary driving ability for perception, cognition, decision-making and control (PCDC). Secondly insensitiveness, in this stage driver is consciousness, may be awakened by the sudden events, and lack normal driving ability for PCDC; As to the steering-wheel operation, the characteristic is low-frequency small-angle steering-wheel operation and sudden   steering-wheel operation. And drowsiness, in this stage the driver lose normal driving capacity for PDDC, run into obstacles, isolation belt or off the lane when running in curve road, and result in fatigue driving accident.

Research shows that the fatigue driving has follows characteristic in time, road shape/type, vehicle speed, and driver's steering-wheel operation. For time characteristics, most fatigue driving occur in the time period between 02:00 to 07:00 and 14:00 to 16:00, for road and vehicle speed, the fatigue driving occur in good road surface and highway, and for driver and behavior, three status of tiredness, insensitiveness, and drowsiness   appears and corresponding steering-wheel operation is implemented.

3   Driver Fatigue Behavior Modeling

3.1   ACT-R Driver Fatigue Model

The declarative knowledge, the procedural knowledge, and model's parameters can be obtained from the characteristic of fatigue related accidents, fatigue driving behavior and the driving environmental conditions. The model is primarily composed of two main parts, the manual controlling part and model part. The manual controlling part implement user's manual controlling function, and the model part includes the chunk type's definition, declarative knowledge, model's first goal and all the procedural knowledge.

3.2   The Principle for Fatigue Status's Judgment

Sometimes the model can judge driving status by several declarative knowledge and procedural knowledge, however, most of the time lots of knowledge are necessary to determine driver's status, even some knowledge are fuzzy and only can be reference[9]. It's essential to quantify the fuzzy knowledge and to unify quantifiable knowledge, and   in order to use unified fatigue judgment criterion in driver fatigue model. The following driver fatigue judgment formula is applied in fatigue driving behavior model.

$$k = \sum_{i=1}^{n} \omega_i S_i \tag{1}$$

Here, K is the index of fatigue, its values is in [0, 1]. If its value is the closer to 1, it indicates that the higher the driver may be fatigue driving; if its value is closer to 0, it indicates the possibility of driver fatigue driving is lower, ω_i is weight of i element in the driver fatigue factors, and Si is the fatigue status's valuesof the i factor.

3.3   The Model's Validation

To validate the model, two scenarios are designed to test the model's effectiveness, the following simulation experiments all set the time to the time period in prone to fatigue driving.

Firstly, a car is running on a straight highway, the vehicle speed is 120km/h. while the car moving, the operation interface prompts there is a left turn ahead with 165 degree angle (the angle, direction generated by model randomly). Under this circumstances, if the operator conduct 5 left-turn operations by key press, and conduct 5 right-turn   operations after promotion of end of turn, the model does not show warning messages. However, if there is no turn operation after prompting message for a period of time (about 5 seconds), the model shows warning message "drowsiness".

Secondly, the car is also driving on a straight highway at beginning, and the vehicle speed is also set to 120km/h. After a period of time (about 10 minutes) there is no turning operation, and the the operator interface prompts that the vehicle deviate from its own lane right 10cm. At this moment, the operator conducts a substantial left-turn steering operation by using keyboard, and the model indicates driving warning message "insensitiveness" within a short time.   By checking the road the car has passed, we know there are slight curve in the road, more than 10 minutes straight moving accumulation make the vehicle deviate from its own lane right 10cm. However, the operator does not adjust vehicle's moving direction according to road's slight curve. As finding the vehicle deviates from suitable lane, he takes a substantial steering wheel operation. Therefore, the model makes a judgment that the driver is in the status of "insensitiveness" [10].

The above two experimental results of fatigue driving behavior model simulation are consistent with fatigue driving situations.

4   Status Warning with Driver Fatigue Model

Based on vehicle performance's output, fatigue driving cognitive behavior model determine whether the driver is fatigue driving or which driving status he is. The model's output, which integrates with other model's output and control strategy, are developed into warning system. The warning system determine vehicle's and driving status, make decision, and finally notify vehicle's ECU (Electronic Control Unit) to implement the decision policy. Figure 1 is the framework for driving status monitoring and warning system including driver fatigue model.

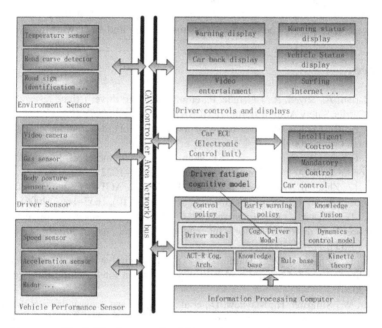

Fig. 1. The framework of driver status warning system

The sensor's data are collected over CAN (for controller area network) bus and transferred to the car operating system. Based on the information, which is collected and processed by sensor's control model, the policy model, database, rule base, knowledge, and intelligence being built on operating system, determine vehicle's and driving status and make decision, and then the decision policy is conducted by ECU. Finally, the system shows the result (warning), or takes measure (control), and achieves the purpose of driver's behavior monitor and driving status's warning [11].

5   Conclusion

The non-invasive driving fatigue detection method, which is on the basis of vehicle performance output and cognitive science theory, has significant advantages in monitoring of driving condition and early warning system. The results show that the output obtained from driver fatigue cognitive behavior model based on ACT-R are satisfactory. Based on analysis of literature and experimental result, the paper proposes the three stages standpoint for driver fatigue that corresponding to the stages that from the waking status to driver fatigue, it makes description of driver fatigue process more intuitive and effective, and lay the foundation of knowledge representation in ACT-R model for driver fatigue. In the light of the close relationship between research on driver fatigue and smart car, a general framework of the fatigue driver status monitoring and early warning system is proposed on the basis of traditional driving behavior model, driver cognitive behavior model, and vehicle dynamics control model.

This work is an ongoing part of the research on intelligent transportation system. Driver fatigue cognitive behavior model combining with other cognitive model, vehicle condition monitoring, and traditional driver model, all of these preliminarily establishes the core part of the driving status monitoring and early warning system.

References

1. Eskandarian, A., Sayed, R., Delaigue, P., et al.: Advanced driver fatigue research. Federal Motor Carrier Safety Administration (FMCSA), USA (April 2007)
2. Yanfei, L.: Researches on driver behavior modeling, Ph.D. dissertation, Zhejiang Univ., Hangzhou, China (2007)
3. Li, L., Feiyue, W., Nanning, Z.: Research and Developments of Intelligent Driving Behavior Analysis. Acta Automatica Sinica 33(10), 1014–1022 (2010)
4. Yanfei, L., Zhaohui, W.: Driver Behavior Modeling in ACT-R Cognitive Architecture. Journal of Zhejiang University (Engineering Science) 40(10), 1657–1662 (2006)
5. Yanfei, L., Zhaohui, W.: Improvement of ACT-R for modeling of parallel and multiprocessing driver behavior. International Journal of Intelligent Control and Systems 12(1), 72–81 (2006)
6. Yanfei, L., Zhaohui, W.: Multitasking Driver Cognitive Behavior Modeling. In: Proceedings of the 3rd International IEEE Conference on Intelligent Systems, pp. 52–57. IEEE (2006)
7. Vanlaar, W., Simpson, H., Mayhew, D., et al.: Fatigued and drowsy driving: A survey of attitudes, opinions and behaviors. Journal of Safety Research 39(3), 303–309 (2008)
8. Oron-gilad, T., Ronen, A., Shinar, D., et al.: Alertness maintaining tasks (AMTs) while driving. Accident Analysis & Prevention 40(3), 851–860 (2008)
9. Gnardellis, C., Tzamalouka, G., Papadakakii, M., et al.: An investigation of the effect of sleepiness, drowsy driving, and lifestyle on vehicle crashes. Transportation Research Part F: Traffic Psychology and Behaviour 11(4), 270–281 (2008)
10. Pinghuang, T., Jiunren, H., Jiliang, D., et al.: Driver fatigue and highway driving: A simulator study. Physiology & Behavior 94(3), 448–453 (2008)
11. Zhaohui, W., Yanfei, L., Gang, P.: A Smart Car Control Model for Brake Comfort Based on Car Following. IEEE Trans. on Intelligent Transportation Systems 10(1), 42–46 (2009)

Simulating the Impact of Mental Models on Human Automation Interaction in Aviation

Sebastien Mamessier and Karen Feigh

Georgia Institute of Technology, Atlanta GA, USA

Abstract. This work proposes a computational approach supporting the simulation of human automation interaction in aviation. The development of an advanced human agent model that accounts for workload limitations, imperfect mental models and consequences on the operator's situation awareness provides new insight for future certification procedures regarding human interaction with complex automated systems.

1 Introduction

Commercial pilots are faced with growing complexity of automated flight systems. Although most of these new systems are known to be robust to small disturbances and failures, humans still play a crucial role for advanced decision making in off-nominal situations and accidents still occur because of poor human-automation interaction. Usual mechanisms to investigate the influence of new automation on human automation interactions includes extensive use of simulation and human-in-the-loop (HITL) experimentation. But simulators and HITL experiments are expensive, time-consuming and not comprehensive as far as diversity of scenarios is concerned. Therefore we need to improve our simulation capabilities by developing realistic computational human agent models taking into account human limitations.

Maintaining a good understanding of the situation including the behavior of the automated flight systems is critical for the flight crews to make appropriate decisions in both nominal and off-nominal cases. Therefore a realistic human agent model should account for the situation awareness of the flight crew. The concept of situation awareness [5] is a good base of projection of the pilot's immediate understanding of the situation but it is not sufficient to explain its evolution. Certain operators are able to maintain a good situation awareness despite of off-nominal external inputs or degraded monitoring capabilities by developing an accurate mental model of the system. However, when the operator has a deficient mental model of the automation, his situations awareness tends to decline and result in loss of control situations.

A key contributor in the difficulty pilots have in maintaining both adequate situation awareness and an accurate mental model is the large number of automation modes, transition rules and their relative opacity to the pilot. This is particularly noticeable for transition scenarios that are rarely faced by the crew. The specifics of these transition scenarios tend to be forgotten but may be

V.G. Duffy (Ed.): DHM/HCII 2013, Part I, LNCS 8025, pp. 61–69, 2013.

critical to fully understand off-nominal situations. As the primary mechanism to import the knowledge of the systems dynamics, rules and procedures to the flight crew, additional training has been the typical response to poor human automation interaction. Enhanced training improves the comprehensiveness of the operator's mental model of the system, but has its limits, especially in light of tight training budgets. And as the mental efforts needed to maintain a good situation awareness are correlated to the number of dynamics/rules to remember and consider, i.e to the complexity of the automated systems, some have begun to question the wisdom of including even more specialized automation into the flight deck, and how to adequately certify future flight deck automation.

This works proposes a computational method to implement mental models and simplified agent training as well as workload limitations into a work simulation tool, taking into consideration implicit knowledge alteration of discrete mode based dynamics and simulate the consequences of inaccurate mental models on Situation Awareness. Such an approach could allow future certification procedures to account for faulty mental models which are a serious cause of human automation interaction breakdowns in aviation.

2 Work Models and Mental Models: Background

2.1 Modeling Work Domains

Vicente [12] defines a work domain as the *The system being controlled, independently of any particular worker, event, task, goal, or interface*. A key part of this effort is to find an adequate formalism for *work domains* before integrating *mental models*. Rasmussen and later Vicente developed an extensive theory of cognitive system engineering that describes the functional structure of these *work domains* [12]. Pritchett et al. in turn, proposed a method to parse such functional descriptions into computational work models [11] while preserving the concept of situated cognition using advanced human agent models. Simulating *work models* has been done using the work simulation framework WMC (Work Model that Computes) used in [11].

2.2 Defining Mental Models

An extensive literature on mental models exists comprised of contributions from multiple scientific communities. System dynamics scientists were the first to introduce the concept of *mental model* with Forrester [7] about industrial dynamics applying this concept to corporate organizations and processes. Psychology and cognitive science also put some effort at defining *mental models* among other cognitive structures whereas Human Computer Interaction was the first field using the concept of *mental models* to address issues in human-in-the-loop systems. Finally, Doyle and Ford drew an extensive survey of the different interpretations of *mental models* of socio-technical systems in these fields to state a precise definition [3], framing the concept of mental models as enduring, but limited internal representations of the system, its environment and procedures.

2.3 Implicit Learning

Forrester was already addressing the changing nature of mental models : "within one individual, a mental model changes with time and even during the flow of a single conversation" in 1971 [8]. Javaux explained how implicit learning alters the knowledge of finite state systems using the concept of Hebbian Learning to update the mental representation of rules as the agent experiences transition scenarios [9]. Hebbian learning has been extensively described in the neuroscience literature [1,2] as a basic model of long-term synaptic plasticity.

3 Creating a Computational Work Model

Based on the approach described by Pritchett et al. [11] and using Work Models that Computes (WMC) as a computational modeling framework, this work introduces a systematic way of breaking down work models into semi-specialized actions to enable more realistic interactions between a human agent and its environment.

3.1 Work Model that Computes (WMC)

WMC (Work Model that Computes) is a simulation framework developed to model realistic work environments, taking into consideration continuous dynamics, discrete actions, human agent models and computing human-related metrics such as Workload and Performance [11.] It has been used to simulate aircraft and Air Traffic Control to test new Continuous Descent Approach patterns at Los Angeles Airport in Kim's work about human-automation function allocation 10.

3.2 Decomposition of Work Model Actions

The fundamental premise behind the WMC simulation modeling framework is that the knowledge of the entire work domain can be captured independently of the agents who are asked to perform the work. However, we want to allow a specific instance of a human agent model to gain knowledge about the system and this knowledge to change over time for example through training. In order to guarantee a generic interfacing between work model and agent models while allowing experienced agents, we need to define a certain number of conceptually different action types.

Continuous Dynamics Actions. WMC is a continuous-time simulation engine. Its therefore capable of integrating numerically differential equations allowing to simulate complex non-linear system dynamics. These actions are executed by a non-human agent and generally include controllers and can implement a variety of numerical integration methods such as Runge Kutta.

Discrete Dynamics Actions. Complex automated systems such as Flight Management Systems comprise discrete modes of operations. Autopilot flight modes is a good example of complex mode transitions potentially confusing the pilot [9]. Since these modes change the control law and the aircraft behavior they have to be implemented by the modeler and their transition rules are assimilated to discrete dynamics actions.

Tasks. Although Vicente excludes task from the definition of work domains, a work model aims to implement the work to be performed, independently of the agent responsible for performing it. However, some attributes of the task such as the its duration and the consequent workload are directly dependent on the agent and are defined while linking a specific agent to the task during the function allocation step of the simulation's initialization. A task are usually atomic actions such as "Engage Autopilot" that can either be performed by the pilot or automation.

Monitoring Actions. Monitoring actions are meant to be executed by human agents. They implement the perception phase and therefore the first level of Situation Awareness. The frequency can either be procedurally fixed to a certain value or set dynamically.

Decision Actions. Decision Actions implement differential behavior. They can be assigned to either automation or human agents. The implementation itself only contains the procedural decision-making rules whereas mechanisms supporting information seeking, consideration of risks come under the implementation of the agents and not the work model. Decision Actions implement the response to change in the environments and therefore can schedule tasks or change the function allocation between agents.

4 Advanced Human Agent

Agents are the other end of a situated work simulation tool such as WMC. They do not have a priori knowledge of the work but are assigned actions from the work model and perform them according to their internal limitations and priorities. An automation agent will execute actions it has been assigned immediately whereas human agents can only undertake a limited number of actions simultaneously thus requiring any additional actions to be delayed depending of their current workload. This works uses the concept of agents introduced by Pritchett et al. [11] and enhances the human performance agent model used by Feigh et al. [6] by adding new constructs believed to account for Situation Awareness and Mental Models as shown in Figure 1. The previous labeling of actions now allows advanced human agents to execute actions differently according to their type. This way, monitoring actions will have an impact on the Situation Awareness and decision actions will depend on it.

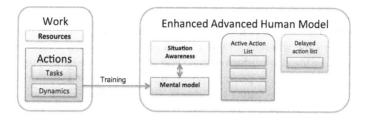

Fig. 1. The implementation of the work model and human model are independent. The mental model get initialized through a generic process that imports knowledge from the work model to an instance of the human model.

4.1 Simulating Situation Awareness (SA)

Situation Awareness is a crucial aspect in the analysis of loss of control situations [5,4]. The temporary loss of important sensors, false alarms or non-consistent information can sometimes be compensated for by a good understanding of the current state of the system and even more through anticipation of likely next actions. Whether the operator has a good or poor situation awareness depends on several factors such as his mental model of the system he is using and the degree of degradation of the situation. Whatever reason is causing an alteration of situation awareness, we need to project this concept onto computational constructs that can be used in simulation.

Perception and Workload (SA Level 1). Situation awareness Level 1 mostly describes the comprehensiveness and accuracy of the operator's perception of available cues about the state of the system [5,4]. Did the driver see the car in his right side-mirror? Did the pilot hear the aural stall warning? and so on. Certain monitoring schemes such as the T-screening for pilots are part of the training and are performed on a recurrent basis depending of the available mental workload. If the pilot is talking on the radio or to his copilot, he might skip one of these monitoring actions and his SA begins to degrade. By having the computational human agent model stacking monitoring actions as well as communication and actual physical actions in a active mental action list with limited capacity, we can simulate a degradation of the monitoring process and situation awareness L1. If the active action list gets saturated, actions get delayed or interrupted and can be even forgotten.

Understanding and Decision-making (SA Level 2) : Bayesian Approach. Situation Awareness Level 2 describes the understanding of the perceived cues, the identification of variables of interest (close to dangerous boundaries for instance), and includes some of the decision making process necessary for the human to consistently operate the system in response to environmental inputs [5,4]. Expert human agents are believed to maintain a belief of the state of the system as well as a degree of confidence that can be high for variables directly monitored on trustful instruments and very low in case of inconsistent or out-of-date information. A novice operator is more likely to apply procedures and rules all the time whereas a more experienced agent will selectively consider risks and other contextual information. The expert will reason using bayesian decision-making. Such an approach doesn't only use the last monitored value of a variable as a basis for decisions but also the degree of belief that one has about it. To model such behaviors, we can introduce the *mental state* of the system as a set of probability distributions. Each of them represents an actual variable of the system and is centered on the current belief of its value and stretched in or out as confidence decreases or increases. By assuming normally distributed belief variables, the mean of the mental variable is the actual belief of the corresponding system's variable and the standard deviation represents the degree of confidence. Using a gaussian representation has many advantages. First, its easy to manipulate and really memory-efficient. Indeed, we only need to store the mean and the standard deviation. Furthermore, this work will address mental models and model-based observers such as Kalman filter and how they change the operator's state representation between or in the absence of available monitoring actions. Kalman filters assumes a gaussian representation of variables. Also these probability distribution implement a bayesian rather than frequentist interpretation of probabilities. This means that the pilot does not sample from the distribution by accessing his working memory but simply reads the expected value, i.e the mean. The standard deviation does not represent his inability to remember or access to the actual value but his confidence in the value of this variable.

Non-gaussian Distribution and Cognitive Dissonance. In some situations, human operators can have a multi-modal belief of certain variables that can lead to inconsistent actions or so-called cognitive dissonances. In the AF-447 accident report by the BEA, the experts conclude several times that pilot flying hesitated between identifying an overspeed or stalling situation leading to non-consistent action sequences and eventually to the crash of the aircraft. In such a case, the mental representation of the speed of the aircraft cannot be fully captured by a gaussian variable. Allowing multi-modal probability distribution, like a sum of gaussian distributions can provide this capability.

4.2   Mental Models

A mental model is comprised of mental (perceived) dynamics of the system that allows the operator to update its mental belief between monitoring actions using the knowledge of covariance between variables and exploit partial observations to maintain a good situation awareness. Moreover, a reliable mental model allows anticipation (SA L3) and a smarter use of the limited available workload. An overview of how mental models fit into the simulation scheme and interact with Situation Awareness is depicted in Figure 3.

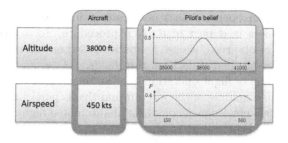

Fig. 2. The operator's belief is generally centered on the actual value of the state it represents. When sensors are not available anymore, the belief can diverge from the actual value and even be multi-modal. In the AF447 accident case, the pilot did not know whether he was in an overspeed or stall situation.

The following introduces two new types of actions that approximate the dynamics actions implemented by the modeler and whose behavior can change in response to implicit learning.

Continuous Mental Dynamics Actions. By contributing to maintaining an accurate mental representation of the state of the world, internal dynamics are an important part of mental models. They reflect and approximate the actual dynamics of the system and inform on operator's expectation. The accuracy of such mental dynamics depend on the training / initial knowledge of these dynamics, the experience/observation that the operator has of the actual dynamics and the amount of cognitive attentional resources available at time t in the WMC Simulation framework. Since agent models don't have a priori knowledge of the work model, the training of the dynamics must be added at the linkage step. The modeler decides which dynamics he would like the human agent to know. Dynamics hidden to the human agent will not update the human operator's belief of the related resources and lead to a lower situation awareness. On the other side, training the operator on too many dynamics might lead to overwhelming his limited mental capacity.

Discrete Mental Dynamics Actions and Implicit Learning. Javaux's work illustrates [9] how the pilot's knowledge of discrete rules, automation mode transition can impact situation awareness and therefore have to be part of the mental model. An inaccurate knowledge of automatic mode reversions of the Autopilot can lead to a problematic mode confusion. Transitions between mode invoke complex engagement conditions and some of them are met rarely enough to have most pilots forget about their importance [9] . Successfully retrieving these rules from long-term memory depends on the available mental resources and the evaluation of the conditions of transitions depend on the accuracy of the pilot's belief.

Moreover, a human operator does not monitor important variables with a fixed time step unless it is part of a given procedure. To determine when a variable has to be re-observed, we use heuristics based on the relative changing rate of the variable and related decision thresholds.

Thousands of hours of flight operation have an unconscious impact on pilot's knowledge and understanding of the aircraft and this is particularly remarkable when it comes to the knowledge of complicated automated flight systems such as autopilot's modes. This alteration of knowledge can be captured by the concept of Hebbian Learning [1,2] based on the Hebb's rule known as a reference to explain synaptic plasticity. This works allows the modeler to integrate Javaux's methodology [9] and account for implicit knowledge alteration although different parameters involved in Hebb's rule still need to be calibrated with real data.

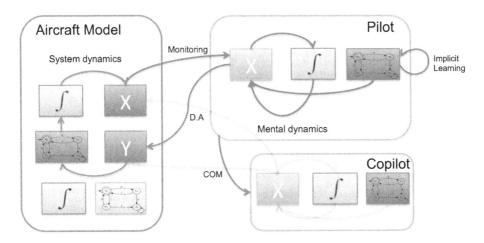

Fig. 3. Overview of the interactions between an aircraft model and a human agent enhanced with mental model capabilities. D.A stands for decision actions, they modify the configuration of the system based on the perceived state of the world. Red arrows represent units of mental activity that contributes to saturate the operator's workload capacity.

5   Conclusion

The implementation of situation awareness capabilities and mental models into WMC is being tested on a case study using the work model initially described in [11,10,6]. This work model simulates air traffic and flight deck operations and communications along the Standard Terminal Arrival Route at the airport LAX and instantiates agents such as the pilot, the co-pilot, air traffic controllers and automation agents. Monitoring patterns and approach procedures were also implemented and the pilot received a basic training on flight dynamics. At this stage of the implementation, the approach scenario exclusively uses the automated flight management system and the pilot remains in a monitoring role.

We can still analyze the evolution of the situation awareness as a result of the monitoring rate and basic internal dynamics which are key parts of the mental model. A quantitative analysis of implicit learning will be part of a future work involving realistic flight scenarios and a complete implementation of the different flight modes.

References

Bi, G., Poo, M.: Synaptic modifications in cultured hippocampal neurons: dependence on spike timing, synaptic strength, and postsynaptic cell type. The Journal of Neuroscience 18(24), 10464–10472 (1998)

Dayan, P., Abbott, L.: Theoretical neuroscience: computational and mathematical modeling of neural systems. Philosophical Psychology 15(4) (2002)

Doyle, J., Ford, D.: Mental models concepts for system dynamics research. System Dynamics Review 14(1), 3–29 (1998)

Endsley, M.R.: Toward a theory of situation awareness in dynamic systems. Human Factors: The Journal of the Human Factors and Ergonomics Society 37(1), 32–64 (1995)

Endsley, M.: Situation awareness global assessment technique (sagat). In: Proceedings of the IEEE 1988 National Aerospace and Electronics Conference NAECON 1988, pp. 789–795. IEEE (1988)

Feigh, K.M., Gelman, G., Mamessier, S., Pritchett, A.R.: Simulating first-principles models of situated human performance. IEEE Transactions on System Man and Cybernetics: Part A (Submitted June 2012)

Forrester, J.: Industrial dynamics, vol. 2. MIT Press, Cambridge (1961)

Forrester, J.: Counterintuitive behavior of social systems. Theory and Decision 2(2), 109–140 (1971)

Javaux, D.: A method for predicting errors when interacting with finite state systems. how implicit learning shapes the user's knowledge of a system. Reliability Engineering & System Safety 75(2), 147–165 (2002)

Kim, S.: Model-based metrics of human-automation function allocation in complex work environments (2011)

Pritchett, A., Kim, S., Kannan, S., Feigh, K.: Simulating situated work. In: 2011 IEEE First International Multi-Disciplinary Conference on Cognitive Methods in Situation Awareness and Decision Support (CogSIMA), pp. 66–73. IEEE (2011)

Vicente, K.: Cognitive work analysis: Toward safe, productive, and healthy computer-based work. Lawrence Erlbaum (1999)

Ergonomics Study of Direct and Indirect Visibility Evaluation at Uncontrolled Intersections Based on Three-Dimensional Computer Simulation

Midori Mori and Noboru Kubo

Kanagawa University, Faculty of Engineering, Yokohama, Japan
mori@kanagawa-u.ac.jp

Abstract. Crossing collisions at intersections account for one-fourth of the total accidents in Japan. This type of accident could be caused by the poor visual environment at intersections, including the lack of indirect visibility provided by traffic convex mirrors. However, no available desk methods have been reported on the proper installation method for such mirrors. This paper discusses the appropriate conditions for direct and indirect visibility. These include mirror visibility simulation technology, which was developed by applying three-dimensional computer graphics software. The simulated mirror images were found to be highly consistent with actual images. The mirror visibility obtained by an optimal mirror installation was found to be desirable in both a simulation and field study. The simulation demonstrated that a slight change in the mirror plate angle greatly influenced the visible distance. In conclusion, the 3DCG simulation method was effective for examining conditions for good direct and indirect visibility at intersections.

Keywords: Visibility Simulation, 3D Computer Graphics, Traffic Convex Mirror, Crossing Collision.

1 Introduction

In Japan, approximately two million crossing collisions occurred at intersections (193,852 cases), the second most frequent pattern among traffic accidents following rear-end collisions (234,993 cases, 32.4%), in 2011. The frequency of crossing collisions accounted for one-fourth of the total accidents (26.1%, 725,773 cases), and 70% of these occurred at urban intersections [1].

Various types of investigations and measures designed for the prevention of traffic accidents have been conducted, focusing mainly on human factors. As a result, safety enforcement and education, rather than engineering redesign or control of the road traffic environment, have been emphasized as preventive measures [2][3]. Ergonomic studies on preventing crossing collisions, however, should focus on what really happened and why accidents occur frequently at uncontrolled intersections. The authors revealed that the risk of a crossing collision depended on the quality of the visual environment at the intersection, including both the direct visibility and the indirect

V.G. Duffy (Ed.): DHM/HCII 2013, Part I, LNCS 8025, pp. 70–77, 2013.
© Springer-Verlag Berlin Heidelberg 2013

visibility provided by traffic convex mirrors at intersections [4]. Our field study revealed that most of the visible ranges in the right/left directions at medium- or smaller-sized intersections in an urban community area were insufficient to confirm safety, and the quality of the direct visibility was associated with the collision frequency. In addition, it became clear that more than half of the mirrors installed at the intersections had severe shortcomings as devices for ensuring crossing safety (Fig. 1). Few stud ies, however, have been conducted on the availability of traffic convex mirrors [5], and the official guidelines regarding mirror installation [6] [7] were considered to be insufficient in terms of their visibility criteria. The authors, therefore, studied the appropriate installation conditions to ensure crossing safety and proposed the following ergonomic guidelines for installing mirrors (three ergonomic requirements): (1) the road lane shall be located in a central part of the mirror image; (2) any blind area shall be deleted in the mirror image; and (3) the road surface markings shall be explicit in the mirror image (Fig. 2) [4] [8].

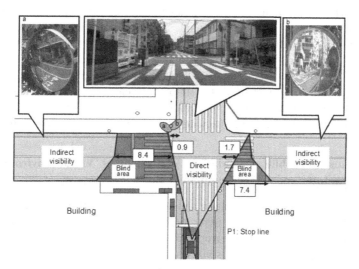

Fig. 1. Example of assessment of direct and indirect visibility at uncontrolled intersection in urban community area

Fig. 2. Example mirror image satisfying three ergonomic visibility requirements for installing traffic convex mirrors

This study aimed to assess the quality of the visual environment at intersections and discuss effective countermeasures for preventing crossing collisions, particularly safety enhancements from the perspective of direct and indirect visibility. There were no available desk methods in civil engineering for examining the conditions for mirror installation or facilitating improvements to supplement direct visibility. Therefore, we developed a highly accurate visibility simulation approach, applying three-dimensional computer graphics (3DCG) software, and discussed the appropriate visibility conditions that ensured crossing safety [9].

2   Method

2.1   Development of Visibility Simulation Approach

A visibility simulation approach, applying 3DCG software, was developed to demonstrate that the direct and indirect visibility can be assessed and improved by installing traffic convex mirrors or adjusting the angle and position of the mirror plate and/or pole. A visibility simulation approach applying the 3DCG software was adopted because it was difficult and time-consuming to examine the range of reflected images in convex mirrors with various curvature changes using a drawing method or two-dimensional CAD software, based on the simple incidence angle/reflection angle data. Therefore, we used the ray tracing function of a multipurpose-type 3DCG software that was available to precisely and efficiently calculate a range of reflected images.

2.2   Systematic Visibility Simulation Assessment of Visual Environment at Typical Intersections for Community Roads

A systematic visibility simulation study and a field experiment in a test course simulating urban community roads were performed to measure and assess the direct/indirect visibility from the driver's viewpoint in a passenger car at an uncontrolled intersection. A systematic visibility simulation study was performed to measure and assess the direct/indirect visibility from the driver's viewpoint at a typical uncontrolled intersection on an urban community road (a 4-m wide minor road and 6-m wide major road).

The Road Traffic Law in Japan requires drivers to drive on the left side of the road, and drivers with lower priority must stop momentarily at a legal stop line when crossing uncontrolled intersections. The road configuration, various items (public/private facilities, buildings, etc.), the visual environment at the eye point of the driver (1.2-m high) at a legal stop line/boundary line of an intersection, and the crossing road were simulated. Optimal solutions that met the condition of a mirror image reflecting the maximum visible distance from the crossing road, as well as the minimum blind areas, were examined to clarify the appropriate conditions (ergonomic visibility requirements).

As one assessment example, the association between the mirror image and the driver's eye point was analyzed by controlling the following dimensions (Fig. 3, Table 1).

1. Independent variables

— Ground height of the driver's eye point (EP) (two values: a truck (1.8 m) and a passenger car (1.2 m))
— Distance from an intersection (three values: 0, 5, and 10 m)

2. Dependent variables: depression angle, horizontal angle of a mirror plate
3. Fixed conditions: horizontal position (M), ground height of mirror plate (2.5 m)

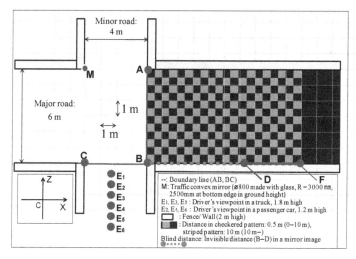

Fig. 3. Diagram of hypothetical intersection for analyzing optimal traffic convex mirror installation based on visibility simulation approach

Table 1. Conditions for visibility simulation assessment of visual environment at typical intersections on community roads

(2) Distance from the intersection	Distance from the intersection [m]		
(1) Driver's eye point (EP)	0	5	10
Truck (anterior bumper-EP: -1.0 m, height: 1.8 m)	E_1	E_3	E_5
Passenger car (bumper-EP: -2.1 m, height: 1.2 m)	E_2	E_4	E_6

3 Results and Discussion

3.1 Development of Visibility Simulation Approach

A visibility simulation approach was developed using 3DCG software. A demonstration test was performed and simulation mirror plans were reproduced to verify the consistency with actual mirror images. High consistency was shown between a simulation study and a field experiment in a test course, in terms of conditions such as the size, position of subject images, blind areas, and the visible distance at the crossing road mirror images (Fig. 4).

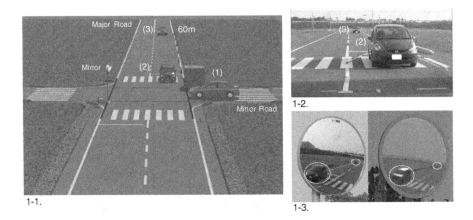

Fig. 4. Example of visibility simulation applying 3DCG software:

1-1. Rendering image: Reproductive simulation of visibility experiment situation on a test course.
1-2. Photo: Visibility experiment situation.
1-3. Mirror image of visibility experiment situation in consideration of the vehicle (1) (Left: Real image, Right: Simulation study).

3.2   Systematic Visibility Simulation Assessment of Visual Environment at Typical Intersections on Community Roads

As one assessment example, indirect visibility simulations to determine the association between a mirror image and the driver's eye point were performed systematically for 36 patterns (combinations for the driver's eye point, Fig. 3, Table 1). 1. Under six conditions (E_1–E_6), the optimal depression angles/horizontal angles of the mirrors (ø800 made with glass, R = 3000 mm) installed at the left corner M were adjusted to meet the following preconditions: a minimum blind distance existed from the crossing road, with a visible distance greater than 50–60 m in the mirror image, where the blind distance was defined as the invisible distance between B and D in a mirror image (Fig. 5). 2. The other mirror images under five conditions were reproduced based on the data for the six optimal depression angles/horizontal angles (E_1–E_6), to assess how the blind distance in a mirror image was affected by the condition.

We observed that there was no condition with a mirror image with no blind areas (BD: 2.0–10.0 m) that ensured a visible distance greater than 50 m. The blind distance was minimum in the E_1 mirror image for the E_6 optimal solution, and in 14 cases (39%), the blind distance was greater than a 4.7-m long passenger car. The blind distances were proportional to the distances from the intersection for the six optimal solutions, as well as for the six conditions in each optimal solution. However, they were inversely proportional to the height of the eye point (Fig. 5 and Fig. 6).

Sometimes drivers had to utilize the mirror at the position distant from the boundary line, about 10 m at a maximum, because of the pedestrian crossings and/or the legal stop line. The theoretical visibility simulation study revealed that a tradeoff problem occurred in intersections, and the indirect visibility provided by mirrors was insufficient for drivers entering the intersections to confirm the presence of a crossing vehicle and avoid a crossing collision. It was necessary to solve these problems systematically to ensure compatibility with direct visibility.

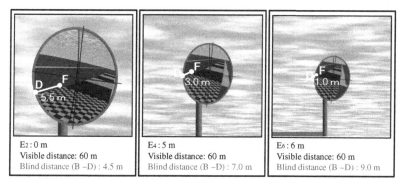

| E₂ : 0 m | E₄ : 5 m | E₆ : 6 m |

E_2 : 0 m
Visible distance: 60 m
Blind distance (B –D) : 4.5 m

E_4 : 5 m
Visible distance: 60 m
Blind distance (B –D) : 7.0 m

E_6 : 6 m
Visible distance: 60 m
Blind distance (B –D) : 9.0 m

Fig. 5. Association between mirror image and driver's eye point: variations in simulated mirror image (E_2, E_4, E_6: passenger car)

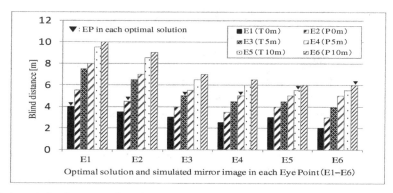

Fig. 6. Association between mirror image and driver's eye point: distribution of blind distances in simulated mirror images

3.3 Mirror Image Matrix Based on Visibility Simulation Study

The difference among the optimal depression angles of the mirrors for the 36 solutions was no more than 2.5°, and the difference among the horizontal angles of the mirrors was 4.5° horizontal angle was 4.5° in the same way. The visibility simulation demonstrated that a slight change in the mirror plate angle greatly influenced the visible/blind distance. These findings suggested that fine adjustments in the depression/horizontal angle of the mirror plate were critical factors affecting indirect visibility.

For these reasons, a mirror image matrix was developed based on the visibility simulation study, to present the variation in the mirror image with a central focus on the optimal solution. This would be available as a tool for examining the conditions for mirror installation or facilitating improvements to supplement direct visibility, as a quick reference chart.

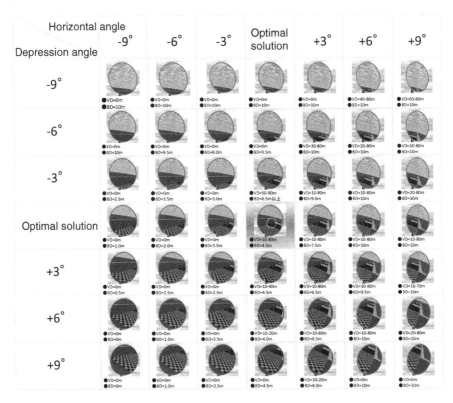

Fig. 7. Mirror image matrix developed based on visibility simulation study: distribution of visible distances/blind distances in simulated mirror images

4   Conclusions

A visibility simulation approach, applying 3DCG software, was developed by the authors. Visibility was assessed and an optimal solution was examined; this solution ensures maximum visible distance at a crossing road with an image having minimum blind areas by installing mirrors or adjusting the angle of the mirror plate based on ergonomic requirements. A visibility simulation demonstrated that slight changes in the angle of the mirror plate and eye point (ground height and horizontal position) significantly influenced the visible/blind distance. These findings suggested that fine adjustments of the depression/horizontal angle and horizontal/vertical position of the eye point were critical factors for realizing adequate indirect visibility for safety.

In conclusion, the visibility simulation approach was efficient and effective for examining the conditions of good direct and indirect visibility and demonstrated that direct and indirect visibility could be improved based on ergonomics guidelines, for example, by adjusting the angle and position of the mirror plate/pole. Crossing collisions are associated with the quality of the visual environment for drivers entering intersections. Thus, visibility improvement by enhancing the direct visibility and/or installing mirrors should be given a high priority.

Acknowledgements. The authors would like to express their deepest thanks for receiving a Grant-in-Aid for Scientific Research (C) from the Japan Society for the Promotion of Science (#21510184) to develop this research project.

References

1. National Police Agency: Statistics 2011 Road Accidents Japan, International Association of Traffic and Safety Sciences, Tokyo (2012)
2. Institute for Traffic Accident Research and Data Analysis: Analysis of Human Factors in Crossing Collision, ITARDA Information, No. 56 (2005)
3. Institute for Traffic Accident Research and Data Analysis: Crossing Collisions in View of Road Environment, ITARDA Information, No. 69 (2007)
4. Mori, M., Horino, S., Kitajima, S., Ueyama, M., Ebara, T., Itani, T.: Ergonomics Solution for Crossing Collisions based on a Field Assessment of the Visual Environment at Urban Intersections in Japan. Applied Ergonomics 9(6), 697–709 (2008)
5. Moukhwas, D.: Road junction convex mirrors. Applied Ergonomics 18, 133–136 (1987)
6. Japan Road Association, Guideline for Traffic Convex Mirror Installation, Japan Road Association (1980) (in Japanese)
7. Japan Society of Traffic Engineers, Design and Plan of Level Crossing-Basic Edition: the 3rd edn. (Revised Version), Japan Society of Traffic Engineers, Tokyo (2007) (in Japanese)
8. Mori, M., Horino, S., Kubo, N., Kitajima, S.: Ergonomics proposal for visibility requirements at urban intersections in Japan for preventing frequent crossing collisions. In: Proceedings of the Applied Human Factors and Ergonomics 2nd International Conference, CD-ROM (2008)
9. Kubo, N., Mori, M., Horino, S.: Study on the conditions for installing traffic convex mirrors with enhanced visibility at intersections applying mirror image simulation. Transactions of the Japan Society of Mechanical Engineers, Series C 76(768), 2154–2159 (2010) (in Japanese)

Prediction of Drowsy Driving Using Behavioral Measures of Drivers – Change of Neck Bending Angle and Sitting Pressure Distribution

Atsuo Murata, Taiga Koriyama, Takuya Endoh, and Takehito Hayami

Graduate School of Natural Science and Technology, Okayama University, Okayama, Japan
{murata,endo}@iims.sys.okayama-u.ac.jp

Abstract. Recently, in Japan, the percentage of the death toll in traffic accidents due to drowsy driving is the most dominant in all death tolls in traffic accidents. Therefore, it is essential for automotive manufacturers to develop a warning system of drowsy driving. A lot of studies are conducted to prevent traffic accident due to drowsy driving, and make an attempt to assess drowsiness by physiological measures such as EEG. However, it is difficult to use such equipment for predicting drowsiness, because it is difficult to equip an automotive cockpit with such equipment due to expensiveness and measurement noise. As more convenient measure used to predict drowsiness, it was examined whether the neck bending angle and the sitting pressure distribution could be used to discriminate the arousal level. The effectiveness of these convenient measures was experimentally assessed. In order to prevent traffic accidents due to drowsy driving, an attempt was made to predict drowsiness (low arousal state) using the change of neck bending angle and sitting pressure distribution. As a result, these measures were found to be useful for evaluating arousal level and predicting arousal level in advance.

Keywords: ITS, prediction of drowsiness, neck bending angle, sitting pressure distribution, COP (Center of Pressure).

1 Introduction

Monitoring drowsiness during driving has been paid more and more attention. The development of system that can monitor drivers' arousal level and warn drivers of a risk of falling asleep and causing a traffic accident is essential for the assurance of safety during driving. However, effective measures for warning drivers of the risk of causing a traffic accident have not been established.

Many studies used psychophysiological measures such as blink, EEG, saccade, and heart rate to assess fatigue. Brookhuis et al. [1] carried out an on-road experiment to assess driver status using measures such as Electroencephalography (EEG) and Electrocardiography (ECG). They found that changes in EEG and ECG reflected changes in driver status. Kecklund et al. [2] recorded EEG continuously during a night or evening drive for eighteen truck drivers. They showed that during a night drive a

V.G. Duffy (Ed.): DHM/HCII 2013, Part I, LNCS 8025, pp. 78–87, 2013.

significant intra-individual correlation was observed between subjective sleepiness and the EEG alpha burst activity. End-of the-drive subjective sleepiness and the EEG alpha burst activity were significantly correlated with total work hours. As a result of a regression analysis, total work hours and total break time predicted about 66% of the variance of EEG alpha burst activity during the end of drive. Skipper et. Al. [3] made an attempt to detect drowsiness of driver using discrimination analysis, and showed that the false alarm or miss would occur in such an attempt. No measures alone can be used reliably to assess drowsiness, because each has advantages and disadvantages.

Murata et al. [4] and Murata et al. [5] made such an attempt to objectively evaluate the drowsiness of drivers using EEG or HRV measures. They succeeded in clarifying the decrease of EEG-MPF or the increase of RRV3 when the participant's arousal level is low. However, it was not possible to predict the drowsiness on the basis of the time series of EEG-MPF or RRV3. Moreover, such equipments to measure an arousal level is too expensive to put these into practical use in automotives. The drowsiness prediction system that should be used in automotive must be less expensive and more convenient. As a more convenient measure for predicting the arousal level, we paid attention to the vertical and horizontal neck bending angle and the change of sitting pressure distribution.

Although detecting the arousal level of a driver automatically by ITS and warn drivers of the drowsy state is an ultimate goal in such studies, it is impossible to develop such a system unless such studies [4,5] are further enhanced and the prediction method on the basis of some useful methodology is established. Few studies made an attempt to predict the arousal level systematically on the basis of physiological measures. Murata et al.[6,7] made an attempt to predict the arousal level using Bayesian theorem or multivariate analysis, and succeeded in the prediction with the accuracy of more than 85%. If a drowsiness prediction system is to put into practical use, more convenient measures which can be easily installed to the automotive cockpit.

As more convenient measure used to predict drowsiness, the neck bending angle and the sitting pressure distribution were used and examined whether these measures can be used to evaluate arousal level like EEH-MPF or RRV3 that had been proven to be effective for evaluating arousal level and succeeded to some extent in predicting the timing where the drowsy state is induced. The effectiveness of these convenient measures was experimentally assessed. In order to prevent traffic accidents due to drowsy driving, an attempt was made to predict drowsiness (low arousal state) using the change of neck bending angle and sitting pressure distribution. First, the time series of these measures were compared between low and high arousal states. The mean values were also compared between the two states. Moreover, the arousal level was predicted using a logistic regression model, and the discrimination percentage was compared among participants, and between low and high arousal states.

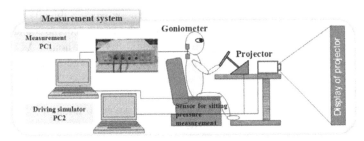

Fig. 1. Outline of measurement apparatus in the experiment

Fig. 2. Placement of goniometer

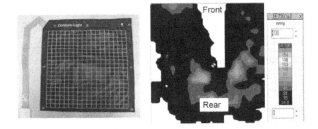

Fig. 3. Measurement system and example of sitting pressure

2   Method

2.1   Participant

Thirteen participants aged from 21 to 22 years old took part in the experiment. The visual acuity of the participants in both young and older groups was matched and more than 20/20. They had no orthopedic or neurological diseases. All provide the experimenter with informed consent on the participation to the experiment.

2.2   Apparatus

The outline of apparatus used in the experiment is shown in Fig.1. Goniometers (DKH) for vertical and horizontal neck bending angle measurement was attached to the back of neck to measure the bend angle of neck as depicted in Fig.2. A measurement system of sitting pressure distribution (Nitta, Conform-Light, See Fig.3) was placed on a driver's seat. Fig.3 also demonstrates the sitting pressure distribution.

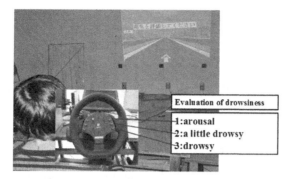

Fig. 4. Experimental setting

2.3   Task, Design and Procedure

While the participant was carrying out a simulated driving task (tracking) task, the bending angle of neck and the sitting pressure distribution were measured. The participant was required to report his or her subjective rating of drowsiness every 1 min. The experiment was continued until the participants fell asleep. The experimental setting is shown in Fig.4. The participant was required to press one of three switched attached on the right side of the steering wheel. The evaluation categories included 1. arousal, 2. a little drowsy, and 3.drowsy.

The participants were required to stay up all night and visit the laboratory. While the participant carried out a one-hour driving simulator task (See Fig.4), the vertical and horizontal bending angle of the neck was measured continuously. In the one-hour driving simulator task, the participants were required to keep the deviation from the moving line as small as possible and to keep the center of the road using a steering wheel. As the participants evaluated their arousal level 60 times during a one-hour experiment, the arousal was classified according to their rating value.

3   Results

The mean change of bending angle every 1 min and the frequency of larger change of center of sitting pressure (COP) were compared between the low and high arousal states. In Fig.5, an example of 420 s-time series of vertical and horizontal bending angle of the neck is depicted. In Fig.6, the horizontal bending angle is compared between the arousal and the drowsy states for eight participants A-M. The corresponding vertical bending angle of the neck is compared between the arousal and the drowsy states in Fig.7. The horizontal bending angle of neck is compared between arousal and drowsy states in Fig.8. The vertical bending angle of neck is compared between arousal and drowsy states in Fig.9.

The change Δ of COP was defined as follows. The coordinate (x_i, y_i) of COP is calculated every 0.02 s (sampling frequency of 50Hz).

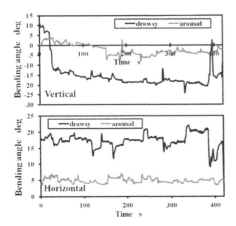

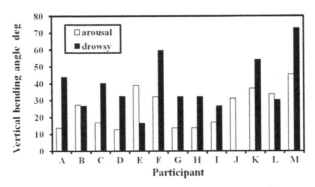

Horizontal
Vertical

Fig. 5. Example of change of vertical and horizontal bending angle with time

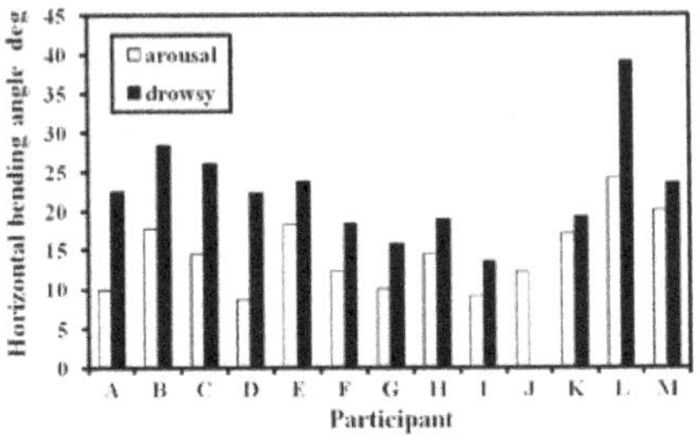

Fig. 6. Comparison of horizontal bending angle between arousal and drowsy states

Fig. 7. Comparison of vertical bending angle between arousal and drowsy states

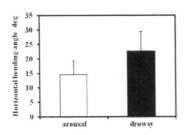

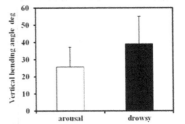

Fig. 8. Horizontal bending angle of neck compared between arousal and drowsy states

Fig. 9. Vertical bending angle of neck compared between arousal and drowsy states

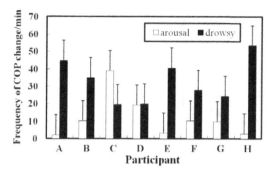

Fig. 10. Comparison of frequency of COP change between arousal and drowsy states from Murata et al.[8]

$$\Delta = \sqrt{(x_i - x_{i-1})^2 + (y_i - y_{i-1})^2} \qquad (1)$$

where (x_i, y_i) and (x_{i-1}, y_{i-1}) represent the coordinate of COP at time i and i-1. After the frequency distribution of the change Δ was obtained for each participant, the number of Δ that is more than 99 % (upper 1%) was counted as change of posture (COP change). The frequency of COP change compared between the arousal and the drowsy states, which was cited from Murata et al.[8], is shown in Fig.10.

The frequency of COP change compared between the arousal and the drowsy states obtained in this experiment is shown in Fig.11. Participants were classified into (i) low drowsy and (ii) high drowsy groups. Five participants A-E and eight participants F-M belonged to (i) and (ii), respectively. In Fig.12, the frequency of COP change for (i) low drowsy group is compared between arousal and drowsy states. The frequency of COP change for (ii) high drowsy group is compared between arousal and drowsy states in Fig.13.

In Fig.14, the total movement of COP/min is compared between arousal and drowsy states. The total movements of COP/min for (i) low drowsy group and (ii) high drowsy group are compared between arousal and drowsy states in Fig.15 and Fig.16, respectively.

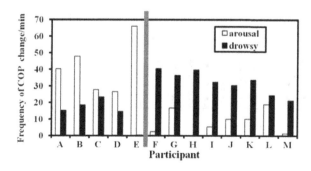

Fig. 11. Comparison of frequency of COP change between arousal and drowsy states

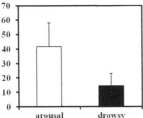
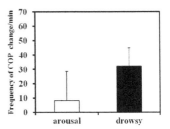

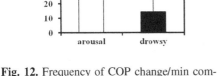

Fig. 12. Frequency of COP change/min compared between arousal and drowsy states for participants A-E (low level of drowsiness)

Fig. 13. Frequency of COP change/min compared between arousal and drowsy states for participants F-M (high level of drowsiness)

The results of logistic regression analysis using the rating of arousal level and one of the four measures (1)COP change/min, (2)bending angle of neck (horizontal), (3)bending angle of neck (vertical) , and (4)total movement of COP/min as dependent and independent variables, respectively, are shown in Fig.17 ((i)low arousal group) and Fig.18 ((ii) high arousal group). For both (i) low arousal and (ii) high arousal groups, the prediction accuracy of (2)bending angle of neck (horizontal) tended to be higher (about 0.8).

4   Discussion

Under the low arousal (drowsy) state, we confirmed that the vertical bending angle, the horizontal bending angle, and the COP change took significantly higher values. As demonstrated in Fig.5, both vertical and horizontal bending angles were different between arousal and drowsy states. Fig.6 and Fig.7 confirmed this tendency. In Fig.8 and Fig.9, the difference between the arousal and drowsy states is depicted. Under the drowsy states, the vertical and the horizontal bending angle got larger. These can be easily guessed to occur under the drowsy state. Although such equipment or a system.

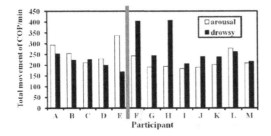
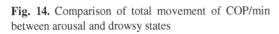
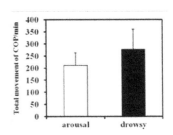

Fig. 14. Comparison of total movement of COP/min between arousal and drowsy states

Fig. 15. Comparison of total movement of COP/min between arousal and drowsy states for (i) high drowsy group (participants F-M)

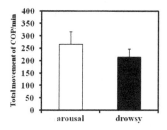

Fig. 16. Comparison of total movement of COP/min between arousal and drowsy states for (i) low drowsy group (participants A-E)

has already been on the market, these are not effective enough to predict the timing of low arousal state. The most important thing is to explore whether we can use these measure not to evaluate the arousal level but to predict the timing of low arousal state to occur in future.

As shown in Fig.11, there were individual differences among thirteen participants. The relaxing such individual differences might lead to higher prediction accuracy. While the result of the frequency of COP change for the participants A-E showed the tendency that the value is larger when the participants are arousal than when the participants were drowsy, this tended to be higher under the drowsy state than under the arousal state for participants F-M. As for the COP change, Murata et al.[8] showed a consistent tendency that the COP change is higher under the drowsy state than under the arousal state (see Fig.10). Synthetically judged, it seems reasonable to think that there exist two patterns in COP change: those for (i) low arousal group and for (ii) high arousal group. Different from neck bending angle (see Figs.7-9) and physiological measures such as EEG, EOG, and ECG, the behavioral pattern observed from the sitting pressure seems to be more influenced by individual differences. As shown in Fig.11, we found two patterns in COP change according to the severity of arousal degradation. The following two patterns were identified. In one pattern ((i) low arousal group in Fig.12), the frequency of COP change is smaller under the drowsy state

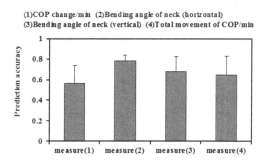

Fig. 17. Comparison of prediction accuracy among predictions using each of four measures (1)-(4) for (i) low arousal group (participants A-E)

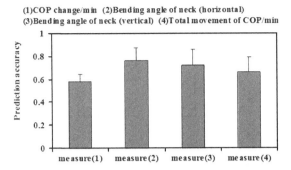

Fig. 18. Comparison of prediction accuracy among predictions using each of four measures (1)-(4) for (ii) high arousal group (participants F-M)

than under the arousal state. Other pattern ((ii) high arousal group in Fig.13) showed a tendency that the COP change is larger under the drowsy state than under the arousal state. Thus, such a finding of the two patterns might help relax individual differences and contribute to higher prediction accuracy.

As shown in Fig.14, Fig.15, and Fig.16, a similar tendency to the frequency of COP change was also observed for the total movement of COP. There existed two patterns of total movement of COP as in Fig.14: ((i) low arousal group in Fig.15) and ((ii) high arousal group in Fig.16). In (i) low arousal group (see Fig.14), the total movement of COP is smaller under the drowsy state than under the arousal state. In (ii) high arousal group (see Fig.16), the total movement of COP tended to be larger under the drowsy state than under the arousal state. In conclusion, these results suggest that the sitting pressure-based evaluation measures must be cautiously used and interpreted by taking the detailed drowsy state into account.

A logistic regression analysis, in which the subjective rating of drowsiness and the biological information corresponded to a dependent variable and an independent variable, respectively, was used to predict the drowsiness. The result is summarized separately for (i) low drowsy and (ii) high drowsy groups in Fig.17 and Fig.18. Although the prediction accuracy of (2) bending angle of neck (horizontal) tended to be higher (about 0.8) for both groups (i) and (ii), predicting the rating score of drowsiness by means of logistic regression analysis that entered a single evaluation measure could not attain high accuracy for other three measures (1) COP change/min, (3)bending angle of neck (vertical), and (4)total movement of COP/min. As mentioned above, individual differences in (1) COP change/min and (4)total movement of COP/min were to some extent relaxed and eliminated by the successful classification of (i) low drowsy and (ii) high drowsy groups. In spite of this, higher prediction accuracy was not obtained with a single evaluation measure. This seems to be the limitation of using behavioral measures such as the bending angle of the COP change for the prediction of drowsy sate. Therefore, future work should add to the more objective measurement technique of drowsiness such as EEG and observe the arousal level of participant more accurately, investigate the correspondence between EEG and the measures used in this study, and make an attempt to enhance the prediction accuracy.

On the basis of the experimental result, it had been suggested that the change of bending angle, the frequency of COP change, and the total movement of COP might be promising for predicting the drowsy state. It must be noted that the two measures derived on the basis of sitting pressure showed different patterns between (i) low arousal (participants A-E) and (ii) high arousal (participants F-M) groups. Future work should use the horizontal and vertical bending angles of the neck together the frequency of COP change and the total movement of COP so that higher discrimination accuracy can be obtained. The use of other convenient measures such as the eye blink together with the measures used in this study might further enhance the prediction accuracy of drowsiness.

References

1. Brookhuis, K.A., Waard, D.: The use of psychophysiology to assess driver status. Ergonomics 36, 1099–1110 (1993)
2. Kecklund, G., Akersted, T.: Sleepiness in long distance truck driving: An ambulatory EEG study of night driving. Ergonomics 36, 1007–1017 (1993)
3. Skipper, J.H., Wierwillie, W.: Drowsy driver detection using discrimination analysis. Human Factors 28, 527–540 (1986)
4. Murata, A., Hiramatsu, Y.: Evaluation of drowsiness by HRV measures - Basic study for drowsy driver detection. In: Proc. of IWCI 2008, pp. 99–102 (2008)
5. Murata, A., Nishijima, K.: Evaluation of Drowsiness by EEG analysis - Basic Study on ITS Development for the Prevention of Drowsy Driving. In: Proc. of IWCIA 2008, pp. 95–98 (2008)
6. Murata, A., Ohkubo, Y., Moriwaka, M., Hayami, T.: Prediction of drowsiness using multivariate analysis of biological information and driving performance. In: Proc. of SIC 2011, pp. 52–57 (2011)
7. Murata, A., Matsuda, Y., Moriwaka, M., Hayami, T.: An Attempt to predict drowsiness by Bayesian estimation. In: Proc. of SIC 2011, pp. 58–63 (2011)
8. Murata, A., Koriyama, T., Hayami, T.: Basic Study on the Prevention of Drowsy Driving using the Change of Neck Bending Angle and the Sitting Pressure Distribution. In: Proceedings of SIC 2012, pp. 274–279 (2012)

Effectiveness of Automotive Warning System Presented with Multiple Sensory Modalities

Atsuo Murata, Michihiro Kanbayashi, and Takehito Hayami

Graduate School of Natural Science and Technology, Okayama University, Okayama, Japan
{murata,kambayashi}@iims.sys.okayama-u.ac.jp

Abstract. Although it is very important to drive safely by drivers themselves, it is impossible to find drivers who do not make mistakes during driving. Therefore, vehicles should be equipped with a system that automatically detect hazardous state and warn if of drivers so that such a preventive safety can contribute to the reduction of traffic accidents due to the oversight of important information necessary for safety driving. This study paid attention to the preventive safety technology, and discussed how the warning should be presented to drivers. It was explored whether simultaneously presenting warning to multiple sensory organs such as visual and auditory systems can promote (quicken) the perception of warning even under the situation, where interference between information of the same sensory modality occurs. The auditory-tactile warning was found to lead to quicker and more accurate reaction to a hazardous scene during a simulated driving.

Keywords: automotive warning, multiple sensory modality, auditory-tactile warning, reaction time, hit rate.

1   Introduction

With the growth of intelligent transportation systems (ITS), such as car navigation systems or hands-free cellular phones, driving is becoming more and more complex. As much of the information provided contains texts and images, drivers are apt to become distracted and inattentive. Driving a car places a characteristically heavy workload on visual perception, cognitive information processing, and manual responses. Drivers often simultaneously perform two or more tasks; for example, they adjust the volume of a radio or CD player and control the air conditioner to adjust the temperature while driving. Such sharing of attention may lead to dangerous situations.

Thus, in driving environment, the visual and cognitive driving workload increases, and the driver-vehicle interaction is getting more and more complicated [1,2]. Consequently, drivers tend to be distracted by a variety of secondary task such as the operation of switches for CD or air conditioner other than driving [3], which increases the risk of inattentive driving.

As the display and control systems of automobile is becoming more and more complex, it is predicted that older drivers are distracted by these systems and cannot cope with such situations. Jones et al.[4] reviewed the utilization of sense of touch as

V.G. Duffy (Ed.): DHM/HCII 2013, Part I, LNCS 8025, pp. 88–97, 2013.

a medium for information representation. They concluded that sense of touch represents a promising means for communication in human-vehicle system. Driver et al. [5], Spence et al. [6,7] and Ho et al.[8-10] showed that the presentation of spatially predictive vibrotactile warning signal can facilitate drivers response to driving event seen through the windscreen or rear mirror. However, in these studies, the presentation of vibrotactile warning signal was to prevent front-to-rear-end collision in a driving simulator. They did not discuss the presentation of tactile signal to warn drivers of right and left dangers. Moreover, they did not compare the effectiveness as a warning signal between auditory and vibrotactile presentations. In driving environment, most information is presented via a visual or auditory stimulus. If the warning signal is presented via a visual or auditory stimulus, the auditory or visual interference with other information might arise. On the other hand, if a vibtotactile warning, that is, tactile interface is used, the possibility of such interference would be sure to reduce. Moreover, although older adults exhibit deficits in various cognitive-motor tasks, older adults' decline of tactile sense seems to be less as compared with visual or auditory sense. On the basis of the discussion above, it is expected that a vibrotactile signal would be very promising as a warning signal especially for older adults.

Recently, the tendencies of multimodal information processing [11,12] and design have emerged as major research topics in complex real-world domains such as military, air traffic operation, or automobile. Presenting information via multiple modalities such as vision, audition, and touch has been expected to be a promising means to reduce transmission errors and enhance safety. A better understanding of cross-modal spatial and temporal links is essential to ensure better application of this property to the automotive warning design. Murata [13] showed the effectiveness of tactile interface for warning presentation in driving environment. However, design technologies of automotive warning system using a principle of cross-modal link have not been established. It is expected that such a cross-modal link between different modalities further enhances the effectiveness of automotive warning system.

The aim of this study was to promote the perception of warning even under the situation, where interference between information of the same sensory modality occurs, by simultaneously presenting warning to multiple sensory organs such as visual and auditory systems. In order to clarify the most suitable method for presenting warning using a cross-modal link between different sensory modalities, the following seven conditions were used in the experiment: (1) visual cue, (2) auditory cue, (3) tactile cue, (4) combination of visual and auditory cues, (5) combination of visual and tactile cues, (6) combination of auditory and tactile cues, and (7) no warning (cue). The aim and hypothesis of the study are summarized in Fig.1. It has been hypothesized that multimodal warning presentation with different modalities is more effective for quickening the reaction to a hazard than unimodal warning presentation.

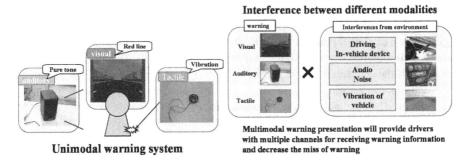

Fig. 1. Aim and hypothesis of the study

The paper is organized as follows: Section 2 shows the experimental method to explore the effectiveness of automotive warning system with multiple sensory modalities. Section 3 summarized the results, and Section 4 discussed the results, and Section 5 considered how the proposed warning system should be utilized for enhancing driving safety.

2   Method

2.1   Participant

Ten participants aged from 21 to 24 years took part in the experiment. All had held a driver's license for 3-4 years. The visual acuity of the participants in both young and older groups was matched and more than 20/20. They had no orthopedic or neurological diseases. All signed the informed consent after receiving a brief explanation on the aim and the contents of the experiment.

2.2   Apparatus

Using a driving simulator system shown in Fig.2, the participants were required to simultaneously carry out a simulated driving task (main task) and the following three secondary tasks: switch pressing, accelerator maneuvering, and judgment of information which is randomly presented on one of the four locations (front, back mirror, right monitor, and left monitor). The experimental front and rear scenes are shown in Fig.3.

2.3   Task

The displays of main task, secondary switch pressing task, accelerator maneuvering, and judgment task of hazard are depicted in Fig.4, Fig.5, Fig.6, and Fig.7, respectively. The displays of eight types of hazard directions are shown in Fig.8-Fig.11.

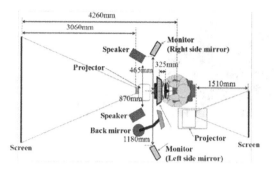

Fig. 2. Explanation of experimental setting

Fig. 3. Scene of experiment (front and rear screen)

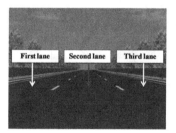

Fig. 4. Display of main task

   In the main task, the participant was required to minimize the deviation from the predetermined line and keep the lane location by maneuvering a steering wheel. The switching task requires the participant to carry out a secondary task such as the adjustment the audio volume using the steering switch. In the accelerator maneuvering, the participant was required to keep the control within the predetermined range using the accelerator. In the judgment task of hazard, the participant was required to react to a visual hazard using an accelerator or a steering switch. In this task, the warning was presented to the participant using the following warning (cue) presentation method: (1) visual cue, (2) auditory cue, (3) tactile cue, (4) combination of visual and auditory cues, (5) combination of visual and tactile cues, (6) combination of auditory and tactile cues, and (7) no warning (cue).

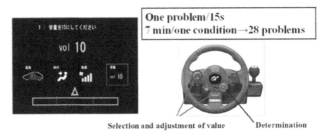

Fig. 5. Display of secondary switch pressing task

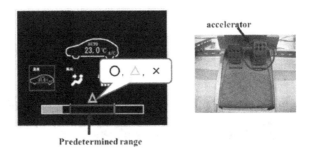

Fig. 6. Display of secondary accelerator operation task

Fig. 7. Display of secondary judgment task of hazard

2.4   Design and Procedure

The experimental condition is summarized in Table 1. The experimental variables were warning presentation method (seven levels). The participant was required to simultaneously carry out a main driving simulator task, a secondary switch pressing task, accelerator maneuvering, and judgment task of hazardous scene displayed either of the front, the back mirror, the right monitor, and the left monitor.

The following measures were used to evaluate the effectiveness of the seven warning condition above: (A) percentage correct in switch pressing, (B) frequency of deviation from the pre-specified range in acceleration maneuvering, and (C) reaction time and accuracy (percentage correct reaction) to the warning cue by steering or braking operation. Hypothesizing that multimodal warning presentation will provide drivers with multiple channels for receiving warning information and decrease the miss of warning, this was experimentally verified.

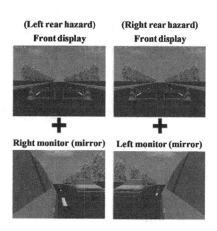

Fig. 8. Display of front hazard, left front hazard, and right front hazard

Fig. 9. Display of left rear and right rear hazards

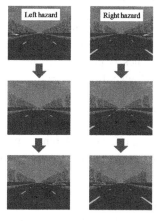

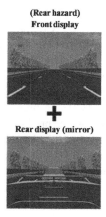

Fig. 10. Display of left and right hazards

Fig. 11. Display of rear hazard

Table 1. Experimental condition

Condition	(1)	(2)	(3)	(4)	(5)	(6)	(7)
Warning method	Nothing	Warning presentation method					
		Visual	Auditory	Tactile	Visual & Audi-tory	Visual & Tactile	Auditory & Tac-tile
Blocking sound	Noise of moving car						
Location of stimulus				Leg		Leg	Leg

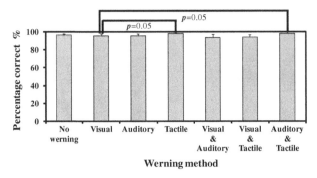

Fig. 12. Percentage correct in switch pressing task compared among seven warning conditions

3   Results

The percentage correct in the switch pressing task is plotted as a function of seven warning presentation condition ((1) visual cue, (2) auditory cue, (3) tactile cue, (4) combination of visual and auditory cues, (5) combination of visual and tactile cues, (6) combination of auditory and tactile cues, and (7) no warning (cue)) in Fig.12. As shown in Fig.13, the reaction time in the braking operation tended to be prolonged for the single-modality condition (visual only, and auditory only) and the visual-auditory combination. In Fig.14, the hit rate of hazardous scenes is plotted as a function of warning presentation condition. Fig.15 compares the miss rate of hazardous scene compared among seven warning presentation conditions above.

A one-way (warning presentation method) ANOVA conducted on the percentage correct in the switch pressing task revealed no significant main effect. A multiple comparison by Fisher's PLSD revealed marginally significant differences between tactile and auditory-tactile presentations, and between visual-tactile and auditory-tactile presentations ($p=0.0584$).

A one-way (warning presentation method) ANOVA conducted on the number of deviation from the lane in the accelerator maneuvering task revealed no significant main effect. A multiple comparison by Fisher's PLSD revealed marginally significant differences between visual and auditory presentations ($p<0.05$).

A one-way (warning presentation method) ANOVA conducted on the reaction time to a hazard revealed a significant main effect of warning presentation method ($F(6,54)=3.873$, $p<0.01$). A multiple comparison by Fisher's PLSD revealed the following significant differences: (no warning, visual) ($p<0.01$), (no warning, auditory) ($p<0.05$), (no warning, visual-auditory) ($p<0.05$), (visual, tactile) ($p<0.01$), (visual, visual-tactile) ($p<0.01$), (visual, auditory-tactile)

($p<0.05$), (visual, auditory-tactile) ($p<0.05$), (auditory, tactile) ($p<0.01$), (auditory, visual-tactile) ($p<0.05$), (tactile, visual-tactile)($p<0.01$).

A one-way (warning presentation method) ANOVA conducted on the reaction time to a hazard revealed no significant difference. A multiple comparison by Fisher's PLSD revealed the following significant differences: (visual, tactile) ($p<0.05$), (visual, visual-tactile) ($p<0.05$), and (visual, auditory-tactile) ($p<0.05$).

Table 2. Summary of the results

Measure	Proper condition
Accuracy in switch pressing	Tactile & auditory-tactile warnings led to higher accuracy.
Reaction time to hazard	Visual, auditory visual-auditory warnings led to slower reaction.
Hit rate	Tactile, visual-auditory, and auditory-tactile warnings led to higher hit rate.
Miss rate	Auditory, tactile, and auditory-tactile warnings led to lower miss rate.

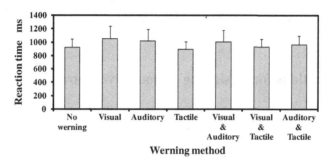

Fig. 13. Reaction time of braking operation compared among seven warning conditions

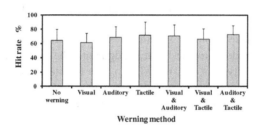

Fig. 14. Hit rate of hazardous scene compared among seven warning conditions

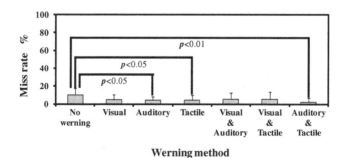

Fig. 15. Miss rate of hazardous scene compared among seven warning conditions

4   Discussion

The braking reaction time for the tactile, and the tactile-auditory combination tended to be shorter (See Fig.8). It tended that the hit rate of tactile only and the auditory-tactile combination was higher (See Fig.9). The auditory-tactile warning led to faster and more accurate reaction to a hazard. The tactile and the tactile-auditory combination improved the accuracy and the speed of the warning perception and the following operation. It might be inferred that the tactile-auditory superiority over other modality combination appeared in this experiment as pointed out by Fujisaki et al. [2].

As a whole, the performance measure such as the reaction time and the hit rate was improved for the cueing condition of tactile only and the auditory-tactile combination. In such a way, the effectiveness of the tactile cue and the combination of auditory and tactile cues was indicated.

5   Implications for Designing Automotive Warning System

The driving task corresponds to a multi-task situation [14] where a main driving task and secondary tasks such as operating an air conditioner or a digital audio system are carried out simultaneously. As pointed out by Wickens at al. [15-18], the interference of perceptual stimuli degraded the cognitive information processing. In almost all of driving environments, drivers receive almost all of information via visual or auditory stimulus. Under such a situation, it was predicted that the presentation of warning via tactile sense would accelerate the processing of stimulus.

The effectiveness of multimodal warning presentation should be explored when directional judgment is added to the hazard judgment. The presentation condition of warning of each modality was determined using the results of unimodal warning experiment. The optimal presentation of each warning must be determined using an experimental setting of multimodal warning. Moreover, as pointed out by Jones [4], the warning condition differs by the attachment location or the number of tactors. Therefore, the optimal warning condition should be determined adaptively according to the experimental setting.

References

1. Gkikas, N.: Automotive Ergonomics-Driver-Vehicle Interaction. CRC Press (2013)
2. Castro, C.: Human Factors of Visual and Cognitive Performance in Driving. CRC Press (2009)
3. Regan, M.A., Lee, J.D., Young, K.L.: Driver Distraction-Theory, Effects, and Mitigation. CRC Press (2009)
4. Jones, L.A., Sarter, N.B.: Tactile displays: Guidance for their design and application. Human Factors 50(1), 90–111 (2008)
5. Driver, J., Spence, C.: Attention and the cross-modal construction of space. Trends in Cognitive Science 2, 254–262 (1998)

6. Spence, C., Driver, J.: Cross-modal links in attention between audition, vision, and touch: Implications for interface design. International Journal of Cognitive Ergonomics 1, 351–373 (1997)
7. Spence, C., Driver, J.: Crossmodal Space and Crossmodal Attention. Oxford University Press (2006)
8. Ho, C., Tan, H.Z., Spence, C.: Using spatial vibrotactile cues to direct visual attention in driving scenes. Transportation Research, Part F 8, 397–412 (2005)
9. Ho, C., Tan, H.Z., Spence, C.: The differential effect of vibrotactile and auditory cues on visual spatial attention. Ergonomics 7(10), 724–738 (2006)
10. Ho, C., Spence, C.: The Multisensory Driver-Implications for Ergonomic Car Interface Design, Ashgate (2008)
11. Ferris, T.K., Sarter, N.B.: Cross-modal links among vision, audition, and touch in complex environmenmt. Human Factors 50(1), 7–26 (2008)
12. Fujisaki, W., Nishida, S.: Audio-tactile superiority over visuo-tactile and audio-visual combinations in the temporal resolution of synchrony perception. Experimental Brain Research 198(2-3), 245–259 (2009)
13. Murata, A., Tanaka, K., Moriwaka, M.: Basic study on effectiveness of tactile interface for warning presentation in driving environment. International Journal of Knowledge Engineering and Software Data Paradigm 3(1), 112–120 (2011)
14. Loukopouls, L.D., Dismukes, R.K., Barshi, I.: The Multitasking Myth-Headlining Complexity in Real-World Operations, Ashgate (2009)
15. Wickens, C.D., Andre, A.D.: Proximity compatibility and information display: Effects of color, space, and objectiveness of information integration. Human Factors 32, 61–77 (1990)
16. Wickens, C.D., Carswell, C.M.: The proximity compatibility principle: Its psychological foundation and relevance to display desiugn. Human Factors 37, 473–494 (1995)
17. Wickens, C.D., Lee, J.D., Liu, Y., Becker, S.E.G.: An Introduction to Human Factors Engineering, 2nd edn. Pearson Education International (2004)
18. Wickens, C.D., Holands, J.G.: Engineering Psychology and Human Performance. Prentice Hall (2000)

Proposal of Automotive 8-directional Warning System That Makes Use of Tactile Apparent Movement

Atsuo Murata, Susumu Kemori, Makoto Moriwaka, and Takehito Hayami

Graduate School of Natural Science and Technology, Okayama University, Okayama, Japan
{murata,moriwaka}@iims.sys.okayama-u.ac.jp

Abstract. We proposed a tactile 8-directional warning system which informs drivers of hazardous traffic situations hidden in 8 directions via tactile apparent movement. The effectiveness of the proposed warning system was compared with that of a warning system by simultaneous two-point stimulation and a system without warning. As a result, the apparent lead to quick reaction and higher hit rate (higher accuracy of hazard perception and recognition) as compared with the simultaneous two-point stimulation. However, this was limited to the front and the rear hazard, and was not true for all directions. The vibrotactile warning system that can recognize hazards from all of eight directions should be developed in future research.

Keywords: warning system, traffic safety, apparent movement, simultaneous two-point stimulation, reaction time, hit rate.

1   Introduction

With the progress of by-wire and information technology, the visual and cognitive driving workload increases, and the driver-vehicle interaction is getting more and more complicated [1,2]. Consequently, drivers tend to be distracted by a variety of secondary task such as the operation of switches for CD or air conditioner other than driving [3], which increases the risk of inattentive driving.

The potential application of tactile sense to the automotive warning system is paid more and more attention for enhancing driving safety [4]. Recently, the tendencies of cross-modal information processing [5-9] and design have emerged as major research topics in the design of automotive warning system. Presenting information via multiple modalities such as vision, audition, and touch has been expected to be a promising means to reduce transmission errors and enhance safety. A better understanding of cross-modal spatial and temporal links is essential to ensure a better application of this property to the automotive warning design. Ho et al. [6-8] showed the effectiveness of vibrotactile warning presentation in driving environment. In traffic situations, many hazards exist ubiquitously. Therefore, the effectiveness of automotive warning must be confirmed using a lot of locations where hazards potentially hide. However, few studies have examined the effectiveness of automotive warning system using

V.G. Duffy (Ed.): DHM/HCII 2013, Part I, LNCS 8025, pp. 98–107, 2013.

Fig. 1. Vibrotransduce Vp216 used as a vibro-tactile stimulus

Table 1. Conditions for producing apparent movement

Duration of stimulation [ms]	125
Inter-stimulus interval [ms]	125
Inter-stimulus distance [mm]	100
Frequency [Hz]	66
Intensity [V]	10

more than two locations. Ho et al. [6-8] explored the effectiveness of tactile warning for front and rear locations. Murata et al. [10] examined how the tactile warning is effective for left and right locations. Moreover, few studies investigated the effectiveness of vibrotactile warning by apparent movement. It is expected that vibrotactile warning by apparent movement can more quickly transmit the directional cues than the simultaneous stimulation of two vibrotransducers or the single-point stimulation.

The aim of this study was to propose a tactile 8-directional warning system which informs drivers of hazardous traffic situations hidden in 8 directions via tactile apparent movement. The effectiveness of the proposed warning system was compared with that of a warning system by simultaneous two-point stimulation and a system without warning. The paper is organized as follows: Section 2 shows the experimental method to explore the effectiveness of tactile 8-directional warning system. Section 3 summarized the results, and Section 4 discussed how the proposed warning system should be utilized for enhancing driving safety.

2   Method

2.1   Participants

A total of five participants aged from 21 to 24 years old took part in the experiment. All had a driver's license. All were healthy, and had no neurological diseased. Informed consent on the participation to the experiment was obtained from all participants after explaining the contents of the experiment briefly.

2.2   Task

The experimental conditions were: warning presentation by apparent movement, simultaneous two-point stimulation, and no warning. The vibrotactile stimuli were presented to the participant via a vibrotranceducer (Vp216) shown in Fig.1. The vibrotranceducers were arrayed on the seat as shown in Fig.2. In a preliminary experiment, the conditions for producing apparent movement were determined as in Tab.1.

Two warning presentation method were used in the experiment. One was the simultaneous two-point stimulation (See Fig.3), and the other was the apparent movement (See Fig.4). In Fig.5, the sketch of experimental setting is depicted.

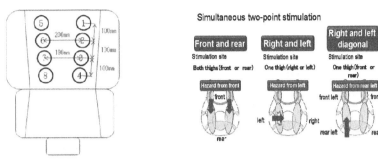

Fig. 2. Array of vibrotransducers on the automotive seat

Fig. 3. Condition of simultaneous two-point stimulation

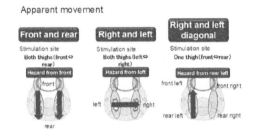

Fig. 4. Condition of apparent movement

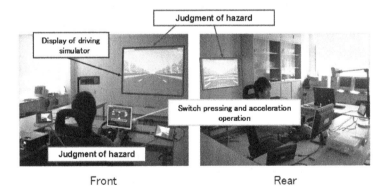

Fig. 5. Sketch of experimental setting

2.3   Design and Procedure

The participants were required to simultaneously carry out the following four tasks: (a) virtual driving task (main task), (b) switch pressing task (secondary task), (c) accelerator operation (secondary task), and (d) judgment of information randomly appearing at 8 directions (front, rear, left, right, front left, front right, rear left, and rear right) around drivers. Each task is explained from Fig.6 to Fig.9. The direction of hazard and how to avoid it are summarized in Fig.10 and Fig.11.

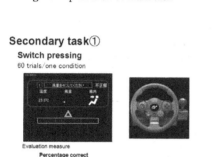

Driving simulator (tracking task)
(10 minutes/ one condition)

Driving
lane

Logicool Driving Force™
GT (Logicool)

Evaluation measure
Number of deviation from lane

Fig. 6. Explanation of main task

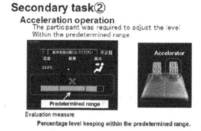

Secondary task③
Judgment of hazardous state
The participant was required to respond as soon as possible and treat this properly

■Steering
■Braking

Evaluation measure
Reaction time, hit rate, miss rate, correct rejection rate and false alarm rate

Fig. 7. Explanation of secondary task (judgment of hazardous state)

Secondary task①
Switch pressing
60 trials/one condition

Evaluation measure
Percentage correct

Fig. 8. Explanation of secondary task (switch pressing)

Secondary task②
Acceleration operation
The participant was required to adjust the level
Within the predetermined range.

Accelerator

Predetermined range

Evaluation measure
Percentage level keeping within the predetermined range.

Fig. 9. Explanation of secondary task (acceleration operation)

2.4   Evaluation Measures

The following measures were used to evaluate the effectiveness of the proposed warning system: (1) frequency of lane deviations, (2) percentage correct in switch pressing, (3) accuracy of accelerator operation, and (4) response time (speed) and accuracy to the hazard. The experiment explored how the evaluation measures were affected by the method of warning presentation (no warning, warning by simultaneous two-point stimulation, and warning by apparent movement).

3   Results

3.1   Hit Rate and Miss Rate

In Fig.12, the hit rate in the judgment of information randomly appearing at 8 directions is plotted as a function of warning condition (apparent movement, simultaneous two-point stimulation, and no warning). The hit rate of the warning by apparent movement was higher than other warning conditions. In accordance with this, the miss rate of the warning by apparent movement was nearly the same with that of the simultaneous two-point vibrotactile stimulation (See Fig.13). In Fig.14, the hit rate to hazard is shown as a function of warning presentation method and direction of hazard

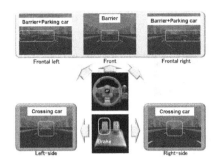

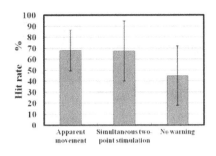

Fig. 10. Direction of hazard and its avoidance -1-

Fig. 11. Hit rate as a function of warning condition

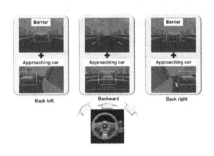

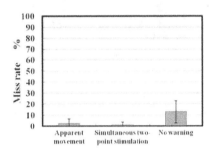

Fig. 12. Direction of hazard and its avoidance -2-

Fig. 13. Miss rate as a function of warning condition

(except for right and left directions). Fig.15 shows the hit rate as a function of warning presentation method and direction of hazard (right and left directions).

A one-way (warning presentation method) ANOVA carried out on the hit rate revealed a significant main effect ($F(2,18)=10.102$, $p<0.01$). Fisher's PLSD revealed a significant difference between apparent movement and no warning ($p<0.01$), and between simultaneous two-point stimulation and no warning ($p<0.01$).A similar one-way (warning presentation method) ANOVA carried out on the hit rate for the right and left directions revealed no significant main effect.

For each direction, Fisher's PLSD further revealed the following significant difference.

Front: Apparent movement and no warning ($p<0.01$)
       Simultaneous two-point stimulation and no warning ($p<0.01$)
Front right: Simultaneous two-point stimulation and no warning ($p<0.01$)
Rear right: Apparent movement and no warning ($p<0.05$)
       Simultaneous two-point stimulation and no warning ($p<0.01$)
Rear: Apparent movement and no warning ($p<0.05$)
Left: Apparent movement and no warning ($p<0.05$)

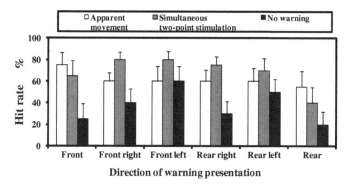

Fig. 14. Hit rate of hazard as a function warning method and direction of warning except for right and left directions

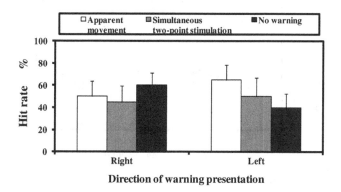

Fig. 15. Hit rate of hazard as a function warning method and direction of warning (right and left directions)

3.2   Reaction Time

The reaction time to a hazard is plotted as a function of warning presentation method and direction of hazard (except for right and left directions) in Fig.16. In Fig.17, The reaction time to a hazard is plotted as a function of warning presentation method and direction of hazard (right and left directions).

For direction of hazard presentation except for right and left directions, a one-way (warning presentation method) ANOVA was conducted on the reaction time to a hazard. A significant main effect of warning presentation method ($F(2,18)=4.438$, $p<0.05$) was detected. Fisher's PLSD revealed significant differences between apparent movement and no warning ($p<0.05$), and between simultaneous two-point stimulation ($p<0.05$).

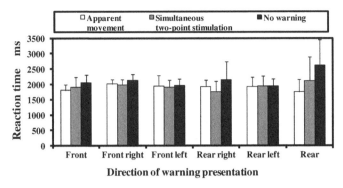

Fig. 16. Reaction time to hazard as a function warning method and direction of warning except for right and left directions

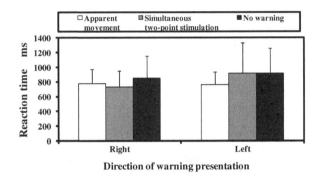

Fig. 17. Reaction time to hazard as a function warning method and direction of warning (right and left directions)

For each direction, Fisher's PLSD further revealed the following significant difference.

Front: Apparent movement and no warning ($p<0.05$)
Rear right: Simultaneous two-point stimulation and no warning ($p<0.05$)
Rear: Apparent movement and no warning ($p<0.05$)
　　　Simultaneous two-point stimulation and no warning ($p<0.05$)

4　Discussion

4.1　Accuracy of Warning Perception

For both front and rear directions, it tended that the warning presentation by apparent movement led to higher hit rate, and was more effective than the warning presentation by simultaneous two-point stimulation as shown in Fig.14. As for other directions, the hit rate for the warning presentation by simultaneous two-point stimulation tended to be higher (See Figs.14 and 15). These results mean that warning presentation should be properly used according to the direction of hazard.

Table 2. Comparison between apparent movement and simultaneous two-point stimulation

Evaluation measure	Comparison between two stimulation methods
Number of deviation from lane	Apparent movement = Simultaneous two-point stimulation
Percentage correct of switch press	Apparent movement = Simultaneous two-point stimulation
Percentage level keeping within the predetermined range	Apparent movement = Simultaneous two-point stimulation
Reaction time	Apparent movement > Simultaneous two-point stimulation (Front, Back, Left)
	Apparent movement < Simultaneous two-point stimulation (Back right, Right)
Hit rate	Apparent movement > Simultaneous two-point stimulation (Front, Back, Right, Left)
	Apparent movement < Simultaneous two-point stimulation (Front right, Front left, Back right, Back left)
Miss rate	Apparent movement = Simultaneous two-point stimulation
False alarm late	Apparent movement = Simultaneous two-point stimulation
Correct rejection rate	Apparent movement = Simultaneous two-point stimulation

4.2 Speed of Warning Perception

For the front hazard, as shown in Fig.16, the warning presentation by apparent movement tended to lead to quick reaction. For the rear right hazard, the warning presentation by simultaneous two-point stimulation tended to lead to quick reaction (See Fig.17). This is also indicative of the proposal that whether warning should be presented via apparent movement or simultaneous two-point stimulation must be determined according to the direction of warning presentation.

4.3 Implication for Automotive Warning Design

The driving task corresponds to a multi-task situation [11] where a main driving task and secondary tasks such as operating an air conditioner or a digital audio system are carried out simultaneously. As pointed out by Wickens at al. [12-15], the interference of perceptual stimuli degraded the cognitive information processing. In almost all of driving environments, drivers receive almost all of information via visual or auditory stimulus. Under such a situation, it was predicted that the presentation of warning via tactile sense would accelerate the processing of stimulus. As expected, it was indicated that the tactile warning system promoted a quick response to hazardous situations. The proposed 8-directional warning system by apparent movement led to higher hit rate. As the simultaneous two-point stimulation seems to have produced confusion among the directions of hazardous situations, this warning system led to slower response time.

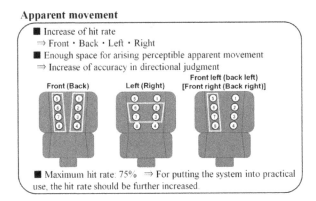

Fig. 18. Summary of results for warning presentation by apparent movement

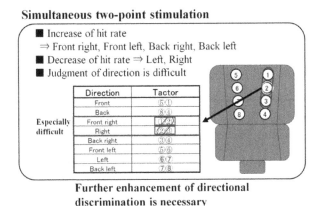

Fig. 19. Summary of results for warning presentation by simultaneous two-point stimulation

However, it must be noted that the hit rate for the warning by apparent movement was about 74%. The reason can be inferred as follows. In this experimental situation, the judgment of information randomly appearing at 8 directions includes (1) warning presentation, (2) appearance of hazardous scene, and (3) avoidance of hazard. In this process, the time to think how the hazard should be avoided is necessary. Even if the hazard was quickly recognized, it is insufficient unless the avoidance action of the hazard was also executed as soon as possible. Therefore, the warning system must be further improved so that the avoidance action after the hazard cognition will be executed fast.

In Table 2, the comparison of two warning presentation methods is listed. Except for the reaction time and the hit rate, no significant differences were detected between two warning presentation methods.

The results for warning presentation by apparent movement and simultaneous two-point stimulation are summarized in Fig.18 and Fig.19, respectively. In conclusion, the vibrotactile warning presentation was in a sense effective for preventing hazard from missing and was helpful to shorten the reaction to hazard (See Figs.12-15). It must also be noted that the following issued related to each warning presentation method must be overcome to put vibrotactile warning system into practical use. As for the warning by apparent movement, more accurate reaction should be attined in some way. Ambiguous perception of direction occurs frequently in the warning presentation by simultaneous two-point stimulation, and this induces delay of directional judgment. The increase of the number of vibrotranceducer installed to the cockpit might solve this problem.

Future work should overcome the issued identified in this experiment so that such a preventive safety driving system should be put into practical use.

References

1. Gkikas, N.: Automotive Ergonomics-Driver-Vehicle Interaction. CRC Press (2013)
2. Castro, C.: Human Factors of Visual and Cognitive Performance in Driving. CRC Press (2009)
3. Regan, M.A., Lee, J.D., Young, K.L.: Driver Distraction-Theory, Effects, and Mitigation. CRC Press (2009)
4. Jones, L.A., Sarter, N.B.: Tactile displays: Guidance for their design and application. Human Factors 50(1), 90–111 (2008)
5. Driver, J., Spence, C.: Attention and the cross-modal construction of space. Trends in Cognitive Science 2, 254–262 (1998)
6. Ho, C., Tan, H.Z., Spence, C.: Using spatial vibrotactile cues to direct visual attention in driving scenes. Transportation Research, Part F 8, 397–412 (2005)
7. Ho, C., Tan, H.Z., Spence, C.: The differential effect of vibrotactile and auditory cues on visual spatial attention. Ergonomics 7(10), 724–738 (2006)
8. Ho, C., Spence, C.: The Multisensory Driver-Implications for Ergonomic Car Interface Design. Ashgate (2008)
9. Spence, C., Driver, J.: Crossmodal Space and Crossmodal Attention. Oxford University Press (2006)
10. Murata, A., Tanaka, K., Moriwaka, M.: Basic study on effectiveness of tactile interface for warning presentation in driving environment. International Journal of Knowledge Engineering and Software Data Paradigm 3(1), 112–120 (2011)
11. Loukopouls, L.D., Dismukes, R.K., Barshi, I.: The Multitasking Myth-Headlining Complexity in Real-World Operations. Ashgate (2009)
12. Wickens, C.D., Andre, A.D.: Proximity compatibility and information display: Effects of color, space, and objectiveness of information integration. Human Factors 32, 61–77 (1990)
13. Wickens, C.D., Carswell, C.M.: The proximity compatibility principle: Its psychological foundation and relevance to display desiugn. Human Factors 37, 473–494 (1995)
14. Wickens, C.D., Lee, J.D., Liu, Y., Becker, S.E.G.: An Introduction to Human Factors Engineering, 2nd edn. Pearson Education International (2004)
15. Wickens, C.D., Holands, J.G.: Engineering Psychology and Human Performance. Prentice Hall (2000)

Evaluation of Drivers Interaction with Assistant Systems Using Criticality Driven Guided Simulation

Stefan Puch[1], Bertram Wortelen[2], Martin Fränzle[1], and Thomas Peikenkamp[2]

[1] Carl von Ossietzky University, 26129 Oldenburg, Germany
{stefan.puch,martin.fraenzle}@informatik.uni-oldenburg.de
[2] OFFIS - Institute for Information Technology, 26121 Oldenburg, Germany
{bertram.wortelen,thomas.peikenkamp}@offis.de

Abstract. Advanced Driver Assistance Systems (ADAS) operate more and more autonomously and take over essential parts of the driving task e.g. keeping safe distance or detecting hazards. Thereby they change the structure of the driver's task and thus induce a change in driver's behavior. Nevertheless it is still the driver who is ultimately responsible for the safe operation of the vehicle. Therefore it is necessary to ensure that the behavioral changes neither reduce the controllability of the vehicle nor the controllability of the hazardous events. We introduce the Threshold Uncertainty Tree Search (TUTS) algorithm as a simulation based approach to explore rare but critical driver behavior in interaction with an assistance system. We present first results obtained with a validated driver model in a simple driving scenario.

Keywords: Guided Co-Simulation, Driver Model, Hybrid Simulation, Risk Analysis, Monte Carlo.

1 Introduction

ADAS have a strong impact on the behavior of drivers and the controllability of vehicles and thus it needs to be demonstrated that the use of an ADAS does not reduce the controllability. The European Code of Practice for the Design and Evaluation of ADAS [4] proposes in more details, how to address these issues during the system development process. It recommends empirical experiments with human drivers as primary instrument for the evaluation process. Unfortunately these experiments are often time consuming and costly. Another option, which is proposed in this paper, is to use a model based approach which integrates executable models of environment, driver and ADAS into a co-simulation.

Although the driver model we use is only an abstraction and does not cover all aspects of human behavior, it still provides some advantages for speeding up the evaluation process. First of all, replacing the human driver by a driver model enables a fully automated simulation and thus a huge amount of different situations can be evaluated in a short amount of time. Such an approach can be useful during an early evaluation phase to identify scenarios which may deserve

V.G. Duffy (Ed.): DHM/HCII 2013, Part I, LNCS 8025, pp. 108–117, 2013.
© Springer-Verlag Berlin Heidelberg 2013

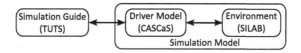

Fig. 1. Setup for the guided simulation as used for the present work

a more detailed analysis by doing experiments with human subjects. Another important issue addresses the risk assessment of the ADAS. Since risky situations are typically very infrequent and the number of tests in empirical experiments is limited, rare events are normally not observed. This issue can be addressed by doing large numbers of simulation as it increases the probability of observing rare events. But performing pure Monte Carlo simulations is not very efficient for this matter, because the largest amount of simulation samples show typically non-critical and mostly similar behavior. As risk assessment is not interested in the average behavior, we present in this paper a heuristic algorithm that guides the simulated driver behavior into critical situations. We furthermore present a first evaluation study of our guided simulation approach. It utilizes a driving simulator study that was conducted with 17 human drivers. Data of this experiment were used to create a cognitive driver model. Human participant and driver model have to interact with an in-vehicle system while driving. We used the TUTS algorithm to guide the driver model behavior into critical situations, where it may hits the pillar of a bridge.

2   Simulation Infrastructure

We propose to use closed-loop simulations of the driver-vehicle-environment system to support the analysis of newly introduced in-vehicle systems. A high-level view on the connection of the driver model, the driving environment and the simulation guide based on the TUTS algorithm is shown in Figure 1. The guide is application independent and is thus not aware of what kind of simulation model it is guiding. In the setup used in the present work, it only guides the behavior of the driver model and not the environment. The driver model, which we employ in our experiments is created using the Cognitive Architecture for Safety Critical Task Simulation (CASCaS). Cognitive architectures are a means to simulate human behavior in a psychologically plausible way. The objective of CASCaS is to supplement the development process of new assistance systems with the possibility of a virtual-human-in-the loop simulation in early design phases. To account for the variations in human behavior, a lot of processes involved in CASCaS contain probabilistic elements (PEs). The TUTS algorithm adjusts the PEs in order to simulate rare behavior. We will give a brief overview on CASCaS and some of its most important probabilistic elements. For more detailed information see [6].

CASCaS is a hybrid architecture consisting of a set of components which are related to different aspects of the human behavior. Like most other CAs, CASCaS simulates goal oriented human behavior. Multitasking is achieved by switching between a set of task goals. A scheduling algorithm dynamically selects in a probabilistic manner from a set of weighted goals the current goal to be executed. The main knowledge processing unit of CASCaS is based on a rule engine, which probabilistically selects from a set of weighted rules in a similar manner as the goal selection algorithm. The rules describe how the cognitive model solves its tasks and achieves its goals. Beyond the selection between finitely many discrete choices, CASCaS also makes use of continuous probability distributions. For a realistic timing of different processes like hand and eye movements or fixation durations, CASCaS adds noise to the calculated durations. The noise is drawn from continuous probability distributions.

3   Threshold Uncertainty Tree Search

In safety-critical environments critical situations are often associated with extreme behavior, which shows up very rarely. Exploring the model behaviour for these rare situations using a pure MC approach is very inefficient. Hence Puch, et al. [3] introduced a concept of an algorithm, that probabilistically guides the simulation into critical situations. We applied this algorithm to the driver model use case presented in section 4. Unfortunately the search speed was very unsatisfying. We elaborated on this aspect and present now as a result the Threshold Uncertainty Tree Search (TUTS) algorithm. TUTS is Monte Carlo-based, meaning that it repeatedly simulates a scenario starting from some initial state, while taking different probabilistic choices. Let S be the set of reachable states and $S_0, S_t \subseteq S$ sets of initial states respectively terminal states which all satisfy a user defined initial condition respectively termination condition. Each simulation run starts in an initial state and stops once a terminal state is reached.

The simulation model (in this case the CASCaS driver model) has to make several choices for all probabilistic elements, that occur during simulation, e.g. the probabilistic selection of a goal. PEs can be divided into two classes: discrete probabilistic elements (DPE) and continuous probabilistic elements (CPE). A DPE e_d is associated with a categorical distribution for a finite set of options denoted by O_{e_d}. A CPE e_c is associated with a continuous probability density function (PDF) denoted by f_{e_c}. We initially assume, that the simulation model only contains DPEs and no CPE. Given an initial state $s \in S_0$ the model behavior b can be characterized by the sequence of probabilistic events $b = o_1, o_2, \ldots, o_{n_b}$, with o_i being the option taken at the i-th event and n_b being the number of events that occur until a terminating state is reached, which might vary for different behaviors. By starting in the same initial state and taking the same sequence of options in different simulation runs, we obtain deterministic behaviors. We call a guidance algorithm with this property a deterministic guidance.

The left part of Figure 2 illustrates an event tree, that was derived by taking successively different available options during multiple simulation runs. Because CASCaS contains many different processes with probabilistic elements, each behavior typically contains a great number of options. This results in very large event trees, because the tree size increases exponentially with its depth.

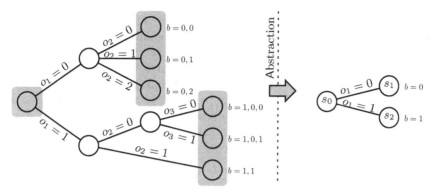

Fig. 2. Only considering events at the gray nodes strongly reduces the event tree

The size of the event tree can be reduced drastically by only considering a subset of important PEs. Let us consider that we are only interested in the events of some PEs that occur in the gray-marked states in Figure 2. The guide will not consider the events of other PEs, which leads to a smaller graph shown in the right part of the figure. This however introduces the problem, that the same sequence of options on two different simulation runs results in the same path of the event tree although the model behavior might differ. Thus the guide is no longer deterministic. If the ignored PEs contribute only marginally to the behavior of the agent, we expect that the observed behaviors in one node are at least similar. Thus a node of the event tree represents a class of similar driving behavior. In section 4 we analyze the similarity of driving behavior within nodes.

In order to deal with CPEs a further source of variance is introduced. Each CPE e_c is discretized by splitting f_{e_c} into a set of q PDFs with equal probability density. The guide selects one of these PDFs and draws a random value, which introduced additional variance. See [3] for details.

In order to drive the model into interesting situations, the TUTS algorithms requires a user defined function, which returns a numerical measure of the criticality $\tilde{c}$ for each simulation run, e.g., the minimum time-to-crash value observed during the simulation run. A user defined threshold τ is used to define the level that separates the acceptable and unacceptable critical situations. The TUTS algorithms attempts to guide the simulation into a region close to the threshold of acceptable and unacceptable situations. Let $C(s)$ be the set of criticality values, that have been observed in all simulation runs, which passed the node s. Consider the event tree on the right side in Figure 2. Being in node s_0 the guide should choose an option ($o_1 = 0$ or 1), that most likely results in a criticality close to τ. We measure the closeness to τ in standard deviations according to the distribution of $C(s)$, by calculating the z-score of τ:

$$z(s) = \frac{\tau - \mu(C(s))}{\sigma(C(s))}$$

To increase the likelihood of observing a criticality of τ when passing s, the guide should prefer options which lead to small absolute z-scores. This is done in a probabilistic way by weighting all options, that the guide can select. A weight $w(s)$ is defined for each node s. With S'_s the set of child nodes of s are denoted. These are the nodes that are reached when selecting an option in state s. The function $t : S, O \longrightarrow S$ defines the parent-child relationship. $t(s, o)$ gives the node, that is reached when option o is selected while in node s. The guide uses the weights of the nodes to probabilistically select from the current set of options $\tilde{O}$. The probability of selecting option $o \in \tilde{O}$ if the current node is s:

$$P(o) = \frac{w(t(s, o))}{\sum\limits_{p \in \tilde{O}} w(t(s, p))} \qquad (1)$$

This means that options that leads to highly weighted states are selected with higher probability. Therefore the states with low z-values should have high weights. The weights are defined by:

$$w(s) = \frac{1}{(z + 1)^{f(s_p)}} \qquad (2)$$

Unless s has been visited twice, $\sigma(C(s))$ does not exist and z is undefined. Therefore, if any selectable child node has not yet been visited twice, the guide selects one of these randomly. In this way the guide explores each branch at least two times. The $f(s_p)$ exponent is used to adjust the weights the more confidence is gained about the distribution of criticality values in $C(s)$. Let s_p be the parent node of s. Thus each sibling uses the same exponent.

Especially for nodes at the top of the event tree the variance of criticality values $\sigma(C(s))$ is high and sibling nodes often have similar mean values $\mu(C(s))$. These nodes are at the beginning of the simulations. Many subsequent decisions influence the criticality of a simulation. This results in high variances and in uncertain mean values for early nodes. In order to take the uncertainty about the z-values into account the function f is used. This function should rise with the certainty of the z-values. This leads to a spreading of weights, the more confident the z-values are. For our use case scenario we used a simple definition of f that creates identical values for the set $S_{\tilde{O}} = \{t(s, o) | o \in \tilde{O}\}$ of all sibling nodes, that can be reached with the current set of options $\tilde{O}$. Let $n_{min} = \min(n_{s'} | s' \in S_{\tilde{O}})$ be the minimum number of visits of any node in $S_{\tilde{O}}$, then we used the following definition for f, with free parameters a and b to adjust the search speed:

$$f(s) = a + b \cdot n_{min}, \quad \text{with } a = 0.5, \quad b = 0.5 \qquad (3)$$

4   Evaluation

In order to evaluate the TUTS algorithm we utilize the setup of a recent driving simulator study [6,7]. Aim of this study was to investigate drivers attention distribution when driving on a curvy road while interacting with a secondary in-vehicle task. We briefly describe aspects of the study that are relevant for the present work. For more details see [6,7].

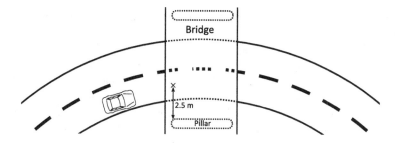

Fig. 3. Distance of bridge pillar to the center of the lane in the driving scenario

4.1 Scenario

The driving scenario consists of a winding road with curve radii between 375 m and 750 m. The drivers were instructed to focus on three goals: (1) Keep the car in the middle of the lane. (2) Keep a constant speed of 100 km/h as closely as possible. (3) Solve some tasks displayed on an in-vehicle display in varying time intervals as soon as possible. This third task is used representatively for the interaction with an infotainment or assistance system displayed in the center console. To meet the requirements of all goals the attention has to be switched between this three tasks and their respective areas of interest (road, speedometer, in-vehicle display).The structure of this scenario is simple. There is no complex task for the driver, no surrounding traffic, road signs or intersections. The most crucial aspect is how drivers distribute their attention among the three goals. If too few attention is paid to keeping the car within the lane, the driver might cross the lane border. Due to this simple structure, we used this scenario as a first use case for the TUTS algorithms, to identify driver model behaviors, where the interaction with the in-vehicle task leads to critical situations.

To demonstrate the functioning of our algorithm, we introduced a single critical point in the scenario. This was done by placing a bridge over the road, which was not present in the original scenario (see Figure 3). The minimum distance from the center of the car to the right bridge pillar was used as a measure for the consequence $\tilde{c}$ of the driving behavior. The pillar of the bridge is placed 2.5 m away from the center of the left lane.

4.2 Simulation

Wortelen, et al. [6,7] developed a driver model using CASCaS, which was able to drive this scenario. The driving behavior and the visual scanning behavior of the driver model has been validated against the behavior of 17 human drivers.

The simulation of the driver model is divided in two phases. In the beginning of each simulation run the driver model accelerates to 100 km/h. Reaching 100 km/h defines the initial states S_0. A simulation run ends 20 m after the car passed the pillar or if a predefined time limit is reached. This defines the terminal states S_t. The time span between initial and terminal state is typically around

8 seconds with small variations. The smallest distance to the pillar is reached approximately 7 seconds after the initial state.

As mentioned CASCaS contains several PEs. It can be configured which classes of PEs the simulation guide considers and which not. The most critical aspect in this scenario is the way in which the driver model switches attention between the three tasks [7]. We therefore assume that the probabilistic element in the selection process for task goals is most relevant for the guiding algorithm. The way in which the driver model executes the tasks is in great parts described by a set of rules, which are selected and executed in a probabilistic manner similar to the goal selection process.

In order to compare the results of our guided simulation we performed three sets of simulations of this scenario. First we did 10,000 simulation runs in a Monte Carlo way without any guidance (MC). Then we used the simulation guide and did 10,000 runs considering only the goal selection DPEs (GS) and 10,000 runs while additionally considering rule selection DPEs (GS+RS). All other PEs are drawn randomly according to their distribution.

4.3   Results

In the algorithm description we assumed that each node of the event tree represents similar behaviors. The PEs not considered by the simulation guide introduce behavioral variance within each node. The variance should be smaller the more PEs the guide considers. But at the same time this increases the size of the event tree. This effect is illustrated in Figures 4. The figures should be read as follows. Every time a node is entered during a simulation the current time distance (Δt) to the point in time when the initial state was reached, and the current lateral position d_L is recorded. The lateral position is measured in meter and is 0 m, if the car is in the center of the lane and increases, when the car drifts to the right lane border and decreases if it drifts to the left lane border. At the end of each 10,000 simulations we calculated for each node the mean values for Δt and d_L and their standard deviation. In the following we only consider nodes that have been visited at least twice and thus have a standard deviation. The x-axis is discretized in 500 ms steps. All nodes with a mean time within each 500 ms window are aggregated.

The solid lines in Figure 4(a) show the mean standard deviation for Δt of all nodes in a 500 ms window. It can indeed be seen that the standard deviation for the GS+RS simulation are much smaller than for the GS simulation, showing that the range of behaviors represented by a node is narrower when goal and rule selection are considered. But at the same time the size of the tree growths much faster in the GS+RS configuration. This can be seen by the dashed lines, which show the number of nodes which have been aggregated in each window.

Data for the lateral position has been aggregated in the same way. In Figure 4(b) the mean standard deviation for d_L within each time window is shown by the thick solid lines. The dashed lines show the total standard deviation, which is calculated over all observed d_L values from all nodes within each time window. If the assumption, that taking the same paths in the event tree leads

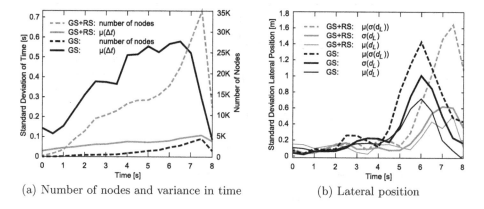

(a) Number of nodes and variance in time   (b) Lateral position

Fig. 4. $\mu(x)$ is the mean over all observations of all nodes with a time interval an $\sigma(x)$ is the standard deviation. $\mu(\sigma(x))$ calculates the standard deviation within a node and averages it over all nodes within a time interval. All values are aggregated over all nodes within a time interval of 0.5 s.

to similar behavior holds, then the standard deviation in each node should be much lower than the total standard deviation. For the GS configuration it can be seen that especially for the last four seconds the mean standard deviation is indeed smaller than the total deviation. However the difference is not very big. By also considering the rule selection DPEs in the GS+RS configuration this difference can be increased. It can be seen that for both configurations during the first 4 seconds the standard deviation does not change much. The same holds for the mean lateral position as indicated by the thin solid lines. Afterwards the mean lateral position of the car in the GS and in the GS+RS configurations drifts towards the bridge pillar. This happens earlier in the GS configuration, where the highest lateral deviation is reached approximately at $\Delta t = 6$ seconds, while the pillar is reached at around $\Delta t = 7$ seconds. In contrast the GS+RS configuration reaches the highest lateral deviation at that time. In future work we will investigate on these differences. A possible reason is, that the guide in the GS configuration controls less aspects of the driver model and is thus not able to guide it as precisely.

The main objective is to explore the driver model behavior and to simulate valid behaviors that show rare and critical consequences far more often than pure Monte Carlo simulations would. In Figure 5 the results for all three configurations are compared. Shown are the frequency distributions of the consequence values $\tilde{c}$ discretized in 0.1 m steps each for 10,000 simulation runs. The distribution for the Monte Carlo simulation is very narrow. In fact 7,272 of the 10,000 runs show a consequence value of around 2.4 m. Nearly all deviations are within the lane boundaries, even though the driver model is interacting with the secondary task.

This is different for the GS and GS+RS configurations. The distributions are strongly biased toward low $\tilde{c}$ values. Especially the GS+RS configuration shows a high number of simulations close to $\tilde{c} = 0$. For the guided simulation

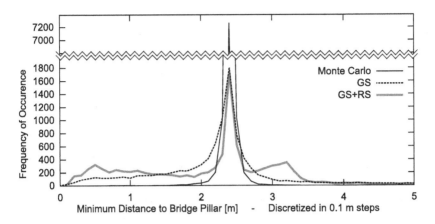

Fig. 5. Frequency distributions of criticality values for all three configurations

configurations also high $\tilde{c}$ values are observed more often. The reason for this is that the guide has to explore the behavior of the model, which might also lead to higher $\tilde{c}$ values. Another reason is, that many options selected by the guide destabilize the lateral control of the driver model, which not only leads to drifts to the right side, but also to the left side.

5   Related Work

A similar approach to ours is found in Hu's work [1]. He presents an efficient model-based simulation engine for risk assessment of complex systems consisting of software, hardware and human elements. Furthermore, he developed a guided simulation process to avoid the slow coverage of Monte Carlo methods. The difference to our approach is that the engineering knowledge about the system is used prior to the simulation to generate a plan as a high level guide. The plan itself contains a list with scenarios of interests and is used as a map for exploration during simulation. Our approach is similar, but does not need a predefined event tree, which is used by Hu. Our tree structure is automatically derived during the simulation. The level of detail of the event tree can be adjusted, ranging from a small and abstract tree up to a fully deterministic one.

The basic idea of the TUTS algorithm was introduced on a conceptual level by Puch, et al.[3]. After first tests with the initial implementation we observed a slow search speed and elaborated on this aspect. The resulting algorithm presented in section 3 is similar to some game theoretic approaches. It shares important ideas of the UCT algorithm (Upper Confidence Bounds applied to Trees) [2], which is a game theoretic planning approach based on rollout Monte Carlo search techniques [5]. Like the UTC algorithm TUTS implements a weighted search within the event tree, that adjusts the search weights according to the confidence of the results achieved during the previous simulations. Though the search criterion of TUTS is different in its nature. This will be described in section 3.

6   Discussion

In this paper we have presented results from a first study to efficiently explore and simulate rare and critical model behavior in a cosimulation of environment, driver and ADAS. We therefore demonstrated the TUTS algorithm and pointed out promising achievements. However the use case was very simple and in future work we aim at more complex scenarios and driver tasks. Currently a driver model is under development which is intended to simulate a number of different highway scenarios like car following, overtaking and merging into traffic flows. An advanced highway assistance system is introduced into the simulation, instead of using an artificial in-vehicle task. Data from simulator experiments with human drivers already have been performed and will be used to validate the driver model. Furthermore we want to provide a concept for the analysis of the resulting event tree. The most relevant paths in the tree should be identified and presented to the system developer in order to reveal critical interaction sequences.

Acknowledgement. This research has been performed with support from the Ministry of Science and Culture of Lower Saxony within the project IMoST II.

References

1. Hu, Y.: A Guided Simulation Methodology for Dynamic Probabilistic Risk Assessment of Complex Systems. Ph.D. thesis, University of Maryland (2005)
2. Kocsis, L., Szepesvári, C.: Bandit Based Monte-Carlo Planning. In: Fürnkranz, J., Scheffer, T., Spiliopoulou, M. (eds.) ECML 2006. LNCS (LNAI), vol. 4212, pp. 282–293. Springer, Heidelberg (2006)
3. Puch, S., Wortelen, B., Fränzle, M., Peikenkamp, T.: Using Guided Simulation to Improve a Model-Based Design Process of Complex Human Machine Systems. In: Klumpp, M. (ed.) Proceedings of the 2012 European Simulation and Modelling Conference, pp. 159–164. EUROSIS-ETI (2012)
4. Servel, A., Knapp, A., Jung, C., Donner, E., Dilger, E., Tango, F., Mihm, J., Schwarz, J., Wood, K., Ojeda, L., Neumann, M., Brockmann, M., Meyer, M., Kiss, M., Flament, M., Kompfner, P., Walz, R., Cotter, S., Winkle, T., Janssen, W.: Code of Practice for the Design and Evaluation of ADAS (2006), http://www.prevent-ip.org
5. Tesauro, G., Galperin, G.R.: On-line Policy Improvement using Monte-Carlo Search. In: Proceeding of Advances in Neural Information Processing Systems 9 (NIPS), Denver, CO, USA, December 2-5 (1996)
6. Wortelen, B., Baumann, M., Lüdtke, A.: Dynamic Simulation and Prediction of Drivers' Attention Distribution. Transportation Research Part F: Traffic Psychology and Behaviour (submitted)
7. Wortelen, B., Lüdtke, A., Baumann, M.: Integrated Simulation of Attention Distribution and Driving Behavior. In: Proceedings of the 22nd Annual Conference on Behavior Representation in Modeling and Simulation (in press)

Effects of Spaceflight Operation Complexity and Training on Operation Error

Meng Wang[1,3], Yijing Zhang[1,3,*], Bin Wu[2,3,*], Pengjie Li[1,3], Shanguang Chen[1,3], Jinwu Zhang[3], and Min Liu[3]

[1] National Key Laboratory of Human Factors Engineering, Beijing, 100094, P.R. China
[2] State Key Laboratory of Space Medicine Fundamentals and Application, Beijing, 100094, P.R. China
[3] China Astronaut Research and Training Center, Beijing, 100094, P.R. China
zyj.acc@gmail.com, wubinacc@sina.com

Abstract. To investigate how the spaceflight operation complexity and training affect operation errors of spaceflight tasks, a two-factor experiment was designed and conducted. Nine participants performed eighteen spacecraft operation units which were divided into three complexity levels during two training stages. Based on the experiment data, the changes of average operation times and errors at the initial and final stages were analyzed; the equations of linear regression between the complexity and the average operation errors were established. The results showed that the average operation errors were significantly raised with the complexity at the initial stage (P=0.03, 0.02). The operation errors of the low and middle complexity levels at the final stage were much less than those at the initial stage ($P<0.05$).The operation errors were significantly correlated to the complexity levels at the two stages. It implies that suitable operation complexity and sufficient training are two of the effective ways to ensure the reliability of astronaut operations during spaceflight.

Keywords: training, operation complexity, operation error, correlation.

1   Introduction

Chinese Manned space program has progressed rapidly after four manned space missions from SZ-5 to SZ-9. The goal of Space Medicine and Medical Engineering has been extended from ensuring the astronauts' safety and health in the early stage to ensuring their working capabilities, improving the operational reliability and maximizing astronauts' contributions.

In space, astronaut, manned spacecraft and space environment constitute a typical man-machine-environment system. All the three aspects are significant to the accomplishment of flight missions. Human aspects: psychological state and training effect will affect the accomplishment of flight mission directly. Machine aspects: inappropriate position of panel or insufficient light will influence the manual control space

---

* Corresponding author.

V.G. Duffy (Ed.): DHM/HCII 2013, Part I, LNCS 8025, pp. 118–125, 2013.
© Springer-Verlag Berlin Heidelberg 2013

operation. Environment aspects: weightlessness, noise or radiation will affect the spatial orientation and the movement control ability of astronauts [1]. Therefore, for manned spaceflights, the reliability of human in system will be particularly important.

Spaceflight operation complexity and training are regarded as the two main influencing factors on astronaut operation error by some previous researches. To improve the training effects of spaceflight operation and finally ensure the reliability of astronaut operation in orbit, a series of researches were conducted in this work to investigate how the two factors affect operation errors of spaceflight tasks. This study would provide theoretical guidance for the design of spaceflight tasks and astronaut training methods in the future, and then the potential human errors in manned spaceflight could be prevented effectively.

2   Method

A two-factor experiment was designed in this study. The independent variables were operation complexity and training. The dependent variable was the number of operation errors which was defined as a deviation from the required action following the operation procedure in this study.

2.1   Participant

Nine male test subjects were recruited from China Astronaut Research and Training Center. They had no operation experience of spaceship panel and Environment Control and Life Support System (ECLSS). All the subjects passed a cognitive test by a multi-dimension psychological test instrument named DXC-VI. The experiment was approved by the ethics committee of China Astronaut Research and Training Center.

2.2   Operation Complexity Evaluation and Operation Unit Selection

Participants were asked to finish 18 simulated spaceflight operation units in the spacecraft panel training platform and ECLSS training platform. The operation complexity of each operation unit was evaluated by entropy based method and subjective evaluation method.

Operation Complexity Evaluation. Xing and Manning reviewed the literature on complexity including articles on general concepts, information complexity, cognitive complexity, and display complexity, and then presented that, while these studies were focused on different areas, they all agreed on three factors associated with complexity: the quantity of basic information elements (size), the variety of elements (variety), and the relationship between elements (rule) [2, 3]. Based on that, the spaceflight operation complexity was defined in previous studies as, the combination of operation tasks, the quantity and the variety of basic information elements and the relationship between the elements included in operation interface. The spaceflight operation complexity can be perceived by astronaut and affect the operation performance. The operation complexity in this study was not related to human factors and environment factors, such as the ability and experience of astronaut and the effect of weightlessness [4, 5].

Subjective and objective evaluation methods were used to determine the complexity level. Subjective evaluation method was implemented by experts' assessments. Objective evaluation method is entropy based method. Finally, the complexity level was determined in terms of the consistent principle of subjective and objective evaluation results. The weighted method would be used to process the results if they were not consistent and the final result would be the complexity value.

On the basis of complexity evaluation index system, a kind of complexity evaluation method based on entropy measure was established (entropy based method for short) [6]. The following four factors were selected to describe the operation complexity: complexity of operation step size (COSS), which evaluates the amount of actions contained in one operation unit, complexity of operation logic structure (COLS), which describes the logical sequence to conduct the activities of one operation unit, complexity of operation instrument information (COII), which denotes the type and number of monitors and controllers in one operation unit, and complexity of space mission information (CSMI) which is related to the difficulty level of the task information for completing one operation unit. Finally, the operation complexity values of spaceflight operations were determined by the weighted Euclidean norm of the four factors [4, 5].

Subjective evaluation method was implemented by experts' assessment. The twelve first batch of astronauts and five main faculties in charge of flight procedure training were recruited into the expert group to evaluate the complexity of each operation unit on a nine-point scale. The average is regarded as the final result of subjective complexity evaluation.

In terms of the complexity range of spaceflight operations, the value of high complexity level is between 2.0 and 2.5, the value of middle complexity level is between 1.5 and 1.8, and the value of low complexity level is between 0.8 and 1.2.

Operation Unit Selection. According to the experiment condition, equipments and operability, the complexities of 25 space operation units initially selected were then evaluated by subjective and objective evaluation methods. Following the consistent principle of subjective and objective evaluation, eighteen operation units were selected for the final experiment. All the units were divided into three operation unit groups. Three spacecraft emergency operations and three ECLSS operations were involved in each group. Each type of operations involved three complexity levels.

2.3   Equipment and Procedure

The experimental equipment included a spacecraft panel training platform, an ECLSS training platform and a data recording software. Participants performed operations on spacecraft panel training platform and ECLSS training platform, in which the operation units could be chosen and the operating states could be recorded. The data recording software were used to record the operation errors and performance of each operation.

The preliminary instruction and basic theories were taught to the participants before the experiment. The formal experiment consisted of initial stage and final stage. Except for the targeted theory instruction and training comment, each participant finished six operation units in each group. Each operation unit was performed five to six times in order.

2.4   Data Processing and Statistic Analysis

The experiment data were processed using Paired Sample T Test in SPSS 15.0.

For each operation unit, the average number of operation errors during the first three times at the initial stage was regarded as the initial training effect and that of the last two times at the final stage was regarded as the final training effect. The changes of average number of operation errors at two stages were analyzed. The equations of linear regression between complexity and average operation errors were established and the coefficients were compared. $P<0.05$ means the difference is significant. $0.05<P<0.1$ means the trend of significant is different.

3   Result

The analysis result of performance shows that the operation success rate was between 98% and 100%, and the operation errors between different participants had no significant statistic meaning. Therefore, the accuracies of all the participants were regarded as high and similar. Based on that, the operation errors were analyzed.

3.1   Comparison between Average Operation Times of Different Complexity Levels at Different Training Stages

Table 1 shows the result of comparison between average operation times of different complexity levels at different training stages. The average operation times of the middle and high complexity levels were more than those of the low complexity level ($P<0.01$). The average operation times of high complexity level were more than those of the middle complexity level ($P<0.05$). These results accorded with the discipline that the operation time prolongs when the complexity level increases. Therefore, the complexity evaluation method used in this study could be proved effectively.

Table 1. Comparison of average operation time of different complexity levels at different training stages ($\bar{x} \pm s, n = 9$)

Complexity level	Initial stage	Final stage	P value
Low	19.90 ± 11.52	14.75 ± 1.60	0.26
Middle	$133.70 \pm 3.00^{\Delta\Delta}$	$64.36 \pm 9.48^{\Delta\Delta}$	<0.01
High	$188.83 \pm 15.23^{\Delta\Delta\#}$	$78.88 \pm 13.34^{\Delta\Delta\#}$	<0.01

Note. $^{\Delta\Delta}$ $P<0.01$, as compared with operation time of low complexity level at the same stage ;

$^{\#}$ $P<0.05$, as compared with operation time of middle complexity level at the same stage.

3.2 Comparison between Average Operation Errors of Different Complexity Levels at Different Training Stages

Table 2 shows the result of comparison between average operation errors of different complexity levels at different training stages. The average operation errors of middle complexity level were more than those of low complexity level significantly ($P<0.05$) at both training stages. At the initial stage, the average operation errors of high complexity level were more than those of low complexity level significantly, while no significant difference existed with those of middle complexity level. At the final stage, the average operation errors of high complexity level were not significantly different with those of middle and low complexity levels. The average operation errors of middle and low complexity levels at the final stage were less than those at the initial stage significantly ($P<0.05$). For the high complexity level, the variation trend is significant ($P=0.064$).

Table 2. Comparison of average operation error of different complexity levels at different training stages ($\overline{x} \pm s, n = 9$)

Complexity level	Initial stage	Final stage	P value
Low	0.35 ± 0.04	0.04 ± 0.03	<0.001
Middle	$1.28 \pm 0.45^{\Delta}$	$0.11 \pm 0.06^{\Delta}$	<0.05
High	$1.99 \pm 0.58^{\Delta}$	0.50 ± 0.66	0.064

Note. $^{\Delta}$ $P<0.05$, as compared with operation errors of low complexity level at the same stage.

3.3 Correlation between Operation Complexity Levels and Operation Errors at Different Training Stages

The equations of linear regression between the operation complexity levels evaluated by entropy based method and the operation errors of each participant on each operation unit are established at both the initial and final stages. Table 3 shows that the regression coefficients and correlation coefficients both decrease at the final stage, compared with those at the initial stage ($P<0.05$). This result demonstrates that the opposite effect of complexity level on operation error reduces after a series of training.

Table 3. Correlation between operation complexity levels and operation errors at different training stages

Complexity measure method	Equations of linear regression		P value
	Initial stage	Final stage	
Entropy based method	Y=6.31X-4.47 $R^2=0.607$, P<0.001	Y=0.492X-0.302 $R^2=0.241$, P=0.038	<0.05

Note. Y, operation errors. X, operation complexity level. P, the value of statistical test probability between regression coefficient of function at the final training stage and that at the first training stage.

4   Discussion

The definitions of complexity in different research fields are different. This study defined the operation error according to the need of astronaut training and the feasibility of measurement and established a complexity evaluation method based on entropy measurement. On the basis of the evaluation model, the effects of spaceflight operation complexity and training on operation error were investigated.

Table 1 shows that with the increase of complexity levels, the operation time lengthened at two stages. Therefore the complexity evaluation method could be regarded as valid. At both the initial and final stages, the average operation errors of middle and high complexity levels were more than those of the low complexity level. Consequently, the operation complexity can be considered as a main influencing factor of operation errors. In space, with the increase of the operation complexity, the requirement on attention and coordination between eyes, hands and brains are more demanding. Meanwhile the astronauts' workload will be heavier, severely affecting the final performance. However, there was no significant difference of operation errors between the middle and high complexity levels. The conceivable reason is that the complexity gap between the two complexity levels is not big enough to reveal the different effects of complexity.

The comparison between Table 1 and Table 2 shows that the differences of operation times are more significant than those of operation errors of different complexity levels. Therefore, the complexity evaluation method used in this study may be more effective on evaluating operation time.

Table 2 shows that the average operation errors of low and middle complexity levels decreased significantly at the final stage ($P<0.05$). This result shows with the training, the operation reliability was enhanced apparently. The occurrence of operation error is closely related to the time of training and the proficiency of skills. Therefore, to ensure the operation reliability in spaceflight, plenty of strict and effective training activities are necessary for astronauts [7]. However the operation errors of high complexity level did not decrease significantly with the proceeding of training. It means that more training is needed to master the high complexity operations.

Table 3 shows that the regression coefficients and correlation coefficients of the equations both decreased at the final stage, compared with those at the initial stage ($P<0.05$). This result shows that the training have a significant effect on the correlation between the operation complexity and operation errors. The ergonomic perspective on human error is that errors arise as a result of incompatibility between the characteristics of the human and task demands [8].Thus, any mismatch between operation capability and task demands will increase error occurrence and potentially challenge safety [9]. One of the basic approaches to managing human error is to establish compatibility between people's capabilities and task demands by using appropriate selection and training methods [10]. Therefore training was one of the countermeasures to decrease the effect of task complexity.

Park et al. noted that the significant correlation between complexity and operation times and errors is the leading basis of judging the effectiveness of complexity evaluation method. If the significant correlation exists and the operation time and error increase with the enhancement of complexity level, then the complexity evaluation method will be regarded as valid and it can be used to predict the operation time and error rate [11,12]. The results of Table 1 and Table 2 show that the variation of operation time and error with the enhancement of complexity level is in accordance with the theory Park presented. Therefore the entropy based method used in this study is valid.

To sum up, this study shows that spaceflight operation complexity and training are of significant effects on operation errors. The complexity evaluation method based on entropy measure is valid in different training stages. However, the influence of training should be considered before predicting the situation of operation error by complexity evaluation. According to the study on effects of spaceflight operation complexity and training on operation error, operation units with high complexity level were verified to lead to astronaut operation error more easily. But with the proceeding of training, operation error rate was reduced apparently. Therefore, high complexity level operations should be avoided when spaceflight missions are designed and arranged. For inevitable high complexity missions, operation skills should be grasped firmly by repeated training. Because of the difference of training stages, the factors have effects on astronaut operation error changes constantly. Consequently, actual flight condition and mission difficulties at different training stages should be taken into account to design pertinent training method. The results in this study provide an important guidance for the design of astronaut training plan in the future and for accomplishment of training mission with high quality with limited time and resource.

Acknowledgements. This work was supported by National Natural Science Fund project (71001092) and National Basic Research Program of China (2011CB711000) and the foundation of National Key Laboratory of Human Factors Engineering (HF2011Z-ZB-04).

References

1. Zhou, Q.X.: The Research of Human Failure and Its Preventive Measures in Manned Spaceflight. Astronaut Center of China 7(3), 18–38 (2001)
2. Xing, J., Manning, C.: Complexity and Automation Displays of Air Traffic Control: Literature Review and Analysis. Federal Aviation Administration, Washington, DC, Report No: DOT/FAA/AM05-4 (2005)
3. Xing, J.: Information Complexity in Air Traffic Control Displays, Beijing, China, July 22-27, pp. 797–806 (2007)
4. Zhang, Y.J.: Spaceflight operation training method based on complexity evaluation (Internal report). Astronaut Center of China (2008)
5. Zhang, Y.J.: Complexity evaluation method and operation performance of spaceflight operation (Doctoral dissertation). The department of industrial engineering at Tsinghua University (2009)
6. Zhang, Y.J., Wu, B., Li, Z.Z., et al.: Operation complexity measure of emergency failure operation procedure in spaceflight. Journal of Astronautics 30(2), 384–390 (2009)
7. Zhou, Q.X., Long, S.Z.: Analysis of Human Operation Antilapse Design In Manned Vehicle. Astronaut Center of China 6, 28–32 (1997)

8. Rasmussen, J.: The definition of human error and a taxonomy for technical systems design. In: Rasmussen, J., Duncan, K., Leplat, J. (eds.) New Technology and Human Error, pp. 23–30. Wiley, London (1987)
9. Fuller, R.: Towards a general theory of driver behaviour. Accid. Anal. Prev. 37, 461–472 (2005)
10. Allahyari, T., Saraji, G.N., Adl, J.: TeimourAllahyari, GebraeilNaslSaraji, JavadAdl. Cognitive Failures, Driving Errors and Driving Accidents. In: Proceeding of International Journal of Occupational Safety and Ergonomics (JOSE), vol. 14(2), pp. 149–158 (2008)
11. Park, J., Jung, W., Ha, J.: Development of the step complexity measure for emergency operating procedures using entropy concepts. Reliability Engineering and System Safety 71(2), 115–130 (2001)
12. Park, J., Jung, W., Ha, J., et al.: The Step Complexity Measure for Emergency Operating Procedures: Measure Verification. Reliability Engineering and System Safety 76, 45–59 (2002)

Predicating the Safety of Airport Approaches Using a Cognitive Pilot Model

Changpeng Yang, Tangwen Yin, and Shan Fu

School of Aeronautics and Astronautics, Shanghai Jiao Tong University, Shanghai, China
sunny280808@sjtu.edu.cn

Abstract. This paper introduces a new cognitive flight operator model (CFOM) that has been developed for predicting the safety of airport approaches. The creation of the CFOM is based on the frequency and percentage of accident associated with Human Factors Analysis and Classification System (HFACS) causal categories by types of operation. Operator capacity limitation, decision heuristics and action error mechanisms are incorporated into the architecture of CFOM to produce the behavior errors. This cognitive model integrated with an environment model consisting of a model of airplane, aircraft dynamics, and flight environment forms Man-Machine-Environment Safety Analysis System (MME-SAS) that canbe used to investigate the cause of human errors and aircraft accident.

Keywords: Human Performance Modeling, Decision Heuristic, Rule Chunk Model.

1   Introduction

Within complex aviation systems around 60% to 80% of accidents and safety compromising incidents are attributable, at least in part, to human error [1-2]. Developing an analysis method or models capable of representing the many multiple potential factors and those factors interacting within the complex and dynamics environment is an effective way to investigate and predict the cause of the accident.

There are many different methods to understand the cause of the pilot errors and accident. The traditional method is accident investigation procedure including the experts review the accident chain that is time consuming and the result is often affected by the background of the expert. Another alternative to predict pilot error is Human Error Identification (HEI) approach [3], the use of this structured method to predict the errors that are likely to be made by operators during task performance. The flaw of this method is that the participants with no experience of HEI method or piloting in general is a significant limitation and is prone to blind spots. Controlled human in the loop (HITL) experimentation provides excellent means for collecting relatively real data, while the HITL simulation are significantly limited in their ability to reproduce a large number scenarios and high cost of HITL simulation.

To remedy the limitation of the methods discussed previously, computational cognitive models of human behavior is developed that can be used to predict the pilot

V.G. Duffy (Ed.): DHM/HCII 2013, Part I, LNCS 8025, pp. 126–133, 2013.
© Springer-Verlag Berlin Heidelberg 2013

error and safety analysis [4]. The computational cognitive models should allow us examine the underlying cause of errors (e.g., system design, operating procedure and pilot capability), providing a tool to investigate error chain and assist redesign the procedure or system to mitigate errors. Several computational cognitive models have been developed to model the pilot error in commercial aviation region [4-5]. However, few models are able to simulate the pilot errors in the approach scenario.

The pilot cognitive model presented in this paper is a combination of a skill- and rule- based model. The skill-based model provides unconscious action such path tracking and stabilization. The part of rule-based model concerns the procedural behavior of the pilot. Both parts integrated together with environment model such as aircraft kinematics and dynamic constraints, aircraft configuration forms a complex dynamic Man-Machine-Environment Safety Analysis System (MME-SAS) to evaluate and predict the pilot error to analysis the safety of the system design and procedure.

2   Basic Principles of Method to Model the Pilot for an ILS Approach

This section describes the basic principles of method to model the pilot for an Instrument Landing System (ILS) Approach; Namely, the assumptions and choices that have been incorporated in this research, and what is not adopted as the scope of this research.

2.1   Flight Task

The selected task occurs in the most important part of every flight: the approach. The approach phase typically consists three segments, including initial approach, intermediate approach and final approach, in which the flight crew performs different actions according to the Standard Operating Procedures (SOPs). As the intermediate and final approaches represent the most complicated and error prone phases during approach, the research only takes into account the phase shown in Fig. 1.

Instrument landing system (ILS) is highly accurate facility by which the airplane is navigated to the runway. ILS consists of three of transmitters –the localizer, the glide slope, and marker beacons [6]. The localizer provides lateral guidance and glide slope provides vertical guidance, and the distance measurement relative to the runway is given by Marker beacons. A precision approach is an approach descent procedure in which navigation equipment aligned with a runway where the glide slope information is given. The crew can execute a precision approach when all ILS systems are available and a clearance is announced by the ATC. In [6], a standard approach ILS procedure is illustrated. The following three parts are used:

- If the heading of the aircraft is aligned with the runway heading, the pilot changes the aircraft configuration, such as deploying the flap according speed limit, using the speed brake to decelerate the aircraft. When the glide slope is intercepted, the crew extends the gear. While in the approach, the flight path angel is nearly $3°$.

- The main activity of the pilot is maintaining the configured aircraft on the glide slope and the localizer with desired speed. While slight undershooting of desired speed is acceptable. In the final approach, the crew monitors the systems, the attitude and flight path of aircraft, and control the aircraft by the difference between the state of aircraft and expectation.
- At the end of approach, landing maneuver is performed. The pilot initializes the flare on a prescribed altitude, controls the thrust lever in the idle position and makes a pitch up command until the main gear touch down the runway.

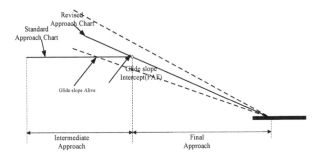

Fig. 1. Revised Approach Chart

As the aim of this work is to develop a cognitive pilot model for ILS approach which is a high precision task. To simplify the modeling, a revised approach chart (see Fig.1) is used in computer simulation. In this chart, only motion in vertical plane was considered, which means the initial heading of aircraft is align with the heading of runway, and there is no crosswind to affect the lateral motion of aircraft. Based on this assumption, the pilot need not control the aileron and rudder surface.

The flare is simulated in HITL simulation while not modeled in the computer simulation because of the optical perception is an important information source during flare, the research only focuses the first two parts of approach.

2.2   Factors Influencing the Safety of Approach

There are so many factors that influence the safety of the approach, the direct factors including meteorological conditions, aircraft, pilot and procedures etc [7]. It is impossible to investigate all the factors which may lead to a pilot error and aviation accidents. In [8], the majority of accident causal factors are classified using the human factors analysis and classification system (HFACS) that is a theoretically based tool used for investigating and analyzing human error associated with accidents and incidents. The unsafe acts of crew are mainly due to aircrew and their environment. For the environment conditions, the casual factors typically associated with aspects of physically environment such as weather and lighting, as for aviation crew, the majority of aviation accidents causal factors are found at unsafe act level, over half of accidents are related to at least one skill-based error and over a third with decision error.

As so many endeavors has been invested to explore the environment constrains using human sensory, biomechanical and control-theoretic pilot model, it is imperative to investigate the aspects of pilot which induces to errors and failure of pilot vehicle system. With respect to the pilot performance modeling, it is tremendous complexity to include all aspects of pilot whereas the pilot performs perception, decision and motor control, often in very tight sequence [9]. In this research, a hypothesis is made that the critical aspects of pilot which affects the safety of aviation will only be modeled, that is capacity limitation, decision and action strategy.

2.3   Framework of Pilot Model

The approach to integrated pilot modeling in this research centers on the development of pilot model in the framework of a cognitive architecture. The cognitive architecture is a general framework to specify the computational behavioral models of human cognitive performance [10]. This architecture can be used to simulate abilities of pilot constrains such as memory decay, limited motor action and foveal versus peripheral visual encoding; and abilities such as learning, decision, perception and motor performance. As such, by abiding all the limitation of pilot model, the cognitive architecture makes the pilot model developed in this framework valid. The pilot model developed in this research is based on this framework. Detail information about the pilot architecture in illustrated in following part

3   Architecture of MME-SAS

The MME-SAS model is framework of models that can be used to evaluate and predict the pilot performance. Pilot cognitive model integrated with environment model (flight dynamic model, automation, weather condition) form a closed loop in which the output of one part servers as the input to another part. The architecture of MME-SAS is illustrated in Figure.2.

3.1   Overview of MME-SAS

The CFOM is a framework of model that predicts human performance. Current aircraft status information indicated on Primary Flight Display (PFD), Navigation Display (ND), and Engine Indication and Crew Alerting System (EICAS) are perceived to determine whether decision must be made. The perceived incoming information through situation awareness process including filtering, comprehension, retrieval and grouping, and ultimately forming situation assessment on the incoming information, this research assumes that incoming information is not distorted and filtered and the situation awareness is sufficient to detect the abnormal event. Following the information pre-processing process, decisions are made based on the result of situation awareness. The output of decision is a stream of actions at "know-how" level, these actions server as the input to environment in which the operators act. The environment dynamically responds to the CFOM's output and feedbacks the system state.

Cognitive activities are influenced by abilities and constraints of operator.

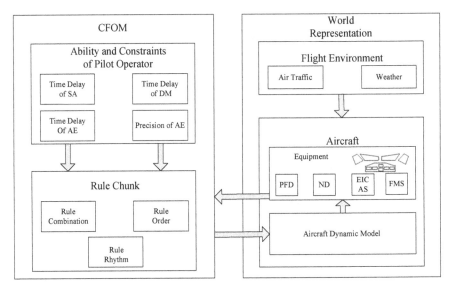

Fig. 2. Architecture of MME-SAS

3.2   Ability and Constraints of Human System

In aircraft system, operator capabilities have great effects on the handling qualities of aircraft. The abilities and constraints of CFOM are expressed by time delay of cognitive activities and control precision. Time delay of operator is divided into time delay for situation awareness, decision making and action execution. Different probability distribution is used to represent the difference and randomness of cognitive characteristic and. For example, the different situation awareness time specifies the time that the operator needs to accomplish the assessment of system state. Sufficient situation awareness needs enough time that may have effect on the safety of system. Control precision reflects the skill proficiency of different operator, meanwhile, the distribution of control strategies provide the error mechanism for slips. Novice and veteran operator can be specified by different control precision.

3.3   Rule Chunk Model

Reason [2] distinguished three categories on human behavior: skill-based, rule-based and knowledge-based. Skill-based behavior assigns stimuli-response in an automatic mode that are routinely practiced (e.g., when the aircraft pitch angle is small than desired angel, the pilot will pull the side lever). Rule based behaviors determine the responses for situations that have been encountered before, such as through training in simulation or experience, are combination of conscious and unconscious process (e.g., routine landing checklist and takeoffs). Lastly, the knowledge-based behavior requires inference to determine a response when other methods have been proven unsuccessful, often the broader and profound of the pilot's knowledge, the more likely a good solution the pilot will make.

The behavior of the pilot model developed in this research is rule-based and skill-based. Namely, the rule-based behavior can model the strategies such as rules, choices and procedures employed by the crew; the skill-based level represents visual scan pattern, situation awareness, and motor action of pilot.

In the CFOM decision phase, using If [certain set of conditions meets] Then [perform one or more action] pairs reflect the experience and knowledge of pilot. Each rule is essentially a condition-action rule that generates specified actions when the condition is satisfied.

The rule-based model includes a rule chunks, using If [certain set of conditions meets] Then [perform one or more action] pairs reflect the experience and knowledge of pilot. Decision strategies specified by rules are different with individual pilot from different countries and airline. It is reasonable to comprise all the possible rules that pilot will used in dynamics environment. However, it is difficult to get the pilot control rule. In this research, several basic pilot skill rules concluding from Flight Crew Training Manual (FCTM) arranged with different order, rhythm and frequency (equation 1, 2, 3) to generate a rule chunk that reveals the different tactics.

$$R_1 R_2 \cdots R_i \cdots R_j \cdots R_{m-1} R_m \xrightarrow{order} R_1 R_2 \cdots R_j \cdots R_i \cdots R_{m-1} R_m \tag{1}$$

$$R_1 R_2 \cdots R_i \cdots R_j \cdots R_{m-1} R_m \xrightarrow{rhythm} R_1 R_2 \cdots R_i \cdots R_j \cdots R_i \cdots R_j \cdots R_{m-1} R_m \tag{2}$$

$$R_1 R_2 \cdots R_i \cdots R_j \cdots R_{m-1} R_m \xrightarrow{order} R_1 R_2 \cdots R_i R_i \cdots R_j R_j \cdots R_{m-1} R_m \tag{3}$$

During action execution phase, operator will output a control on throttle, flap lever, throttle lever, speed brake lever, landing gear lever or other control equipment if any decisions are made to change the aircraft status. Denoting $\delta_e, \delta_t, \delta_s, \delta_l, \delta_f$ as elevator deflection, throttle position, speed brake position, landing gear status and flap deflection. T_{SA}, T_{MD}, T_{AC} denote situation awareness, decision making and control time delay respectively. Note that control precision provides the pilot control error that exists on all action or motor control. The output of control can be expressed as below:

$$\delta_a = \left[\delta_{a0} + P_{\delta_e} \right] \tag{4}$$

δ_a and δ_{a0} are aft-control and pre-control value, P_{δ_e} is control increments.[] is an operator for saturation constraint of controls.

3.4   Representation of External Environment

The external environment is the environment in which the flight crew, in aviation domain, the external environment represents the aircraft's handling quality, performance characteristics, flight deck displays and instrumentation, and the atmosphere and air traffic. The fidelity of external environment mostly is a difficult decision point, a high-fidelity environment can closely represent the response of pilot action and provide the pilot more accurate and real flight information. On the other hand, a high-fidelity of external environment can be time consuming and expensive. In this research, a simple aircraft kinematic equation is constructed to simulate the continuous aircraft status by referring[11], the simplification incorporates the most significant impact on action/response feedback mechanism.

4   Results of Computer of Simulation

MME-SAS is simulated based on the basic principles and assumptions, as explained in the previous section. The mission in the simulation can be view as the management of aircraft's attitude to maintain desired height and speed during approach and landing phase. The mission begins with an initial point where the aircraft status is balanced and ends with touchdown point on the runway, pilot try to keep the path angle with glide slope equal to -1:29.

In order to simplify the approach process, the simulated virtual pilot should conform to a revised approach chart that prescribes the pilot action. Although the MME-SAS should work for any aircraft type, however, a Boeing 747 aircraft is used in the simulation. The aircraft model is modeled based B747-100 documentation [12], so the SOPs that are modeled in computer simulation are based on the SOPs that are for B747.

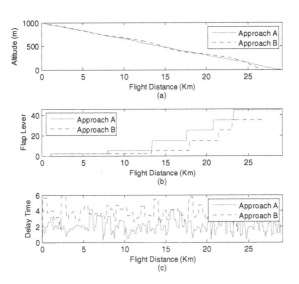

Fig. 3. Results of two different approaches

Two different approaches are simulated to reveal the linkage between operator capabilities with the flight safety. The results are illustrated in Fig.3.Obviously the touchdown points in approach A and approach B are (289221m, 0, 0) and (268517m, 0, 0) respectively, we can conclude that the approach A is more successful than approach B with respect to flight trajectory. Fig.3(b) shows that for approach B, the flaps is not fully deployed that only 30°is used by the pilot. The reason for this is showed by Fig.3(c) that the pilot time for B is larger than for A, meaning that the time delay affect the pilot performance greatly. It can be concluded that the time delay of approach B showed in Fig.3(c) cannot be used to design the aircraft automation system.

5   Conclusion

In this paper, a computational model of pilot behavior combined with aircraft and flight environment model is built in this paper forms a MME-SAS that links the human factors and handing quality of aircraft with the performance of flight. Computer simulation results show that MME-SAS can be used to investigate the cause of pilot error and accident.

Acknowledge. This work is supported by National Basic Research Program (973 Program) of China under Grant No.2010CB734103.

References

1. Shappell, S., Wiegmann, D.: U.S. naval aviation mishaps 1977-92: Differences between single- and dual-piloted aircraft. Aviation, Space, and Environmental Medicine 67, 65–69 (2006)
2. Reason, J.: Human error. Cambridge University Press, New York (1990)
3. Shorrock, S.T., Kirwan, B.: Development and application of a human error identification tool for air traffic control. Applied Ergonomics 33, 319–336 (2002)
4. Gray, W.D.: Integrated models of cognitive systems. Oxford University Press, New York (2007)
5. Mark, R., Anderson, C.C., Greg, D.: Flight test maneuver design using a skill- and rule-based pilot model. In: IEEE International Conference on Intelligent Systems, pp. 2682–2687 (1995)
6. Nolan, M.: Fundamentals of Air Traffic Control. Wadsworth Publishing Company, Belmont (1994)
7. Monique, H., Theo, V.H., Max, M.: Flight Mechanical Evaluation of Approaches. Journal of Aircraft 48(3) (May-June 2011)
8. Scott, S., Cristy, D., Kali, H., Carla, H., Albert, B., Douglas, A.W.: Human error and commercial aviation accidents: Analysis using the human factors analysis and classification system. The Journal of the Human Factors and Ergonomics Society, 49–227 (2007)
9. Byrne, M.D., Pew, R.W.: A History and Primer of Human Performance Modeling. Reviews of Human Factors and Ergonomics 5, 225 (2009)
10. Meyer, D.E., Kieras, D.E.: A computational theory of executive cognitive processes and multiple-task performance: Part1. Basic mechanisms. Basic mechanisms. Psychological Review 104, 3–65 (1997)
11. Zipfel, P.H.: Modeling and Simulation of Aerospace Vehicle Dynamics. American Institute of Aeronautics and Astronautics, Inc., Reston (2000)
12. Hanke, R.C., Nordwall, D.R.: The Simulation of a Jambo Jet Transport Aircraft. Modeling Data, vol. II, NASA Rept. D6-30643, 1–647 (September 1970)

Pilot Performance Models

Xiaoyan Zhang and Hongjun Xue

School of Aeronautics, Northwestern Polytechnical University, Shanxi Xi'an 710072,
P.R. China
zxyliuyan@sina.com, xuehj@nwpu.edu.cn

Abstract. Pilot as the controller of the aircraft whose performance is key for aviation safety. This paper investigated three main pilot models at present. The models all can solve the problems they are expected to well, but there is no model that has integrated architecture for pilot information processed. According to the characters of pilot executing tasks, the paper built the architecture of "pilot in the loop" model. The model is dynamic and has the ability to simulate the interaction of human-machine, and can also reflect the micro mechanism and macro behavior of pilots. The difficulties of modeling have been analyzed and the methods to solve the problems have also been put forward.

Keywords: pilot modeling, human in the loop, cognitive model, control model, Fitts' law.

1   Introduction

More than two-thirds of all aircraft accidents are attributed to pilot error. Identifying when equipment and procedures do not fully support the operational needs of pilots is critical to reducing error and improving flight safety [1, 2]. And the capabilities, limitations of pilot will be basis of the new flight deck design. But the latent design flaws cannot be discovered in nominal scenarios but in off-nominal scenarios which can induce serious pilot error and flight accidents. The off-nominal scenarios are not so easy to be designed and executed in experiment research and the flight accidents in off-nominal scenarios are always rare. There is not enough data to investigate for the pilot performance research. The researchers have been built many pilot models such as optimal control model, ACT-R, Air-MIDAS and so on to investigate pilot performance both in nominal and off-nominal scenarios [2, 3]. There are pilot control models for flight quality, and cognitive models for the display system design and evaluation and error prediction, and also anthropometry pilot models for flight deck layout design and evaluation. The current models can evaluate design, predict pilot error and discover the latent design flaws, but they are not perfect because of not covering the whole process of flight task by pilot, and they can only find partial key latent design "flaws", or evaluate parts of cockpit design or the model is rough and cannot simulate pilot performance correctly. The model writers' team had built is based on the current model, but aimed at the real and whole pilot flight task process both in nominal and off-nominal scenario such as atrocious weather condition.

V.G. Duffy (Ed.): DHM/HCII 2013, Part I, LNCS 8025, pp. 134–140, 2013.
© Springer-Verlag Berlin Heidelberg 2013

2   Extensive Understanding of Pilot Behavior

Effective pilot models require extensive understanding of the task and the domain environment and the pilot behavior in order to produce valid and meaningful results. Flight task is complicated. The task will be accomplished successfully both by ATC (Airplane Traffic Controller) and pilots. The pilot is the one who receives information and also the one who makes decision and performs. The job is high art needed, which requires the performers to react to the variable environments sensitively and properly. The unique performance of flight task induces special cognitive and operational performance of pilot.

The processes of pilot to execute a typical flight task can be divided into cognitive process and motor process. The cognitive process begins at stimulus produced by the cockpit, and ends up with the decision made. Before he can manipulate an airplane the pilot is expected to learn lots of declarative knowledge, and also should have the capability to transform declarative knowledge to procedure knowledge as quickly and precisely as he can. During the task there is huge information such as flight path, airplane state, and also the environment out the window and so on for him to choose and he is expected to make decisions from the cognitive quickly and effectively. This is cognitive process. The motor process begins right after cognitive process, and ends up with an action over. When the decision is checked out, pilot is expected to do actions effectively following the instruction. During the whole task, pilot is expected to follow the pilot operation procedure strictly, and there is no chance for pilot to make mistake even a tiny one.

From the process we can learn that pilot works under high workload and pressure, the cognitive process is pivotal for the success of whole task, but its success cannot assure the ultimate success. The current model can simulate the cognitive process well or see the human as a function. None of the present model can simulate the whole process well. But for the pilot modeling, every specific character should be simulated correctly.

3   Overview of Typical Pilot Models

The human pilot behavior during flight tasks is a fundamental component of the overall aircraft control loop. From an initial review of past efforts in pilot behavior modeling, they can be classified as two different kind pilot performance models, which are pilot control models and cognitive models. Each kind model will be described in model development, and significant findings for the aviation community.

3.1   Control Model [4, 5, 6]

Over the years, there has been a large amount of research in the input-output representation of manual control, with significant contributions especially for modeling linear and pseudo-linear tracking tasks. The model based on control theory has been passed through three phases from Transfer-function model, optimal control model to fuzzy control model. A variety of techniques were used based on frequency domain methods, as well as algorithmic time domain methods.

The control model is focused on flight quality concerned with pilot performance, such as PIO (Pilot-Induced- oscillations). The pilot is considered as controller of the plane and the pilot is just a part of transfer function. The model is effective to evaluate flight quality and the affection of pilot for the flight, but from the model we cannot analysis the detail behaviors of pilot and the specific influence can also not be acquired.

Control model is always built based on control theory. And the general model is expressed as transfer function G(s).

The control model is maturity enough for users to predict system performance and initial optimization. But the essential limitation is that the model cannot consider the pilot performance precisely which is always considered as a part of transfer function and the particular performance of pilot in nominal or off-nominal cannot be concluded. The limitation leads to the simulation results not so accurate and reduces the results reliability.

3.2   Cognitive Model

Cognitive model focuses on how human reacts on the stimulus, especially on the process of thinking and then how to decide. The theory of cognitive model is information processing which generally divides the cognitive process into three parts which is perception, thinking and decision and response [7]. Thinking and decision is the hot point and also the most important for all research. There are also various models especially for this process. And attention acts on the whole process.

The cognitive models were mainly developed by NASA in 2001[1, 8] and also the beginning of the model for engineering. The primary goal of the project was to develop and extend human modeling capabilities while gaining knowledge regarding aviation operations and supporting emerging capabilities and technologies that increase aviation safety. The two aviation domain problems addressed by the models are: Airport surface (taxi) operations and Synthetic vision system (SVS) operations. There are five models:

1. Adaptive Control of Thought-Rational (ACT-R);
2. Improved Performance Research Integration Tool/ACT-R hybrid (IMPRINT/ACT-R);
3. Air Man–machine Integration Design and Analysis System (Air MIDAS);
4. Distributed Operator Model Architecture (D-OMAR); and
5. Attention-Situation Awareness (A-SA).

The usefulness of five cognitive models to the design and evaluation of new technology is determined to a significant extent by the core capabilities – visual attention allocation, workload, crew interactions, procedures, situation awareness, and error prediction. There are two significant functions which are error prediction and mitigation and display design and information allocation. But the model framework had not covered the whole process, which induced that the model could not predict pilot error except cognitive error and evaluate manipulate and control system.

However, the five cognitive models indicate that the art of human performance models has advanced to a level of maturity. They are now considered important tools in the aircraft design, analysis and evaluation.

3.3   Anthropometry Pilot Models

Anthropometry models conclude kinetics model, kinematics model and biodynamic model and so on. For the engineering use, a perfect anthropometry model always considers the kinetics, kinematics and some biodynamic of manikin.

The current anthropometry model is very well-developed and there are various softwares containing these models for system design and evaluation, especially for ergonomics design and evaluation. CATIA/DELMIA, JACK, RAMSIS all are the typical manikin models and widely used in aviation. And the Chinese pilot anthropometry data can be imported into the software to build the Chinese pilot manikin model. The anthropometry data of Chinese pilot comes from GJB 4856-2003 (Human dimensions of Chinese male pilot population).

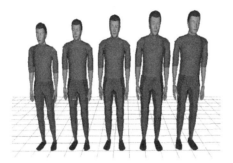

Fig. 1. Chinese pilot model in JACK

The anthropetry model of pilot has been widely used in aircraft design, analysis and evaluation. But the instruction is limited in the system layout or the operation analysis. What the objects think and what they would do if the scene changed is not considered in the anthropometry models and so is the dynamic simulation and evaluation.

Fig. 2. Chinese pilot model in CATIA

3.4   Fitts' Law

The operation of buttons on panel in the cockpit is defined as "target-pointing" operation, and Fitts' law deprived from information theory is most used to investigate accuracy and time of the operation [10]. There are various formats of Fitts' law. Many people have done some amazing job to perfect the law since 1954. The work concludes different movement types, different operators, and different equipments and so on.

The initial format of Fitts' law [11] is:

$$MT = a + b \cdot ID \tag{1}$$

Where a, b is the experienced parameter of the particular task, and ID is index of difficulty and is the function of the target width (W in the following expression), and distance from the initial position (A in the following expression).

$$ID = \log_2(\frac{2A}{W}) \tag{2}$$

The most widely used expression is as follows:

$$T = a + b \log_2(A/W + 1) \tag{3}$$

Although Fitts' law is widely used for the interface design and evaluation, it just considers the last part of the whole operation task, and the whole process of thinking is just omitted. Maybe we can also say the whole process of thinking is represented by a macro parameter ID (index of difficulty). This is not so strict for research.

4   Integrated Pilot Performance Model

The pilot model has already be used in design and evaluation, but from an initial review of past efforts in modeling, it was recognized that no single modeling architecture or framework had the scope to address the full range of interacting and competing factors driving pilot actions in dynamic, complex environments [1]. The research team has built an integrated pilot performance model which can compensate the architecture flaws of other models and expand multiple modeling efforts. The architecture of the model is shown in figure 3.

There are three main parts: simulation environment, pilot model and ground guide. Simulation environment includes world environment, airplane itself and the flight dynamics model to support flight; Pilot performance model is based on the process pilot executes flight task which roughly divided into four parts, and during every process the attention will join in and affect the actions, while ground guide part receives information from the environment and then guides pilot.

All the three parts constitute the whole flight process, and pilot is the centre obviously. The pilot performance model is built based on the process pilot executes tasks. For the model, we consider the motor module has equal importance to the perception module which is different from the previous models. The two aspects of previous models are apt to imbalance. Motor is only a factor for the whole model, and most of them had just used one-dimension Fitts' Law to simulate the human operation. The inadequate consideration of motor induces the model is not as accurate as it was. The model based on the task process takes "operation" as important as it is. The builders have been extending Fitts' Law to three-dimension to simulate human real operation and predict operation error both in nominal and off -nominal scenarios. Not just for the motor performance and the other performances of pilot would be investigated in the new-built model. To enable model development, information would be collected from task analyses and objective data and subjective ratings in the closed loop both in nominal and off -nominal scenarios.

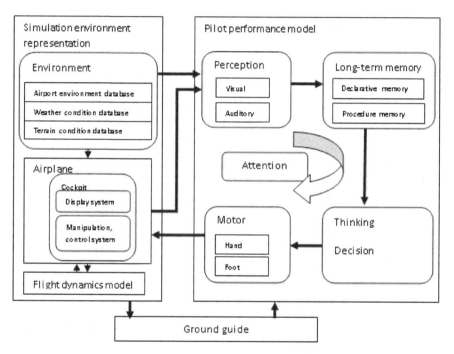

Fig. 3. Architecture of integrated pilot performance model

5   Conclusion and Discussion

Each pilot model has its own advantages and disadvantages. But each model has extended its capabilities significantly to answer important aviation domain questions and has shown considerable efforts for the human performance model development. As mentioned before, however, the integrated pilot performance model can simulate pilots more roundly and accurately. There are two major improvements of the new model. First the model can be used to simulate pilot operation easily and precisely. The model built based on the whole task and the operation part is put the same as the cognition. The three-dimension Fitts' Law would be used to model pilot operation results, and the design "flaws" induced by operate equipment would be found. And the error probability model would be used to predict human errors, especially the error induced by operation. After all, since we consider operation as a big part of the model, the problems about operation would be solved accordingly. For example, by the model we have the ability to check if the procedure is reasonable.

However, we still have huge work to do to perfect the model. The motor module is not only a three-dimension Fitts' Law model, the module should be effective in both nominal and off-nominal scenarios and also have the ability to predict errors caused by operations. And the off-nominal scenarios are not so easy to be designed and executed in experiment research and the flight accidents in off-nominal scenarios are always rare. There is not enough data to investigate for the pilot performance research. How to get the data to support the model is also a big problem.

Another problem is how to validate model. The appropriate validate method is pivotal.

Acknowledgement. The paper is granted under National Basic Research Program of China (No.2010CB734101).

References

1. Leiden, K., Keller, J.W., French, J.W.: Context of Human Error in Commercial Aviation (Techniacal Report). Micro Analysis and Design, Inc., Boulder (2001)
2. Gluck, K.A., Pew, R.W. (eds.): Modeling human behavior with integrated cognitive architectures. Lawrence Erlbaum Associates, Mahwah (2005)
3. Foyle, D.C., Hooey, B.L., Byrne, M.D., Corker, K.M., Deutsch, S., Lebiere, C., Leiden, K., Wickens, C.D.: HUMAN performance models of pilot behaviors. In: Proceedings of the Human Factors and Ergonomics Society 49th Annual Meeting, pp. 1109–1113. HFES, Santa Monica (2005)
4. Liu, X., Li, R.: A surey on study of human operation model. Journal of System Simulation 11(4) (1999) (in Chinese)
5. 刘兴堂，李润玲. 人控制模型研究综述. 系统仿真学报 11(4) (1999)
6. Yu, L., Wang, Z., Qiu, L.: The study on pilot /flight control system and pilot model. Electronics Optics & Control (1) (2001) (in Chinese)
7. 于黎明，王占林，裘丽华. 人机控制与驾驶员模型研究. 电光与控制 (1) (2001)
8. Long, S.Z., Chen, H.: Research on Human Fuzzy Control Model in Man-Machine-Environment Systems. In: The 33rd International Congress of Aviation and Space Medicine, pp. 138–141 (1985)
9. Anderson, J.R.: The architecture of cognition. Harvard University Press, Cambridge (1983)
10. Foyle, D.C., Hooey, B.L.: Human performance modeling in aviation. CRC Press (2007)
11. Schmiedl, C.: An overview and evaluation of modern human interface devices. Proseminararbeit Technische Informatik, 1–13 (2010)
12. Langolf, G.D.: An Investigation of Fitts' Law Using a Wide Range of Movement Amplitudes. Journal of Motor Behavior 8, 113–128 (1976)

Part II

Human Factors and Digital Human Modeling in Healthcare

Supporting Conversation for People with Dementia by Introducing a Computer-Based Third Element to the Interaction

Norman Alm[1], Arlene Astell[2], Gary Gowans[3], Maggie Ellis[2],
Phillip Vaughan[3], and Richard Dye[1]

[1] School of Computing, Dundee University, Scotland, UK
{nalm,rdye}@computing.dundee.ac.uk
[2] School of Psychology, University of St Andrews, Scotland, UK
{aja3,mpe2}@st-andrews.ac.uk
[3] Duncan of Jordanstone College of Art and Design, Dundee University, Scotland, UK
{g.m.gowans,p.b.vaughan}@dundee.ac.uk

Abstract. The principle of introducing a third element to a stressful communicational encounter, to which both participants can direct their attention, and which can provide prompts for communication, has a wide potential applicability. We have developed a system to support the communication of older people with dementia, which uses this principle. The approach has uses in many settings in which there is a cognitive or emotional blockage to communicational flow, several of which are described.

Keywords: assistive technology, cognitive prostheses, dementia, autism, cognitive impairment.

1   Computer-Based support for dementia

Dementia is the loss of cognitive abilities, particularly the use of working (short-term) memory, usually as a result of Alzheimer's disease or stroke. Dementia occurs primarily in older people, and while it does not affect all of them, its rate of occurrence rises steeply from about 1 in 10 over 60 to 1 in 2 of those over 90 [1,2]. As our population balance shifts towards the older end of the spectrum, the incidence of dementia will increase dramatically. Because of the high level of human effort currently required in caring for people with dementia, designing assistive technology will be a growing priority until a way of reversing this debilitating condition can be found.

Among the skills which dementia degrades is the ability to communicate. Finding ways to promote communication in people with dementia is vitally important. Communication is such a fundamental part of being human that when people are no longer able to interact successfully they are treated as somehow less than human. This dehumanization is, sadly, commonly seen in the treatment of people with dementia.

We have developed a computer-based communication support system which can assist older people with dementia to interact more successfully with relatives and

V.G. Duffy (Ed.): DHM/HCII 2013, Part I, LNCS 8025, pp. 143–149, 2013.

carers. The system, called CIRCA, consists of two parts. A conversation support system prompts the user's long term memories by means of touchscreen access to reminiscence material drawn from public archives [3]. Also included is a set of interactive games, playable via the touchscreen, which have been developed specifically to be useable and enjoyable for people with dementia [4].

The system was developed a multidisciplinary team of software engineers, psychologists, and designers. Potential users and their families and professional carers were involved throughout the design process. User-Centred Design was particularly important in this case because of the complexity of the problem being addressed [5].

2   Conversation Support through Reminiscence Materials

Without an operating working memory, interaction becomes very difficult. Long-term memory, however, can remain relatively well-preserved with dementia, so conversations based on reminiscence are possible, if long term memories can be prompted. Our system can stimulate long term memories by providing the person with dementia and a carer with a touchscreen based hypermedia presentation of material from the past : photos, music, video clips, graphics and text, all accessible in a flexible and engaging manner. Using this system allows people with dementia to once again have a conversation with relatives and carers.

In comparing this system with using traditional reminiscence aids, we found that the person with dementia was offered a choice of reminiscence materials more often when using our system. We also found that the person with dementia chose reminiscence materials more often when prompted when using the system. The traditional sessions were characteristically a series of one question from the carer followed by one response from the person with dementia. The sessions with the prototype system were more of a conversation, with each person contributing an equal amount, and control of the direction of the conversation being shared [6].

3   Interactive Games Playable by People with Dementia

The system also includes a set of interactive games and activities, accessible through the touchscreen display, which were specifically designed to engage and entertain people without the need for an intact working memory. A great deal of thought and experimentation went into identifying effective activities and prompting methods. The aim of the project was to design a touchscreen system which would engage the attention of a person with dementia for a significant period of time. At the start of the project there was little or no knowledge in the field about how a person with dementia would interact with a touchscreen system. We therefore adopted a rapid prototyping and testing method to derive the design requirements.

Our initial assumptions about the requirements were as follows:

1. Require little working memory to use
2. Activities to be familiar for the user

3. Should prompt the user using either animation, text or voice
4. Behave predictably
5. Be enjoyable
6. Require little or no skill

The activities all used 3D graphics to create a visual approximation of the actual activity. We tried to design these activities to suit a wide range of abilities. The 3D objects generated on the touchscreen behaved in a similar way to physical objects. To help keep users engaged the activities rewarded the users' interactions with animation and sound effects. The activities could be enjoyed as shared or as individual activities, depending on the level of severity of the dementia.

To give the system the most challenging evaluation, activities were tested by people with dementia using the touchscreen on their own with no-one else present in the room. A video camera was used to observe them from an adjacent room.

In the testing sessions, the activities which had a clear goal and required some level of skill proved to be most popular. From users' comments they seem to realise that there is a skill required and then got a sense of achievement when they mastered it. One surprising and welcome observation was that the performance of the users with dementia appeared to improve with use. This may have been because procedural memory - the memory of how to perform a task - was being used.

4   A Helpful Third Element in an Interaction

As a result of widespread demand from participants in the project for a version of the system which they could keep, a company was set up by the inventors to make the system available to care homes and day-care centres in the UK. A number of care homes and day care centres in the UK have now had the experience of CIRCA, in some cases for three years.

The reminiscence system and the set of interactive games in fact grew out of two separate research projects, with different aims for people with dementia: communication in the first project and entertainment in the second. Feedback from the users of the two systems show us that in addition to their individual functions, both the reminiscence support and the games can be seen as part of one system, which enables interaction where communication is problematic. The reminiscence system provides touchscreen access to material which both partners in the interaction can enjoy exploring and commenting on together. The games provide touchscreen access to activity which, as well as being used individually, can be used by two people taking part in together, communicating with each other throughout.

Both systems have been carefully designed to achieve separate effects. However, we have found that a session with the reminiscence material, as well as prompting conversation, involves mutual enjoyment of the material presented. On the other hand, a games session, as well as providing enjoyment, triggers a great deal of communication.

One feature which is in operation here is that a third element has been introduced into the face-to-face encounter that draws the attention of the interactants to itself and alters the interaction from a direct one to one which it mediates. This has proved helpful in assisting the interaction to be more relaxed and enjoyable.

There is a theoretical background for this effect. When two people interact face-to-face, a certain amount of psychological effort is required for both parties. This has been termed 'face-work' by Goffman [7]. In any interaction, the individual wishes to establish and then to maintain a positive impression of themselves. If they are inconsistent with how they project themselves to others, they risk being embarrassed or discredited. There is always a certain amount of work required to maintain this equilibrium. This effort naturally increases hugely with a problematical communication situation such as interacting when dementia is present.

The simple expedient of providing a focus of attention for the interactants external to themselves can be of great assistance in making the encounter more relaxing. In this new situation the task becomes, not the difficult one of managing the face-to-face interaction, but the relatively easier one of jointly attending to and reacting to something of interest. The mutual attention and reacting provide a more relaxing and enjoyable basis for interaction than a direct face-to-face encounter which must be negotiated. If what is being attended to is itself an active participant, such as a computer generated interactive display, so much the better: achieving engagement and a sense of conversational flow is significantly enhanced. Interacting with a person who has dementia is aided by making use of a scrapbook of photos, but it is considerably easier if the artefact you are using is itself interactive and inventively engaging.

What is lost with dementia and what can be partially regained here is a sense of conversational momentum. This has a connection with the work on the experience of 'flow' [8]. Research on this phenomenon has highlighted the fact that it is often possible to achieve a state of flow— a state of concentration or complete absorption with the activity at hand and the situation. It is a state in which people are so involved in an activity that nothing else seems to matter. They lose track of themselves and completely indentify with what is going on. The experience is associated with a very happy state of mind.

When a conversation or an interaction 'flows' it moves along without any apparent effort by the participants [9]. The opposite situation occurs when it constantly falls on participants to decide deliberately on what the next move in the conversation or interaction might be. In the case of a relative or carer interacting with someone who has dementia, this is more or less the case for every conversational or interactional move - an effortful and often tiring and stressful experience for them.

5   Other Applications of This Principle

This principle of introducing a third element to a problematic communicational encounter, to which both participants can direct their attention, which both can control, but which can also provide prompts for communication, has a wide potential applicability.

5.1   Communication Support for People with Autism

Work to help people with autism has shown that they often experience an 'emotional overload' when spoken to directly. An indirect approach, through for instance a mutual activity, can establish a bond that would be impossible to make by direct interaction [see, for example 10, 11]. The person with autism seems to be experiencing a magnified form of the effort which we all need to put into interacting with others [12].

The Picture Exchange Communication System (PECS) was developed to help children with autism communicate more effectively [13]. The user learns to exchange single pictures for items or activities they want. Eventually the communication can be expanded to include multiple pictures making up a 'sentence'. The system was designed as an application of operant conditioning, but is interesting to note that it also makes use of the 'third element' principle in that the user does not need to communicate verbally but can make use of a picture card handed to the other person. As noted, people with autism can be overwhelmed by the emotions involved in direct interaction with others. In addition to its other features, the PECS system seems to provide a way of making an interaction less direct and thus less threatening.

5.2   A Low-Technology Communication Framework

Another communication support system that has made use of this third element principle to make communication possible where it was difficult or impossible before is the Talking Mats system. Talking Mats is a low-technology communication framework to help people with communication difficulties to express their views and opinions more effectively [14, 15].

The system uses a mat, such as a doormat or carpet tile, to which symbols and pictures can be attached by hook and loop tape. Symbols representing emotions are placed along the top to form a visual rating scale. The emotions can be as simple as 'positive', 'neutral' and 'negative' or more detailed, depending on the user. A relevant topic is discussed and a symbol representing it is placed at the bottom of the mat. As the session progresses the user expresses their view by placing pictures representing various aspects of the topic on the mat, grouping them underneath the rating symbols.

Talking Mats have been used with a number of different sorts of people: people with dementia, with a learning disability, with autism and with communication difficulties due to physical impairment. Even if the person can communicate, the system can often still be helpful as a support for discussions to clarify and confirm, and often increases the person's confidence to put forward their point of view. It has been proved useful for example in working with children who are in care to help them express their views.

5.3   The Role of Activities in Dementia Care

In the field of dementia care there has been a growing realisation that providing engaging activities in care homes is not a matter of an added extra, but is an essential part of good care. Training programmes offer staff help in devising continuous activities that are suitable for residents who are focused on 'living in the moment' [16, 17]. Residential home regimes have been created which require having a number of activities going on at any one time, all the time, with varying levels of ability catered for [18,19].

It might be argued that to have this degree of activity in what is in fact someone's home is not appropriate. However, the key point here is that we are dealing with dementia, which makes the person's subjective experience of their home quite different from a person who is cognitively intact. The reason having the continuous presence of activities is vital should be clear from the analysis above: they provide a valuable 'third element' that allows participants to interact with others without any effort needing to be applied to managing the interaction explicitly.

A possible inhibitor to the widespread adoption of this approach is the staff time and effort involved. Residential and day care staff working with people who have dementia are often fully occupied with the basic daily tasks to ensure that the people in their care are safe and healthy. Here technology may be able to play a role, by providing support for staff in creating activities which people with dementia can successfully take part in and enjoy. As with the CIRCA system, such technology must require a minimal effort for staff to learn to use and employ successfully. Their design must incorporate the latest hardware and software advances to increase ease of use and engaging power. Their development should include input from people with dementia and their carers, even though this is difficult in practice, in order to ensure that any systems developed meet real needs.

6   Conclusion

The development of a communication support system for people with dementia has shown that there are a number of ways to provide a 'scaffolding' structure that assists a person with cognitive impairments to regain the ability to communicate. Observing the use of a set of interactive games which were later developed specifically for people with dementia showed the researchers that, for the person with dementia, sharing the experience of these games with a carer was also a form of communication support, and a great deal of communication and enjoyable interaction took place alongside the playing of the game. Looking at the two systems, it was clear that the procedure of introducing a third element into a problematic interaction could in itself sometimes be useful in turning the attention of the interactants away from the stressful job of managing a difficult encounter and directing them to the third element in the interaction, engaging both in a form of mediated interaction. Other examples of this phenomenon in operation have been given. The third element need not involve technology, as demonstrated by the examples of PEC symbols, Talking Mats, and activities based environments for people with dementia. However, where the third element provided is a computer based system there is the potential through careful design to significantly magnify and enhance this effect.

References

1. Jorm, A.F., Korten, A.E., Henderson, A.S.: The prevalence of dementia: a quantitative integration of the literature. Acta Psychiatrica Scandinavica 76, 465–479 (1987)
2. Wimo, A., WInblad, B., Aguero-Torres, H., von Strauss, E.: The magnitude of dementia occurrence in the world. Alzheimer Disease and Associated Disorders 17, 63–67 (2003)
3. Alm, N., Dye, R., Gowans, G., Campbell, J., Astell, A., Ellis, M.: A communication support system for older people with dementia. IEEE Computer 40(5), 35–41 (2007)
4. Alm, N., Astell, A., Gowans, G., Dye, R., Ellis, M., Vaughan, P., Newell, A.F.: An interactive entertainment system usable by elderly people with dementia. In: Stephanidis, C. (ed.) UAHCI 2007 (Part II). LNCS, vol. 4555, pp. 617–623. Springer, Heidelberg (2007)
5. Abras, C., Maloney-Krichmar, D., Preece, J.: User-Centered Design. In: Bainbridge, W. (ed.) Encyclopedia of Human-Computer Interaction. Sage Publications, Thousand Oaks (2004)
6. Astell, A., Ellis, M., Bernardi, L., Alm, N., Dye, R., Gowans, G., Campbell, J.: Using a touch screen computer to support relationships between people with dementia and caregivers. Interacting with Computers 22, 267–275 (2010)
7. Goffman, E.: Interaction Ritual: Essays on Face-to-Face Behavior. Anchor Books, New York (1967)
8. Csikszentmihalyi, M.: Flow: The Psychology of Optimal Experience. Harper and Row, New York (1990)
9. Tannen, D.: Conversational Style: Analyzing Talk Among Friends. Oxford University Press, Oxford (1984) (revised. ed. 2005)
10. Caldwell, P., Horwood, J.: From Isolation to Intimacy: Making Friends without Words. Jessica Kingsley, London (2007)
11. Caldwell, P.: Intensive interaction: getting in touch with a child with severe autism. In: Zeedyk, M.S. (ed.) Promoting Social Interaction for Individuals with Communicative Impairments: Making Contact. Jessica Kingsley, London (2008)
12. Bowman, S., Hinkley, L., Barnes, J., Lindsay, R.: Gaze aversion and the primacy of emotional dysfunction in autism. In: Gorayska, B., Mey, J. (eds.) Cognition and Technology, pp. 267–301. John Benjamins Publishing Company, Amsterdam (2004)
13. Charlop-Christy, M.H., Carpenter, M., Le, L., LeBlanc, L.A., Kellet, K.: Using the picture exchange communication system (PECS) with children with autism: assessment of PECS acquisition, speech, social-communicative behavior, and problem behavior. Journal of Applied Behavior Analysis 35(3), 213–231 (2002)
14. Murphy, J., Gray, C.M., Cox, S., van Achterberg, T., Wyke, S.: The effectiveness of the Talking Mats framework with people with dementia. Dementia: International Journal of Social Research and Practice 9(4), 454–472 (2010)
15. Murphy, J., Oliver, T.M.: The use of Talking Mats to support people with dementia and their carers to make decisions together. Health & Social Care in the Community Health and Social Care in the Community 21(2), 171–180 (2013)
16. Sheard, D.: Being: An Approach to Life and Dementia. Alzheimer's Society, London (2007)
17. Dementia Care Matters, http://www.dementiacarematters.com (last accessed January 22, 2013)
18. Zeisel, J.: I'm Still Here: A Breakthrough Approach to Understanding Someone Living with Alzheimer's. Little, Brown, New York (2009)
19. Hearthstone Care Homes, http://www.thehearth.org (last accessed January 22, 2013)

"Using Digital Interactive Television to Promote Healthcare and Wellness Inclusive Services"

André Baptista, Ágata Dourado Sequeira, Iolanda Veríssimo, Célia Quico, Mário Cardoso, and Manuel José Damásio

Centro de Investigação em Comunicação Aplicada, Cultura e Novas Tecnologias (CICANT) / Universidade Lusófona de Humanidades e Tecnologias (ULHT), Lisbon, Portugal
{andreprb,agata.sequeira,
verissimo.iolanda}@gmail.com,
{celia.quico,p4287,mjdamasio}@ulusofona.pt

Abstract. The potential of digital interactive television (iDTV) to promote original services, formats and contents that can be relevant to support personal health care and wellness of individuals, namely elderly people, has not been fully explored yet in the past. Therefore, in a context of rapid change of the technological resources, in which the distribution and presentation of content comes associated to new platforms (such as digital terrestrial TV and IPTV), it is important to identify the configurations that are being developed for interactive digital TV (iDTV) that may result in relevant outcomes within the field of healthcare and wellness, with the aim of offering complementarity to the existing services and contents made available today via the traditional means and media.

This article describes and discusses the preliminary results of the first part of the research project iDTV-HEALTH: Inclusive services to promote health and wellness via digital interactive television. These first results suggest that iDTV solutions may represent a real contribution to bring healthcare and wellness to the target population, namely as a supplement to health services provision.

Keywords: Healthcare, wellness, digital, television, ICTs.

1 Introduction

The social practice of television is changing in highly contingent ways [1] and this project occurs in the context of a profound transformation of this medium in function of the emergence of new technological platforms, such as digital terrestrial television (DTT) and IPTV, as well as new mobile communication technologies such as WimAX and Long Term Evolution (LTE). Therefore, and in the context of the adoption of new technologies for the production and distribution of TV content, the project intends to evaluate the satisfaction and potential generated by a iDTV service as a way to support personal health care and wellness and facilitate access to the view of information and contents, namely on what concerns its ability to increase levels of social capital amongst target group.

The information and communications technology (ICT) have had an important role in the progress of the health area, intervening in the procedures for the management of

V.G. Duffy (Ed.): DHM/HCII 2013, Part I, LNCS 8025, pp. 150–156, 2013.

health systems and facilities, closing the gap between these services and the health professionals. Furthermore, the ICT systems open new possibilities of autonomy, allowing, among other aspects, individuals to have access to scientific information about any disease, to monitor their health condition without having to travel repeatedly to a medical office and to safeguard their welfare in an informed manner and in accordance to their individual and social contexts.

According to data from the market studies company Marktest, in 2012, the largest consumers of TV in Portugal are, by age group, the individuals with more than 64 years, who watch TV daily 5h15m08s daily (44.2% more than the average of the population), followed by the group between 55 and 64 years, with 4h15m24s [2]. These figures, together with the fact that peoples' thoughts about health services are highly influenced by media news and information about health [3,4] indicate that TV, more specifically interactive TV (iDTV), can be an excellent platform of health content distribution among the Portuguese seniors, contributing decisively for the development of E-health services.

E-health, the delivery of health information and services via the Internet and related technologies [5], provides new opportunities for interventions aiming health issues, which enable message targeting and tailoring based on users preferences and needs due to the flexible nature of digital media. Using E-health services can also be more appealing to users than traditional information brochures because it is possible to use more audiovisual information [6] and consequently to improve learning due to a continuous interactivity [7].

One of the biggest issues that could limit efficiency of E-health interventions is Health literacy. Health literacy is the ability to read, understand and act correctly with the provided information related to Health. When patients have low levels of health literacy, their ability to perceive and act with the proper medical information available is poor, and they may even put his health at risk [8,9]. Low health literacy can be found and is more common on the elderly, ethnic minorities and those of lower socioeconomic status, which are consequently the most vulnerable groups to health disparities and chronic health conditions [8,9]. In order to a better understanding of the literacy levels of a given population for a more effective intervention, there are already several health literacy measures such as Rapid Estimate of Adult Literacy in Medicine (REALM) [10], Test of Functional Health Literacy in Adults (TOFHLA) and his short version (S-TOFHLA) [11] and Newest Vital Sign (NVS) [12].

It has been shown that E-health interventions designed specifically to meet the needs of low health literate audiences can both be educational and user friendly [13]. Such interventions have been evaluated favorably and considered effective in large surveys with participants of variable degrees of literacy – both low and high health literate users [14,15]. In this sense this project will focus on individuals over 55 years of age with low levels of technological literacy and health professionals.

Therefore, iDTV will fruitfully serve as a contact point between users and health and wellness services professionals, and using these new tools will allow us to extend health care from the typical hospital or clinic to the patient's home, and the diagnosis, treatment and rehabilitation effectiveness will be augmented with the use of a continuous patient record, enhancing their quality of life and keeping their autonomy at home, while preserving safety [16]. It is the capacity for preparing selected information and blending the concerns of both production and distribution platforms that makes iDTV a valid possibility for aiding health care services in the future.

For this first stage, the proposed research design combines quantitative and qualitative methods, namely:

- Semi-structured interviews with stakeholders, with the involvement of key-people in institutions such as the Portuguese health care system, as well as representative from medical doctors and nurses and, finally, users of the national health service;
- Cross-sectional inquiry to a representative sample of the Portuguese population/target group about health and the new information and communication technologies - internet, mobile phones and iDTV.

2   Overview of the Quantitative Survey

The quantitative survey was applied to 1,207 individuals aged 18 to 93 years (average age 45.63), of which 47.6% were male (n=574) and 52.4% were female (n=633). The data analysis from the quantitative survey indicates that out of the 1.207 participants, 99.6% answered that they have at least one TV set at home. The most common situation found was two TV sets per household, with this option being chosen by 40.3% of participants. Regarding TV consumption habits, 26.4% of the participants said that they watch TV for approximately 120 minutes per day. Then, the participants were asked to indicate, from a given list, which digital services considered more interesting and which they utilized.

Regarding to the most interesting services, TV Guide (63.1%) and High Definition Channels (62.3%) were the services that participants mentioned more. Relevant for this study is the percentage that the Health and Wellness service obtained, being the third most chosen digital TV service with 61.7%. For those over 55 years of age, who represent the target age group of this research project, the most interesting digital TV service was the Health and Wellness service, with 47.2% of the subjects considering this to be a service of their interest. Finally, about which digital TV services are currently more utilized, the TV Guide (34.2%) and the High Definition Channels (34%) were at the top for these respondents. On the other hand, the Audio-Description service is the less chosen with only 1,3% of participants in this survey claiming to use such digital TV service. The Health and Wellness services are mentioned by 4.2% of the respondents. The same happens in the age group above 55 years old.

As shown in previous results, the use of digital TV services is not yet a very common practice for the users. The two main reasons evoked by the participants on why this happens were because they "don't have access" (49.9%) and "because they don't need" (33.2%).

Next, the participants were questioned if they feel any type of difficulties when using digital TV services and 69.6% of the respondents claimed to have no difficulty, 14.1% said that they have little difficulty, 11.8% replied to have some difficulty, 3.1% declared that they have much difficulty, while 1.4% of the respondents stated they can't use it. People who argued to have some kind of difficulty were asked to indicate what were the main difficulties using a digital TV service were: about half (50.6%) of respondents said that their main difficulty was not knowing what the functions of the remote TV buttons were. The item "I don't know what the services stood for" was the second option most chosen, by 29.8% of the participants.

The next question focused on the content or functionalities or utilities which may be included in a future health digital TV service. Thus, a list with several functionalities was given and the participants were asked to indicate what they would like to see included in a digital TV health service. The possibility of doing medical appointments was the most selected options by the interviewees (35%). The second most selected option was to contact emergency care (32.5%). To verify the pharmacies timetables was third among the functionalities considered most useful by the participants (28.7%). The functionalities which obtained a lesser degree of interest in this survey were educational games and monitoring patients and treatments, with 1.7% and 3.2% respectively. Analyzing the data focusing only on respondents over 55 years old, the scenario remains broadly the same.

Regarding the question about the most important aspects of a digital TV health service, there were two items that stood out in the participants' selections – total sample and over 55 years old group: "user friendly" and "free of charge" are the essential features that the respondents indicated as most important to incorporate a future digital TV service.

Somehow in order to determine the perception of respondents over the potential that usefulness of a health digital TV service could have for him/herself and his/her family, we asked all the participants to classify the degree of usefulness, from 1 (not useful) to 10 (very useful). The average of all answers is 7.22 and the number 8 is the most often chosen classification with 18.1%. This is another indicator that a service of this kind would be well regarded by the interviewees.

The last question of this questionnaire requested the participants to say how frequently they use the presented sources in a given list to gather information and clarify doubts about health, using a scale between 1 (Never) and 5 (Always). After analysis, the most used sources by the respondents are doctors, nurses, pharmacists, family and friends. Next, below the professional knowledge, and relevant to this study, appears the TV which can be more used than the therapists, patients' associations and books to seek for health information.

A special care to have in the development of this digital platform is the fact that there is a high probability that approximately half of the Portuguese population may have limited health literacy. The Newest Vital Sign – NVS – assessment was used to attempt to gauge the level of health literacy of our respondents.). After the data analysis, it was found that 51.7% of individuals presented a high probability (+50%) of limited health literacy, while 22.6% of the respondents may have limited literacy. Lastly, only 25.7% have an adequate health literacy level.

These data will allow a particular focus in the development of this platform for iDTV in order to adapt it as best as possible to the target population.

3 The Qualitative Study Results: iDTV as a Useful Resource for Healthcare Providers

A set of 13 interviews was collected- 4 by e-mail, and 9 face to face - between September and December 2011. The set of questions posed focused on the possibilities of applications in digital TV in the context of healthcare and wellness.

After using the software NVivo as a tool to support content analysis, it was possible to extract, in relation to the role that respondents consider that ICT should play in the provision of health care and welfare, three fundamental aspects: the answers that highlight information; those who privilege the role of communication and those who consider that they can have a relevant role in what concerns mobility and accessibility.

In what concerns the informative role, it was indicated that ICTs in health can have a relevant saying in minimizing the consequences of low health literacy, increasing the level of health information and in particular about chronic diseases, and in making health information more understandable to the common health services user. It is also relevant to add that in what concerns the insurance activity, ICTs are stated to make easier the access to information of the clients' portfolio of each healthcare provider easier, as well as the choice the user makes of these providers.

As for the communication role, it was mentioned that the essential ICTs role in healthcare should be: to make communication easier between healthcare professionals (which would include the discussion of diagnosis, the exchange of clinical opinions among medical staff, etc.); to make communication easier between healthcare professionals and the users of healthcare services, through monitoring, remote doctor's appointments, etc.

Finally, in what concerns the role of ICTs as enablers of the conditions of accessibility and mobility, the following aspects are to be highlighted: ubiquity of the physical support; physical demobilization (meaning that it may allow for remote appointments, previous sorting out of emergency cases, to remotely sort symptoms, etc.); National healthcare services to become less congested.

Still, as for potentially negative aspects of ICTs as resources for the access to healthcare, several aspects were mentioned: low levels of technological literacy that don't allow their extended use; too much of an out-of-context and general information that ends up being of no practical use; the costs such resources would involve and the difficulties in maintaining an effective structure.

4 Discussion and Next Steps

As we can see and according to the data previously mentioned from Marktest, a large majority of people spend more than two daily hours watching TV. This element combined with the fact that TV is for the interviewees, right after to healthcare professionals, the most trusted source to gather information about health, appears as a further incentive for the awareness of the potential of digital interactive TV to promote services, formats and original content that may be relevant to the area of Health and Wellness.

The data analysis from the quantitative survey also specifies that a digital service to promote health and wellness is indicated as a helpful service and regarded as the most interesting by the target population. This indicates that the target population is concerned about their health and welcomes anything that will help them stay healthy. Yet, it is vital that this application (app) can be free of charge for the users to secure his success, because this condition is the second most important aspect of a digital TV health service for interviewees.

On the other hand, we can verify that using digital TV services is not yet a common task with all provided digital services obtaining low percentages when the individuals were asked by their usage rate of digital TV applications. About half (49.9%) of the respondents say that they don't use TV digital services because they don't have access to them in their home. Thus, for a health app to be as much as possible accessible to everyone, one first step to be taken is to reach an agreement with TV service providers in order to cover the population. Second step is to present the app to the healthcare professionals, so that they talk to their patients about the included features and help them to search for the easiest way to get the app.

Moreover, in relation to the level of health literacy, the data shows that 51.75% of individuals have a high probability of limited literacy. Therefore, on the development of a future health and wellness digital service it is essential that these factors are taken into account to easily develop an app designed specifically for the low literate groups, helping them to have a positive usage of it. Doing this will allow the users to see the real benefits of using such app at the same time that they are being encouraged to learning new forms of protecting their health.

And what do the users expect to find in a health app or service via digital TV platform? Analyzing the most chosen utilities by the respondents when enquired what they would like to see included in a future health app, we can see that their favorites are the utilities that could help them to do several tasks at home that normally force them to go out to resolve them, like the possibility of doing medical appointments, consulting pharmacies schedules or messaging with healthcare professionals. This is a positive aspect because it will allow, as Stankovic stated, an enhanced autonomy to people by letting them take care of their health issues easily, being the possibility of doing this without leaving their home, the most positive feature.

The stakeholders put emphasis on three key aspects of the role that ICTs should play in health care and welfare: inform, simplify communication between health professionals and users and facilitate the accessibility and mobility conditions. These key characteristics match with the population's requests that we saw in the quantitative survey. But they also pointed several potentially negative aspects like the lower level of technological literacy, the decontextualized and generalized information and the costs and difficulties inherent to maintaining an efficient structure. To minimize these aspects, a possible health app must be user friendly, both software and hardware (the unknown functions of the TV remote control were the main reason named by respondents for the existence of difficulties when using a digital app), all the available in-app content and information should be supervised by health professionals to guarantee its quality and the right entities partnerships must be wisely chosen to make a future health app project financially viable, at the same time that assures its credibility.

Consequently the results show that iDTV solutions could represent a real contribution to deliver healthcare to the target population, namely as a supplement to health services provision in order to avoid unnecessary visits to the health centers or hospitals.

Currently, our research team is focusing on the development of an iDTV portal solution for Smart TV, mobile and PC, where the users will have the possibility to obtain credible and rigorous information about diabetes (mostly in video format), to access useful tips and contacts about the disease and to monitor basic indicators related to Diabetes.

References

1. Green, J.: Why do they call it TV when it´s not on the box? "New" television services and "old" television. Media International Australia 126, 95–106 (2008)
2. Yearbook Communication 2010/2011. OberCom,
   `http://www.obercom.pt/client/?newsId=28&fileName=`
   `anuario1011.pdf`
3. Brodie, M., et al.: Communicating Health Information Through the Entertainment Media. Health Affairs 20(1) (2001)
4. Turow, J.: As seen on TV: Health Policy Issues in TV´s Medical Dramas. Kaiser Family Foundation Report, University of Pennsylvania (2002)
5. Eysenbach, G.: What is e-health? Journal of Medical Internet Research 3(2), e20 (2001)
6. Campbell, M., Honess-Morreale, L., Farrell, D., Carbone, E., Brasure, M.: A tailored multimedia nutrition education pilot program for low-income women receiving food assistance. Health Education Research 14(2), 257–267 (1999)
7. Gustafson, D.H., McTavish, F., Stengle, W., Ballard, D., Hawkins, R., Shaw, B.R., Landucci, G.: Use and Impact of eHealth System by Low-income Women With Breast Cancer. Journal of Health Communication 10, 195–218 (2005)
8. Ad Hoc Committee on Health Literacy. Health Literacy: Report of the Council on Scientific Affairs. Journal of the American Medical Association 281, 552–557 (1999)
9. Nielsen-Bohlman, L., Panzer, A., Kindig, D. (eds.): Health Literacy: A Prescription to End Confusion. National Academy of Sciences, Washington (2004)
10. Davis, T.C., Long, S.W., Jackson, R.H., Mayeaux, E.J., George, R.B., Murphy, P.W., Crouch, M.A.: Rapid estimate of adult literacy in medicine: a shortened screening instrument. Family Medicine 25(6), 391–395 (1993)
11. Parker, R.M., Baker, D.W., Williams, M.V., Nurss, J.R.: The Test of Functional Health Literacy in Adults: a new instrument for measuring patients' literacy skills. J. Gen. Intern. Med. 10(10), 537–541 (1995)
12. Weiss, B., Mays, M., Martz, W., Castro, K., DeWalt, D., Pignone, M., Mockbee, J., Hale, F.: Quick Assessment of Literacy in Primary Care: The Newest Vital Sign. Annals of Family Medicine 3, 514–522 (2005)
13. Whitten, P., Love, B., Buis, L., Mackert, M.: Health Education Online for Individuals with Low Health Literacy: Evaluation of the Diabetes and You Website. Journal of Technology in Human Services 26(1), 77–88 (in press)
14. Mackert, M., Love, B., Whitten, P.: Patient education on mobile devices: An e-health intervention for low health literate audiences. J. Inf. Sci. 35, 82–93 (2009)
15. Mackert, M., Whitten, P., Garcia, A.: Evaluating e-Health Interventions for Low Health Literate Audiences. Journal of Information Science 35(1), 82–93 (2008)
16. Stankovic, J.A., Cao, Q., Doan, T., Fang, L., He, Z., Kiran, R., Lin, S., Son, S., Stoleru, R., Wood, A.: Wireless Sensor Networks for In-Home Healthcare: Potencial and Challenges. In: HCMDSS 2005 (2005)

Homecare Risk Management: Nursing Issues Related to Technology

Juliana J. Brixey and James P. Turley

University of Texas Health Science Center at Houston
School of Biomedical Informatics
7000 Fannin, Suite 600, Houston, TX, USA 77030
{Juliana.J.Brixey,James.P.Turley}@uth.tmc.edu

Abstract. Traditional risk management may not address the needs of technology being introduced into homecare situations for nurses. We propose to augment traditional risk management with insights from Prevention through Design and The 8 Rights giving a more technology focus to risk management.

1 Introduction and Background

The goal of this paper is to propose an expanded view of risk management to address the technology which is rapidly coming to the homecare setting. Technology has the ability to create unintended side effects. We believe that with proper risk management that these side effects can be minimized. The future role of risk management in homecare is twofold. The first is to monitor and protect the client given the limits of current technology. The second will monitor and assess the potential for increased risk to the client as a result of the technology. The first role of healthcare is to "do no harm". Findings from a recently published study indicate the introduction of EHRs and DSS can lead to numerous unintended consequences[1]. A core aspect of risk management in homecare would be to pre-emptively assess the implications of the current and future technologies to minimize the unintended consequences of the technology. This would be true whether it was a direct result of the technology or a consequential result in clinical care. As a result of the proliferation of HIT, EHRs, and PHRs in homecare a new paradigm of risk management is emerging from the intersection of socio-medical problems and socio-technical approaches.

The problem space for risk management in homecare is well summarized by the AHRQ Report:

> "Home health care clinicians seek to provide high quality, safe care in ways that honor patient autonomy and accommodate the individual characteristics of each patient's home and family. Falls, declining functional abilities, pressure ulcers and non-healing wounds, and adverse events related to medication administration all have the potential to result in unplanned hospital admissions. Such hospitalizations undermine the achievement of important home health care goals:

V.G. Duffy (Ed.): DHM/HCII 2013, Part I, LNCS 8025, pp. 157–162, 2013.

keeping patients at home and promoting optimal well-being. Nevertheless, the unique characteristics of home health care may make it difficult to use—or necessary to alter—interventions that have been shown to be effective in other settings. Therefore, research on effective practices, conducted in home health care settings, is necessary to support excellence and evidence-based care."2

The AHRQ report indicates that that homecare addresses a wide range of acute and chronic health care needs. Homecare can expose social-medical problems different from those associated with hospital care with resultant risk management issues. For example, the homecare treatment of acute and chronic health conditions can involve the use of Health Information Technology (HIT) once reserved for hospitals. The patient/client and significant others are increasingly using HIT such as glucose monitors, infusion pumps, ventilators, sleep apnea machines and other medical devices. In homecare, HIT is being used in both direct client care and in adjunct components to that care. In terms of direct client care, EHRs are being used to both record the elements of direct client care and with increased DSS to directly control the quantity and quality of direct client care. DSS will become more directive in domains where the evidence is sufficient to direct "evidence based best practices". Moreover, patients/clients are recording their own health information in personal health records (PHRs). Using PHRs, patients control access to the health information. This is in sharp contrast to clinician controlled access to heath in the patient has limited access to their own health information. The addition of patient specific outcomes and interventions in PHRs will become future resource to be mined to create new areas of evidence based care.

Homecare companies may be small. As noted in 2000, 16% of healthcare agencies have 5 or fewer employees. These smaller organizations may lack the sophistication to complete comprehensive risk management.3

Homecare is becoming more integrated into the continuum of health care services. To accomplish this we will need to view a more pervasive model of HIT used in homecare and that will communicate with other health care delivery areas.4 The HIT integration will demand not only standards for communication and data structures but will also require standardization of outcomes and homecare interventions.

Moreover, emerging HIT is being introduced into homecare to facilitate aging in place. The near future requires HIT to address directly the specific needs of the socio-medical problems related to homecare. Examples of social-medical problems include monitoring that medications and treatments are completed; they are usually a combination of people interacting and tasks that need to be completed. HIT may allow that monitoring from a distance, introducing new social dynamics. As the AHRQ2 report indicates, mobility is one of the chief concerns in homecare. The "smart home" will allow practitioners to monitor mobility within the home using sensors. These sensors, whether monitored by external humans, family members or artificial intelligence, to determine whether the target patient/client is ambulatory within the home to indicate whether there is a risk for falls or reduced immobility which leads to pneumonia, pressure ulcers, and deep vein thrombus. These same sensors could be used to monitor 'safe vs. unsafe' activity within the home indicative of bodily functions such as continence and performance activities related to cooking and other activities of daily living (ADLs). These sensors will become part of the pervasive computing network noted above.

2   Identified Homecare Risks

The National Institute for Occupational Safety and Health developed the National Occupational Research Agenda (NORA). NORA[5] identified a number of risks in the healthcare arena that have particular import for homecare. These include:

1. Work related musculoskeletal disorders
2. Slip, Trip and Fall Incidents
3. Violence
4. Hazardous Drugs
5. Chemical Hazards
6. Sharps injuries and Bloodborn Pathogens
7. Other infectious diseases.

Taylor and Donnelly[6] cite a different set of risks to homecare workers. They noted that workers were "visiting at all hours and in all seasons, homecare workers faced many and varied hazards ranging across access issues, hygiene and infection, manual handling, aggression and harassment, domestic and farm animals, fleas and safety of home equipment. Something accepted unquestioningly as a 'normal' hazard of life by the client (perhaps over decades) may be unacceptable to the homecare worker or (possibly) the employing organization". The issue of perspective and relative value of 'risk' will vary between the professionals and the patients with geographic and value perspectives as well. Similar to the NORA list they identified:

1. Physical risks moving patients and equipment
2. Violence from other family members and the environment

Other identified risks included:

1. Environmental Risks
    (a) Internal to the home situation (e.g. lack of running water)
    (b) External to the home (e.g. animals, travel during winter etc.)
2. Patient/Family lifestyle choices
3. In-home safety issues (e.g. electrical wiring, sanitation, heat etc.)
4. Conflicts on how to decide care protocols.

While there are a variety of 'lists of risk', issues of injury to workers, from the setting, the environment and the tasks to be accomplished are always present. The environmental risks are ever present. While the environmental risks may vary between urban and rural settings and by geographic locations e.g. whether the category is a major one. Likewise the potential for violence is an ongoing concern for homecare providers. Taylor and Donnelly summarized this as "Homecare is not a panacea for the high costs of institutional care. There are significant hazards facing homecare workers in the homes of clients including health hazards, injuries in moving and handling, verbal abuse and aggression. Such hazards were a major concern for the managers of homecare workers.".6

3   Risk Management by Prevention

The introduction of technologies into home care will demand new areas for risk management in the homecare setting. The prevention of unintended consequences from the technology is an overarching goal. The settings for homecare are less standardized than other healthcare settings as the setting is usually the patient/client's home. Homecare providers have less control over the environment, increasing the difficulty in risk management.   Prevention through design resulted from a NIOSH initiative launched in 2007.[7] The Prevention through Design Model involves three major components to achieve the goal:

1. Strategic Input
    (a) Research
    (b) Education
    (c) Practice
    (d) Policy
2. Strategic Planning
    (a) Incorporating occupational safety and health considerations
3. Implementation
    (a) Designing systems with the goal of reducing injuries and risk.

Prevention through design incorporates the usual steps in risk management:

1. Information Sharing
2. Risk Identification
3. Risk Assessment
4. Risk Management

And it more formally includes the research, education and practice policies to infuse the Risk Management Model with information external to each situation. The additional information gives a move complex view of the elements which can abate risk.

4   Risk Management by Design

We will present a comprehensive framework based on socio-technical approaches to the use of technology in health care and a multi-dimensional understanding of the impact of technology in health care to frame a better understanding of risk assessment in healthcare technologies. Sittig and Sing1 identified eight 'rights':

1. Right Hardware or Software
2. Right Content
3. Right Interface
4. Right Personnel
5. Right Workflow and Communication
6. Right Organizational Characteristics
7. Right State and Federal Policies and Regulations
8. Right Monitoring

We propose creating a grid using the identified categories of Prevention through Design and The 8 Rights identified by Sittig and Sing will create a model to better inform the steps in the risk management process. Figure 1 gives an example of how Prevention through Design and The 8 Rights can be combined. The resulting information grid is then used to 'inform' the risk management process.

	Hard-ware Soft-ware	Con-tent	Inter-face	Per-sonnel	Work-flow Comm.	Organiza-tional Character.	Pol-icy	Moni-toring
Input								
Research								
Education								
Practice								
Policy								
Planning								
Safety								
Implemen-tation								
Design								

Fig. 1. Integration of Prevention through Design and The 8 Rights

The combination of Prevention through Design and the 8 Rights give a richer framework for risk analysis.

5   Conclusions

Conventional risk management may not address the requirements of technology being introduced into homecare environments for nurses. We caution that the interaction between technology and the variables inherent in homecare settings warrant continued and cautious scrutiny.

References

1. Sittig, D., Singh, H.: Eight Rights of Safe Electronic Health Record Use. JAMA 302(10), 1111–1112 (2009)
2. Ellenbecker, C.H., Samia, L., Cushman, M.J., Alster, K.: Patient Safety and Quality in Home Health Care. Patient Safety and Quality: An Evidence-based Handbook for Nurses (2008), http://www.ahrq.gov/qual/nurseshdbk/
3. BLS.: 2000 Standard Occupational Codes (2000), http://www.bls.gov/oes/2002/oes_stru.htm
4. Armrich, A., Mayora, O., Bardram, J., Troster, G.: Pervasive Healthcare: Paving the Way for a Pervasice, User-centered and Preventive Healthcare Model. Methods of Information in Medicine 49(1), 67–73 (2010)
5. NIOSH.: State of the Sector: Healthcare and Social Assistance – Identification of Research Opportunities for the Next Decade of NORA (2009), http://www.cdc.gov/niosh/docs/2009-139/pdfs/2009-139.pdf
6. Taylor, B.J., Donnelly, M.: Risks to Home Care Workers: Professional Perspectives. Health, Risk & Society 8(3), 239–256 (2007), http://dx.doi.org/10.1080/13698570600871695
7. Lamba, A., Heckel, P.: Practice designing out hazards in the real world. Prof. Saf. 58(1), 34–40 (2013), http://www.asse.org/professionalsafety/search/index3.php

Facilitators' Intervention Variance and Outcome Influence When Using Video Games with Fibromyalgia Patients

Anthony L. Brooks and Eva Petersson Brooks

Aalborg University Esbjerg, Niels Bohrs vej 8, Esbjerg, Denmark
{tb,ep}@create.aau.dk

Abstract. 22 adult females diagnosed as suffering Fibromyalgia syndrome (FMS) participated in two explorative studies investigating potential benefits from playing gesture-controlled video games. A main goal was researching potentials of commercial gaming systems with inbuilt Internet connectivity toward home-based self-driven adaptable 'telerehabilitation' targeting means to increase tolerance to pain and thus, augmenting quality of life for sufferers. Beside this, an aim was to study variance between facilitator formal and informal intervention approaches and to analyze potential influence on outcomes; this is the core focus of this paper. Typical to FMS studies, high patient drop out numbers resulted in limited compliance. Informal facilitator intervention (non-therapist) resulted in significantly higher outcome scores (increased tolerance indicators/reported pain threshold) when compared to a formal therapeutic intervention approach. Findings, whilst not conclusive, offer a point of departure to discuss how intervention approach influences outcomes and patient benefit, especially when a self-driven training regime is designed.

Keywords: Fibromyalgia, Video Games, Pain, Facilitator Intervention.

1 Introduction

Two explorative studies investigating potentials for Fibromyalgia Syndrome (FMS) patients playing gesture-controlled video games was undertaken to explore use as an intervention to motivate participation in training.

Notable from the studies was that outcomes were significantly different, such that the positive indicators from study-A were not apparent from study-B. In querying these results (A/B), an analysis of the video material suggested a major difference in the approaches taken by the different facilitators. 'A' was conducted systematically yet non-formal in a playful way, whereas 'B', whilst also being systematic, was more formal in line with a traditional therapeutic approach. The implication of such different intervention strategies is thus explored as the core of this contribution.

Fibromyalgia is a lifelong condition involving widespread musculoskeletal pain and tenderness, fatigue, sleep disturbance, and functional impairment, without any known structural or inflammatory cause. It affects patient life quality and is costly in

V.G. Duffy (Ed.): DHM/HCII 2013, Part I, LNCS 8025, pp. 163–172, 2013.

terms of consultations, prescriptions and sick leave. The main aims of therapy are to reduce symptoms, to improve function, and to help patients adapt to the condition. The medical communities are split between treatments with some believing it psychosomatic while others acknowledge that medication is possible whereby physical exercise can assist improvements.

An overall goal of this research, which is conducted in the Esbjerg region of southwest Denmark, was to augment patient motivation to participate and exercise and thus raise their energy level, tolerance and threshold before onset of the fibromyalgia pain. By using contemporary, affordable, and widely popular video gaming systems (that are already present in many Danish homes), it was hypothesized that new opportunities to achieve these goals as well as to augment social interactions via playing with family members, peers, and friends would further stimulate, motivate, and sustain the intervention strategy. The goal of this publication is to explore the impact of patient mindset from intervention influences between the playfully supportive strategies toward an enjoyable experience (study-A) versus a methodological formalized structure clearly based on targeting therapeutic output (study-B).

The next section introduces selected related researches on video games in rehabilitation, therapy and treatment; alternative control via gesture; related intervention strategies; and specific research targeting pain distraction. The following sections detail methods, the session design, and results. A discussions section critically reflects on the different intervention approaches by the facilitators that are speculated as being influential in such applied research and practices in the field. A closing section concludes the findings whilst clearly stating their speculative nature. This section furthermore includes a 'next-step' future research proposal that targets to strengthen the work beyond speculation to stimulate peer discussions on the topic.

2   Related Work

Playing VR games has been shown to distract a patient/player so that (s)he focuses on the gameplay rather than any pain sensations [1]. This can result in a more enjoyable experience and thereby improve motivation to comply with the training.

"Acute pain is shown to be noticeably reduced in children and adult sufferers once engaged in video game activity," says Charles Friedman, D.O. of Pain Relief Centers in Pinellas Park. "These video games do certainly play a role in relieving some pain through both distraction and movement," says Friedman. "Even if you've never played video games, engaging in any sort of active gaming will reduce your pain level and even increase pain tolerance," says Friedman.[1]

Using an exploratory approach [2] investigated the influence of movement on how players experience video games through the systematic collection and analysis of data

---

[1] http://www.brashgames.co.uk/2010/11/29/
video-games-ease-the-pain/   (np).

obtained from interviews; questionnaires; video observations; and a motion capture system. Achievement and relaxation were gamer-reported motivators of the play (i.e. boxing), which was evident in the gameplay via two corresponding movement control strategies. Such motivators are acknowledged as pain distractors. Outcomes from this study point to four movement-specific items influencing immersion in movement-based interaction: natural control, mimicry of movements, proprioceptive feedback, and physical challenge. These were reflected from a design perspective in respect of physical activity and emotional wellbeing. Accordingly, based on input from the patients' doctor, we have used a gesture-controlled game (held handset) as motivators and in line with studies on Energy Expenditure (EE) during Wii Sports game activities of typically developed (TD) adults and with positive results [3]. [4, 5] similarly report on cerebral palsy and chronic stroke patients using the Wii to achieve more active lifestyles.

Methods to assess game systems use in rehabilitation via psychometric evaluation to provide a personalized and automated training is exemplified by [6]. However, research of video games in Fibromyalgia has been found lacking. Also, despite the numerous studies on video games in healthcare, it has been difficult to find researches that focus on facilitator intervention approaches and strategies.

The first authors' prior research highlights how the use of tailored accessible interactive causal environments that empower digital game playing, art making, and robotic device control via gesture (i.e. play and creativity), has realised potentials in the field of healthcare rehabilitation and therapy. Included are early conceptualizations on use of Internet connectivity for *Telerehabilitation* evolving to *TeleAbilitation* [7], including for home training of pain tolerance. A common factor in this body of work has been how immersion and engagement in the playful and creative activities distract from the patient's impairment. Similar distraction strategies via video games are used by [8],[2] which is used as a pain-management tool for patients undergoing agonizing medical treatments whereby the need for potent narcotics is reduced: This a strategy also used in [9]. Thus, synthesizing these approaches, a home-based pain management tool can be acknowledged as appropriate. However, a concern would be extensive computer and video game usage that may indirectly cause non-FMS pain that would confuse diagnosis and progress. In line with this is a related study with 791 adolescent where the frequent use of computer and video games was found to not be associated with the presence of pain and musculoskeletal pain syndromes [10].

This paper's second author is an authority on non-formal learning that is innate within such interactive environments where the motivation of the participant aligns with embodied challenges such as researched in many contemporary education situations. Petersson [11] underlines that through gameplaying activities, the FMS participant determines the course of (inter)actions and, thereby, experiences autonomy in the form of actions that are selected from a range of possible choices. To select among these choices is to grasp affordances [12], i.e. to perceive and to act upon

---

[2] http://www.hitl.washington.edu/projects/vrpain/
index_files/SCIAMFin.pdf

something in a particular way. This operation is an immediate and reciprocal action with an interactive character, which relates the participant's action to the concept of interaction. In this way, a dialogue is initiated as a part of the participant's input in the form of movement (feed-forward) and the response from the game system (feedback). This creates motivators in the form of iterative feed-forward-to-feedback loops. Halliday [13, p. 68] terms such turn-taking activities as speech acts and emphasizes:

An 'act' of speaking /.../ might more appropriately be called an 'interact': it is an exchange in which giving implies receiving, and demanding implies giving in response.

Feed-forward and feedback evolves as an iterative loop encourages exploration and development of skills and competencies. In terms of [14] the competencies in question are those involved in the mastery of the gameplay. Bruner describes the exploration as an exercise, through which the participant can augment his or her actions to new limits of already achieved skills. When the participant becomes absorbed by the gameplay-based exercise, the exploration develops into play. Intense concentration of the exploration and the gameplay is core as a basis for non-formal learning [11, 15, 16]. Here, where the conditions are created so that the feed-forward-to-feedback loop provides an invitation to explore and, then, to begin to play and to continue playing, the gameplay can be considered as active creation of meaning (or learning), and not just use of a game. [11] states that the use and the design of such gameplaying interventions are dependent on idiosyncratic tendencies. How to use and overcome possible constraints in such situations is a crucial facilitator consideration. In the context of this paper, the facilitator contemplations are suggested to also include framing consideration in terms of formal- and non-formal-based mindsets in order to create appropriate motivators for therapeutic gameplay interventions.

3   Method

The study as such included two pilot studies: A and B. A [17] investigated gesture-based control of video games to promote and motivate self-driven home-based aerobic exercise (AE) training regimes to improve pain threshold associated to FMS. 10 patients were randomized to 10 sessions each led by a nonmedical 'game-savvy' PhD Medialogy student. Control was treatment-as-usual (TAU) patients via the patient's doctor who conducted pre- and post- interviews, tests, and VAS registrations of pain, disturbed sleep, lack of energy, and depression. Included was patient-reported global subjective improvement or otherwise. A Nintendo Wii was used with a sports compilation game 'Sports Resort' with the Wiimote MotionPlus accessory to increase accuracy of gesture. Only two completed the study.

Study B [18] was conducted with two occupational therapist students as session facilitators of 12 participants. Three game platforms were studied: the MS Kinect, Sony MOVE, and Nintendo Wii, with 5 game sessions of one hour being played by each patient in regular lab visits (=15 sessions each). Control was again treatment-as-usual (TAU) patients and collection of data by the doctor as in study-A. High dropouts were again apparent with only 7 completing all sessions.

3.1   Procedure

In both studies an introduction session guided the patients to be able to play the games. In study A, the Wii 'Sports Resort' compendium game was used where patients could select the specific gameplay and level.

Similar games were used in study B.

In both studies, a 107 cm screen size TV was used for the patient to monitor the gameplay that mirrored input motion. The use of a large screen size had been found optimal in prior research where optimum experiences, immersion, and engagement was reported by participants where interactions were mirrored as a direct and immediate response delivered on a one-to-one scale [19, 20, 21, 22, 23, 24, 25]. In study A the facilitator supported where necessary targeting fun experiences from the play situation rather than evoking a therapeutic-focused intervention.

The Wiimote handset was enhanced via the MotionPlus accessory for extra sensitivity. The test area was set-up with a tape marker for the patients' gameplay start position consistency between sessions. Data collection was via three cameras with different viewing angles were routed to 1, 2, and 3 inputs of a Roland V-4 four-channel video mixer (figure 1).

The component output from the game console was split and routed to the input of channel 4 and to the TV. This was to enable a quadrant view of patient activity so that stimuli and responses could be automatically synchronized to optimize intervention/interaction analysis.

VAS registrations of: pain, disturbed sleep, lack of energy, and depression were among the tests, conducted by the patients' doctor, as well as interviews questioning global subjective improvement. Outcome measures and interviews were at baseline and at treatment completion.

Fig. 1. Two quad screen views (left = session 2, right = final session)

The complexity of researching a disabling condition such as fibromyalgia where much is still being debated on the disease itself (e.g. psychosomatic versus medication/exercise) as well as the innate challenges of assessing human condition in general, means that each case is individual when considering progress.

Whilst initial results are positive, a reflection on the generic viability against the TAU control in such a limited study is speculative due to the large drop out of 8 from 10 patients. However, the significance of the findings in this pilot study led to a follow-on comparative study (including handheld device for motion tracking versus non-handheld) with 39 patients invited under the same doctor.

Thus, study B was conducted with two occupational therapist students replacing the Medialogy student as session facilitator. Three game platforms were studied: the MS Kinect (non-handheld), Sony MOVE (handheld), and Nintendo Wii (handheld), with 5 game sessions of one hour being played by each patient in regular lab visits (total =15 sessions each patient). This is detailed next where the formal data collection process is outlined.

Data collection process.

- Data collection at the clinic (pre- and post-programme) (VAS etc.)
- Data collection – Home =ADL-Q (Completed and brought at the baseline interview)
- Data collection at Aalborg University Esbjerg/SensoramaLab (test site)

  1. Baseline interview + Platform 1 game selection
  2. Platform 1 – Session 1
  3. Platform 1 – Session 2
  4. Platform 1 – Session 3
  5. Platform 1 – Session 4
  6. Platform 1 – Session 5
  7. Platform 2 – Game selection + Session 1
  8. Platform 2 – Session 2
  9. Platform 2 – Session 3
  10. Platform 2 – Session 4
  11. Platform 2 – Session 5
  12. Platform 3 – Game selection + Session 1
  13. Platform 3 – Session 2
  14. Platform 3 – Session 3
  15. Platform 3 – Session 4
  16. Platform 3 – Session 5

- Data collection – Home = ADL-Q (Completed and brought at the post-intervention interview)
- Data collection at AAUE/SensoramaLab = Post-intervention interview (2 handheld video cameras recorded)

4   Results

Facilitator in vivo observations and multiple angle (3) video recordings synchronized to the game play provided substantial data to analyze study-A. Outcome measures were at baseline and completion. Short-term results were positive of those patients who completed the study (n = 2). 50% drop out at study commencement suggested a skeptical patient attitude. Further dropouts (n = 3) were due to a car accident (n = 1) and recurrence of pain (n = 2). Both patients who completed showed significant motion improvements and substantial rise in reported onset of pain threshold indicators (VAS) and each purchased a Wii for home training following the study. Follow up interviews and tests are undertaken to question compliance and long-term outcomes.

Videos were analyzed and further viewed by a representative from the Danish Fibromyalgia union. The videos clearly indicated a common pattern that, following initial trepidation and caution by the patients, and once comfortable, the patients' dynamic motions were stimulated via the gameplay so that a new level of engagement and motion was evident by the end of each session. The Danish Fibromyalgia union expert evaluated positively.

In study-B doctor interviews the patients who dropped out informed that after the training session they got worse and he suggests this may explain their stopping. When interviewing and testing those who completed there was no significant change on pain (pre-post) and negative on fatigue (pre-post). Participants stated that they did not take notice of pain symptoms while playing and that playing VR games was a fun way of doing manageable exercise. The session facilitators said that those who completed mentioned less pain and more energy while they played. They were observed as seeming very focused and enjoying themselves and "lifted" when they are leaving post-session. Although no general reduction in pain was attained, participants did see VR games as a good way of doing exercise. Participants stated that they did not take notice of pain symptoms while playing and that playing VR games was a fun way of doing manageable exercise. Most participants did not engage in a lot of exercise at baseline, because they related this with increased pain and fatigue, but playing VR games they managed to be physical active for 30 minutes and had fun with it. Reasons could be that playing VR games was not being perceived as exercise but as play.

5   Discussions

The medical doctor who reported significant results between pre- and post- VAS outcomes and other collected data substantiated the findings from study-A, yet was confounded at the negative outcome from study-B, suggesting the only explanation as *"the two first patients had a special positive personality"*. This study looked further into the videos from the sessions and reflected on preliminary comments. In study-A, the video games engaged the patients to previously unseen dynamics of motion gesture and participation. They also had lots of fun both in the gameplay and interactions with the facilitator and this was analyzed as offering positive reinforcement and scaffolding for the patient playing the game. One patient reported using the training sessions as a family event (she brought her daughters to the sessions for encouragement). The other patient used sessions as a self-training regime without family support and would change into a Lycra aerobics outfit. Her approach was that this was her private time and space. Both of these were session participants that evolved to become self-driven eventually without researcher intervention. Notable was that the two patients that completed all sessions each purchased the Nintendo Wii for home use. This is in line with a report by Dr. Ben Hertz, a director of Occupational Therapy at the Medical College Georgia [26], who explained that in a study with Parkinson's disease and the Wii participants showed significant improvements in rigidity, movement, fine motor skills and energy levels. Perhaps most impressively, most participants' depression levels decreased to zero. The report states that about 60 per cent of the study participants decided to buy a Wii themselves, suggesting that that speaks volumes for how the study made them feel. The play aspect, which was a major issue in study-A where the facilitator was the games-oriented PhD student, was also reported positive in study-B as patients preferred to think of the activity as play versus training and this motivated participation. However, the video footage of session gameplay suggests a different priority for the facilitators in their approach to intervention such that study-B therapist facilitators had 'therapy' as a priority. Thus, a question arises whether the facilitator mindset affects the patient mindset and subsequently reported outcomes. This speculation is complex to prove due to the challenges inherent of researching humans is a subjective and qualitative manner, and especially over only a short period where findings are limited.

6   Conclusions

FMS, by its nature, presents a challenge for full study compliance and dropouts should be expected [27, 28]. The studies presented were no different with many stopping to attend for many reasons. However, the results between the studies were significantly different, thus necessitating a closer analysis of what had happened to cause the changes. The facilitator intervention was thus observed according to non-formal approach analogized from [11]. When outcomes between comparative studies are so significantly different questioning of variances is an obvious thing to do. In querying A/B results, video analysis suggested a major difference in the approaches taken by the different facilitators with study-A being conducted systematic yet informal, whilst study-B, whilst also systematic, was more formal in line with a traditional therapeutic approach. The implication of effect impact on patient mindset from intervention influence between a playful yet supportive strategy toward an enjoyable experience (study-A) versus a methodological formalized structure clearly based on targeting therapeutic outcome (study-B) is thus explored as the core of this contribution. With advances in such game-based systems prevalent alongside their increased use in healthcare, this contribution posits the need to consider patient mindset influence by facilitator intervention, suggesting further research with this focus to establish additional strategy models that are not framed in traditional formality but more open to improvised yet systematic and adaptive intervention. An example of such a model is the Zone of Optimized Motivation (ZOOM) as emergent from the first author's body of research [e.g. 3, 4, 5, 6, 7]. Such models are posited required to support the predicted future service industry trained personnel shortages of those that care for impaired, aged, and others in need. It is envisaged that such healthcare facilitators will increasingly use ICT in their practices and likely increasingly collaborate across disciplines with non-therapists, and especially with those capable of creatively programming such ICT.

Conflict of Interest Statement. The authors have no conflict of interest to disclose.

Acknowledgements. Dr.. Hans-Jakob Haga and patients from www. reumaklinikdanmark.dk; Danish Fibromyalgia union; Gudmundur Bogason; Jesper Mortensen; Lola Qvist Kristensen. Eva Ejlersen Wæhrens for allowing use of ADL-Q. Study-A was supported by the Aalborg University Esbjerg. Study-B was supported by the Danish Occupational Therapist Association.

References

1. Taylor, M.J., McCormick, D., Shawis, T., Impson, R., Griffin, M.: Activity-promoting gaming systems in exercise and rehabilitation. J. Rehabil. Res. Dev. 48, 1171–1186 (2011)
2. Pasch, M., Bianchi-Berthouze, N., van Dijk, B., Nijholt, A.: Movement-based Sports Video Games: Investigating Motivation and Gaming Experience. Entertainment Computing 9(2), 169–180 (2009)
3. Miyachi, M., Yamamoto, K., Ohkawara, K., Tanaka, S.: METs in adults while playing active video games: a metabolic chamber study. Med. Sci. Sports Exerc. 42(6), 1149–1153 (2010)
4. Hurkmans, H.L., Ribbers, G.M., Streur-Kranenburg, M.F., Stam, H.J., van den Berg-Emons, R.J.: Energy expenditure in chronic stroke patients playing Wii Sports: a pilot study. J. Neuroeng. Rehabil. 14(8), 38 (2011)
5. Hurkmans, H.L., van den Berg-Emons, R.J., Stam, H.J.: Energy expenditure in adults with cerebral palsy playing Wii Sports. Arch. Phys. Med. Rehabil. 91(10), 1577–1581 (2010)
6. Cameirão, M.S., Badia, S.B., Oller, E.D., Verschure, P.F.M.J.: Neurorehabilitation using the virtual reality based Rehabilitation Gaming System: methodology, design, psychometrics, usability and validation. Journal of NeuroEngineering and Rehabilitation 7(48) (2010)
7. Brooks, A.L.: TeleAbilitation: GameAbilitation. In: Kumar, S., Cohn, E.R. (eds.) Telerehabilitation, Health Informatics, pp. 225–238. Springer Publishing Company (2012)
8. Hoffman, H., Chambers, G.T., Meyer III, W.J., Arceneaux, L.L., Russell, W.J., Seibel, E.J., Richards, T.L., Sharar, S.R., Patterson, D.R.: Virtual Reality as an Adjunctive Non-pharmacologic Analgesic for Acute Burn Pain During Medical Procedures. Annals of Behavioral Medicine 41(2), 183–191 (2011)
9. Morris, L.D., Louw, Q.A., Grimmer-Somers, K.: The effectiveness of virtual reality on reducing pain and anxiety in burn injury patients: a systematic review. Clin. J. Pain. 25(9), 815–826 (2009)
10. Zapata, A.L., Moraes, A.J.P., Leone, C., Doria-Filho, U., Silva, C.A.A.: Pain and musculoskeletal pain syndromes related to computer and video game use in adolescents. European Journal of Pediatrics 165(6), 408–414 (2006)
11. Petersson, E.: Non-formal Learning through Ludic Engagement with in Interactive Environments. Doctoral dissertation, Malmoe University, School of Teacher Education, Studies in Educational Sciences (2006)

12. Gibson, J.J.: The Ecological Approach to Visual Perception. Houghton Mifflin, Boston (1979)
13. Halliday, M.A.K.: Spoken and written language. Oxford University Press, Oxford (1985)
14. Bruner, J.S.: Organization of early skilled action. Child Development 44, 92–96 (1973)
15. Petersson, E.: Editorial: Ludic Engagement Designs for All. Digital Creativity 19(3), 141–144 (2008)
16. Petersson, E., Brooks, A.: ArtAbilitation®: An Interactive Installation for the Study of Action and Stillness Cycles in Responsive Environments. In: Proc. of Stillness – CADE – Computers in Art and Design Education Conference, Perth, Australia, pp. 159–170 (2007)
17. Brooks, A.L., Petersson, E.: Perceptual game controllers and fibromyalgia studies. In: Sharkey, P., Klinger, E. (eds.) 9th International Conference Series on Disability, Virtual Reality, and Associated Technologies (ICDVRAT). Reading University Press, UK (2012)
18. Mortensen, J., Lomquist, L., Brooks, A.L., Petersson, E.: Fibromyalgia women's experience with three different movement-based gaming consoles and the effect on daily living. Scandinavian Journal of Occupational Therapy (2013)
19. Brooks, A.L.: Virtual interactive space (V.I.S.) as a movement capture interface tool giving multimedia feedback for treatment and analysis. In: Proc. Int. Congress World Confed. Phys. Therapy (WCPT), Yokohama, Japan (1999), Available from Science Links Japan, http://sciencelinks.jp/j-east/article/200110/000020011001A0418015.php
20. Brooks, A.L., Camurri, A., Canagarajah, N., Hasselblad, S.: Interaction with shapes and sounds as a therapy for special needs and rehabilitation. In: Sharkey, P., Sik Lányi, C., Standen, P. (eds.) 4th Intl. Conf. on Disability, Virtual Reality and Assoc. Technologies, pp. 205–212. University of Reading Press, Veszprém (2002)
21. Brooks, A.L.: Patent US6893407 - Communication method and apparatus (2000)
22. Brooks, A.L.: SoundScapes: The Evolution of a Concept, Apparatus, and Method where Ludic Engagement in Virtual Interactive Space is a Supplemental Tool for Therapeutic Motivation (PhD dissertation). Sunderland University Press (2006/2011)
23. Peterson, E., Brooks, A.L.: Virtual and Physical Toys: Open-Ended Features for Non-Formal Learning. CyberPsychology & Behavior 9(2), 196–198 (2006)
24. Brooks, A.L.: HUMANICS 1 – a feasibility study to create a home internet based tele-health product to supplement acquired brain injury therapy. In: Sharkey, P., Brown, D., Mc Crindle, R. (eds.) 5th International Conference Series on Disability, Virtual Reality, and Associated Technologies (ICDVRAT). Reading University Press, UK (2004)
25. Brooks, A.L.: TeleAbilitation: GameAbilitation. In: Kumar, S., Cohn, E.R. (eds.) Telerehabilitation, Health Informatics, pp. 225–238. Springer Publishing Company (2012)
26. Hertz, B.: Medical College of Georgia. Occupational Therapists Use Wii For Parkinson's Study. ScienceDaily (2008), http://www.sciencedaily.com/releases/2008/04/080407074534.htm (Accessible)
27. Busch, A.J., Schachter, C.L., Overend, T.J., Peloso, P.M., Barber, K.A.: Exercise for fibromyalgia: a systematic review. J. Rheumatol. 35(6), 1130–1144 (2008)
28. Rossy, L.A., Buckelew, S.P., Dorr, N., Hagglund, K.J., Thayer, J.F., McIntosh, M.J., et al.: A meta-analysis of fibromyalgia treatment interventions. Ann. Behav. Med. 21(2), 180–191 (1999)

The Causal Analysis of Requested Alterations for Pressure Garments

Chia-Fen Chi, Chih-Hsiang Lin, and Hung-Wei Cheng

Department of Industrial Management,
National Taiwan University of Science and Technology
43 Keelung Road, Section 4, Taipei, Taiwan 106
chris@mail.ntust.edu.tw

Abstract. The purpose of this study was to examine altered pressure garments requested by burn patients, in Taiwan. Three hundred forty-two pressure garments needing alterations were collected from 127 burn patients at the Sunshine Foundation Organization, an nonprofit organization for burn patients to identify the major defects found in these pressure garments and their causes. Causes of required alterations were classified according to a hierarchical coding scheme focusing on poor fit, discomfort, component part, fabric and sewing, and cosmetics to identify systematic problems for each garment type. The result of our analysis indicated that the majority of the pressure garment alterations were related to poor fit in circumferential and longitudinal dimensions of the various body parts, incorrect position and size of openings for eyes, nose, ears, and mouth, or inappropriate length or position of zippers. Information derived from this causal analysis can be applied in helping to reduce the recurrence of alterations in pressure garment, thus improving the quality and effectiveness of pressure therapy.

Keywords: pressure garment, defect analysis, causal analysis.

1 Introduction

Optimal scar management requires that pressure garments be worn by burn patients for at least 23 hours a day and for at least 9 months to 2 years to provide adequate, consistent and sustained pressure (Cheng, et al., 1996; Williams, Knapp, & Wallen, 1998). Previously, the majority of researchers on pressure garments have indicated that patients were not satisfied with their garments and therefore were not wearing them long enough (Brown, 2001). Johnson, et al., (1994) found that only 41% of pressure garment wearers were fully compliant with their treatment. Problems with movement, appearance, fit, comfort, swelling of extremities, rashes and blistering all resulted in a low compliance rate (Macintyre & Baird, 2006). Interestingly, the clinicians had a different perception from the patients. Stewart, et al. (2000) indicated that clinicians were largely unaware of their patients experiences of excessive skin friction caused by the garments and that not a single clinician believed that the garments were poorly constructed. The clinicians' apparent lack of attention to the effects of poor

V.G. Duffy (Ed.): DHM/HCII 2013, Part I, LNCS 8025, pp. 173–182, 2013.

garment construction and fit mitigates against the implementation of simple interventions to improve garment comfort (Stewart, et al, 2000).

Alterations can be done to improve fit and to provide more consistent pressure to a certain scar areas or to help patients to lessen their difficulties in donning garment, maintaining personal hygiene and relieving discomfort (Pratt & West, 1995). Each alteration takes time and other resources from the garment providers and cause some inconvenience for the client. Fewer alterations required is an important quality for custom-made pressure garments because reliability of fit with the first garment ordered is indicated by 90% out of 101 burn centers, as one of the key factors used in the selection of a manufacturer (Ward, 1993). Mays, Jones, Holloway, et al., (1990) suggested that the causal analysis of alteration (defect) provide a much better understanding of why an error occurred and how to prevent its reoccurrence. Since there are some reoccurring causes behind these alterations, by identifying alterations and putting them into categories can determine what areas need to be addressed in order to improve the quality and productivity of pressure garments.

You, Wang, Luo, et al. (2002) stated that wearing pressure comfort is one of the most important factors influencing a wearer's sensation of comfort for these tight-fitting garments and are basically determined by garment fit, fabric extensibility and garment style. In the current study, factors related to garment fit were singled out to indicate possible deficiency or human errors in patient measurement or other pressure garment making factors. In some cases, problems could also arise from the irregularity of a body shape (eg, patient with a hunch back) or change in body size of burn patients. Our study aims to articulate and differentiate the causes of needed alterations into orthogonal and consistent categories (Chi, Chang, and Ting, 2005; Chi, Yang, and Chen, 2008) because this choice of a classification leaves little room for confusion and the set of causes are sufficient enough to cover the seven major pressure garment making stages and include all alteration cases (Chillarege, Bhandari, Chaar, et al., 1992). Through a systematic collection and analysis of the causes of alteration, we can prevent the recurrence of alterations and reach a consensus concerning the quality of a pressure garment. This study collected and analyzed 342 requested alterations from a local Taiwan workshop to identify the causes of alterations for preventing recurrence and thereby save cost, time, and reduce the inconvenience of the burn patients, who are required to use pressure therapy.

2   Methods

2.1   Data Collection

This study analyzed 342 alterations and/or repairs requested by 127 clients of the Sunshine Organization between in 2007. For each alteration, the following information was collected: age, gender, garment types, causes of alterations and corrective measures that were completed, to fix any problem. The Sunshine Foundation was founded in 1981 to provide professional recovery services for burn survivors which includes their physical, psychological, and social rehabilitation. Burn patients were referred to the pressure garment workshop of the Sunshine Foundation after being treated, diagnosed, and assessed by medical doctors at Taiwan hospital burn centers. A service team composed of 4 occupational therapists, 3 physical therapists, 2 sewing technicians, and 1 general assistant was made available to all burn patients. In 2006, a total of 2633 pressure garments were custom-made for 530 burn patients by the Sunshine Organization. This accounted for more than one-third of the total 1,458 of burn patients in 2006, assuming that all burn patients received pressure therapy.

Table 1. Pressure garment types produced and altered in 2006 and 2007

		Make	Alter-nation	Alternation vs. Made Ratio	Zipper	Hook	Velcro	Elastic Belt
2006	Mask	143	377	2.6	34	0	0	0
	Collar	92	53	0.6	0	0	12	0
	Vest	201	488	2.4	0	38	0	1
	Sleeves	594	1014	1.7	164	0	0	2
	Gloves	759	1145	1.5	182	0	0	0
	Pants	279	732	2.6	73	45	0	0
	Stockings	125	79	0.6	13	0	0	1
	Foot glove	435	432	1.0	51	0	0	0
	Finger glove	5	33	6.6	0	0	0	0
	Total	*2633*	*4353*	*1.65*	*517*	*83*	*12*	*4*
2007	Mask	159	452	2.8	32	1	0	0
	Collar	72	62	0.9	0	0	0	0
	Vest	248	580	2.3	0	68	0	17*
	Sleeves	753	1139	1.5	154	0	0	33*
	Gloves	969*	1299	1.3	229	0	0	0
	Pants	356*	725	2.0	73	71	0	0
	Stockings	98	66	0.7	16	0	0	4*
	Foot glove	538	569	1.1	49	0	0	0
	Finger glove	74	0	0.0	0	0	0	0
	Total	*3267*	*4892*	*1.5*	*553*	*140*	*0*	*54*

* Significant at 0.05 based on one-tail t statistic.

The design and fabrication of a pressure garment at the Sunshine Foundation followed the seven major stages: (1) patient measurement, (2) selection of garment design, (3) fabric selection, (4) drafting a pattern, (5) cutting a pattern from fabric, (6) sew the garment together, (7) fitting the garment to the patient, as described in Pratt & West (1995) with some variations to its sequence.

Alteration was at no extra cost for burn patients to ensure compliance. In 2006, about 4,353 alterations were made for various reasons, while only 2633 garments were made during this same period of time (See Table 1). Some garment types required a significant greater number of alterations, such as finger gloves (6.6 alterations), masks (2.6 alterations), pants (2.6 alterations), and vests (2.4 alterations). On an average, each pressure garment required 1.65 alterations. Regarding the 616 alterations which were made on the components, including zippers, hooks, Velcro and the elastic belt, the zippers in particular represented 84% of all components. Before the formal data collection stage, an open-ended descriptive survey was used to collect qualitative description on the causes and corrective measures of 40 alterations. After an extensive review of the collected survey and literature (Williams, Knapp & Wallen, 1998; Stewart, Bhagwanjee, Mbakaza, et al., 2000; Cheng, Chan, Fong, et al., 1996) and several discussions with the service team at the Sunshine Organization, the causes of garment alterations were categorized into major categories such as problems related to garment fit, garment comfort, component parts, fabric and sewing, and cosmetics. Each category was further divided into a hierarchical list of choices targeting potential improvements in the making of pressure garment and service processes (See Table 2). On the other hand, corrective measures were categorized into garment sewing, component alteration, cut hole or adjust the opening, and alter garment design, each followed by a list of choice as shown in Table 2. Eventually, a data collection form including personal information of the patient, and list of causes for alteration and corrective measures, along with a garment pattern chart was composed. The data collection form was filled out by 3 trained occupational therapists and 1 physical therapist, because burn patients or their caretakers could hardly verbalize these alterations.

2.2   Statistical Analyses

All recorded data was classified into useful categories for frequency distribution and other analyses. Cramer's V and Phi coefficient analysis, based on Chi-square, were used to examine the dependency trend between factors (Kurtz, 1999) and levels of factors, respectively. Where expected frequencies were less than 5, Fisher's exact test was used in place of Chi-square (Mehta, Patel, Senchaudhuri, 1992).

3   Results

The garment types and design options of 342 alterations were tabulated in Table 2. The majority of garment alterations were caused by poor fitting, particularly garment that were too loose (144 times), too tight (64 times), or change in body size (22), incorrect position or size of opening (12), too short (11), collar too high (9), too long (7), and garment displacement created by activity (7). It was found that some of these garments became too loose due to a gradual decline in the skin-and-garment interfacial pressure. For those garments that were too loose, too long, and too short cases, seven cases indicated that an error had occurred, especially when measuring gloves (2), pants (2), sleeves (2), and foot gloves (1). Some of these measurement errors were caused by the misreading of the figures. An incorrect garment pattern was indicated in 5 cases including masks (3 too loose, 1 too tight), and gloves (1 too loose). Other cases included missing the mix-axilla, when taking measurement for a sleeve or the reduction rate was incorrect when drafting the pants. Only about 20 alterations were caused by garment discomfort, such as excessive friction between garment and skin (10), uncomfortably hot to wear (4), difficult for open wound healing (3), difficult to put on or take off or use the toilet (3), and difficult for proper burn wound healing (3).

Table 2. Information collected on 127 burn patients and 342 garment alterations

Factor	Frequency	Percentage
Garment Type Gloves (gauntlet, mitten)	86	25.1
Vest (long-sleeved, short-sleeved, shoulder strap)	74	21.6
Panty and brief	57	16.7
Face mask, head band, chin strap	50	14.6
Sleeve (shoulder flap with sleeve)	40	11.7
Foot glove	23	6.7
Stocking and anklet	7	2.1
Collar	5	1.5
Causes of Garment Alterations		
Poor fit		
Too loose	144	29.8
Too tight	64	18.7
Change in body size	22	6.4
Incorrect position or size of opening	12	3.5
Too short	11	3.2
Neck collar too high	9	2.6
Too long	7	2.0
Garment displacement created by activity	7	2.0
Discomfort		
Excessive friction between garment and skin	10	2.9
Uncomfortably hot to wear	4	1.2
Difficult to put on and take off or use the toilet	3	0.9
Difficult for burn wound healing	3	0.9
Component part		
Poorly positioned component	9	2.6
Defective component	6	1.8
Fabric and sewing		
Tear/hole Wear/friction	18	5.3
Break in the seams	8	2.3
Cosmetics		
Exposed garment	5	1.5
Corrective measures		
Garment sewing		
Reduce circumstances to the problem area	135	39.5
Add circumstances to the problem area	50	14.6
Reduce length	25	7.3
Increase length	17	5.0
Mended holes /breaks in the seams	26	4.9
Adding double layer on a specific area	5	1.5
Insert soft lining over fragile area	4	1.2
Cut open along the seam	5	1.5
Component alterations		
Reposition the component	29	8.5
Insert or add a component	14	4.0
Replace component	6	1.8
Soft pad to fill up the concave area	6	1.8
Cut hole or adjust the size and position of opening	17	5.0
Alter design		
Alter sleeved vest into sleeveless	3	0.9

Association Between Factors And Between Levels of Factors. The Cramer's V coefficients indicate that significant associations exist between garment types and causes for alteration (V=0.32, p<0.01) and between causes of alteration and corrective measures (V=0.66, p<0.01). Table 3 identified the distinctive cause of alteration for each garment type. Garment too loose (30 cases, φ=0.15) and incorrect in size or the position of the opening (8 cases, φ=0.28) were significantly associated with alterations of the mask. These alterations of the mask which was too loose were mainly for the ears (7 cases), chin (7), neck (6), nose (3), and cheek (1). For incorrect sizes or positions of the opening, month (3), eyes (1), ears (1), and nose (1) were the major problem areas. Alteration of the collar was related to the Adam's apple or the fitting of another piece of garment, such as the mask (2 cases, φ=0.28).

Alterations for the vest was mainly associated with the collar being too high (7 cases, φ=0.22), uncomfortably hot to wear (3 cases, φ=0.14) or exposed garment (5 cases, φ=0.23). A machine operator, deliveryman and the mother of an active child reported that pressure garments were uncomfortably hot to wear. Neckline (4 cases) and sleeve (1 case) were examples causing the garment exposure problems and resulting in poor cosmetics.

Glove alterations were significantly associated with garments that were too short (6 cases, φ=0.12), poorly positioned zippers (5 cases, φ=0.12) and a break in the seam (6 cases, φ=0.18). Six clients whose garments were too short indicated that their gloves were too short in the little (2) and ring fingers (1), or they developed contracture and deformity in their knuckle (2), or it was not long enough to cover the scar on the back of their hand close to the wrist (1). These poorly positioned zippers were all caused by zippers being placed too close to the scar and resulted in pain and discomfort.

Alteration on pants was significantly associated with the difficulty of putting on and taking off of garments or when children wanted to use the toilet (3 cases, φ=0.21). Excessive friction was the cited main cause for the alteration of anklet (2 cases, φ=0.22) and complaints were actually about the zippers. Changes in body size was due to children growth process (4 cases), diminished edema (2 cases), and weight loss (1 case) resulted in the alteration of foot gloves (7 cases, φ=0.26). Clients reported sliding loose gloves and tightness of web space within gloves that were too loose or too tight, respectively. For vest garments that were too loose, under the arm pit, at the side of the breast, neckline, or shoulder were the major problem areas while arm pits, arms, shoulders, the stomach, and sleeve cuffs were related to vests that were too tight. Similarly, stomach, waist, buttock, calf, and lower leg problems were the major areas for both too tight and too loose fitting pants.

4   Discussion

This study developed a classification system in which to categorize the causes for alterations and to determine what areas need to be addressed for improving the quality of these garment. The result of our analysis indicated that the majority of pressure garment alterations were related to poor fitting in circumferential and longitudinal dimensions for various body parts. Therefore, it can be expected, that the fit affects the comfort and the wear life of a garment (Brown & Rice, 1988), and the fit is determined by pattern making and pattern making begins with the body measurements (Hudson, 1980). Fit is even more difficult to be achieved since in pressure garments, fit means applying sufficient pressure by fabric to have certain curative effects for each treatment stage (Ng, 1994). This finding leads us to look into the process of taking measurements of burn patients. In order to obtain detailed and correct measurements from the burn patients, a typical cycle for measuring garments includes burn scar assessment, selection of garment design, posture positioning, identification of landmarks, taking measurements, recording and checking measurements.

All occupational therapists and physical therapists at the Sunshine Foundation were required to have 36 hours of training regarding human body measurements including: human anatomy, garment fabrication, fabric design and analysis, measurement tools, and measurement skills. However, it was found that measurement errors cannot be fully prevented due to a number of factors which include subject positioning, imprecision in landmark location, and instrument applications (Meunier & Yin, 2000) which will be elaborated upon as follows. Some pressure garment manufacturers such

Table 3. Significant association between cause of alterations and garment types

	Mask	Collar	Vest	Gloves	Pants	Anklet	Foot glove	Sleeves
Garment too loose	30 0.15^{++}	2 $^f -0.01$	22 -0.13^*	33 -0.04	24 0.00	4 $^f 0.04$	10 0.01	19 0.04
Incorrect position of opening	8 $^f 0.28^{++}$	0	1 $^f -0.06$	0	3 $^f 0.04$	0	0	0
Neck collar too high	0	2 $^f 0.28^{++}$	7 $^f 0.22^{++}$	0	0	0	0	0
Uncomfortably hot to wear	0	0	3 $^f 0.14^+$	0	1 $^f 0.02$	0	0	0
Expose garment	0	0	5 $^f 0.23^{++}$	0	0	0	0	0
Garment too short	1 $^f -0.03$	0	0	6 $^f 0.12^+$	0	0	1 $^f 0.02$	3 $^f 0.09$
Poorly positioned component	0	1 $^f 0.13$	3 $^f 0.05$	5 $^f 0.12^+$	0	0	0	0
Break in the seams	0	0	2 $^f 0.01$	6 $^f 0.18^{++}$	0	0	0	0
Difficult to put on and take off	0	0	0	0	3 $^f 0.21^+$	0	0	0
Excessive friction against skin	0	0	4 $^f 0.08$	3 $^f 0.02$	0	2 $^f 0.22^+$	1 $^f 0.02$	0
Change in body size	2 $^f -0.04$	0	4 $^f -0.02$	4 -0.04	1 $^f -0.09$	0	7 $^f 0.26^{++}$	4 $^f 0.05$

In each cell, the three numbers give number of cases, the Cramer V value and significance level, respectively. Only cause with significant φ coefficients are listed.

++: φ value is positive and significant at 0.01.; +: φ value is positive and significant at 0.05.

**: φ value is negative and significant at 0.01. ; *: φ value is negative and significant at 0.05.

f: Fisher's exact test is used instead of φ.

as Bio-Concepts Inc. provided instructions on the correct body posture for measurement taking procedures including each body part. However, some burn patients in our study had difficulty maintaining the suggested posture for being measured. Also, the postural differences and breathing movement generate greater variability for waist and chest circumferences (Meunier & Yin, 2000) and caused measurement errors for pants and vests, respectively. Landmarks are placed on the body to assist with accurate measurements. The measurement reliability on female subjects was poorer than for those of males due to the difference in the amount and pattern of adiposity. Female bony landmarks are generally less developed than in males and thus more difficult to palpate (Bennett & Osborne, 1986). In our study, burn patients with body parts covered by fat tissue were found to have greater difficulties for obtaining reliable body measurements.

Regarding instrument applications, most measurements are taken with tapes and typically based on feel-by-hand, such as "use retractable tape to take circumference measurements and tighten the tape until it is snug but not snug enough to wrinkle the skin (Bio-Concepts Inc., 2003). In general, a portable 3-D computer graphics system is more accurate and consistent for taking body measurement, but the advantage are not outweighed due to its cost, to justify its practical use for collecting anthropometric data from burn patients. Regarding alterations pertaining to component or optional features, zippers seemed to be the major concern, since both the position and length of zipper are critical and can cause fitting or excessive friction problems because they are stiffer than the rest of the garment. After extensive discussion with members of the Sunshine Foundation workshop and one of the zipper manufacturers, problems associated with zippers can be roughly divided into: (1) the derailment of zipper or teeth, (2) inappropriate position or length of the zipper, and (3) the poor stitching quality of the zipper. Each may require additional data collection and analysis on garments with defective zippers to look for root causes and strategy for improvement.

Concerning the incorrect position and size of openings, eyes, nose, ears, and the mouth seemed to be the most difficult parts. Current work practice at the Sunshine Foundation is to mark opening positions on finished masks fitted directly on the client, then cutting the opening according to the marks on the garment to reduce errors. This work practice had shown to improve the problems with openings.The analysis regarding causes for alterations for pressure garments only stands as an initial step for a complete defect prevention program. Numerous changes had occurred because of the causal data of alterations collected by the occupational therapists and a physical therapist who designed and made the pressure garments. As a result of this defect analysis, the charts of eight major garment types initially designed to mark and collect the cause and location of the alterations had been developed into measurement charts for taking measurements. Figure 1 presents the measurement chart for the mask before and after the defect analysis was conducted. Besides, because of this defect analysis, service team members can learn from their mistakes and become aware of the quality status of their garments. Defect data on the pressure garments was collected between March and September in 2007. Data included monthly total made, alterations, alteration vs. made ratio, number of alterations on zipper, hooks, Velcro and elastic belts in 2007 was compared with those in 2006 to see if there was any significant change during and after the defect analysis had been conducted. From the paired t test statistics, it was found that the sleeves, gloves, and pants had a significant greater number of total made while mask and foot gloves had a significant greater number of total alterations, in 2007. Although no significant difference was found in the alteration vs. made ratio, the overall ratio had been reduced from 1.65 to 1.50. Alterations on finger gloves were eliminated since it was more feasible to construct new finger gloves. In the long run, since each of these causes can be directly related to the seven steps of garment making process for improving the design and manufacturing process, standardized operating procedure could be developed and modified gradually from findings of the causal analysis.

Landmark position	Size in inches or cm	Landmark position	Size in inches or cm	Landmark position	Size in inches or cm
a~b		f~g		f~d	
b~c		g~h		g~c	
c~d		h~i		h~b	
d~e		i~j		j~b	
e~f		j~k		k~a	
ℓ		c~m		Desired pressure	
		m~n			

Fig. 1. The mask measurement chart showing a before and after defect analysis

5   Conclusion

Three-hundred-and-forty-two alterations requested by 127 clients of the Sunshine Organization were collected and analyzed for the current study. A categorization system was developed to facilitate the coding and analysis of causes and corrective measures on pressure garment alterations for the improvement of the design, selection of fabric material, and workmanship for the making a pressure garment. The current study developed a systematic classification scheme for the causal analysis of identifiable causes regarding pressure garments produced by a Taiwan custom-made pressure garment workshop. This classification scheme and the analytical approach can be applied to the analysis of other custom–made or ready-to-wear pressure garment manufacturers.

References

1. Bennett, K.A., Osborne, R.H.: Interobserver measurement in anthropometry. Human Biology 58(5), 751–759 (1986)
2. Bio-Concepts Inc., Measuring for custom-made pressure garments. Bio-Concepts Inc., Phoenix (2003)
3. Brown, C.A.: A comparison of the outcomes of two clinical audits of burn pressure garment satisfaction and compliance in Saudi Arabia. Burns 27, 342–348 (2001)
4. Brown, P., Rice, J.: Ready-to-wear apparel analysis, 2nd edn. Prentice-Hall, Upper Saddle River (1998)

5. Cheng, S., Chan, A., Fong, S., Lam, M., Leung, A., Lee, P., Tsang, J., Wong, J., Wu, A.: Outcome studies for burn patients in Hong Kong: patients' satisfaction. Burns 22(8), 623–626 (1996)
6. Chi, C.-F., Chang, T.-C., Ting, H.-I.: Accident Patterns and Prevention Measures for Fatal Occupational Falls in the Construction Industry. Applied Ergonomics 36, 391–400 (2005)
7. Chi, C.-F., Yang, C.-C., Chen, Z.-L.: In-Depth Accident Analysis of Electrical Fatalities in the Construction Industry. International Journal of Industrial Ergonomics (2008) (in press)
8. Chillarege, R., Bhandari, I.S., Chaar, J.K., Halliday, M.J., Moebus, D.S., Ray, B.K., Wong, M.Y.: Orthogonal defect classification—A concept for in-process measurements. IEEE Transactions on Software Engineering 18(11), 943–955 (1992)
9. Hudson, P.B.: The role of fit and fashion in apparel quality. Bobbin 21(11), 108–122 (1980)
10. Johnson, J., Greenspan, B., Gorga, D., Nagler, W., Goodwin, C.: Compliance with pressure garment use in burn rehabilitation. Journal of Burn Care and Rehabilitation 15, 180–188 (1994)
11. Kroemer, K.H.E.: Engineering Anthropometry. In: Salvendy, G. (ed.) Handbook of Human Factors and Ergonomics. John Wiley & Sons, New York (1997)
12. Kurtz, N.: Statistical Analysis For The Social Sciences, p. 316. Allyn & Bacon, MA (1999)
13. Mays, R.G., Jones, C.L., Holloway, G.J., Studinski, D.P.: Experiences with defect prevention. IBM Systems Journal 29(1), 4–32 (1990)
14. Macintyre, L., Baird, M.: Pressure garments for use in the treatment of hypertrophic scars—an evaluation of current construction techniques in NHS hospitals. Burns 31, 11–14 (2005)
15. Macintyre, L., Baird, M.: Pressure garments for use in the treatment of hypertrophic scars—a review of the problems associated with their use. Burns 32, 10–15 (2006)
16. Mehta, C.R., Patel, N.R., Senchaudhuri, P.: Exact stratified linear rank tests for ordered categorical and binary data. J. Computational and Graphical Statistics 1, 21–40 (1992)
17. Meunier, P., Yin, S.: Performance of a 2D image-based anthropometic measurement and clothing sizing system. Applied Ergonomics 31, 445–451 (2000)
18. Ng-Yip, F.: Medical clothing-the stress relaxation and shrinkage of pressure garments. International Journal of Clothing Science and Technology 64, 17–27 (1994)
19. Pratt, J., West, G.: Pressure Garments: A manual on their design and fabrication. Butterworth-Heinemann Ltd., Oxford (1995)
20. Stewart, R., Bhagwanjee, A.M., Mbakaza, Y., Binase, T.: Pressure garment adherent in adult patients with burn injuries: An analysis of patient and clinician perceptions. The American Journal of Occupational Therapy 54(6), 598–606 (2000)
21. Ward, R.S.: Reasons for the selection of burn-scar-support suppliers by burn centers in the United States: a survey. Journal of Burn Care & Rehabilitation 14(3), 360–367 (1993)
22. Williams, F., Knapp, D., Wallen, M.: Comparison of the characteristics and features of pressure garments used in the management of burn scars. Burns 24, 329–335 (1998)
23. You, F., Wang, J.M., Luo, X.N., Li, Y., Zhang, X.: Garment's pressure sensation (1): subjective assessment and predictability for the sensation. International Journal of Clothing Science and Technology 14(5), 307–316 (2002)

Towards Enhancing the Acoustic Models for Dysarthric Speech

Kuruvachan K. George and C. Santhosh Kumar

Machine Intelligence Research Lab., Amrita School of Engineering, Amritanagar,
Coimbatore, India
kg_kuruvachan@cb.amrita.edu

Abstract. Dysarthria is a set of congenital and traumatic neuromotor disorders that impair the physical production of speech. These impairments reduce or remove the normal control of the vocal articulators. The acoustic characteristics of dysarthric speech is very different from the speech signal collected from a normative population, with relatively larger intra-speaker inconsistencies in the temporal dynamics of the dysarthric speech [1] [2]. These inconsistencies result in poor audible quality for the dysarthric speech, and in low phone/speech recognition accuracy. Further, collecting and labeling the dysarthric speech is extremely difficult considering the small number of people with these disorders, and the difficulty in labeling the database due to the poor quality of the speech. Hence, it would be of great interest to explore on how to improve the efficiency of the acoustic models built on small dysarthric speech databases such as Nemours [3], or use speech databases collected from a normative population to build acoustic models for dysarthric speakers. In this work, we explore the latter approach.

1   Introduction

Dysarthria [4] is a speech disorder due to a brain, nerve or muscle damage resulting in lack of control on the muscles of tongue, mouth, larynx or vocal cords that produce speech. The muscles may be weak, completely paralyzed, or the coordination between them might have failed. The speech of dysarthric patients is poorly audible, improperly pronounced, or without any rhythm or speed and of very poor quality. Due to the poor quality of dysarthric speech data, the performance of a speech recognition system build on speech data collected from the normative population will be very bad.

In most kinds of motor speech disorders articulatory gestures are typically slow, even when the speaking syllable rate is faster than normal as in the case of dysarthria associated with Parkinsons disease [1]. Speech temporal impairments can include unclear distinction between adjacent phonemes due to imprecise placement of articulators, slower speech rates, and rhythmic disturbances, to name a few [2]. Thus, it may be seen that the distorted temporal dynamics of the speech signal is one of the important reasons that causes degradation in the quality of dysarthric speech[2]. Further, it is also observed that formant trajectories of dysarthric patients are inconsistent across repetitions [1].

V.G. Duffy (Ed.): DHM/HCII 2013, Part I, LNCS 8025, pp. 183–188, 2013.
© Springer-Verlag Berlin Heidelberg 2013

There are many difficulties in building a good quality acoustic model for dysarthric speech:

1. Collecting large dysarthric database is extremely difficult, due to the small percentage of the population with this disorder.
2. Labeling dysarthric speech is extremely difficult due to the poor quality of the speech signal.

Yet, the importance of acoustic models for computer assisted recognition of dysarthric speech is no less important. Usually, people with dysarthria needs treatment from specialist clinics, mainly for the therapy sessions to improve the patient's speaking skills. Often, this means traveling long distances for the therapy. A good quality acoustic model, and fairly reasonable recognition accuracy can help build low cost computer assisted therapy tools for the dysarthric patients.

Since it is difficult to get large dysarthric speech databases for languages across the world, it would be of great interest if we can build acoustic models using speech databases of the normative population, and then transform these models to dysarthric speech for improved performance.

2   Maximum A Posteriori (MAP) Adaptation

Maximum a posteriori adaptation(MAP)[5] can be used for adapting the existing phone models. MAP is a speaker independent adaptation technique. It uses prior knowledge about the model parameters to adapt the present models. In this approach, model parameters are estimated and modified in such a way that the likelihood of the adaptation data to be generated by the adapted model is maximized. In MAP, the model parameter estimate is considered as a random variable, which has prior probability distribution. Using this prior probability, we calculate the posterior probability, the maximum posterior probability is considered as the adapted model estimates. The new model with adapted model parameters are generated with the MAP estimate, utilizing the knowledge about the prior parameters, weights and the adaptation data.

The update formula for a single stream system for state j and mixture component m is,

$$\hat{\mu}_{jm} = \frac{N_{jm}}{N_{jm} + \tau}\bar{\mu}_{jm} + \frac{\tau}{N_{jm} + \tau}\mu_{jm} \tag{1}$$

where τ is a weighting of the a priori knowledge to the adaptation speech data and N is the occupation likelihood of the adaptation data, defined as,

$$N_{jm} = \sum_{r=1}^{R}\sum_{t=1}^{T_r} L_{jm}^r(t) \tag{2}$$

where μ_{jm} is the speaker independent mean and $\bar{\mu}_{jm}$ is the mean of the observed adaptation data and is defined as,

$$\bar{\mu}_{jm} = \frac{\sum_{r=1}^{R}\sum_{t=1}^{T_r} L_{jm}^r(t)o_t^r}{\sum_{r=1}^{R}\sum_{t=1}^{T_r} L_{jm}^r(t)} \tag{3}$$

The amount of adaptation data required for MAP adaptation is relatively high. The performance goes down as the amount of adaptation data available becomes less. In this work the MAP adaptation is performed for the phone models trained on the speech data collected form normative population feeding sufficient amount of the adaptation data collected from dysarthric patients.

3   Maximum Likelihood Linear Regression(MLLR)

Unlike MAP adaptation, Maximum Likelihood Linear Regression(MLLR)[6] needs relatively less amount of adaptation data, and is usually used for speaker adaptation of the speaker independent acoustic model. In this technique, the parameters of the speaker independent (MAP adapted) phone models are modified based on the linear transformation (regression) matrix . MLLR adaptation makes use of the available adaptation data to formulate the regression matrix. This regression matrix is calculated and refined using the forward-backward algorithm [7] and it maximizes the likelihood of the adaptation data.

A particular distribution, s, is characterized by a mean vector, μ_s and a covariance matrix C_s. Given a parameterized speech frame vector o, the probability density of that vector being generated by distribution s is $b_s(o)$

$$b_s(o) = \frac{1}{(2\pi)^{n/2}|C_s|^{1/2}}e^{1/2(o-\mu_s)'C_s^{-1}(o-\mu_s)} \tag{4}$$

where n is the dimension of the observation vector.

The adaptation of the mean vector is achieved by applying a regression matrix W_s to the extended mean vector ξ_s to obtain an adapted mean vector $\hat{\mu}_s$

$$\hat{\mu}_s = W_s\xi_s \tag{5}$$

where W_s is an $n \times (n+1)$ matrix which maximizes the likelihood of the adaptation data, and ξ_s is defined as

$$\xi_s = [\omega, \mu_1, ..., \mu_n]' \tag{6}$$

where ω is the offset term for the regression.

For distribution s, the probability density function for the adapted system becomes

$$b_s(o) = \frac{1}{(2\pi)^{n/2}|C_s|^{1/2}}e^{1/2(o-W_s\xi_s)'C_s^{-1}(o-W_s\xi_s)} \tag{7}$$

In our work, we use MLLR technique to adapt only the mean vectors of the MAP adapted phone models as it requires relatively less training data compared to adapting mean, variance and mixture weights.

4   Experiments and Results

Our baseline system uses mel frequency cepstral coefficients(MFCC), with zero mean subtraction, and delta and acceleration coefficients appended. We use 13

MFCC coefficients, and this makes the total number of features in the acoustic model to 39. For training the acoustic models, we split the data speakerwise into training and test set. Training data consisted of data from speakers, BB, BK, BV, FB, JF, KS, LL. Speakers MH, RK, RL, and SC are used for testing. 20 per cent of the speech from every speaker is used for adaptation of the acoustic models, and the remaining 80 per cent for testing. Nemours database is phonetically transcribed using the TIMIT[1] transcriptions. The database is recorded at 16 kHz. Acoustic models trained on the training data are MLLR adapted using the adaptation data to generate the speaker dependent acoustic models. For small amounts of adaptation data, MAP adaptation was seen to be ineffective, and hence not MAP adaptation was not performed on this acoustic model. Table 1 lists the phone recognition accuracy of the acoustic model trained on Nemours data and tested on Nemours data, with and without adaptation.

Table 1. Phone recognition accuracy of the baseline acoustic model trained using the TIMIT, and Nemours databases on the Nemours test set

Train data	Adaptation	Accuracy
NEMOURS	NO	31.83%
NEMOURS	MLLR	36.31%

Next, we built another acoustic model using the TIMIT database, recorded at 16 kHz desktop quality speech. We then MAP adapted this acoustic model using the Nemours training data to transform the acoustic model from the normative population feature space to the dysarthric feature space. It was observed that the performance of the MAP adapted acoustic model is better than the baseline acoustic models trained using the Nemours database. Fig.1 illustrates schematically how different adaptation techniques are applied on the baseline system built using the TIMIT database. Table 2 lists the performance of the acoustic model trained on TIMIT, when tested without any adaptation, and with MAP, and MAP+MLLR adaptation using the Nemours data.

Table 2. Phone recognition accuracy after MLLR adaptation

Train data	Adaptation	Accuracy
TIMIT	NO	29.69%
TIMIT	MAP	32.67%
TIMIT	MAP + MLLR	39.61%

It may be noted from Tables 1 and 2 that training the acoustic model on speech data from a normative population, and adapting the models to the dysarthric

---

[1] http://www.ldc.upenn.edu/Catalog/LDC93S1.html

speech is better than training the models on the dysarthric speech. This is perhaps due to the ability of the acoustic models built using TIMIT to learn the consistent aspects of the speech better than the acoustic model trained using the Nemours database. Subsequently, adaptation transforms the models to the Nemours feature space for improved performance.

Fig. 1. Sequence of model training, adaptations and testing

All phone recognition experiments in this work are performed using a phone loop without using any language models. All phones has three states each, and evry phone state use 64 Gaussians to model the probability distribution, as this was found to be the optimum configuration empirically. No Gaussians are shared between phone states [8][9].

It may be noted that the performance of the acoustic models may be further enhanced by using bigram/trigram phone language models, or performing the experiments for word recognition with word language models. Using triphone acoustic models also may considerably enhance the phone recognition accuracy of the acoustic models.

5 Conclusion

Dysarthric phone/speech recognition has always been very challenging mainly due to the unavailability of enough amount of well labeled speech data, and the poor quality of the dysarthric speech. Often getting a labelled dyarthric speech database for many of the world languages is extremely difficult, if not impossible. It would be of great interest to explore building acoustic models using speech from a normative population that is much easily available, and then adapt these acoustic models using a small amount of dysarthric speech. It was seen that for small amounts of speech data, it is advantageous to train acoustic models on speech from a normative population and then adapt the acoustic models to the dysarthric feature space. By doing this, we may be able to get an improved phone recognition accuracy over a phone recognition system built on the dysarthric speech alone.

References

1. Weismer, G., Tjaden, K., Kent, R.D.: Can articulatory behavior in motor speech disorders be accounted for by theories of normal speech production? Journal of Phonetics 23, 149–164 (1995)

2. Duffy, J.: Motor Speech Disorders: Substrates, Differential Diagnosis, and Management. Mosby, St. Louis (2005)
3. Menendez-Pidal, X., Polikoff, J.B., Peters, S.M., Leonzio, J.E., Bunnell, H.T.: The Nemours database of Dysarthric speech. In: Proceedings of the Fourth International Conference on Spoken Language Processing, Philadelphia, USA (1996)
4. Murdoch, B.E. (ed.): Dysarthria: A Physiological Approach to Assessment and Treatment, ch. 1. Stanley Thornes Publishers Ltd., UK (1998)
5. Gauvain, J.L., Lee, C.H.: Maximum a posteriori estimation for multivariate Gaussian mixture obser-vations of Markov chains. IEEE Transactions on Speech and Audio Processing 2, 291–298 (1994)
6. Leggetter, C.J., Woodland, P.C.: Maximum likelihood linear regression for speaker adaptation of continuous density hidden Markov models. Computer Speech and Language 9, 171–185 (1994)
7. Young, S., Jansen, J., Odell, J., Ollason, D., Woodland, P.: The HTK book. Cambridge University Engineering Department, Cambridge (2003)
8. Deller, J.R., Hsu, D., Ferrier, L.J.: On the use of Hidden Markov Modelling for recognition of dysarthric speech. Computer Methods and Programs in Biomedicine 35, 125–139 (1991)
9. Reynolds, D.A.: A Gaussian Mixture Modeling Approach to Text-Independent Speaker Identification. Ph.D. thesis, Georgia Institute of Technology (1992)

Supporting a Participant-Centric Management of Obesity via a Self-improving Health Game*

Philippe J. Giabbanelli[1,2], Penny Deck[2], Lisa Andres[4], Thecla Schiphorst[3], and Diane T. Finegood[2]

[1] MoCSSy Program, Interdisciplinary Research in the Mathematical and Computational Sciences (IRMACS) Centre
[2] Department of Kinesiology and Biomedical Physiology
[3] School of Interactive Arts and Technology
Simon Fraser University, Canada
[4] IgnitePlay
{giabba,pennyd,thecla,finegood}@sfu.ca,
lisaandres@igniteplay.com

Abstract. A majority of American and Canadian adults are currently obese or overweight. Despite the urgency in tackling this issue, current interventions have not yet been able to provide sustainable weight loss, in part due to the difficulty of maintaining engagement over an extended period of time. Emerging trends in self-management have led to the design of new health tools in HCI that can improve individual engagement. In this paper, we propose to combine health games with recommender systems. The former has a demonstrated ability in promoting behaviour change, while the latter is able to personalize user experience. This approach goes beyond traditional health games, as the recommender system's personalization provides players with options tailored to the specific factors shaping their weight, thereby allowing for a high degree of customization which is sought after but difficult to achieve in weight interventions. Focusing on what matters for each individual can also be used to initiate dialogue with a health-care provider, which sets the stage for increased agreement on treatment and can lead to improved health outcomes.

1 Introduction

Obesity is a major public health issue in Canada and other developed countries, associated with a reduced quality of life for individuals and an increasing health-care cost to society [1, 2]. As obesity is a chronic disease, long-term support is critical. Current interventions struggle to maintain successful weight loss beyond one to a few years [3]. One of the reasons for this failure lies in the difficulty of sustaining engagement of individuals. Emerging trends in self-management suggest that engagement may be increased by creating interventions that integrate patients' values, experiences and perspectives [4].

---

* Research funded by the Canadian Institutes of Health Research (MT-10574). We thank the MoCSSy Program for providing facilities.

Achieving such an integration is highly complex given the tremendous heterogeneity of obese individuals [5, 6]. Existing interventions address this complex problem by using simple and generic solutions that "would be sufficient only for those individuals who receive the appropriate intervention by chance" [7]. Practitioners have acknowledged that the wide diversity of obese individuals requires comprehensive tools that explore the myriad factors relevant to an individual's weight [8]. The design of such new health tools is seen in HCI through the increasing focus on personalization of user experience [9].

A *Recommender System* is the approach of choice when searching for a relevant item (*e.g.*, what a patient values) among a very large choice (*e.g.*, the set of all values that patients could have). Recommendation algorithms are at the core of websites such as Amazon, which are able to suggest relevant items to users based on information about their past purchases [10]. Therefore, they could be used to automatically and quickly elicit what matters to patients; whereas the same task would be challenging and very time consuming for practitioners. In this paper, we propose to embed recommender systems in *Health Games* [11], which are games that aim to improve a dimension of health such as the player's physical or emotional well-being. Previous research has found that games promoting healthy behaviour change are associated with positive outcomes [11] such as an increase in knowledge and change in attitude [12]. There has been little research within HCI that explores recommender systems which use a customer's psychosocial and demographic characteristics to promote self-management of healthy activity. Our framework combines the ability of recommender systems to find relevant factors with the strength of Health Games to motivate individuals to act on those factors. Such a tool can contribute to address patient diversity in weight-loss interventions, providing a personalized experience that improves long-term engagement.

1.1 Contribution of the Paper

The principal contributions of the present work can be summarized as follows:

- We detail the design of an innovative combination of health game and recommender system to find and act on factors relevant to individuals' weight.
- While health games focus on diet and physical activity, our combination allows them to take a comprehensive approach to individuals' weight-being.
- The combination that we suggest can improve our understanding of heterogeneity and support sustained behaviour changes.

1.2 Organization of the Paper

The rationale and key technical details of our framework are summarized in Section 2. Its implementation is exemplified in Section 3 via the case of the health game *IgnitePlay*. Finally, we discuss the potential of the framework in supporting a participant-centric management of obesity.

2 Framework

Our architecture at the intermediate level is summarized in Figure 1. The health game collects information on participants' psycho-social factors via entertaining activities.

This information serves to identify relevant factors for the individual and suggest evidence-based steps for change. This tool capitalizes on the potential of intrinsic motivation to support efficient interventions. The information collected by the health game is also passed on to a recommender engine which uses sophisticated data mining techniques to predict the psycho-social factors most relevant to an individual based on observed behaviour, allowing the game to adapt to the participant. Further, the integration of this information into mobile and desktop software utilizes the engine's ability to quickly tailor factors in order to support primary care practitioners in performing comprehensive assessments of their patients. This directly addresses the need stated by practitioners for algorithms that are able to explore the maze of psycho-social factors contributing to obesity [8]. Finally, the game offers support for monitoring improvements and can deliver regular reports to both the practitioners and patients, thereby facilitating continuous communication as well as increasing the efficacy of treatment via self-monitoring.

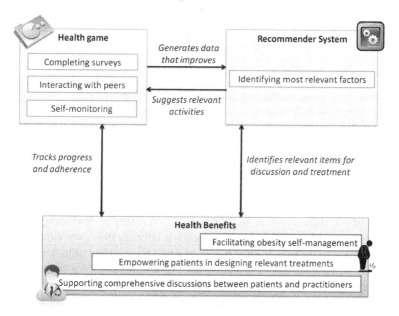

Fig. 1. Intermediate level workflow

Technical details on the health game independently of the other components illustrated in Figure 1 can be found in [13]. In order to ensure a seamless linkage between the health game and the recommendation engine, we need to efficiently extract relevant factors from in-game behaviour. Performing correlations between the given player's behaviour and the behaviour of all other players is straightforward (e.g., using Pearson's correlation coefficient or cosine similarity) but prohibitive time-wise. Therefore, we use techniques developed to ensure real-time answers and modest hardware requirements. Intuitively, these techniques spend time organizing the data (e.g., when there is a low-load on the server) so that recommendations can be quickly performed (e.g., at peak time). Practically, the similarity between game activities is computed before intensively requesting the recommender system to infer a player's liking of activities that have not been tried yet. The inferred answer is then estimated using the player's past behaviour on activities that have been tried, and the similarity of these activities to the activity that has not been tried (Figure 2). The efficiency of the recommender system in regard with the game will be examined by means including assessing the participant attitudes through Quality of Life (QOL) metrics utilizing self-monitoring techniques [14, 15]. The contribution of the recommender system to facilitating discussions between practitioners and participants will also be analyzed by comparing QOL metrics prior and after integration of the tool.

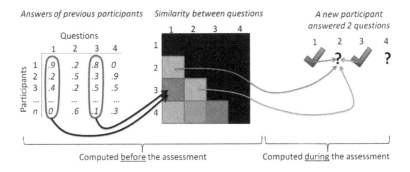

Fig. 2. Key steps in an item-based nearest neighbor recommendation system

3   Implementation: The Case of *IgnitePlay*

IgnitePlay, a Canadian company, is creating *SpaPlay*, a social game that makes it fun for users to adopt a healthy lifestyle. *SpaPlay* uses mixed reality by rewarding players with points for doing healthy real-world activities while building their own virtual island spa resort (Figure 3). As the player earns points, she will level up and unlock spa buildings, site features, mini-games and virtual currency. Players will also earn coupons for products and services that support their healthy lifestyle by leveling up in the game. Players can earn points for doing spontaneous activities like climbing the stairs or eating a piece of fruit (Sparks). They can also earn points by going on health Quests which allow them to do a series of activities towards a common goal. In the beginning the player will level up quite easily and receive frequent rewards but as she improves, she will need to do a greater number of Sparks and Quests to achieve subsequent levels. This leveling up and reward system provides the player will a greater amount of extrinsic motivation in the beginning when it is required but allows the player to rely more on intrinsic motivation as she starts to see improvements in her health and well being.

A pilot evaluation of this design was conducted on 14 female volunteers, aged 25 to 50, and concluded that the game "showed initial success [...] to hook and sustain participant's interest" [13]. Monitoring the most recent version of the game over the past two months confirmed these earlier findings. Figure 4 shows that the total number of activities played is increasing as the game is being deployed, while the estimated number

Fig. 3. Main user interface in *IgnitePlay*

of weekly activities per user remains in a range that suggests a sustained interaction. In particular, player engagement for the IgnitePlay alpha product was found to be high compared to what is expected for mature social games. Playnomics Quaterly US Player engagement study for the third quarter of 2012[1] found that only 5% of players acquired at the beginning of the quarter were still active, whereas for IgnitePlay 15% of testers either remained for a whole quarter or leveled up to the maximum level available in the beta product at the time. Furthermore, 23% of IgnitePlay players returned after one day which is comparable to that of other social games which is 25%.

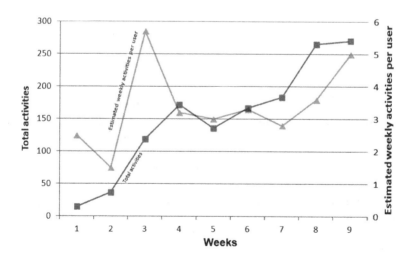

Fig. 4. Weekly trends of *IgnitePlay* since January 2013

The results suggest that this game could be beneficial to sustain the engagement of its target population, primarily adult obese women. The game has made room for

---

[1] http://www.insidesocialgames.com/wp-content/uploads/2012/10/ Playnomics_Q3-report_Final-copy.pdf

recommended activities (Figure 5), which are currently implemented using a heuristic. Moving to the recommender system detailed in Figure 2 would yield several benefits compared to the current implementation. First, a recommender system is able to navigate through the maze of the many possible factors that could shape one's weight: using it would lead to a more comprehensive set of activities, beyond the usual 'move more and eat better' approach. Second, it is important to clarify why a user should follow a recommendation, and recommender systems can highlight the logic behind the result (*e.g.*, "90% of those who enjoy doing this activity like you also enjoyed doing this spark"). These benefits could reinforce the game's ability to sustain engagement, while benefiting the player's weight management.

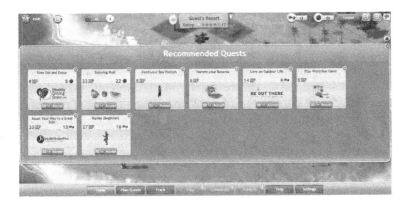

Fig. 5. *IgnitePlay*'s current recommendations, centred on physical activity and nutrition

4   Discussion

Most adults in Canada and the United-States are currently obese or overweight. The inadequacy of current interventions is partly due to the difficulty of sustaining long term engagement. Novel solutions in HCI can contribute to facing this challenge. In this paper, we proposed to develop and test a tool which combines a health game and recommender system in order to support adults in a sustained weight management. This tool capitalizes on the ability of Health Games to promote behaviour change, and combines it with the strength of recommender systems to find factors that matter to individuals. While the primary participant is the player, the resulting game should also be viewed in relation to the broader health-care system. In particular, the game could benefit the patient-practitioner communication.

Communication with a health care provider is an essential component to fostering patient empowerment and personalization of care [16, 17]. Impaired communication reduces empowerment, and has an array of negative effects such as patient dissatisfaction and the failure to provide personalized weight interventions [18–20]. Research has shown that a key component of successful communication is agreement between health care providers and patients [21, 22]. The proposed Health Game allows for identification of the unique combination of factors that are most relevant to each individual. This facilitates patients' ability to articulate their individual needs, in turn opening channels for improved communication with practitioners and supporting patient empowerment.

Focusing on the factors that shape an individual's weight offers the degree of customization needed to adequately address the heterogeneity of obese adults. This heterogeneity is currently poorly understood, and exposing practitioners to it can encourage a shift in their perceptions about obesity away from a "one-size-fits-all" approach. By collecting a vast amount of data from players, the game can also be key to a better understanding of heterogeneity. The initial database on which the recommender system would rely is currently being collected [6], but only its automatic update by the proposed system is necessary to ensure the system's relevance over time.

5 Conclusion

Health games have been increasingly popular but typically focused on diet and physical activity. This project utilizes health games together with recommender systems to face the specific needs of obesity: a comprehensive assessment of the driver shaping one's weight, which will improve on our understanding of heterogeneity and support the design of relevant treatments.

References

1. Anis, A., Zhang, W., Bansback, N., Guh, D., Amarsi, Z., Birmingham, C.: Obesity and over-weight in canada: an updated cost-of-illness study. Obesity Reviews 11(1), 31–40 (2010)
2. Wang, Y., Beydoun, M., Liang, L., Caballero, B., Kumanyika, S.: Will all americans become overweight or obese? estimating the progression and cost of the us obesity epidemic. Obesity 16, 2323–2330 (2008)
3. Obesity in canada: a joint report from the public health agency of canada and the canadian institute for health information (2011),
   http://www.phac-aspc.gc.ca/hp-ps/hl-mvs/oic-oac/assets/pdf/oic-oac-eng.pdf
4. Carman, K.L., Dardess, P., Maurer, M., Sofaer, S., Adams, K., Bechtel, C., Sweeney, J.: Patient and family engagement: a framework for understanding the elements and developing interventions and policies. Health Affairs 32(2), 223–231 (2013)
5. Harkaway, J.: Obesity and systems research: the complexity of studying complexities. Families, Systems and Health 18(1), 55–59 (2000)
6. Deck, P., Giabbanelli, P.J., Finegood, D.T.: Exploring the heterogeneity of factors associated with weight management in young adults. Third National Obesity Summit (2013)
7. Epstein, L., Myers, M., Raynor, H., Saelens, B.: Treatment of pediatric obesity. Pediatrics 101(2), 554–570 (1998)
8. Sharma, A., Padwal, R.: Obesity is a sign - over-eating is a symptom: an aetiological framework for the assessment and managment of obesity. Obesity Reviews 11(5), 362–370 (2009)
9. Dubberly, H., Mehta, R., Evenson, S., Pangaro, P.: Reframing health to embrace design of our own well-being. Interactions, 56–63 (2000)
10. Jannach, D., Zanker, M., Felfernig, A., Friedrich, G.: Recommender Systems: An introduction. Cambridge University Press (2011)
11. Ferguson, B.: The emergence of games for health. Games for Health Journal 1(1), 1–2 (2012)

12. Baranowski, T., Baranowski, J., Cullen, K., Marsh, T., Islam, N., Zakeri, I., Honess-Morreale, L., deMoor, C.: Squire's quest! dietary outcome evaluation of a multimedia game. American Journal of Preventive Medicine 24(1), 52–61 (2003)

13. El-Nasr, M., Andres, L., Lavender, T., Funk, N., Jahangiri, N., Sun, M.: Igniteplay: Encouraging and sustaining healthy living through social games. In: 2011 IEEE International Games Innovation Conference (IGIC), pp. 23–25 (November 2011)

14. Chu, K., Wong, C.Y., Khong, C.W.: Methodologies for evaluating player experience in game play. In: Stephanidis, C. (ed.) Posters, Part I, HCII 2011. CCIS, vol. 173, pp. 118–122. Springer, Heidelberg (2011)

15. Hori, Y., Baba, A.: Evaluation and classification of digital games using qol measurements. In: 2010 IEEE International Conference on Virtual Environments Human-Computer Interfaces and Measurement Systems (VECIMS), pp. 93–98 (September 2010)

16. Anderson, R.M., Funnell, M.M.: Patient empowerment: Myths and misconceptions. Patient Educ. Couns. 79(3), 277–282 (2010)

17. Alpay, L., van der Boog, P., Dumaij, A.: An empowerment-based approach to developing innovative e-health tools for self-management. Health Informatics J. 17(4), 247–255 (2011)

18. van den Brink-Muinen, A., Verhaak, P., Bensing, J., Bahrs, O., Deveugele, M., Gask, L., Leiva, F., Mead, N., Messerli, V., Oppizzi, L., Peltenburg, M., Perez, A.: Doctor-patient communication in different european health care systems: relevance and performance from the patients' perspective. Patient Educ. Couns. 39(1), 115–127 (2000)

19. van den Brink-Muinen, A., Verhaak, P., Bensing, J., Bahrs, O., Deveugele, M., Gask, L., Nead, N., Leiva-Fernandez, F., Perez, A., Messerli, V., Oppizzi, L., Peltenburg, M.: Communication in general practice: differences between european countries. Fam. Pract. 20(4), 478–485 (2003)

20. Zolnierek, K.B.H., DiMatteo, M.R.: Physician communication and patient adherence to treatment: a meta-analysis. Med. Care 47(8), 826–834 (2009)

21. Starfield, B., Wray, C., Hess, K., Gross, R., Birk, P., D'Lugoff, B.: The influence of patient-practitioner agreement on outcome of care. Am. J. Public Health 71(2), 127–131 (1981)

22. Krupat, E., Rosenkranz, S., Yeager, C., Barnard, K., Putnam, S., Inui, T.: The practice orientations of physicians and patients: the effect of doctor-patient congruence on satisfaction. Patient Educ. Couns. 39(1), 49–59 (2000)

Feedback-Based Self-training System of Patient Transfer

Zhifeng Huang[1], Ayanori Nagata[1], Masako Kanai-Pak[2], Jukai Maeda[2],
Yasuko Kitajima[2], Mitsuhiro Nakamura[2], Kyoko Aida[2],
Noriaki Kuwahara[3], Taiki Ogata[1], and Jun Ota[1]

[1] Research into Artifacts, Center for Engineering (RACE),
The University of Tokyo, Chiba, Japan
[2] Faculty of Nursing, Tokyo Ariake University of Medical and Health Sciences, Tokyo, Japan
[3] Department of Advanced Fibro-Science, Kyoto Institute of Technology, Kyoto, Japan
zhifeng@race.u-tokyo.ac.jp

Abstract. In this paper, we propose a self-training system to assist nursing students to learn nursing skills. The system focuses on the task of transferring a patient from a bed to a wheelchair. In the system, two Kinect sensors were applied to measure the posture of the trainees and patients and an automatic evaluation method was used to classify the trainees' performance in each skill as correct or incorrect. A feedback interface based on a checklist was designed to help the trainees check whether they performed correctly. The system is designed for the trainees to operate by themselves. A control test was performed to measure the training effects of the system. The results show that the growth rate of the group that trained with feedback (79%) was higher than the group that trained without feedback (48%).

Keywords: self-training system, patient transfer, Kinect sensor, nursing skills, feedback.

1 Introduction

In a nurse's daily work, many physical tasks are related to lifting or moving patients, such as bathing, dressing, and transferring a patient from a bed to a wheelchair [1]. In carrying out these heavy-workload tasks, it is easy to cause injury to both the patient and the nurse [2–4]. In order to avoid these problems, nurses need to concentrate on the patient and also apply their nursing skills. However, it can be difficult for nursing students to master the many complicated skills required. As a result, it is important to find an efficient way to help nursing students to learn these skills. One solution is to provide a self-training system that can monitor the performance of trainees automatically and then instruct them to improve their nursing skills.

Previous studies of nursing skills have focused mainly on the analysis of nurses' motion [5], economic evaluation [6, 7], or patient comfort [8], but none have involved the construction of a self-training system. However, training systems have been proposed for a variety of other physical tasks such as worker posture [9], aerobics

V.G. Duffy (Ed.): DHM/HCII 2013, Part I, LNCS 8025, pp. 197–203, 2013.

[10], dance [11], and Tai Chi [12]. Yet these systems were limited as they were designed for a single person. Currently, no research focuses on a physical multiperson task.

To achieve our long-term goal, and focusing on the nursing skills of transferring a patient from a bed to a wheelchair, we initially developed a sensor system to measure and evaluate the performance of trainees based on Kinect sensors [13, 14]. However, a feedback method and interface were not involved. Therefore, the aim of this study was to provide a feedback method for instructing trainees to improve their nursing skills when transferring a patient from a bed to a wheelchair. In addition, an interface was proposed to enable trainees to operate the system themselves. Thus, the trainees could train themselves with the system.

The paper is structured as follows: Section 2 details the proposed the system composition, automatic evaluation method, the interface and the feedback method; Section 3 describes the experimental setup and the results; and Section 4 is our conclusion.

2   Methods

2.1   Overview of the Self-training System

A prototype self-training system for patient transfer was proposed (Fig. 1(a)). The system comprised a multi-Kinect sensor system, a liquid crystal display, a mouse, and a keyboard.

The multi-Kinect sensor system was designed to measure the posture information of trainees and patients, and the states of the wheelchair. The sensor system contained two Kinect sensors (Microsoft, Fig. 1(b)), two computers, and a router. One sensor was installed on the ceiling, and the other was set up at the side of the bed. The connected computers recorded and processed the data of each Kinect sensor, respectively. In order to synchronize the image data from the two sensors, the computer was connected to a router and communication was based on the Transmission Control Protocol / Internet Protocol.

The liquid crystal display, the mouse, and the keyboard constituted the operation interface for trainees to manipulate the system and to review the feedback results.

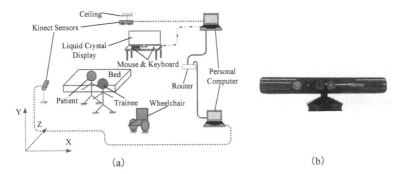

(a)   (b)

Fig. 1. System architecture: (a) the schematic of the system; (b) the Kinect sensor

2.2   Automatic Evaluation Method for Patient's Performance

To indicate the performance of the trainees as correct or incorrect in each evaluation item, an automatic evaluation method [13, 14] was performed. In the method, color markers were attached to the body joints of both trainees and patients for posture measurement (Fig. 3(c)). First, using the order of the skills and the features of the three-dimensional trajectory of the patients' heads, the trainees' motions were recognized to identify the images where the skills were performed. Second, according to each item, the related posture information of both patients and trainees was measured by combining the color and the depth information. For example, the three-dimensional positions of the trainees' waists were measured for checking whether the trainees lowered the center of gravity of their bodies. Finally, according to the contents of the items, two methods were carried out to classify the performance of the trainees as correct or incorrect. One method was to detect whether the related body joints were inside the predefined region (Fig. 3(a) and (b)), and the other used the thresholds determined in our previous experiment [13] (Fig. 3(c) and (d)).

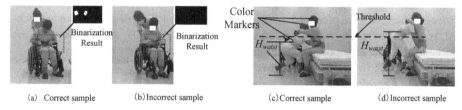

(a) Correct sample   (b) Incorrect sample   (c) Correct sample   (d) Incorrect sample

H_{waist}: Height of the nursing student's waist

Fig. 2. Examples of the evaluation methods. In (a) and (b), a trainee's performance is classified by detecting whether the target body joints are inside the predefined region; (a) correct sample: the trainee grasped the patient's forearm; (b) incorrect sample: the trainee grasped the patient's abdomen. In (c) and (d), a trainee's performance is judged by a threshold determined in [13]; (c) correct sample: the trainee's waist is low enough; (d) incorrect sample: the trainee's waist is too high

2.3   Operation Interface

The trainees themselves could operate the interface, using the mouse and the "Esc" key to manipulate the system. The interface used five images that indicated the system's five stages. The images were displayed on the screen according to the trainees' operation. Fig. 3 depicts the flow chart of the interface. First, when the system was started, a guidance image appeared describing the system's operation. Next, the trainees clicked the "Start" button on the screen to inform the system that training was to commence. Then the system recorded the image sequences of the training process. When the training process was finished, the trainees went back to the screen and clicked the "Stop" button. Thus, the system stopped recording and started to evaluate the performance of the trainees and display the feedback. When the trainees were ready to train again, they could click the button inside the feedback image and return to the preparation image for the next training session.

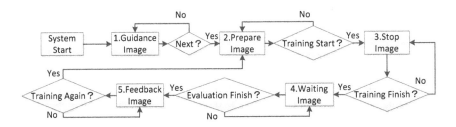

Fig. 3. Flow chart of the operation interface

2.4   Feedback Method

As we described in Section 1, nurses need to concentrate on the patient's state during the transfer process. The feedback should not distract trainees during the transfer process. Therefore, we proposed an asynchronous feedback method based on a checklist and demonstration video. The checklist included 20 skills. All results from the skills' evaluation were provided after the trainees had finished the transfer process.

The feedback image comprised five parts (Fig. 4): 1) the total result (percentage-complete) of all skills to give the trainees an overview of their performance; 2) the evaluation result of each skill to help trainees check whether they performed in the correct way; 3) a list detailing each skill; 4) the buttons, including a "Full Demo"

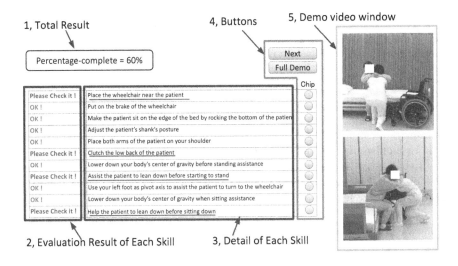

Fig. 4. The feedback image

button to review the demonstration of the entire process, the "Chip" buttons to review each skill's corresponding demonstration, and a "Next" button to start the next training; and 5) a window for displaying the demonstration videos. In the checklist, each item was indicated as correct or incorrect. For a correct performance, an "OK!" label was attached to the corresponding skill. If trainees performed the skill incorrectly, a "Please Check it!" label and the underlined in red was attached.

3   Evaluation of the Proposed System

3.1   Purpose

A control test was carried out to examine whether the system helped trainees to improve their skills compared with using a textbook and demonstration videos without any feedback on their performance.

3.2   Participants

Ten freshman nursing students were employed as the trainees. The students were assigned randomly into an experimental group and a control group, each having five students. A woman, 160 cm in height, was employed as the mock patient who was assumed unable to stand up on her own but could maintain a standing posture once she had been assisted to her feet.

3.3   Procedures

The experimental environment was set up in the training rooms of Tokyo Ariake University of Medical and Health Science (TAU) to simulate a patient room. To simulate the self-training, only the trainees and the mock patient were inside the training rooms.

The experiment comprised four sections: i) Learning period; ii) Pretest; iii) Training period; and iv) Posttest. First, each group was given 7 minutes to learn the skills of patient transfer. This amount of time enabled the trainees to watch the demonstration video at least twice. To ensure uniformity of the learning conditions, the textbook and demonstration video from TAU were used as the teaching materials. Next, each group took the pretest to record their initial scores. The students were then asked to perform the patient transfer in 20 minutes. The experimental group trained with the proposed system, while the control group trained without any feedback, but could use the textbook and demonstration video to review the skills freely. Finally, the students took the posttest to record their final scores.

A nursing teacher evaluated the pretest and posttest using the same checklist described in Section 2.4. The teacher evaluated the performance of trainees in each task and indicated whether they were correct or incorrect. Students scored one point for every correct task and no points for incorrect tasks. Thus, the full score of the checklist was 20 points.

3.4   Results and Discussion

Table 1 shows the scores of the pretests and posttests in each group. Fig. 5 depicts the average improvements. In the experimental group, the average score of the pretest was 8.6 (SD = 3.0) and the average score of the posttest was 15.4 (SD = 2.5). In the control group, the average score of the pretest was 9.6 (SD = 4.2) and the average score of the posttest was 14.2 (SD = 2.5).

Equation 1 defines the growth rate, G_r, of the average score:

$$G_r = \frac{\overline{S}_{post} - \overline{S}_{pre}}{\overline{S}_{pre}}. \tag{1}$$

Here, $\overline{S}_{pre}$ is the average score of the pretest and $\overline{S}_{post}$ is the average score of the post-test. The growth rates of the experimental and control groups were 79% and 48%, respectively.

The result of the control test revealed that participants who trained with feedback from the system progressed more quickly than those without feedback. Although the individual score increased in each group, the increase in the experimental group was more stable than that of the control group. In the control group, the improvement in the skills depended more on the individual trainee.

Table 1. Results of the pretest and posttest for each group

Experimental Group				Control Group			
Participant	Pre	Post	Increase	Participant	Pre	Post	Increase
1	11	17	8	1	10	14	4
2	9	14	5	2	4	10	6
3	6	14	8	3	13	16	3
4	12	19	7	4	14	16	2
5	5	13	8	5	7	15	8

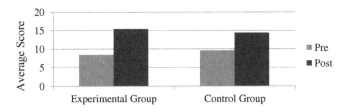

Fig. 5. The average pretest and posttest scores for each group

4   Conclusion

In this paper, a self-training system was proposed for assisting nursing students to improve their skills with a focus on transferring a patient from a bed to a wheelchair. The system was able to check automatically as correct or incorrect the performance of trainees in each skill. The nursing students could view their evaluation results using the feedback method, which was based on a checklist. In addition, the system was designed to be operated by the students themselves. The control test results highlighted the benefits of the proposed self-training system. In the experimental group (utilizing the system), the growth rate of the average score was up to 79%. This rate was higher than that for the control group (48%), where students trained without any feedback.

Acknowledgements. This work was supported by MEXT/JSPS KAKENHI (23593194, 24300079).

References

1. Garg, A., Owen, B.D., Carlson, B.: An Ergonomic Evaluation of Nursing Assistants' Job in a Nursing Home. Ergonomics 35, 979–995 (1992)
2. Menzel, N.N., Brooks, S.M., Bernard, T.E., Nelson, A.: The Physical Workload of Nursing Personnel: Association with Musculoskeletal Discomfort. Int. J. Nurs. Stud. 41, 859–867 (2004)
3. Smedley, J., Egger, P., Cooper, C., Coggon, D.: Manual Handling Activities and Risk of Low Back Pain in Nurses. Occup. Environ. Med. 52, 160–163 (1995)
4. Hignett, S.: Work-related Back Pain in Nurses. J. Adv. Nurs. 23, 1238–1246 (1996)
5. Hignett, S.: Posture analysis of nursing work. Appl. Ergon. 27, 171–176 (1996)
6. Garg, A., Owen, B., Beller, D., Banaag, J.: A Biomechanical and Ergonomic Evaluation of Patient Transferring Tasks: Bed to Wheelchair and Wheelchair to Bed. Ergonomics 34, 289–312 (1991)
7. Garg, A., Owen, B., Beller, D., Banaag, J.: A Biomechanical and Ergonomic Evaluation of Patient Transferring Tasks: Wheelchair to Shower Chair and Shower Chair to Wheelchair. Ergonomics 34, 407–419 (1991)
8. Kjellberg, K., Lagerstrom, M., Hagberg, M.: Patient Safety and Comfort During Transfers in Relation to Nurses' Work Technique. J. Adv. Nurs. 47, 251–259 (2004)
9. Ray, S.J., Teizer, J.: Real-time Construction Worker Posture Analysis for Ergonomics Training. Adv. Eng. Inform. 26, 439–455 (2012)
10. Davis, J.W., Bobick, A.F.: Virtual PAT: A Virtual Personal Aerobics Trainer. In: Workshop on Perceptual User Interface (1998)
11. Chan, J.C.P., Leung, H., Tang, J.K.T., Komura, T.: A Virtual Reality Dance Training System Using Motion Capture Technology. IEEE Trans. Learn. Technol. 4, 187–195 (2011)
12. Chua, P.T., Crivella, R., Daly, B., Hu, N., Schaaf, R., Ventura, D., Camill, T., Hodgins, J., Pausch, R.: Training for Physical Tasks in Virtual Environments: Tai Chi. In: Proceedings of 2003 Virtual Reality, Pittsburgh, pp. 87–94 (2003)
13. Huang, Z., Nagata, A., Kanai-Pak, M., Maeda, J., Kitajima, Y., Nakamura, M., Aida, K., Kuwahara, N., Ogata, T., Ota, J.: Development of a Nursing Self-training System for Transferring Patient from Bed to Wheelchair. In: Proceedings of the SICE Annual Conference, Akita, pp. 246–254. SICE (2012)
14. Huang, Z., Nagata, A., Kanai-Pak, M., Maeda, J., Kitajima, Y., Nakamura, M., Aida, K., Kuwahara, N., Ogata, T., Ota, J.: Posture Study for Self-training System of Patient Transfer. In: Proceedings of IEEE International Conference Robotics and Biomimetics (ROBIO 2012), Guangzhou, pp. 842–847. IEEE (2012)

A Comparative Analysis of the Educational Effectiveness of Leaflet and Website for Low-Literate Patients – A Case Study of Immigrant Mothers in Taipei

Yah-Ling Hung[1], Kai-Ren Chen[2], Catherine Stones[3], and Thomas Cassidy[3]

[1] Dept. of Communication Arts, Fu Jen Catholic University, Taiwan
[2] Dept. of Public Health, Fu Jen Catholic University, Taiwan
[3] School of Design, University of Leeds, UK
030872@mail.fju.edu.tw

Abstract. Low health literacy has been associated with poor outcomes in health care. Recent research suggests that good health educational material can help to reduce the literacy barrier and enhance health outcome. Immigrant populations are vulnerable to serious health disparities, and language barriers may further exacerbate their limited health literacy in accessing health care information. Yet, ways to help low-literacy parents to look after their children by applying health educational material are still at an early stage of development. The purpose of this study is to compare the educational effectiveness of leaflet and website to deliver knowledge related to children allergy healthcare for immigrant mothers with low literacy, thus establishing design guidelines of health educational materials for low-literate patients. The study was implemented in five stages, including a focus group interview, the development of testing media, a reliability and validity test, a pre-post knowledge test, and a usability survey.The findings revealed the problems low-literate patients usually encountered at the clinic, the pediatric information they most needed, the way they were able to acquire knowledge of children's healthcare, and the media they usually used to access information. Moreover, the results demonstrated that the leaflet intervention, as well as the website intervention, had a positive outcome. However, there was no significant difference between the influence of design intervention made by the leaflet and by the website. The findings also showed that the criteria used by low-literate patients to evaluate health educational material could be analyzed in terms of the quality of information, presentation, and appeal. An assessment checklist related to the design of health educational materials for low-literate patients was also listed.

Keywords: Design Intervention, Health Literacy, Low-literate Health Education, Health Educational Material Design.

1 Introduction

1.1 Research Background

Low health literacy has been associated with poor outcomes in health care, which include higher health care costs, a worse assessment of one's own degree of health,

V.G. Duffy (Ed.): DHM/HCII 2013, Part I, LNCS 8025, pp. 204–213, 2013.
© Springer-Verlag Berlin Heidelberg 2013

and less success in managing chronic diseases (National Institute of Health, 2002). Recent research suggests that good health educational materials can help to reduce the literacy barrier and enhance health outcome, they can help modify attitudes, shape positive behaviors, and improve patients' self-prevention. However, the majority of health educational materials are constructed for well-educated users rather than those with low literacy skills. This begs the question of whether or not various health educational materials have the same effect on low-literate patients.

Immigrant populations are vulnerable to serious health disparities, and language barriers may further exacerbate their limited health literacy in accessing health care information. According to the Ministry of the Interior, a total of 44622 new immigrants were registered on the census of Taipei city in 2012, and their number of newborn babies was 14220, which accounted for 5.87% of the total number of new babies born in Taipei. This research considers a specific group within Vietnamese and Chinese immigrant mothers in Taipei, most of who have low levels of education and have married into poor families. Therefore, their children might not get good care because of low socio-economic status. Recent surveys indicate that more than 20 per cent of children in Taiwan suffer from allergies. Children with chronic diseases are highly dependent on their parents in the management of their health care. Yet, ways to help low-literate parents to look after their children by applying robustly designed health educational materials are still at an early stage of development.

The past decade has seen a great proliferation of research into low-literacy health communication, such as information and communication technologies (Mishra et al., 2007; Allison & Ricardo, 2011), health education for low-literate patients (Andersen et al., 2008; Ndwe et al., 2010; Choi & Bakken, 2010), consumer-centered health information design (Weitzman et al., 2009; Rubinelle et al., 2009), and service-learning technology for low-literate patients (Houston et al., 2006; Wexler et al., 2011). Past studies related to low literacy health communication cover diverse disciplines ranging from health science to health education, information technology, and health care application. However, they mainly focus on exploring the effectiveness of health promotional platforms from the perspective of information providers and consumers, while comparative analyses of the educational effectiveness of various media for low-literate users from the perspective of designers are comparatively rare.

1.2   Purpose of This Study

The purpose of this study is to compare the educational effectiveness of leaflet and website to deliver knowledge related to children allergy healthcare for immigrant mothers with low-literacy, thus establishing design guidelines of health educational materials for low-literacy patients. Even though leaflet is relatively inexpensive to create and provides valuable information for populations, the benefit of its one-size-fits-all approach varies from person to person. With the recent advances in computer technology, website, which combine texts, pictures, audio, and video, seem to be welcome, but whether or not their versatile presentations affect low-literate patients' health knowledge is not yet known. Considering the issues of concern above, the primary research objectives of this study are described below:

- To survey current strategies, methodologies, and tools to design health educational materials for low-literate patients
- To compare the educational effectiveness of leaflet and website to deliver children's health care knowledge to users with low literacy.
- To set up guidelines for the design of health educational materials for low-literate patients.

2   Literature Review

2.1   Design Interventions (Leaflets VS. Websites)

There has been a huge proliferation of research into health-based design interventions in the past decade, most of which focused on the educational effectiveness of paper-based and web-based media. For example, Jan et al. (2007) attempted to determine whether or not a web-based multimedia asthma educational and monitoring program would improve the knowledge and health status of children and caregivers. 164 pediatric patients with persistent asthma were enrolled for a 12-week controlled trial. The results showed that the adherence rates of therapeutic and diagnostic monitoring, the global assessment of asthma control, the knowledge of asthma self-management, and the quality of life of caregivers were all significantly higher in the intervention group. Moreover, Yardley et al. (2010) conducted two in-depth qualitative studies to compare the effectiveness of paper-media and web-based media for providing medical care for flu. 47 participants were randomly placed into two groups to explore the influence of the tested media that delivered health care information about cold or flu symptoms. The results showed that users often felt overwhelmed by the quantity of information provided in paper-based media, and they wanted to have greater control of how information is accessed in web-based media.

Since paper-based media are typically created for the general population, they do not really consider the specific characteristics of prospective consumers. On the contrary, web-based media is based upon the principle of "market segmentation" which aims to find a specific group of consumers for a particular product or service. Indeed, targeted information is well suited to meet the needs of targeted populations. Compared to the function of one-size-fits-all paper-based media, web-based media can tailor information which applies to people with similar characteristics, allowing interventions to effectively target high-risk groups. Furthermore, since displaying photographs and video clips in a web browser does not require the use of additional expensive hardware, it can be generated inexpensively. Conversely, printed educational booklets are costly to produce and update. (Richards et al. 1998; Ahern et al. 2010; Kreuter et al. 2010).

	Leaflet	Website
1	Static Media	Dynamic media
2	Portable	Portable but expensive (smart phone)
3	Initially inexpensive	Initially expensive
4	One-way communication	Interactive communication
5	One-size-fits-all	Tailor target users
6	General population	Market segmentation
7	No IT skills needed	Basic skills needed
8	No feedback	Allow feedback

2.2   Low-Literacy Health Education

Health literacy is the degree to which individuals have the capacity to obtain, process, and understand basic health information and services needed to make appropriate health decisions and follow instructions for treatment (American Medical Association Foundation, 2008). It is important to examine health literacy because low health literacy has been associated with poor health-related outcomes, which include hospitalization rates, poor adherence to prescribed treatment and self-care regimens, increase medication or treatment errors, failure to seek preventive care, lack of skills needed to navigate the health care system, disproportionately high rates of diseases and mortality, and the increased use of emergency rooms for primary care (H. L. Bankson, 2009; Choi & Bakken, 2010).

A growing number of studies are now available to shed some light on the development and evaluation of practicable health care applications for low-literate users. For example, Ishibashi & Nakajima (2004) developed a courseware to provide illiterate people with knowledge of preventing infectious diseases. They suggest that, rather than providing highly valuable satellite-assisted telemedicine systems to support high income doctors, a low valuable multimedia-assisted public health courseware will be far more cost-effective to engage in a project targeting poverty-stricken levels of society which are more susceptible to disease. It is undeniable that improving the knowledge of preventative measures of the low-literate population could reduce social risk and cost. Furthermore, Andersen et al. (2008) created an adaptive web-based kiosk system to deliver appropriate information about smoking cessation to low-literate Hispanics (Mexican- Americans). The study was implemented in three stages, including a focus group interview, the development of a website, and a field testing and usability survey. The results showed that Hispanics were just as likely to use technology as Non-Hispanics, and that a kiosk was an appropriate way to collect data about the population of a clinic. In addition, Medhi et al. (2011) developed and tested three prototypes of mobile phone with a text-free interface, such as a spoken dialogue system, a graphical interface, and a live operator. They conducted an ethnographical study of the barriers to usability encountered by 90 low-literate subjects in India, Kenya, the Philippines, and South Africa. The results showed that first-time low-literate users found textual interfaces to be unusable and the greatest number of tasks were completed using a graphical interface. They also found that a live operator was up to ten times more accurate than a text-based interface, and a spoken dialogue system could be used by those who felt more comfortable and familiar with speech. The broad range of the available testing methods makes it difficult to choose the best usability assessment plan, which is what the study and methodology described in this paper intends to investigate.

2.3   Design for Low-Literate Users

As the volume of health education materials rises, the need to evaluate its effectiveness becomes more critical. Evaluation is the crucial part of developing a healthcare application. It motivates the designer, and explains the guidelines related to concrete projects and problem-solving.

> *"Health message design is an audience-centred process; it is designed primarily to respond to the needs and situation of the target audience, rather than to the needs and situation of the message designers or sponsoring organizations."* (Maibach & Parrott, 1995,   p167).

Nevertheless, how can the benefits of design be maximised to meet the special needs of poor readership? Scholars have produced a host of design guideline to help low-literate patients to learn. These can be summarised as follows:

1. Information design: (1) Limit information to a specific objective; (2) Use short sentences and paragraphs; (4) Use plain language and avoid medical jargon; (3) Write in a conversational style; (5) Adopt a vivid and friendly tone; (6) Use headings and sub-headings to help reinforce the flow and content; (7) Provide an adequate amount of text on each page; (8) Divide the information content into several unique classifications.
2. Presentation design: (1) Ensure that the cover is attractive; (2) Use ample white spaces to clarify the layout; (3) Use a large font size to improve the readability of the content; (4) Closely link pictures to text or captions; (5) Minimise distracting details in pictures; (6) Use simple drawings to illustrate concepts; (7) Use real photos rather than fake cartoons; (8) Use bullets and other graphic devices to highlight key messages.
3. Interaction Design: (1) Interaction is invited via questions, responses, suggested action ; (2) Design user- friendly interfaces; (3) Provide users with control and freedom; (4) Consistency style of webpage design; (5)Voiding scrollbars, drop-down menus and multiple windows; (6) Use large link buttons adequately spaced apart; (7) Easy to recover from errors; (8) Short time to download and quickly feedback.
4. Appeal design: (1): The material closely matches the race, language, and experience of the target audience; (2) Offering information to meet users' needs; (3) The content of the website is easy to browse; (4) The source of the content is credible and up to date; (5) The authority and attribution are clearly recorded; (6)The advertisement and content are obviously compartmentalised; (7) Provide a discussion area for users to communicate with each other; (8) Offering professional on-line consultation.(Gillespie, 1993; Doak et al., 1996; Harvey& Fleming, 2003; Houts et al., 2006; Andersen et al., 2008; Cassell et al., 2010; Green & Tones, 2010; Choi & Bakken, 2010; Hung & Stones, 2011).

3   Methodology

The study was implemented in five stages, including a focus group interview, the development of testing media, a reliability and validity test, a pre-post knowledge test, and a usability survey. Before commencing the primary research, ethics approval was granted by Fu Jen Catholic University and the University of Leeds.

Firstly, a focus group interview was conducted with 10 Vietnamese volunteer interpreters who have lived in Taiwan for years to provide a translation service for immigrant mothers consulting physicians. This ensured they had good knowledge of cultural and sociological issues the mothers experience on a regular basis. This brainstorming meeting at the Taipei Immigrant Hall was two hours in duration and explored the problems involved in health communication for low-literacy users and their media use. What was attained from their feedback served as a reference for the further development of usability testing media and the implementation of Pre-Post knowledge testing.

Secondly, a leaflet and a website were developed, both including the same healthcare information relating to the causation, symptoms, treatment and prevention of children's allergies. All the information and questionnaires for this research were created at secondary school level or lower to meet the standard of immigrant mothers' readability. All of the text, layout design and operating function in the testing media were integrated and converted using the computer software, Photoshop, Illustration, Flash and Dreamweaver, a combination of Adobe multimedia-development application systems.

Thirdly, a reliability and validity test was conducted by a paediatric allergy specialist, a paediatric clinical nurse, a Vietnamese translator, a new immigrant mother, and a professional researcher to ensure that all the questions in the questionnaire were good indicators to measure the important variables in this study. A 5-point Likert-type scale of response options ranging from strongly disagree to strongly agree was used to elicit endorsement of a particular statement, with higher scores indicating the higher appropriateness.

Fourthly, 64 immigrant mothers from Vietnam and China were randomly placed into two groups to explore the educational effectiveness of leaflets and websites respectively. The leaflet group was presented with the leaflet, whereas the website group was presented with the website. Both groups were asked to fill out the knowledge testing questionnaire before and after the trial. Thus, this research could measure their memory recall of the presented materials. The pre-test included demographic information and a questionnaire to test their knowledge. The post-test included the same questions as those contained in the pre-test, as well as a usability survey to assess the participants' user satisfaction.

Fifthly, each participant was asked to complete a questionnaire to evaluate the usability of the presented media. This consisted of 21 items of evaluation criteria, including the quality of information, presentation, and the appeal of the media in question. These evaluation criteria were informed by recent studies from evaluation literature and references collected from former focus group interviews. A five-point Likert Scale was used for every question, with higher scores indicating the higher appropriateness. The rating scale for measuring the appropriateness of the question-naire was scored from 1= very unimportant, 2=unimportant, 3=no opinion, 4=important, 5=very important.

3.1   Data Analysis

1. In order to examine whether there were significant differences between the results shown in the pre-test and the post-test of using the leaflet as a media, a Pair T-test was applied. Table 1 shows the results: there were significant differences between the pre-test and the post-test of using the leaflet as a media. (t=-11.259, *** p < .001)

Table 1. Pair T-test (Leaflet)

		Mean	Mean Difference	t-value
Leaflet	Pre-test	13.50	2.97	-11.259***
	Post-test	16.47		

2. In order to examine whether there were significant differences between the results shown in the pre-test and the post-test of using the website as a media, a Pair T-test was applied. Table 2 shows the results: there were significant differences between the pre-test and the post-test of using the website as a media. (t=-9.063, *** p < .001)

Table 2. Pair T-test (Website)

		Mean	Mean Difference	t-value
Website	Pre-test	14.44	3.03	-9.063***
	Post-test	17.47		

3. In order to examine whether there were significant differences between the effectiveness of health intervention made by the leaflet and by the website, an independent sample t-test was applied. Table 3 shows the results: there was no significant difference between the effectiveness of health intervention made by the leaflet and by the website (t=-0.147, p>.05).

Table 3. Independent Sample t-test (Leaflet VS. Website)

	Media	N	Mean	Std. Deviation	Sig.	t-value
Educational	Leaflet	32	2.97	1.49	.884	-.147
Effect	Website	32	3.03	1.89		

4. In order to examine whether there were significant differences between the educational effect and the user's "educational level", One-Way ANOVA test was used. Table 4 shows the results: there were significant differences between the educational effect and the user's "educational level", (F=4.435, P<.01). By using the Scheffe multiple-comparison test, we can see only those who acquired primary education and those who acquired secondary education show the significant differences.

Table 4. One-Way ANOVA (Educational Effect VS Education Level)

	1	2	3	4	F	Sig.	Scheffee Post Hoc Comparison
Mean	2.00	3.70	2.95	1.75	4.435	.007*	(1,2)*

5. In order to examine the criteria used by low-literate patients to evaluate health educational material, Descriptive Statistics / Frequencies test was used. Chart 2 showed the results: **Chart. 1. Usability Evaluation Survey**

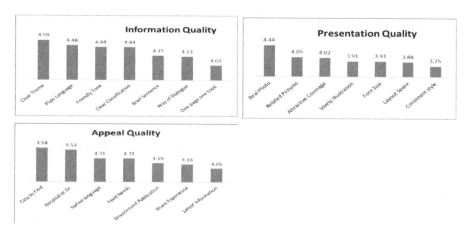

4   Discussion and Conclusion

The findings showed that the problems the immigrant mothers usually encountered in the clinic could be ranked as "which doctor to see", "cannot understand the prescription", "too shy to ask questions", "cannot understand what the doctor says", and "the doctor cannot understand what I say". This illustrates a fundamental concern to resolve the problems involved in doctor-patient communication among members of low-literate populations. The findings also showed that the most needed pediatric information for immigrant mothers when their children were sick can be ranked as "how to give care", "common symptoms", "trigger factors", "side effects", and "when to see a doctor". What is achieved from above might serve as a reference for further health promotional media design. Most of the immigrant mothers would ask their doctors, families and friends about the knowledge of children's healthcare, and only 48% of them indicated that they would make use of health educational materials. The media the immigrant mothers usually accessed to acquire information about their children's healthcare were ranked as television, brochures, books, internet, and DVD respectively. Moreover, most of the demographic factors did not have an impact on the educational effectiveness, apart from the user's "educational level". Low-literate users performed significantly better than highly literate ones, which proved that these two testing media had been well-designed for low-literate users and well-accepted by them. It is also probably because the users with high literacy are not as compliant as the users with low literacy to receive any suggestion from health educational materials. In addition, the results showed that the leaflet intervention had a positive outcome, as well as the website intervention. However, there was no significant difference between the influence of design intervention made by the leaflet and by the website. This is probably because both testing media were designed with the same content and were short of adequate probability sampling.

The findings also showed that the criteria used by low-literate patients to evaluate health educational material could be analyzed in terms of the quality of information, presentation, and appeal. Most of the participants agreed that the quality of information and appeal were more important than the quality of presentation. An assessment checklist of design of the health educational materials for low literacy patients is as follows:

1. Information design: 1. It conveys clear themes; 2. It is written in a friendly tone; 3. It uses plain language; 4. Information classification is very clear; 5. It represents information in the way of a dialogue; 6. It has brief descriptive sentences; 7. One topic is shown on one page
2. Presentation design: 1. Real photos help to understand information. 2. It has an attractive coverage (homepage); 3. Related pictures are placed right next to the description; 4. The layout space of the content is well situated; 5. The font size is suitable for reading; 6. Lovely illustrations are very attractive; 7. The colors and background are consistently designed.
3. Appeal design: 1. If it is easy for users to find the information they want; 2. If the media contains information of hospitals or doctors; 3. If it is written in users' native language; 4. If it offers information to meet users' needs; 5. If someone else's caring experiences are related in the media; 6. If it presents the latest information; 7. If it is published by the government.

This research has two major limitations, one of which is the use of probability sampling, while the other is the reliability of the questionnaire survey. It was very difficult to recruit low-literate participants because of the consent form for ethical reasons, while some feedback from the questionnaire may have been distorted because of embarrassing and upsetting issues. This research is an experiment that integrates design, communication and public health. Its findings are expected to be valuable, not only for providers and consumers, but also designers of health educational materials. Future studies are needed to identify which of the characteristics of low-literacy patients influence their ability to learn about health information. Identifying these factors and incorporating solutions into a health intervention may help to bridge the learning gap related to patients' literacy status.

Acknowledgement. The authors gratefully acknowledge the Taiwan National Science Council which funded this research, No: NSC 101-2410-H-030 -047 –SSS.

References

1. Ahern, D., Kreslake, J., Phalen, J.: What is eHealth: Perspectives on the Evolution of eHealth Research. In: Krep, G.L. (ed.) Health Communication. Health Communication and new information technologies (eHealth), vol. 4, pp. 267–287. SAGE Publications Ltd., London (2010)

2. American Medical Association Foundation. Health literacy. The Foundation, Boston (2008), http://www.ama-assn.org/ama/pub/category/8115.html (accessed: 150811)

3. Andersen, P., Andersen, S., Youngblood, E., Colmenares, E.: Health education kiosk for low-literacy patients served by community-based clinics. In: 2008 IEEE International Symposium on Technology and Society, pp. 1–9 (2008)

4. Bankson, H.L.: Health Literacy: an exploratory bibliometric analysis, 1997-2007. J. Med. Libr. Assoc. 97(2) (April 2009)

5. Cassell, M., Jackson, C., Cheuvront, B.: Health Communication on the Internet: An Effective Channel for Health Behaviour Change? In: Krep, G.L. (ed.) Health Communication. Health Communication and new information technologies (eHealth), vol. 4, pp. 17–42. SAGE Publications Ltd., London (2010)

6. Choi, J., Bakken, S.: Web-based education for low-literate parents in Neonatal Intensive Care Unit: Development of a website and heuristic evaluation and usability testing. International Journal of Medical Informatics 79(8), 565–575 (2010)

7. Green, J., Tones, K.: Health Promotion: planning and strategies. Sage Publication (2010)

8. Houts, P., Doak, C., Doak, L., Loscalzo, M.: The role of pictures in improving health communication: A review of research on attention, comprehension, recall, and adherence. Patient Education and Counseling 61(2), 173–190 (2006)

9. Hung, Y.-L., Stones, C.: A Comparative Study of Children's eHealth Design between East and West: A Case Study of a Children's Health Website in China, Taiwan, the UK, and the US. In: Robertson, M.M. (ed.) EHAWC 2011 and HCII 2011. LNCS, vol. 6779, pp. 129–138. Springer, Heidelberg (2011)

10. Ishibashi, Y., Nakajima, I.: The database which creates multilingual web information on preventing infectious diseases. In: Proceedings of the 6th International Workshop on Enterprise Networking and Computing in Healthcare Industry - Healthcom 2004 (IEEE Cat. No.04EX842), pp. 129–132 (2004)

11. Jan, R.-L., Wang, J.-Y., Huang, M.-C., Tseng, S.-M., Su, H.-J., Liu, L.-F.: An Internet-based interactive telemonitoring system for improving childhood asthma outcomes in Taiwan. Telemedicine Journal and e-Health 13(3), 257–268 (2007)

12. Kreuter, M., Strecher, V., Glassman, B.: One Size Does Not Fit All: The Case for Tailoring Print Materials. In: Krep, G.L. (ed.) Health Communication. Health Communication and health promotion, vol. 2, pp. 151–168. SAGE Publications Ltd., London (2010)

13. Maibach, E., Parrott, R.L. (eds.): Designing health messages: approaches from communication theory and public health practice, Thousand Oaks, Calif. Sage Publications, London (1995c)

14. Medhi, I., Patnaik, S., Brunskill, E., Gautama, S.N., Thies, W., Toyama, K.: Designing mobile interfaces for novice and low-literacy users. ACM Transactions on Computer-Human Interaction 18(1) (April 2011)

15. Yardley, L., Morrison, L.G., Andreou, P., Joseph, J., Little, P.: Understanding reactions to an internet-delivered health-care intervention: accommodating user preferences for information provision. BMC Medical Informatics and Decision Making 10, 52 (2010)

Effect Evaluation of Recreational Coloring Carried Out at Pay Nursing Home

Shinichiro Kawabata[1], Nasu Maki[2], Akiyoshi Yamamoto[3], Yoshiyuki Kida[1], Noriaki Kuwahara[1], Akihiko Goto[4], and Hiroyuki Hamada[1]

[1] Kyoto Institute of Technology, Matsugasaki, Sakyo-ku, Kyoto 606-8585 Japan
{Shinichiro Kawabata,Yoshiyuki Kida1,Noriaki Kuwahara, Hiroyuki Hamada}hhamada@kit.ac.jp
[2] Soliton Corporation Co., Ltd., 8C06 ASTEM, 134 Chudoji-minamimachi, Shimogyo-ku, Kyoto city, Japan
[3] City Estate Co., Ltd., 1-7-7-CE, Nishi Honmachi Building, Nishi Honmachi, Nishi-ku, Osaka City, Japan
[4] Osaka Sangyo University, 3-1-1 Nakagakiuchi, Daito City, Osaka, Japan

Abstract. Aging has becoming a serious problem to be solved in wide area of the world. In this study coloring was taking place at the pay nursing home for the aged tenant as part of the recreation, and the influence to the tenant was verified. It was suggested that the coloring showed effect to improvement s for reducing the frequency of wandering around and petition of excretion of the tenant. Coloring is easily done compared to painting and descriptions, also regardless to the needing care degree, more over a care worker's burden can also be reduced. As the result shows, coloring is suggested as an activity that should be taken as one of the recreations at the pay nursing home.

Keywords: key words Coloring recreation, Dementia, Nursing home.

1 Introduction

The population of the world is aging at an accelerated rate. It has becoming a serious problem in wide area of the world as shown in Figure 1. The number of elderly people are increasing for more than threefold since 1950, from approximately 130 million to 419 million in the year 2000. The number of elderly people is now increasing by 8 million per year, and by 2030, this increase will reach to 24 million per year. The most rapid acceleration in aging will occur after 2010, when the large post World War II baby boom cohorts begin to reach age of 65. Declining fertility rates combined with steady improvements in life expectancy over the latter half of the 20th century have produced dramatic growth in the world's elderly population. People aged 65 and over now comprise a greater share of the world's population than ever before, and this proportion will increase for more years.

As of October 1, 2010, the elderly population aged 65 and over became 29.6 million people to be the highest ever in Japan. Moreover the proportion of the population of the total population over the age of 65 was also recorded the highest of 23.1%.

V.G. Duffy (Ed.): DHM/HCII 2013, Part I, LNCS 8025, pp. 214–222, 2013.
© Springer-Verlag Berlin Heidelberg 2013

When this tendency continues, one person in four people comes to enter the age of senior citizen in 2015.

The numbers of dementia patients are also increasing. Therefore, various measures for dementia prevention are taken place in many places. In Japan, transcribing a sutra is performed from ancient times for mental concentration, nevertheless there are difficulties for the aged person to transcribe a sutra because writing a Chinese character is very delicate work. Accordingly, coloring which is more easily carried out was paid to attention.

When starting coloring, people needs to observe the original picture carefully. At this time, lobus occipitalis that take charge of the sight work. Moreover, to understand the original picture accurately, the temporal lobe that takes charge of the memory works to refer from the memory the shape and the color sow in the past. The parietal lobe cooperates when the balance of the entire picture is gripped. As written above coloring has the effect to activate a widespread area of the brain. In this study coloring was taking place at the pay nursing home for the aged tenant as part of the recreation, and the influence given to the tenant was analyzed. As an early stage of this experiment we tried to verify the optimal writing equipment for coloring, which can give more effective influence to the brain activity during coloring.

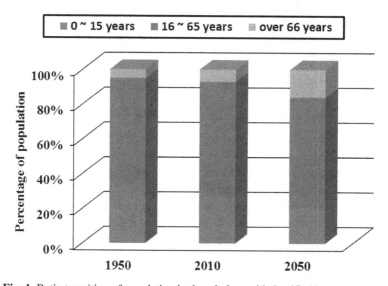

Fig. 1. Ratio transition of population in the whole world classified by generation

2   Experiment

2.1   Selection of Writing Instrument for Coloring Recreation

2.1.1   Change of Brain Activity by Difference of Writing Instruments
As an early stage of this study, experiment for effective evaluation to find the optimal writing instrument during coloring was carried out. The coloring experiment was

carried out with four kinds of writing instruments, such as crayon pastel (SAKURA COLOR PRODUCTS CORP), color pencil (MITUBISHI PENCIL CO., LTD.), felt-tipped pen (Too Corporation.), and color brush pen (soliton corporation CO. LTD.). Four writing instruments are shown in Figure 2. These four writing instruments are commonly used instruments for coloring. The brain activity in each case was measured.

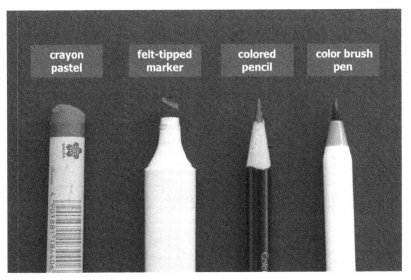

Fig. 2. Four kinds of writing instruments for coloring

2.1.2   Experiment

Electroencephalograph of Digital Medic co.,Ltd, shown in Figure 3 was used to measure the brain activity. Five postgraduates cooperated in this experiment as a test subject. To make experimental conditions impartial, each test with different writing instrument was conducted in the same time zone of a different day using the same laboratory with a tranquil environment. The used sketch design of the picture is shown in Figure 4. The sequential order for coloring the grain of the grape was been determined to make equal condition between the subjects.

After having installed the electroencephalograph, test subject will close eye for 1 minute to record the brain wave at the rest situation, subsequently after that start coloring work for three minutes to record the brain wave during coloring. Assuming that the brain waves at the time of eye closure as 100%, the brain waves of alpha wave and beta wave under coloring work in progress was compared.

Fig. 3. Electroencephalograph of Digital Medic co.,Ltd,

Fig. 4. Used sketch designs for coloring experiment

2.1.3   Results and Discussion

The results of the beta wave brain activity of four different writing instruments are shown in Figure 5 and the result of the alpha wave brain activity are shown in Figure 6. Color brush pen and color pencil showed the high value of Beta wave, which of 139% compared to rest condition. Beta wave is related with active thinking and concentration, therefore by using color brush pen and color pencil the user can achieve more concentration of the brain.

The lowest value for the alpha wave was color brush pen by 93% compared to rest condition. It is suggested that color brush pen has softest tip compared to other writing instruments. Thereby the test subject had to be vividly aware to hand movement of not only the XY-axis of left to right, but also to the Z-axis of up and down movement, leading alpha wave to decline consequently.

From these results color brush pen is demonstrated as the writing instruments which can give most stimulation to the brain.

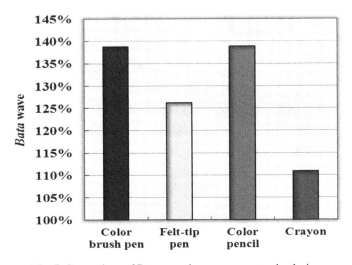

Fig. 5. Comparison of Beta wave between at rest and coloring

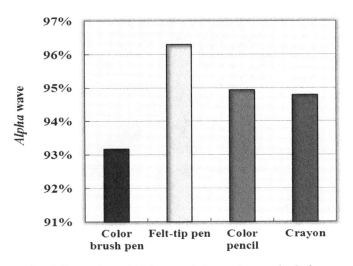

Fig. 6. Comparison of Alpha wave between at rest and coloring

2.1.4   Experiment

In the experiment mentioned earlier, the color brush pen was demonstrated as the most appropriate writing instrument for coloring recreation. For the second part of the experiment, the thickness of the brush was carried to verification using the same experimental method. Ten test subjects have cooperated in this experiment. The value of beta wave using ordinary size brush and extra thin brush was compared.

2.1.5   Results and Discussions

The result for the changes of beta wave by difference of the thickness of writing brush is shown in Figure 7. The value for ordinary size brush was 136% compared to at rest condition and the value for extra thin brush was 154% compared to rest condition. It is suggested that handling the thinner brush which is more sharply pointed, needs more concentration to handle, causing beta wave to increase. The result shows that extra thin brush is the most appropriate writing instrument for coloring recreation taken place at pay nursing home.

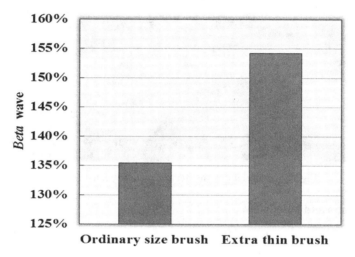

Fig. 7. Comparison of Beta wave between at rest and coloring using ordinary size brush and extra thin brush

3   Coloring Recreation Taken Place at Pay Nursing Home

3.1   Experiments

The experiment of coloring recreation using color brush pen was carried out to pay nursing home tenant. Five tenants who have more behavior problems comparatively with other tenant, such as wandering around, petition of excretion and unnecessary nurse calls were chosen as a test subject. Each coloring recreation was operated for approximately thirty minutes and the frequency of the coloring recreation was two or three times a week, changing according to physical condition of the tenants. The experiment was conducted for three months and the frequency of wandering around, petition of excretion was recorded. Additional experiment was carried out to one other test subject to find out the relationship between number of nurse calls and sleeping time of the tenant when working on coloring. Checking of sleeping hour was operated once in every fifteen minutes where usually operates once in an hour.

Furthermore, in order to verify the influence of stopping coloring recreation, as for this subject the coloring experiment was stopped after two month and follow-up observations were carried out. The scenery of coloring recreation is shown in Figure 7.

Fig. 8. Scenery of coloring recreation at pay nursing home

3.2   Results and Discussion

3.2.1   The Frequency of Wandering around and Petition of Excretion

The result for the frequency of wandering around and petition of excretion is shown in Figure 8. The average number of   wandering around and petition of excretion for five test subject have decreased approximately 40% after three month of coloring recreation. According to the commentary of the physical therapist, the decrease of wandering around frequency and petition of excretion occurred as a result to the plural domains such as cerebral cortex and basal nuclei, cerebellum, the brainstem were activated concurrently by feeling strain increased caused by the effect of coloring. It is estimated that result occurred especially by the change in the function of frontal lobe participating in an accomplishment function.

3.2.2   The Result for Number of Nurse Calls and Sleeping Time

The result for number of nurse calls and sleeping time is shown in Figure 9. After starting the experiment, the number of nurse call decreased dramatically. Due to this change, the hours of sleeping time increased up to average of 4.5 hours per day to 7.9 hours per day in maximum. The number of the nurse calls increased up to 87 times and hours of sleeping time declined again to average of 4.8 hours per day after having finished coloring experiment. This result shows accordance to the research which mentioned about decrease of nurse calls when coloring was carried out at pay nursing home (e.g., Kawabata 2010). Furthermore, as for the increase of nurse calls and decrease of sleeping hours after stopping coloring experiment, it is suggested that coloring should be carried out continuously to gain effective influence.

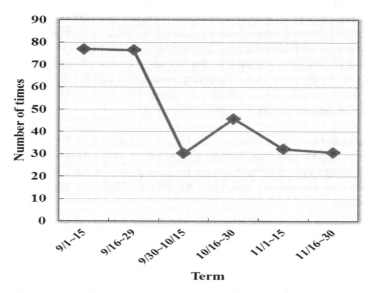

Fig. 9. Average frequency of wandering around and petition of excretion

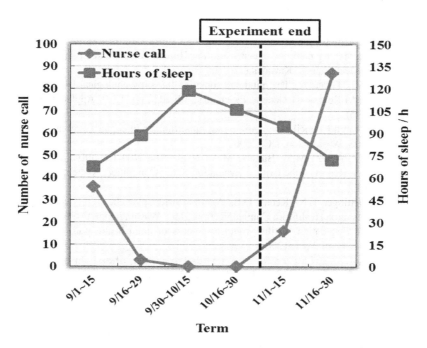

Fig. 10. Results for number of nurse calls and sleeping time

4   Conclusions

In this study, optimal writing instrument for coloring is suggested as extra thin color brush pen. The number of wandering around frequency and petition excretion of the tenant at nursing home decreased due to working on coloring recreation. Coloring is easily done compared to painting and descriptions, also regardless to the needing care degree. More over a care worker's burden can also be reduced because the time for handling unnecessary nurse calls, wandering around and petition of excretion can be reduced. As the result shows, coloring is suggested as an activity that should be taken as one of the recreations at the pay nursing home.

Acknowledgments. The authors would like to acknowledge Professor Hiroyuki Hamada, an associate professor Noriaki Kuwahara, an associate professor Yoshiyuki Kida of Kyoto institute of technology, an associate professor Akihiko Goto of Osaka sangyo-university for making this work possible and for their encouragement and helpful discussions.

References

1. Japanese brain Health society: brain Health news No. 15 (2006)
2. Tanaka, H., et al.: Effect that "memories coloring paper" gives to slight dementia patient acknowledgment function, psychology function, and side of daily life. Journal of Rehabilitation and Health Sciences 7, 39–42 (2009)
3. The Management and Coordination Agency, white paper on aging society (2005)
4. The Ministry of Health, Labour and Welfare nursing care for elderly people society Nursing care for elderly people in 2015 (2003)
5. Recreation to nursing facilities tenant. Coloring Human Factors and Ergonomics Society 55th Annual Meeting, e.g., Kawabata (2010)
6. Eisendrath, S.J., Feder, A.: The mind and somatic illness: psychological factors. In: Goldman, H.H. (ed.) Review of General Psychiatry, 4th edn., pp. 13–9. Appleton and Lange, Norwalk (1995)
7. National Research Council. The aging mind: opportunities in cognitive research. National Academy Press, Washington, DC (2000)
8. Hendrie, H.C., Albert, M.S., Butters, M.A., et al.: The NIH Cognitive and Emotional Health Project, Report of the Critical Evaluation Study Committee. Alzheimers Dement 2, 12–32 (2006)
9. Himes, C., Oettinger, E.N., Kenny, D.E.: Aging in stride: plan ahead, stay connected, keep moving. Caresource Healthcare Communications, Inc., Washington, DC (2004)
10. ASA-MetLife Foundation. Attitudes and awareness of brain health poll. San Francisco: American Society on Aging (2006),
http://www.asaging.rg/asav2/mindalert/brainhealthpoll.cfm
11. Graham, J.E., Rockwood, K., Beattie, B.L., et al.: Prevalence and severity of cognitive impairment with and without dementia in an elderly population. Lancet 349, 1793–1796 (1997)
12. Lopez, O.L., Kuller, L.H., Fitzpatrick, A., Ives, D., Becker, J.T., Beauchamp, N.: Evaluation of dementia in the cardiovascular health cognition study. Neuroepidemiology 22, 1–12 (2003)
13. Bynum, J.P.W., Rabins, P.V., Weller, W.E., Niefeld, M., Anderson, G.F., Wu, A.: The impact of dementia and chronic illness on Medicare expenditures and hospital use. Am. Geriatr. Soc. 52, 187–194 (2004)

A Study for Conducting Waves by Using the Multi-channel Surface EMG

Tomohiro Kosuge[*], Naoaki Itakura, and Kazuyuki Mito

Department of Informatics, The University of Electro-Communications, Chofu, Tokyo, Japan
{tomo23,ita,mito}@se.uec.ac.jp

Abstract. The surface electromyogram (EMG) is recorded as the interference electric potential generated by motor units in muscle. Therefore, it may be possible to analyze the muscle contraction mechanism in order to examine the composition of the interference signal of the surface EMG. We herein propose a new method by which to analyze the composition of the surface EMG. The proposed method involves searching conducting wave which mean similar waveforms considered same wave appearing during several channels by using multi-channel surface EMG, and we can analyze surface EMG as a set of conducting waves. The proposed method is referred to as the multi-channel method for conducting waves (m-ch method). We analyzed multi-channel EMG using the proposed method.

Keywords: EMG, surface EMG, MFCV, motor unit.

1 Introduction

Muscular activity is investigated by analyzing the action potential in muscle fiber, primarily in the field of clinical medicine [1] and [2]. The conduction velocity of potentials, i.e., the muscle fiber conduction velocity (MFCV), is measured by needle electrodes, and recent studies have measured the MFCV by surface electromyography rather than using needles because surface electromyography is a non-invasive technique [3]. The surface electromyogram (EMG) is mainly used to analyze the frequency and amplitude of EMG signals [4]. The conducting velocity is calculated based on the average response to a pair of EMGs and the delay time of these added signals [5] and [6].

Surface EMG is recorded as an interference wave of action potential that is generated by some of motor units in muscle. If composition of the interference wave can be analyzed, we may be able to examine the mechanism of muscular contraction, for example activity of motor units.

On the other hand, previous studies have analyzed multi-channel surface EMG, which is measured from multiple electrodes arranged in a line [7], [8], and [9]. These studies examined waves considered to be caused from motor units and examined the change of waves by conducting to search similar waveforms from surface EMG of

---

[*] Corresponding author.

V.G. Duffy (Ed.): DHM/HCII 2013, Part I, LNCS 8025, pp. 223–231, 2013.
© Springer-Verlag Berlin Heidelberg 2013

several channels [7], [8], and [9]. However, to judge which waveform we should examine is subjective and time consuming. Therefore, we herein proposed a new method for analyzing multi-channel surface EMG in order to examine the mechanism of muscle activity. The proposed method involves dividing the surface EMG into zero-crossing sections comparing the waveforms quantitatively section by section. Conducting waves are similar waveforms that appear in several channels and are considered to be the same wave. We can examine various data, including the conducting velocity and the amplitude of each conducting wave, over multiple channels. We refer to the proposed method as the multi-channel method for conducting waves (m-ch method). We used the m-ch method to analyze conducting waves from multi-channel EMG.

2   Experiment

We performed a number of experiments in order to obtain data for the analysis (Fig. 1). We measured the multi-channel surface EMG by electrodes aligned along the surface of the biceps brachii muscle of each subject. The electrodes were made of silver and were 1 mm in diameter and 10 mm in length. The distance between electrodes was 5 mm. We placed the electrode on the belly of muscle so that the major axis of the electrode was aligned with the muscular fibers. We used 17 electrodes and measured 16-ch EMG from each electrode interval by using bipolar law. For 16-ch EMG, 1 ch is set to the shoulder side and 16ch is set to the elbow side.

We used amplifiers with a high cut of 1 kHz and a low cut of 5 Hz. The amplifiers had an amplification rate of 80 dB and a sampling frequency of 5 kHz. The EMGs were recorded on a PC. The number of subjects was five and the subjects were all males in their 20s. The subject kept his elbow joint at a 90-degree angle while seated, and his maximum muscular strength was measured (100% MVC). The subject then held four loads (10%, 20%, 30%, and 40% MVC) with the same posture for 15 s. The subject held the same load three times, for a total of 12 trials. The order of the trails was random, and the subjects took one-minute breaks between trials.

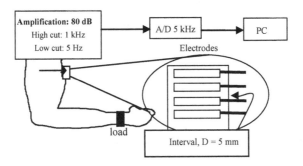

Fig. 1. Experimental system

3   Method

We developed the m-ch method in order to analyze multi-channel surface EMG by examining conducting waves. In order to obtain conducting waves, we first divided EMG signals in sections between points of electrical potential crossing zero from minus to plus (Fig. 2). For each section, we search other sections which appear nearby in time (within 10 ms) in the adjacent channel, and compare the waveforms to examine their similarity. Since these sections have different wavelengths, the coefficient of correlation cannot be calculated between sections. As such, sections are calculated a re-sampling to restore the analog signals, in pseudo-simulated Eq. (1).

$$x_a(t) = \sum_{k=-\infty}^{+\infty} x_a(k\Delta t) \cdot \frac{\sin\left[\dfrac{\pi}{\Delta t}(t - k\Delta t)\right]}{\dfrac{\pi}{\Delta t}(t - k\Delta t)}$$

(1)

where Δt is the sampling interval, $x_a(k\Delta t)$ are the sampling data, and $x_a(t)$ are pseudo-analog data restored from the sampling data.

In order to perform re-sampling, we analyze sections with any sampling frequency (Fig. 2). After re-sampling, the coefficient of correlation is calculated for the two sections in order to determine the similarity of the waveforms. In this study, we refer to the value of the coefficient of correlation of sections as the similarity ratio. The similarity ratio is used in a conducting condition to judge to be a conducting wave and is obtained as follows:

$$R_{xy} = \max[\gamma_{xy}(\tau)]$$

$$\gamma_{xy}(\tau) = \frac{\{\phi_{xy}(\tau) - m_x m_y\}}{\sqrt{\{\phi_x(0) - m_x{}^2\}\{\phi_y(0) - m_y{}^2\}}}$$

(2)

where R_{xy} is the similarity ratio, m_x and m_y are the averages of potential of each zero-crossing section, ϕ_x and ϕ_y are the autocorrelation coefficients, and ϕ_{xy} is the cross-correlation coefficient.

The denominator of γ_{xy} in Eq. (2) is the amplitude of each section. However, the difference in amplitude cannot be examined through this calculation. Then, the amplitude ratio for one conducting condition is calculates as follows:

$$G_{xy} = \frac{\sqrt{\{\phi_x(0) - m_x{}^2\}}}{\sqrt{\{\phi_y(0) - m_y{}^2\}}}$$

(3)

The wavelength ratio is also needed for a conducting condition for judging wavelength similarity:

$$L_{xy} = \frac{L_x}{L_y}$$

(4)

where L_x and L_y are the wavelengths of each section.

In order to judge to be a conducting wave based on the similarity of waves, we set thresholds for the conducting conditions for the similarity ratio, the amplitude ratio, and the wavelength ratio. If a pair of sections satisfies the conducting conditions, these sections are considered to represent a conducting wave, i.e., the same wave is considered to appear in two channels.

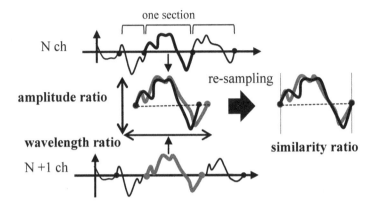

Fig. 2. Judging sections to be a conducting wave

The m-ch method involves the comparison of zero-crossing sections. So to apply this method to a section repeatedly in adjacent channel, we can get conducting wave appearing in multiple channels (Fig. 3). Moreover, we can analyze the change of a wave in conducting process to examine sections considered a same conducting wave in each channel.

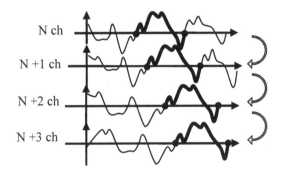

Fig. 3. Conducting wave in multiple channels

The conduction velocity is calculated by dividing the distance between the electrodes by the delay time of the conducting wave, as follows:

$$v_{xy} = \frac{D}{\frac{1}{2}(\Delta t_1 + \Delta t_2)}$$

(5)

where vxy is the conduction velocity, and D is the distance between the electrodes. In order to calculate the delay time of the waves, sections are divided at the midpoint.

In a section of next cannel, we set a dividing point. We calculate the coefficient of correlation between first half of each section, and the coefficient of correlation between each last half. We move the dividing point and calculate them to search the point where the average of two value of the coefficient of correlation is highest. When we find such dividing point, we calculate delay time of midpoint of each part of section ($\Delta t1$, $\Delta t2$). The average of these delay time is then considered to be the delay time of the waves (Fig. 4).

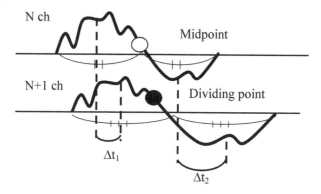

Fig. 4. Calculation of the conduction velocity

To use this method, we can get conducting waves appearing in multiple channels. Then, we add the number of conducting channels as a condition of wave to analyze.

When analyzing waves in more than three channels, there is the possibility that noise is included in sections which considered a conducting wave. Some of this noise will satisfy the conducting conditions but the delay time is too small. This noise appears to originate from a commercial power supply or electrical noise. Moreover, this noise has an abnormally fast conduction velocity. In order to counteract this noise, we calculate the variation index of the conduction velocity as calculated by each channel and add this index as a conducting condition.

4   Results and Discussion

4.1   Comparison of Methods

We compared the results obtained using the m-ch method and results obtained by the averaged response. In order to perform the m-ch method, we set thresholds of the conducting conditions: the similarity ratio, the amplitude ratio, and the wavelength ratio. We set the values of these three conditions to over 0.9. Moreover, we examined two-channel conducting waves in order to compare with the result using the averaged response. In order to calculate EMGs the averaged response, we set an electric potential threshold to search addition sections and set time width of the section.

The part of EMG from the point which electric potential exceed the threshold is considered to be an addition section. All addition sections are calculated the averaged response and we consider the result as an added wave. In the EMG of the next channel, the same time sections are calculated the averaged response as the added wave of this channel.

We compared two added waves in order to calculate the maximum value of the coefficient of correlation for each of the waves. The velocity was calculated based on the time lag of the starting points of the two waves when the coefficient of correlation was the highest. In the present study, we set the electric potential threshold to twice the RMS value of the EMG data and set the time period of the added section to 1 s.

The results obtained using the averaged response is shown as one value of velocity from two EMG data. In contrast, the result using the m-ch method is shown as many conducting waves. Each wave contains data such as conduction velocity, amplitude, wavelength, and number of conducting channels. Thus, we can analyze EMG in greater detail.

Figure 5 shows the distribution map for the amplitude and conduction velocity of the conducting waves appearing in a pair of channels, the velocity calculated using the synchronization addition is shown as a dotted line.

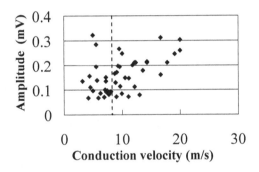

Fig. 5. Results of two methods (Sub1, ch 7-8, 20% MVC)

The velocity which calculated by using the averaged response is affected by the value of threshold and time width of the adding section, so the value of velocity is vague. The conducting waves obtained by the m-ch method have various velocities, which appears to indicate the existence of elements which caused by each muscular fiber.

We should examine these elements using conducting waves in order to clarify the mechanism of muscle activity.

4.2   Difference in Muscle Activity for Different Loads

We analyzed the difference in muscle activity for different loads in order to examine conducting waves using the m-ch method. In this analysis, in consideration of the conducting wave having a bigger change of the amplitude during channels than wavelength and waveform, we set the conducting conditions as follows: similarity ratio and wavelength ratio > 0.9, amplitude ratio > 0.7. We examined four-channel conducting waves in order to obtain more reliable results, as compared to two-channel conducting waves. We set the variation index of the conduction velocity to be less than 10%.

In order to examine the amplitude of the conducting waves for each load compared with 100% MVC, we calculated the relative amplitude as a ratio normalized with respect to the amplitude of the wave for 100% MVC.

We compared the conducting waves obtained by the EMG when the subject held each load. The relative amplitude versus the conduction velocity of the conducting wave is shown for two loads, 10% MVC and 40% MVC, in Figs. 6 and 7, which show the four-channel conducting waves from all channels for the two subjects.

In the case of 40% MVC load for both subjects, conducting waves having large relative amplitude increased from the case of 10% EMG load.

Examining the conduction velocity in the case of 40% EMG load, conducting waves having large velocity increased from the case of 10% EMG load in subject A. However, Subject B did not should such as significant a difference.

We think the difference of the distribution map of conducting waves show the effects of working muscular fiber and recruitment of motor units.

The increase in relative amplitude is thought to be caused by the change in the interference with recruitment of motor units resulting from a change of working muscle. As more waves interfere with each other, the amplitude increases. As such, the change in amplitude appears to be caused by the working of motor units.

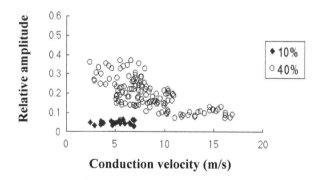

Fig. 6. Difference in conducting waves according to load (Sub A)

We believe the difference in the change of conduction velocity was caused by the effect of working muscle fiber. High-velocity waves are thought to be caused by fast muscles, and low-velocity wave are thought to be caused by slow muscles. Since the

10% MVC load did not require a great deal of power, slow muscles worked harder. In contrast, the 40% MVC load required fast muscles to work harder, generating high-velocity waves. The difference in velocity between subjects appears to indicate a difference in the composition of the muscular fiber. Specifically, compared to Subject B, Subject A appears to have more fast muscle or to need to use fast muscle more in the case of the 40% MVC load.

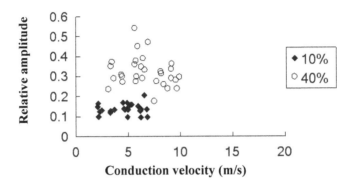

Fig. 7. Difference in conducting waves according to load (Sub B)

5   Conclusions

We proposed a new method of analyzing multi-channel surface EMG. Using the proposed method, we were able to find numerous conducting waves in EMGs and were able to examine these EMGs in detail. Analyzing the composition of conducting waves, we think that we can examine mechanism of the activity of muscle for example recruitment of working motor units and composition of muscular fiber. We analyzed differences in conducting waves generated by different loads. We believe that the proposed method can be used to analyze changes in EMGs caused by muscle fatigue or movement, for example. In the future, the results obtained by the proposed method should be compared with results obtained by another method of analyzing muscle activity.

References

1. Willoson, R.G.: Analysis of electrical activity in healthy and dystrophic muscle in man. Neurol. Neurosurg. Psychiat. 27, 386–394 (1964)
2. Rose, A.L., Willison, R.G.: Quantitative electromyography using automatic analysis: studies in healthy subjects and patients with primary muscle disease. Neurol. Neurosurg. Psychiat. 30, 403–410 (1967)
3. Preece, A.W., Wimalaratna, H.S.K., Green, J.L., Churchill, E., Morgan, H.M.: Non-invasive quantitative EMG. Electromyogr. Clin. Neurophysiol. 34, 81–86 (1994)
4. Ohashi, J.: Effects of contraction level on the changes of surface electromyogram during fatiguing static contractions. Ann. Physiol. Anthrop. 12(4), 229–241 (1993)

5. Arendt-Nielsen, L., Zwarts, M.J.: Measurement of muscle fibre conduction velocity in humans: techniques and applications. Clin. Neurophysiol. 6, 173–190 (1989)
6. Farina, D., Merletti, R.: Methods for estimating muscle fibre conduction velocity from surface electromyographic signals. Med. Biol. Eng. Comput. 42, 423–445 (2004)
7. Zwarts, M.J., Stegeman, D.F.: Multichannel surface EMG: basic aspects and clinical utility. Muscle Nerve. 28, 1–17 (2003)
8. Holobar, A., Zazula, D.: Correlation-based decomposition of surface electromyograms at low contraction forces. Med. Biol. Eng. Comput. 42, 487–495 (2004)
9. Farina, D., Pozzo, M., Merlo, E., Bottin, A., Merletti, R.: Assessment of muscle fiber conduction velocity from surface EMG signals during fatiguing dynamic contractions. IEEE Trans. Biomed. Eng. 51, 1383–1393 (2004)

Implementing Scenarios as an Evaluation Method of the Patient-Physician Interaction in Decision Aids

Curtis V. Lauterbach and Jeremiah D. Still

Missouri Western State University, Saint Joseph, MO, USA
{clauterbach,jstill2}@missouriwestern.edu

Abstract. Decision aids are being used in the exam room to assist physicians with diagnosing. Past research on computer-based decision aids examined perceived physician capabilities and degree of liability, and their impact on the patient-physician interaction. However, no one has contrasted the use of physical aids (physician's desk reference) with computerized aids on these characteristics. In this study, participants were given a scenario in which they took on the role of the patient and were asked to rate the physician's capabilities and degree of liability given a negative outcome. There were no significant differences between the no types (computer, physical, or no) employed on physician capabilities or liability. However, we suggest that scenarios can effectively be used to assess the impact of decision aids on the physician-patient interaction.

Keywords: scenario, decision aid, patient-physician interaction.

1 Introduction

Evaluating the user experience is very important in Human-Computer Interaction (HCI) as correcting design flaws leads to the development of better experiences. One area growing exponentially is medical devices, especially within the domain of decision aids in Electronic Medical Records (EMRs). These designs are strenuously scrutinized because they assist the physician in recording the patient-physician interaction and generating a differential diagnosis.

The patient-physician interaction can be improved or harmed by decision aids. Decision aids are known to affect patient compliance, patient perception of physician capabilities, and, in some instances, liability in malpractice cases. Decision aids take on physical and electronic forms. Traditionally, physical aids such as a physician's desk reference were ubiquitous. The physician created a differential by using their clinical knowledge, which they cross referenced against their desk references. However, now computer aids allow physicians to input patient symptoms and compare their differential diagnosis with that of the computer's to exhaust the possibilities thereby reducing the incidence of misdiagnosis.

V.G. Duffy (Ed.): DHM/HCII 2013, Part I, LNCS 8025, pp. 232–239, 2013.

Computer-based decision aids have been used since the 1960's. In addition to providing an exhaustive search during diagnosis, computer-based aids are not subject to forgetting. It has been shown that recertification scores decrease over the years – as reported by the American Board of Internal Medicine – suggesting that some medical knowledge may be less accessible over time (Leigh, Young, & Haley, 1993; Ramsey et al., 1991). Therefore, it would be logical for physicians' computer aid usage to increase over the years. As a caveat, although it is logical for people to use computer aids more as their medical knowledge declines, that does not mean they are more likely to actually use them. They may gain a tacit knowledge, e.g., "gut feeling", about their craft over the years allowing them to make better diagnoses and that knowledge cannot be captured in these test scores. However, the benefit to computer aid usage is clear; computer aids have been shown to increase correct diagnosis from 39.5% to 45.9% (Friedman, Elstein, & Wolfe, 1999). A 6.4% increase in diagnosis accuracy is substantial considering its real-world impact on patients.

The goal of this research project was to first replicate Arkes, Shaffer, and Meadow's 2007 study to see the effects of physician use of different diagnostic aids on participant's ratings of physician effectiveness and liability. Second, we hoped to further explore the role computer decision aids play in patient-physician interactions compared to traditional physical aids. Through this process we introduce some of the history of the medical decision making literature, patient-computer-physician interaction findings, and methods for evaluating the patient-physician interaction. Finally, we discuss the use of scenarios as a new explorative method to test potential computer interactions intended for use in high risk situations.

1.1   History of Computerized Decision Aids

Decision aids have been an integral part of medical diagnostics for decades and have been shown to significantly reduce medication errors (Bates, Teich, & Lee, 1999). There are different types of decision aids. Traditional physical aids (e.g., research articles) and computer decision aids summarize and organize information obtained from clinical findings to assist physicians in determining a differential diagnosis. As early as 1960 computer decision aids were designed and used Bayesian analysis to provide information from clinical findings and reviewed the existing literature.

In 1968, Gorry and Barnett developed a method for converting new clinical findings into a form usable for generating differential diagnoses. Between 1972 and 1983 the INTEREST-1 system was developed for a similar purpose; it reviewed all available literature in its database and generated a differential diagnosis (Miller, 2009). In 1984 the Quick Medical Reference (QMR) was developed. This system used the existing knowledge base from the INTEREST-1, reviewed clinical findings, and provided information on how relevant the information was to the current case

(Miller, 2009). Later, guidelines stemming from various medical associations (e.g., American Heart Association) were built into the diagnostic aids providing physician with valuable, up-to-date information (Pennachio, 2004).

Currently, there are many suggestions regarding how to design future decisions aids. The following points represent some of the concerns pertinent to future design. In terms of accuracy and aid evaluation, decision aids should be able to generate the same differential as an unaided physician, the test cases used should mimic those in the real world, and the aids should be evaluated on their ability to solve medical cases with and without a physician (Miller, 2009; Promberger & Baron, 2006). In regards to interactions, the aid should not interfere with patient-physician interaction, the aid should follow the physician's thought process, it should present a list of possible diagnosis based on clinical findings, and the aid should alleviate paper work (Ridderikhoff & Van Herk, 1997).

1.2   The Patient-Computer-Physician Interaction

Patients interact with physicians in a wide variety of settings and EMR are employed in many of those settings (Chen, Ngo, Harrison, & Duong, 2011). EMRs have been used in the family practice, general hospital, specialty clinics, and most recently the emergency and operating rooms. Although decision aids are now included in EMRs, some physicians opt not to use them. Many believed that the use of a computer-based decision aid will reduce trust and rapport (Cruickshank, 1984; Larkin & Kelliher, 2011; Potter, 1981). This could result, in part, from the device acting as a physical barrier and from eye contact being broken as the physician switches between patient and the computer (Chen, Ngo, Harrison, & Duong, 2011; Scott, & Purves, 1996). Similarly, Bristowe and Patrick (2012) reported that computer-based aids can lead to feelings of less autonomy and disengagement, fewer resolved concerns, and a significant reduction in the ability to ask questions. Additional studies have found that patients also experience feelings of disengagement and feel as if the physician withheld information (Roter, Frankel, Hall, & Sluyter, 2006; Rouf, Whittle, Lu, & Schwartz, 2006; Waitzkin, 1984).

Research by Arkes, Shaffer, and Meadow (2007) examined the effect of electronic decision aids on ratings of professionalism, thoroughness, length of visit, diagnostic capability, and overall satisfaction of physicians. Physicians who used decision aids were rated lower. Medical students evaluated the physicians similarly. Shaffer, Probst, Merkle, Arkes, and Meadow (2012) found that physicians were perceived as being more effective when they did not use a decision aid and when they sought a colleague's advice. However, Pezzo and Pezzo (2006) reported that medical students reading mock court transcripts of malpractice cases, gave physicians less liability when they had followed the recommendations of a decision aid.

Although there are potential negative aspects associated with use of a decision-making aid, the potential exists for positive interactions. For example, Frankel et al.

(2005) reported that a simple movement of the computer screen had a positive effect on patient-physician interaction. Chen, Ngo, Harrison, and Duong (2011) examined this interaction further using an apparatus referred to as "Computers on Wheels" (COW). Physicians initially placed the apparatus in front of themselves while obtaining clinical findings and switched their attention between the COW and patient. The physician then positioned it to where physician and patient could view the diagnosis and treatment together. Based on these findings, it was suggested that the physician should have the COW close to them when entering their orders and initiate eye contact when the patient asked follow-up questions.

1.3   Methods for Evaluating the Patient-Computer-Physician Interaction

We focus on evaluating the patient-physician interaction and the role a decision aid plays. The exam room is a dynamic setting in which a tremendous amount of information is passed between the patient and the physician in order to reach a diagnosis and, ultimately, treatment. This setting presents many challenges for testing user experience, such as the confidential nature of the shared information. Therefore, alternative methods such as questionnaires, standardized patients, and scenarios ought to be used.

Questionnaires provide a common method for gathering information. Bieber, Muller, Nicolai, Hartmann, and Eich (2010) developed a survey to measure the quality of the patient-physician interaction. Previous questionnaires focused too heavily on quality of care without objective measures and were also criticized as being biased by social desirability, clinical, and socio-demographic variables. However, their Questionnaire on Quality of Physician-Patient Interaction (QQPPI) was found to have high reliability and did not appear to be biased by social desirability (Bieber, et al, 2010). Questionnaires are not the only method available to researchers. Linder et al. (2005) used standardized patients to evaluate a new decision aid. These patients were trained to present conditions that mimic what a physician would experience in a real medical case (Tamblyn, 1990). Linder et al. found that the standardized patient was treated like an actual patient, were able to evaluate physicians, and were realistic in their ability to display medical cases. Standardized patients are now being used in instances when the interaction between the patient and physician impacts the use of the system.

Traditionally, scenarios have been used in the design process to show how users would interact with the system. They also can be used to discover what activities, functions, and needs ought to be considered when designing the system (Sharp, Rogers, & Preece, 2007). Therefore, information collected via scenarios can help design teams see how users interact with the system. In this light, it seems reasonable to assume that scenarios could prove useful in examining physician decision-making aids. We will not be the first to apply scenarios to the study of medical decision making as they have been used to determine how patients view their physician's capabilities.

This method was selected over the others due to its easy of employment. It afforded us an easy way to contrast traditional and electronic decision aids. Please note that this study does not set out to test which method would be the most effective.

2   Methods

Ninety-three undergraduate students (70 female) who were enrolled in introductory psychology courses participated in this study. We examined the effects of decision aids (no aid, computer aid, physical aid) on perceived physician effectiveness. A between-subjects design was used with participants distributed equally across the three conditions.

After informed consent was obtained, the participants read a scenario in which they took the role of a patient suffering from deep vein thrombosis. This scenario was taken directly from Arkes, Shaffer, and Medow (2007) and it depicted the interaction between a patient and physician. For each of the experimental groups, the physician could employ no aid, use a computer aid or a physical aid within the scenario. The participants read a scenario, which described the scene and interactions. The inclusion of a physical aid as a comparison condition is unique to this study. Next, participants used a seven-point likert scale (the same as Arkes et al., 2007) to rate the physician's effectiveness.

The survey focused on five key patient-physician interaction dimensions identified by the medical decision making literature; we added an additional question intended to gage liability. These are the dimensions and respective questions used in the survey: 1. Thoroughness: did the physician completely address the condition, 2. Length of visit: did the physician spend enough time to adequately diagnose the condition, 3. Diagnostic capabilities: did the physician appear to know how to assess the condition and what tests to order, 4. Professionalism: was the physician behaving appropriately, 5. Overall satisfaction: was the patient happy with their physician interaction, 6. Liability: how severe should a punishment be, given a negative outcome.

3   Results

A Kruskal-Wallis test was conducted that compared participant ratings on the perceived effectiveness of the physician given the different types of decision aids used. Mean rank for each condition appear in Table 1. A higher ranking indicates a better rating of the physician on that characteristic. There were no significant differences between the three aids on thoroughness ($H(2) = .04, p > .05$), length of visit ($H(2) = .26, p > .05$), diagnostic capabilities ($H(2) = 1.08, p > .05$), professionalism ($H(2) = 2.16, p > .05$), overall satisfaction ($H(2) = .33, p > .05$), or liability ($H(2) = 2.04, p > .05$).

Table 1. Mean Ranks for Physician Characteristic per Aid Type

Physician Characteristic	Aid Type	Mean Rank
Thoroughness	None	46.24
	Computer	47.35
	Physical	47.40
Wait	None	45.50
	Computer	46.68
	Physical	48.82
Diagnostic Capabilities	None	50.68
	Computer	46.56
	Physical	43.76
Professionalism	None	51.79
	Computer	47.05
	Physical	42.16
Satisfaction	None	46.65
	Computer	49.06
	Physical	45.29
Liability	None	42.37
	Computer	46.79
	Physical	51.84

4   Conclusion

Previous research on computer-based decision aids examined perceived physician capabilities and their impact on the patient-physician interaction. However, no one has contrasted the use of computerized aids with physical ones. Participants were given a scenario either containing a computerized, physical, or no decision aid in which they took on the role of the patient and were asked to rate the physician's capabilities and degree of liability given a negative outcome. The results indicated no significant differences, on any dimension, across the conditions.

This result stands in contrast to findings in the medical decision literature in which differences have been demonstrated between ratings of physician interactions using computer-based aids and those using no aid. Although our manipulation did not produce significant differences, our study introduces designers to an accepted measure of a physician's effectiveness that has already been established in the medical decision making literature. In addition, understanding how decision aids are viewed by both patients and physicians can help developers create interfaces that are useful and provide good patient-physician interaction. These improvements could lead to increased diagnostic accuracy, patient compliance, and decrease stress amongst medical staff.

Although it is important to develop these technologies, medical decision making is high risk. Patients in these situations may feel intimidated or even depersonalized when observers are in the exam room. As such they may withhold vital information that may lead to an incorrect diagnosis. These factors can preclude the use of several methods commonly used to evaluate interactions.

We believe that scenarios give the participant a situation mimicking the flow of information in a medical exam without the associated risk. Further, scenarios can be used to evaluate this interaction in different settings, such as the emergency room, physician training. They also provide a chance to evaluate communication between medical professionals, which normally is difficult to achieve given the associated privacy and liability issues. Ultimately, scenario use could facilitate the development of improved designs and improved patient-physician interactions.

References

1. Arkes, H.R., Shaffer, V.A., Medow, M.A.: Patients derogate physicians who use a computer-assisted diagnostic aid. Medical Decision Making 27(2), 189–202 (2007)
2. Bates, D.W., Teich, J.M., Lee, J.: The impact of computerized physician order entry on medication error prevention. Journal of American Information Association 6(4), 313–321 (1999)
3. Bieber, C., Muller, K.G., Nicolai, J., Hartmann, M., Eich, W.: How does your doctor talk with you? Preliminary validation of a brief patient self-report questionnaire on the quality of physician-patient interaction. Journal of Clinical Psychological Medical Settings 17(2), 125–136 (2010)
4. Bristowe, K., Patrick, P.L.: Do too many cooks spoil the broth? The effect of observers on doctor-patient interaction. Medical Education 46(8), 785–794 (2012)
5. Chen, Y., Ngo, V., Harrison, S., Duong, V.: Unpacking exam-room computing: Negotiating computer-use in patient-physician interactions, CHI, Vancouver, Canada, pp. 3343–3352 (2011)
6. Cruickshank, P.J.: Computers in medicine: patient's attitudes. The Journal of the Royal College of General Practitioners 34(259), 77–80 (1984)
7. Frankel, R., Altschuler, A., George, S., Kinsman, J., Jimison, H., Robertson, N.R., Hsu, J.: Effects of exam room computing on clinician-patient communication: a longitudinal qualitative study. Journal of General Internal Medicine 20(8), 677–682 (2005)
8. Friedman, D.P., Elstein, A.S., Wolf, F.M.: Enhancement of clinicians'diagnostic reasoning by computer-based consultation: a multisite study of 2 systems. JAMA 282, 1852–1854 (1999)
9. Gorry, P.N., Barnett, G.O.: Experience with a model of sequential diagnosis. Computers and Biomedical Research 1(5), 490–507 (1968)
10. Larkin, K., Kelliher, A.: Designing flexible EMR systems for recording and summarizing doctor-patient interactions, CHI, Vancouver, Canada, pp. 1609–1614 (2011)
11. Leigh, T.M., Young, P.R., Haley, J.V.: Performances of family practice diplomats on successive mandatory recertification examinations. Academic Medicine 68(12), 912–918 (1993)
12. Linder, J.A., Rose, A.F., Palchuk, M.B., Chang, F., Schnipper, J.L., Chan, J.C., Middleton, B.: Decision support for acute problems: The role of the standardized patient in usability testing. Journal of Biomedical Informatics 39(6), 648–655 (2005)
13. Miller, R.A.: Computer-assisted diagnostic decision support: history, challenges, and possible paths forward. Advances In Health Science Education 14(S1), 89–106 (2009)

14. Pennachio, D.L.: Clinical guidelines sword or shield? Medical Economics 81(12), 22–24 (2004)
15. Pezzo, M.V., Pezzo, S.D.: Physician evaluation after medical errors: Does having a computer diagnostic aid help or hurt in hindsight? Medical Decision Making 26(1), 48–56 (2006)
16. Potter, A.R.: Computers in general practice: the patient's voice. Journal of Royal of General Practioners 31(232), 683–685 (1981)
17. Promberger, M., Baron, J.: Do patients trust computers? Journal of Behavioral Decision Making 19(5), 455–468 (2006)
18. Ramsey, P.G., Carline, J.D., Inui, T.S., Larson, L.O., Gerfo, J.P., Norcini, J.J., Wenrich, M.D.: Changes over time in the knowledge base of practicing internists. JAMA 266(8), 1103–1107 (1991)
19. Ridderikhoff, J., Van Herk, E.: A diagnostic support system in general practice: is it feasible? International Journal of Medical Informatics 45(3), 133–143 (1997)
20. Roter, D.L., Frankel, R.M., Hall, J.A., Sluyter, D.: The expression of emotion through nonverbal behavior in medical visits: Mechanisms and outcomes. Journal of General Internal Medicine 34(S1), S28–S34 (2006)
21. Rouf, E., Whittle, J., Lu, N., Schwartz, M.D.: Computers in the exam room: Differences in physician-patient interaction be due to physician experience. Journal of General Internal Medicine 22(1), 43–48 (2006)
22. Scott, D., Purves, I.N.: Triadic relationship between doctor, computer and patient. Interacting with Computers 8(4), 347–363 (1996)
23. Shaffer, V.A., Probst, C.A., Merkle, E.C., Arkes, H.R., Meadow, M.A.: Why do patients derogate physicians who use a computer-based diagnostic support system? Medical Decision Making 33(1), 1–11 (2012)
24. Sharp, Rogers, Preece: Interaction design: Beyond human-computer interaction, 2nd edn., pp. 505–506, 558. Wiley, NJ (2007)
25. Tamblyn, R.M., Klass, D.K., Schanbl, G.K., Kopelow, M.L.: Factors associated with the accuracy of standardized patient presentation. Academic Medicine 65(S9), 55–56 (1990)
26. Waitzkin, H.: Doctor-patient communication. Clinical implications of social scientific research. JAMA 252(17), 2441–2446 (1984)

Plantar Pressure Gradient Angles to Evaluate Risk of Diabetic Foot Ulcer

Chi-Wen Lung[1], Ben-Yi Liau[2], and Yih-Kuen Jan[3]

[1] Department of Creative Product Design, Asia University, Taichung, Taiwan, ROC
[2] Department of Biomedical Engineering, Hungkuang University, Taichung, Taiwan, ROC
[3] Departments of Kinesiology & Community Health and Computational
Science & Engineering, University of Illinois at Urbana-Champaign, Champaign, IL, USA
cwlung@asia.edu.tw

Abstract. Diabetic foot ulcers remain one of the most serious complications of diabetes mellitus. Peak pressure gradient (PPG) has demonstrated to contribute to the development of diabetic foot ulcers. This study used the time-varying directions of instantaneous PPG angle to evaluate the risk of diabetic foot ulcers. A total of 14 participants were studied, including 7 diabetics and 7 non-diabetic controls. The peak plantar pressure (PPP), PPG, and PPG angle at the great toe were calculated from plantar pressures obtained by the F-scan plantar pressure measurement system during walking. The results showed that the PPP and PPG in the diabetics were significantly higher than in the controls, but the PPG angle in the diabetics was significantly lower than in the controls. This study provides evidence that the diabetics are associated with higher PPP and PPG and lower PPG angle as compared to non-diabetics. The proposed PPG angle may improve our understanding of the influence of PPG on the risk for diabetic foot ulcers.

Keywords: diabetic foot ulcers, peak pressure gradient, plantar pressure.

1 Introduction

Diabetes mellitus (DM) is the seventh leading cause of death by disease in the United States [1]. The one of most serious complications of DM is the diabetic foot ulcers [2]. DM causes not only a reduced or loss of protective sensation in the foot, but also changes in the soft tissues of the foot as well as the dryness of the skin, that can lead to excessive formation of callus. These changes affect ambulatory function that may lead to a high peak plantar pressure (PPP) in diabetics. The repetitive high PPP insults to the plantar surface of the diabetic foot have been shown to be associated with the development of foot ulcers. However, Lavery and colleagues [3] suggested that the plantar pressure alone is not adequate to predict the development of skin breakdown and other factors should be explored.

Mueller and colleagues [4] introduced the peak pressure gradient (PPG) to further quantify the changes of plantar pressure distributions in diabetics. The high PPG may contribute to the skin breakdown because they cause large shearing stresses within the

V.G. Duffy (Ed.): DHM/HCII 2013, Part I, LNCS 8025, pp. 240–247, 2013.
© Springer-Verlag Berlin Heidelberg 2013

plantar soft tissues [4]. Although the introduction of the PPG concept has provided a new assessment to understand the development of diabetic foot ulcers, the quantification of the PPG patterns require further investigation and classification [5]. For example, the current definition of the PPG does not quantify the time-varying directions of instantaneous PPG angle (PPG angle), which may be used to estimate the plantar shear directions.

Shear stresses may be an important factor in locating where the skin breakdown occurs in diabetics [6]. The measurement devices of the plantar shear stress are currently being used only in the research environments due to a large size of the sensors [7-9]. However, the PPP and PPG measurements, based on the thin sensors of the plantar pressure mapping device, are easier to obtain in the clinical settings [4, 10, 11]. The PPG may be used to estimate the shear stress for predicting potential trauma to the plantar soft tissues [11, 12]. We postulate that the PPG angle may provide additional information to quantify the PPG patterns. Theoretically, the PPG angle may increase at the distraction of the pressure in concert (Fig. 1a), and decrease at the concentration of the pressure in indentation (Fig. 1b). The purpose of this study was to develop a new method to quantify time-varying directions of instantaneous PPG as defined as the PPG angle in this study in diabetics with peripheral neuropathy.

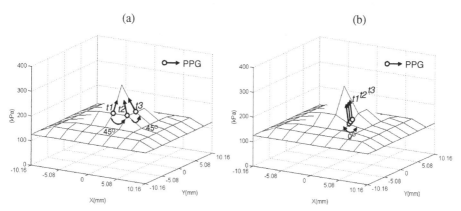

Fig. 1. The time-varying directions of peak plantar gradient (PPG). (a) Distraction pattern: the angles of the time 1 to time 2 is $45°$ ($t1$-$t2$), and time 2 to time 3 is $45°$ ($t2$-$t3$). (b) Concentration pattern: the angles of the time 1 to time 2 is $0°$ ($t1$-$t2$), and time 2 to time 3 is $0°$ ($t2$-$t3$). Although the PPG values in (a) and (b) are close, the average of the changes in angles, PPG angles, are very different ($45°$ v.s. $0°$).

2   Methods

2.1   Participants

Fourteen volunteers were recruited, including 7 type 2 diabetics (3 males) and 7 non-diabetic healthy controls (4 males). Subjects with gross foot deformities (except minor toe clawing) and prior foot amputations/major surgeries were excluded for a more homogeneous population. The demographic data of the control group were: age 23.1±3.4 years, weight 60.8±14.0 kg, height 1.66±0.12 m, body mass index (BMI) 21.9±3.7 kg/ m2. The demographic data of the diabetic group were: age 44.7±11.9 years, weight 85.3±19.9 kg, height 1.68±0.08 m, BMI 30.1±6.9 kg/m2. The fasting blood glucose level and duration of diabetes were 143.3±61.0 mg/dL and 7.3±7.6 years. All diabetics had peripheral neuropathy as confirmed by inability to sense a 5.07 Semmes-Weinstein monofilament on at least four locations of the plantar foot. This study was approved by an institutional review board. The research protocol was explained to the volunteers who signed an informed consent form.

2.2   Plantar Pressure Measurements

The F-scan system (Tekscan, Boston, MA, USA) was used to collect the plantar pressures data during walking at a self-selected pace in standardized shoes (Fig. 2) [13-15]. Each F-scan in-shoe sensor contains 960 sensing pixels. The size of each pixel is 5.08 x 5.08 mm. A sensor was placed between the subject's sock and the insole of the shoe. All subjects wore ambulatory shoes with a 1-inch heel (Altrex, Teaneck, NJ). The shoe was worn with its standard insert and a thin cotton sock. Subjects wore the sensor inside the shoe for 3-5 min walking before calibration for adequate sensor acclimatization [13, 14]. The sensor was calibrated according to the manufacturer's guidelines. Subjects were allowed to walk at their chosen walking speed, and data were collected at 200 Hz during two walking trials immediately after calibration.

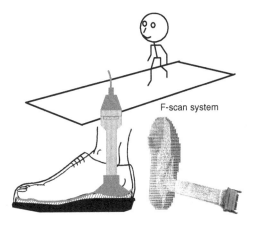

Fig. 2. The F-scan system was used to collect the plantar pressures data during walking at a self-selected pace in standardized shoes

2.3   Data Analysis and Statistics

ASCII files with data from the three middle steps were processed by Matlab codes to determine the PPP and PPG in the 1st toe regions at risk for diabetic foot ulcers [16, 17]. The pressure was determined in a defined area [a 3x3 box of F-Scan sensels

(231.3 mm2)] around the nodes (spacing equal to half the length of the sensor) which were generated using the bicubic polynomial spline function. A pressure data on the plantar surface of the foot may be characterized by the PPP and PPG. The PPP is defined as equation (1)

$$PPP = max\,(p) \tag{1}$$

where p is the pressure distribution on the plantar region surface. The PPG was calculated by determining the greatest difference in pressure from one node (half sensel apart) to the next according to rows, columns, and by diagonal (Fig. 3) [4]. The PPG at the PPP locations can be calculated as equation (2)

$$PPG = max\left(\left.\frac{\partial p}{\partial r}\right|(x_p, y_p)\right) \tag{2}$$

where $(\partial p / \partial r)\,|\,(x_p, y_p)$ (space rate of change of pressure on the plantar surface) is the directional derivative of pressure p at the node of the plantar region (x_p, y_p) on the plantar surface in any direction given by the vector $\vec{r}$. Each node accompanies eight pressure gradients in eight directions. The time-varying directions of the PPGs (PPG angle) (Fig. 3) was the average of the changes in angles as equation (3).

$$PPG\ angle = \frac{1}{N-1}\sum_{i=1}^{N-1}(\alpha_{i+1} - \alpha_i) \tag{3}$$

where N is the time over the half of the peak pressure gradient, where α is the angle of the PPG direction in the time of i.

The differences in the PPP, PPG, and PPG angle between diabetics and controls were examined using the Student t test [18, 19]. The values were presented as the mean ± standard deviation. The level of the significance was set at 0.05.

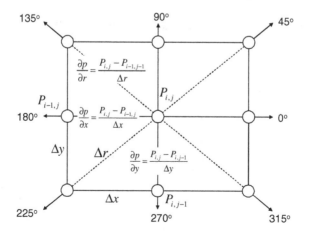

Fig. 3. Calculation of the Peak pressure gradient (PPG) and the time-varying directions of the PPGs (PPG angle)

3   Results and Discussion

The PPP value at the 1st toe was significantly greater in the diabetics (566.2±234.8 kPa) as compared to the controls (313.9±104.2 kPa, p<.05, Fig. 4A). The PPG value at the 1st toe was significantly greater in the diabetic group (128.9±53.8 kPa/mm) as compared to the control group (51.5±16.5 kPa/mm, p<.05, Fig. 4B). The PPG angle at the 1st toe was significantly smaller in the diabetic group (14.6 o±19.0o) as compared to the control group (48.1 o±32.4o, p<.05, Fig. 4C).

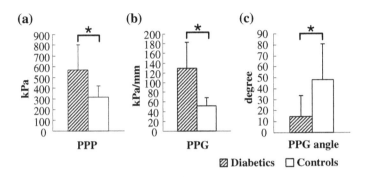

Fig. 4. The comparison of peak plantar pressure (PPP), peak pressure gradient (PPG), and peak pressure gradient angles (PPG angle) in the controls and diabetics; * indicates $p < .05$

The results support our hypotheses that the plantar pressure has higher values in the PPP and PPG in of diabetics during the shoes walking, but smaller values in the PPG angle. The proposed new variable, PPG angle, were able to further define the PPG patterns in diabetics and could provide additional insight into the mechanism of the influences of PPG on the development of diabetic foot ulcers.

The mean PPP were 165% at the 1st toe of the diabetics than controls in this study. These results are consistent with the literature. Zheng et al. [20] demonstrated that the Young's modulus (elasticity) of plantar tissues of the diabetic foot increased at the 1st toe. Perry and colleagues [6] also indicated that the diabetes-associated stiffening of the plantar soft tissues that the pad of the 1st toe may cause this abnormal PPP. Our results support that the 1st toe is higher stiffness and risk for foot ulceration during the walking [21].

The mean PPG were 214% in the 1st toe in the diabetics than in the controls. The increase in PPG at the 1st toe in diabetics may be attributed to a significant limitation of motion at the metatarsophalangeal joints. The exact pathogenesis of the limited joint mobility in diabetics is unclear, but is thought to be related to the progressive stiffening of the collagen-containing tissues due to accumulation of advanced glycation end products (AGEs) [22]. The diabetic foot with limited motion at the metatarsophalangeal joints significantly reduce shock absorbing ability and may cause an abnormal plantar pressure distribution [23]. Fernando el al. [24] showed that the limited joint mobility may be a major factor in causing abnormally high PPP and contribute to the foot ulceration. The authors also proved that the abnormal plantar foot pressures alone did not predict the location of foot ulcers. Our results of the PPP and PPG in the diabetic and control groups support the principle of assessing both the PPP and PPG to predict diabetic foot ulcers.

As expected, the mean PPG angle was at the 1st toe in the diabetics than in the controls in this study. Ahmed et al. [25] reported that the most common sites of diabetic foot ulcers was in the planter surface of the 1st toe. About 33% of diabetics develop callus at the 1st toe. Plantar callus is associated with the high vertical and shear forces in diabetics. When callus is removed, plantar pressures are reduced by 32.1% in diabetics [26]. This finding indicates that callus may act as a foreign body elevating the plantar pressures. As high shear stresses are associated with foot ulcers [27], the high PPG angle in diabetics may be negatively related with shear stresses. This may imply the use of foot pressure mapping system to measure PPP and PPG (PPG angle) should be promoted in clinical settings due to its ease of use. Further studies need to establish the relationship between PPG angle and shear stresses. Calluses are generally not harmful, but may sometimes lead to the changes in PPG angles that may aggravate the risk for foot ulcerations.

4   Conclusions

This study provides evidence that diabetics are associated with higher PPP and PPG and lower PPG angle compared to non-diabetics. The proposed PPG angle may improve our understanding of the influence of PPG on the risk of diabetic foot ulcers. Such knowledge may contribute to the prevention of diabetic foot ulcers.

Acknowledgements. This study was initiated at the University of Oklahoma Health Sciences Center supported by the Oklahoma Center for the Advancement of Science and Technology (HR09-048) to Dr. Yih-Kuen Jan, and was completed at the University of Illinois at Urbana-Champaign.

References

1. NDIC: National Diabetes Statistics 2011. National Institutes of Health (2011)
2. van Schie, C.H.M.: A review of the biomechanics of the diabetic foot. The International Journal of Lower Extremity Wounds 4, 160–170 (2005)
3. Lavery, L.A., Armstrong, D.G., Wunderlich, R.P., Tredwell, J., Boulton, A.J.M.: Predictive value of foot pressure assessment as part of a population-based diabetes disease management program. Diabetes Care 26, 1069–1073 (2003)
4. Mueller, M.J., Zou, D., Lott, D.J.: "Pressure gradient" as an indicator of plantar skin injury. Diabetes Care 28, 2908–2912 (2005)
5. Jan, Y.K., Lung, C.W., Cuaderes, E., Rong, D., Boyce, K.: Effect of viscoelastic properties of plantar soft tissues on plantar pressures at the first metatarsal head in diabetics with peripheral neuropathy. Physiol. Meas. 34, 53–66 (2013)
6. Perry, J.E., Hall, J.O., Davis, B.L.: Simultaneous measurement of plantar pressure and shear forces in diabetic individuals. Gait & Posture 15, 101–107 (2002)

7. Yavuz, M., Erdemir, A., Botek, G., Hirschman, G.B., Bardsley, L., Davis, B.L.: Peak plantar pressure and shear locations: relevance to diabetic patients. Diabetes Care 30, 2643–2645 (2007)
8. Cong, Y., Tak-Man Cheung, J., Leung, A.K.L., Zhang, M.: Effect of heel height on in-shoe localized triaxial stresses. Journal of Biomechanics 44, 2267–2272 (2011)
9. Stucke, S., McFarland, D., Goss, L., Fonov, S., McMillan, G.R., Tucker, A., Berme, N., Cenk Guler, H., Bigelow, C., Davis, B.L.: Spatial relationships between shearing stresses and pressure on the plantar skin surface during gait. Journal of Biomechanics 45, 619–622 (2012)
10. Smith, K.E., Commean, P.K., Mueller, M.J., Robertson, D.D., Pilgram, T., Johnson, J.: Assessment of the diabetic foot using spiral computed tomography imaging and plantar pressure measurements: a technical report. Journal of Rehabilitation Research and Development 37, 31–40 (2000)
11. Lott, D.J., Zou, D., Mueller, M.J.: Pressure gradient and subsurface shear stress on the neuropathic forefoot. Clinical Biomechanics 23, 342–348 (2008)
12. Zou, D., Mueller, M.J., Lott, D.J.: Effect of peak pressure and pressure gradient on subsurface shear stresses in the neuropathic foot. Journal of Biomechanics 40, 883–890 (2007)
13. Pitei, D.L., Lord, M., Foster, A., Wilson, S., Watkins, P.J., Edmonds, M.E.: Plantar pressures are elevated in the neuroischemic and the neuropathic diabetic foot. Diabetes Care 22, 1966–1970 (1999)
14. Mueller, M.J., Strube, M.J.: Generalizability of in-shoe peak pressure measures using the F-scan system. Clinical Biomechanics 11, 159–164 (1996)
15. Nicolopoulos, C.S., Anderson, E.G., Solomonidis, S.E., Giannoudis, P.V.: Evaluation of the gait analysis FSCAN pressure system: clinical tool or toy? The Foot 10, 124–130 (2000)
16. Armstrong, D.G., Lavery, L.A., Bushman, T.R.: Peak foot pressures influence the healing time of diabetic foot ulcers treated with total contact casts. Journal of Rehabilitation Research & Development 35, 1–5 (1998)
17. Lung, C.W., Jan, Y.K.: Soft tissue biomechanics of diabetic foot ulcers. In: Ruiz, A.J.C., Mendoza, J.M.A. (eds.) Soft Tissue: Composition, Mechanisms of Injury and Repair, pp. 1–32. Nova Science Publishers, Hauppauge (2012)
18. Salsich, G.B., Mueller, M.J., Sahrmann, S.A.: Passive ankle stiffness in subjects with diabetes and peripheral neuropathy versus an age-matched comparison group. Physical Therapy 80, 352–362 (2000)
19. Klaesner, J.W., Hastings, M.K., Zou, D., Lewis, C., Mueller, M.J.: Plantar tissue stiffness in patients with diabetes mellitus and peripheral neuropathy. Archives of Physical Medicine & Rehabilitation 83, 1796–1801 (2002)
20. Zheng, Y.P., Choi, Y.K., Wong, K., Chan, S., Mak, A.F.T.: Biomechanical assessment of plantar foot tissue in diabetic patients using an ultrasound indentation system. Ultrasound in Medicine & Biology 26, 451–456 (2000)
21. Gefen, A., Megido-Ravid, M., Azariah, M., Itzchak, Y., Arcan, M.: Integration of plantar soft tissue stiffness measurements in routine MRI of the diabetic foot. Clinical Biomechanics 16, 921–925 (2001)
22. Burns, S., Jan, Y.K.: Diabetic foot ulceration and amputation. In: Kim, C.T. (ed.) Rehabilitation Medicine, pp. 1–20. InTech Publisher, Croatia (2012)
23. Zimny, S., Schatz, H., Pfohl, M.: The role of limited joint mobility in diabetic patients with an at-risk foot. Diabetes Care 27, 942–946 (2004)

24. Fernando, D.J., Masson, E.A., Veves, A., Boulton, A.J.: Relationship of limited joint mobility to abnormal foot pressures and diabetic foot ulceration. Diabetes Care 14, 8–11 (1991)
25. Ahmed, M.E., Tamimi, A.O., Mahadi, S.I., Widatalla, A.H., Shawer, M.A.: Hallux ulceration in diabetic patients. The Journal of Foot and Ankle Surgery 49, 2–7 (2010)
26. Pitei, D.L., Foster, A., Edmonds, M.: The effect of regular callus removal on foot pressures. The Journal of Foot and Ankle Surgery 38, 251–255 (1999)
27. Manorama, A.A., Baek, S., Vorro, J., Sikorskii, A., Bush, T.R.: Blood perfusion and transcutaneous oxygen level characterizations in human skin with changes in normal and shear loads — Implications for pressure ulcer formation. Clinical Biomechanics 25, 823–828 (2010)

Explicit Tracking in the Diagnostic Process for Hand Dermatological Practices

Luca Mazzola[1,2], Sara Marceglia[1,*], Stefano Bonacina[1], Francesco Pinciroli[1], Fabio Ayala[3], Ornella De Pitá[4], and Paolo Pigatto[5,**]

[1] Politecnico di Milano - Piazza Leonardo da Vinci 32, 20123 Milano (MI) Italy
sara.marceglia@polimi.it
[2] Universitá della Svizzera italiana - Via Buffi 13, 6900 Lugano (TI) Switzerland
[3] Universitá di Napoli Federico II, Napoli, Italy
[4] Servizio di Allergologia ed Immunologia Clinica e di Laboratorio,
Istituto Dermopatico dell'Immacolata, Roma, Italy
[5] Universitá degli Studi di Milano, Milano, Italy

Abstract. The complexity of the medical diagnostic practices is faced nowadays mainly with an extensive and long education and with on-the-job training for GPs. Despite these efforts, a big part of the diagnostic process remains implicit in the everyday practicies of skilled professionals. This project aims at an explicit tracking of this ability through the filling-in of an additional importance level for the voices in the Electronic Medical Record. The collected data leads to the extraction of rules that can empower a Decision Support System for hand dermatological practictioner with suggestios and/or diagnoses distribution probability for a specific situation.

1 Background

In almost every country in the world, the education of medical practitioners is complex and requires a relevant amount of resources, in terms of both time effort and skilled professionals dedicated to teaching. After the first educational level, the second level is required to train a fully operational general practitioner (GP).

A relevant issue in GP education is the diagnostic process. The diagnostic reasoning and ability are firstly learnt by observation of - and interactions with

---

* Corresponding author.
** On behalf of the *"Ambulatorio della Mano"*. The *Ambulatorio della Mano* is: S. Amato, Ospedale Civico di Palermo; G. Bornacina, Azienda Ospedaliero-Universitaria Maggiore della Caritá, Novara; P. Calzavara-Pinton, Spedali Civili di Brescia; S. Calvieri, La Sapienza Universitá, Roma; M. Congedo, Ospedale Vito Fazzi, Lecce; A. Cristaudo, Istituto Dermatologico San Gallicano IRCCS, Roma; C. Crosti, Universitá degli Studi di Milano; F. Cusano, Ospedale Rummo, Benevento; M. Gola, Universitá degli Studi di Firenze; P. Lisi, Universitá degli Studi di Perugia; P. Patrone, Azienda Ospedaliero-Universitaria, S. Maria della Misericordia, Udine; C. Potenza, Polo Pontino, La Sapienza Universitá, Roma; M. Travaglini, Ospedale A. Perrino, Brindisi.

V.G. Duffy (Ed.): DHM/HCII 2013, Part I, LNCS 8025, pp. 248–257, 2013.

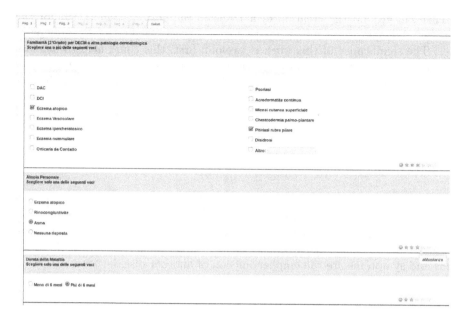

Fig. 1. The user interface of the specialized *EMR* implemented for the diagnosis of hand skin diseases

- training supervisors or advisors during medical education, and then improved by the growing experience in everyday practice [1]. Making a diagnosis requires evaluating a large number of objective and subjective parameters that are not always available all together, and that may be acquired during the process itself, thus introducing uncertainty.

In dermatology, hand skin pathologies are difficult to be diagnosed because they are characterized by similar signs and symptoms [2] that can be correctly interpreted only by highly experienced and trained specialists. Recently, the differential diagnostic process ([3], [4], [5]) has been applied to hand skin pathologies. Performing a differential diagnosis, timely recognizing the disease and promptly referring the patient to the appropriate specialized center are hard tasks for an inexperienced GP. Wrong diagnoses and thus inadequate therapies or treatments can worsen patients conditions.

2   Objective and Significance

The objectives of this work are: first, to track the diagnostic process performed by specialized dermatologists about the differential diagnosis of hand skin pathologies characterized by similar signs and symptoms; second, to test whether the information collected during the tracking would support better uncovering of the process [5]; third, to design and develop a computerized system that can enable GPs in diagnosing hand skin pathologies appropriately [6] and [7].

This will ground the creation of a Decision Support System (DSS) for the differential diagnosis of hand skin pathologies that will facilitate GPs daily practices. The significance of this work is twofold: first, this could help to increase the correctness rate of diagnosis performed by the GPs - or at least to make them aware of the need of a second specialized consultation. Second, the collected information and the implicit diagnostic pathway (or rules) can lead to better understand the usual way of reasoning followed by specialists for hand skin disease diagnosis.

3   Methods

We designed and implemented a specialized Electronic Medical Record (EMR) system [8], to support the process of differential diagnosis of hand skin pathologies. Specifically, the pathologies considered are divided in two classes: primary hand skin pathologies and secondary hand skin pathologies in which the hand signs and symptoms are the epiphenomenon of another disease:

1. **Primary pathologies**
   (a) DAC (Contact Allergic Dermatitis)
   (b) DCI (Irritant Contact Dermatitis)
         i. DAC + DCI
   (c) Atopic eczema
         i. Atopic eczema + DCI
   (d) Vescicular eczema
   (e) Hyperkeratotic eczema
   (f) Nummular eczema
2. **Secondary - other pathologies**
   (a) Psoriasis
   (b) Palmoplantar keratoderma
   (c) Superficial cutaneous mycoses
   (d) Continuous acrodermatitis
   (e) Pityriasis rubra pilaris

Based on this list of pathologies and their signs and symptoms, we designed the EMR contents together with trained specialists [9] belonging to the Italian reference centers for hand dermatology called "Ambulatorio della Mano", thus ensuring its clinical correctness and usefulness[1].

Then, the implemented EMR was re-assessed by specialists in the field who did not participate in its design, to prevent from possible biases introduced by personal experiences of the designers.

The EMR comprises an explicit tracking system that records a personal score (in a 0-5 range) given to the collected information by the specialist during a patient encounter. The question underlying the scoring phase is: how much was this

---

[1] For the full list of the fields included in the EMR and the scales adopted, please contact: *Paolo Pigatto – pigatto@unimi.it*

information (e.g. patient's gender, age, parts of the hand with altered skin) important/useful to diagnose patient's disease? The scoring phase allows to uncover a crucial step of diagnostic reasoning usually implicit in specialists decision.

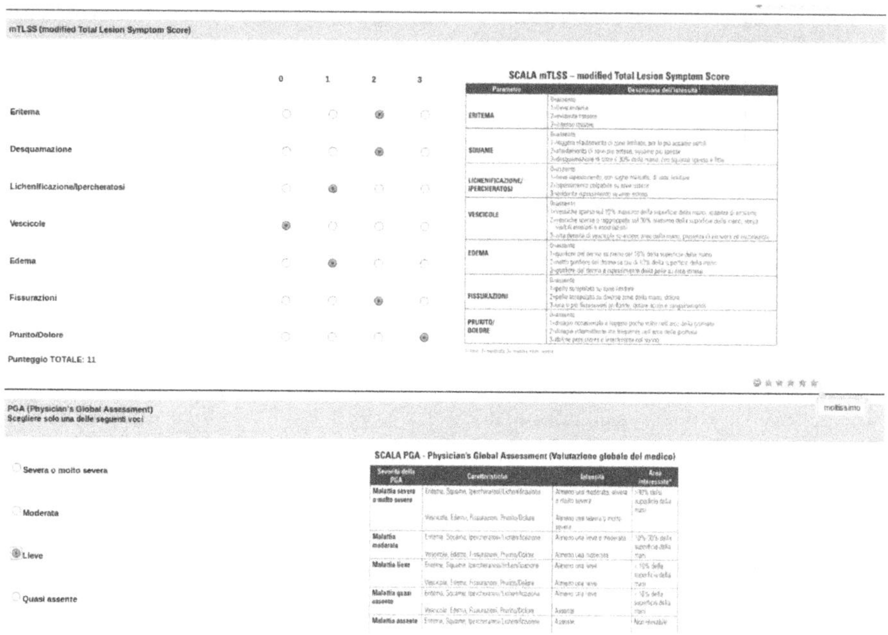

Fig. 2. The input forms for Modified Total Lesion Symptom Score ($mTLSS$) and Physician's Global Assessment (PGA) scales

More than one visit is needed to finalize the diagnostic process as either different symptoms spontaneously emerged during time, or the results of prescribed diagnostic tests become available. So, the EMR system is able to track patients in all the encounters they attended. This is achieved by pre-filling out forms with patient information, after the patient identification code is inserted. Furthermore, the system facilitates the practitioners by providing a list with all the visits attended by a patient, in order to allow run-time consulting of the patient medical history.

We included in our EMR system the results of standard evaluation scales (Fig. 2), like the modified Total Lesion Symptom Score (mTLSS) and the Physician Global Assessment (PGA) [10]. We implemented the EMR as a web application based on Apache web Server, PHP pages and MySQL database.

As the aim of the dataset collection was to explicit the underlying process and mine for diagnostic reasoning adopted, through data analysis we created a set of associations and rules able to suggest not only the possible diagnosis given an information dataset, but also the next possible diagnostic step (e.g., a test to be prescribed to reach a diagnosis, or a symptom to monitor). To do so, data

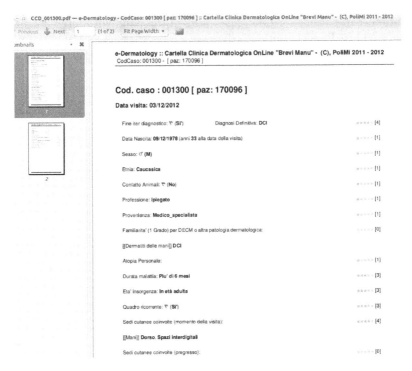

Fig. 3. The stored *EMR* record as a *PDF* file. It is available for reviews by GP, in case of new visits.

analysis used the additional inputs (the 0-5 scores) both to verify the rules and associations identified, and to formulate specific rules.

4   Results

4.1   The Electronic Medical Record [*EMR*] Developed

We developed a specialized EMR system able to collect in a distributed, secure and authenticated way the data about patient's visits from 16 reference centers for hand skin diseases in Italy.

The EMR system is divided in 5 different sections:

- personal information [2]
- demographical information
- physiological conditions
- pathological conditions
- contact reaction tests *[optional]*

---

[2] The identification of the patient is achieved through an ID assigned by the center, and its association with the name is managed outside this system, in every single diagnostic center. In this way we guarantee a strong separation between medical data and personal identification ones.

After the access by protected protocol to the website using the authentication codes provided, each center can manage its own patients, inserting a new visit, retrieving the ones already executed, or inserting an update for an already enrolled patient.

The EMR comprises relevant patient's personal data and an assessment of signs, symptoms and laboratory tests results together with a 5 star-based score of the importance of each single information for the current diagnostic process. In the EMR, the diagnosis field could be labeled as definitive or as temporary. This means requiring more exams or waiting for new signs/symptoms to raise.

To guarantee a secure identification of the patient, the system requires to insert the patients code twice for crosschecking. If the codes inserted are different, an alert will be generated and the two fields (mandatory for the saving of the record inside the system) are deleted. On the other side, if the patient code already exists, the persistent information (such as birth date, residence, gender) will be preloaded in the form, making the filling out of new visit report form quicker.

At the end of the process, the doctor can save or print a PDF compact version - Fig. 3 - of the medical record for the local archive. These files are also optimized for being printed on paper in gray tones. For example, the standard scales are reported in a text format (Fig. 4), the chosen level for each sub-index is highlighted with bold characters and the * symbols (e.g., *1*), while the assessed importance (the number of stars) is clearly reported [5].

4.2   The DataSet

We collected data regarding more than 1.300 visits. More than the 85% were usable for the subsequent analyses, while the others were affected by errors in the data stored and therefore excluded. Table 1 presents the distribution of the diagnoses, grouped as temporary diagnosis requiring further visits (28%), and final diagnosis (72%). The column *AVG(Stars)* shows the average values for the assessed importance (as number of stars) given by the specialists. They are aggregated in two sets, the first, for the attributes filled out for all cases (labeled as *Mand.*, for mandatory) and the second, for the attributes that make sense only for the differential diagnoses of the contact dermatitis (labeled as *Opt.*, for optional).

4.3   The Decision Support System [*DSS*]

The final objective of this data collection and the following analyses is the development of a Decision Support System for the diagnosis of hand skin diseases devoted to inexperienced GPs. It can be made available to them as a web accessible service or as a stand-alone application, distributed on a portable device, such as USB memory stick, for example. The possibility to store the output of

Table 1. Distribution of the diagnoses in the raw dataset

Diagnosis	—Records—		— Type —		—AVG(Stars)—	
	Nr.	Perc.	Final	Nr.	Mand.	Opt.
Contact Allergic Dermatitis *[DAC]*	248	18.18 %	0	100	2.24	0.61
			1	148	1.71	0.97
Irritant Contact Dermatitis *[DCI]*	207	15.18 %	0	65	2.29	0.19
			1	142	1.89	0.48
Psoriasis *[other]*	205	15.03 %	0	34	2.03	0.20
			1	171	2.34	0.06
Vescicular eczema	175	12.83 %	0	37	2.34	0.11
			1	138	2.47	0.24
DAC+DCI	173	12.68 %	0	40	2.25	0.28
			1	133	1.76	0.92
Atopic eczema	107	7.84 %	0	21	2.62	0.02
			1	86	2.25	0.27
Hyperkeratotic eczema	92	6.74 %	0	28	2.44	0.07
			1	64	2.09	0.23
Atopic eczema + DCI	84	6.16 %	0	20	2.37	0.19
			1	64	2.31	0.79
Nummular eczema	25	1.83 %	0	14	2.54	0.02
			1	11	2.27	0.47
Palmoplantar keratoderma *[other]*	9	0.66 %	0	0	–	–
			1	9	1.27	0.18
Superficial cutaneous mycoses *[other]*	8	0.59 %	0	0	–	–
			1	8	2.31	0.10
Continuous acrodermatitis *[other]*	4	0.29 %	0	1	1.65	0.00
			1	3	1.92	0.00
Pityriasis rubra pilaris *[other]*	2	0.15 %	0	0	–	–
			1	2	0.98	0.00
[[EMPTY]]	*25*	*1.83 %*	0	16	1.28	0.09
			1	9	2.20	0.31
Total	1363	100,00%				

each visit as a PDF file – compacted in a double-sided A4 sheet, through optimized data representation, see Fig. 3 – could be a further advantage of the system. This allows the GP to create a personal and portable digital archive, and to provide a physical copy of the visit report to the patient (fulfilling local regulations).

The software will be just a prototype for research purposes and its user interface will initially be only available in Italian. It is expected to be localized easily, when needed. As far as the USB memory stick is concerned, it can be internally based on an Apache web server and a MySQL database, accessed using a web browser, reusing the developed user interface.

Possible Ideas for the DSS. This tool consists of the EMR empowered by two functionalities:

e-Dermatology :: Cartella Clinica Dermatologica OnLine "Brevi Manu" - (C), PoliMi 2011 - 2012
CodCaso: 001300 - [paz: 170096]

mTLSS: totale = 5					★★★★★ [3]
Eritema	0	*1*	2	3	
Desquamazione	0	*1*	2	3	
Lichenificazione/Ipercheratosi	0	*1*	2	3	
Vescicole	*0*	1	2	3	
Edema	0	*1*	2	3	
Fissurazioni	*0*	1	2	3	
Prurito/Dolore	0	*1*	2	3	

PGA: Malattia **Quasi assente**   ★★★★★ [3]

Quadro clinico corrente: **Eritemato-desquamativo, Eritemato-edematoso**   ★★★★★ [4]

Simmetricita': ☞ **(No)**   ★★★★★ [3]

Quadro clinico pregresso: **Eritemato-desquamativo, Eritemato-edematoso**   ★★★★★ [3]

Evoluzione quadro clinico: **Cronica (> 6 mesi)**   ★★★★★ [4]

Fattori implicati: *Nessuna informazione sui fattori implicati dichiarati*   ★★★★★ [0]

Dermatite da contatto: ☞ **(No)**   ★★★★★ [0]

Cartella inserita il *2012-12-03 09:23:39*

Fig. 4. A detail of the stored *EMR* record. On the top, the compact representation of *mTLSS* and *PGA* scales.

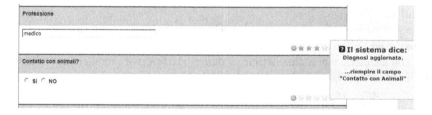

Fig. 5. The final DSS thought: suggestion box filled with an indication *[MOCKUP]*

- The *Suggestion box*. It suggests which attribute should be filled-out, based on the information just provided to the current EMR. In the Fig. 5, the system suggests to fill out the attribute contact with animals.
- The *Rank of Diagnoses*. The probability of each diagnosis is expressed as a percentage (Fig. 6). Only a set probability are shown, but not reordening or hiding are provided, to enforce the idea that the real choice is performed by the – human – medical professional. In fact, the percentages are indicative values from the data extracted, based on statistical and computational methods, such as frequency and co-occurrences, in accordance with experiences in other fields [11].

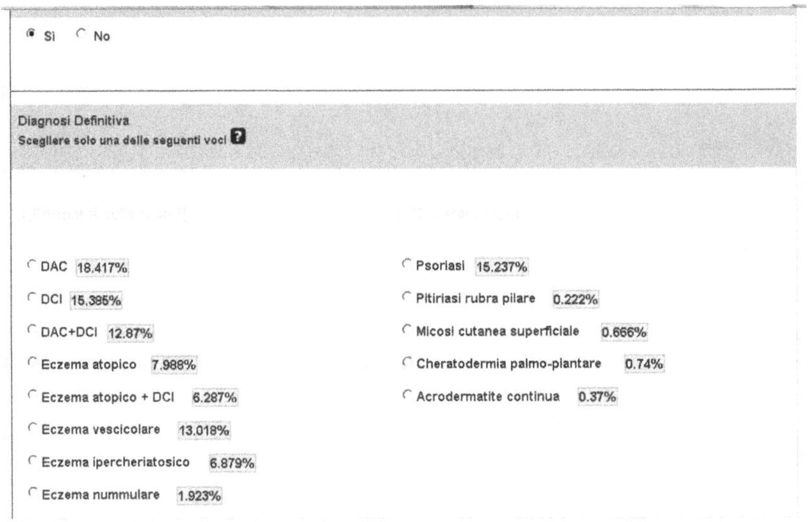

Fig. 6. The final DSS thought: suggestion on the probability for each pathology [MOCKUP]

5   Conclusions

The system we created provides evidence that tracking the implicit information as used by specialists during the diagnostic process allows to obtain relationships and rules supporting inexperienced GPs in the autonomous primary management of hand skin diseases.

The software application created works as a stand-alone service from a USB memory stick, allowing the GP to bring it with him *anywhere anytime.*

At the moment when this article is being written, we are starting validating the identified rules, with the support of all the specialists included in the panel of *'Ambulatorio della Mano".* The next steps will be the distribution of the developed DSS – on USB memory stick – to a group of the GPs of the Italian public National Health System.

After that, we expect to ask them to fill-out an online questionnaire regarding the different aspects of the system: from usability issues to the perceived usefulness in the everyday diagnostic practices. We also planned to recollect back the information stored in some of the distributed memory sticks, after proper anonymization procedure. We may then analyze and check if the rules found in the initial phase are confirmed by more data on one side and to explore the real usage in the daily practices on the other one.

Acknowledgment. The research was partially supported by the funds generously provided by *ALLMIRALL.* Authors want to thanks *ContentEdNet* for the recruitment and coordination of the 16 centers participating in the experimentation. We acknowledge all the specialists involved for their hard work and factual collaboration towards the good end of the project.

References

1. Kassirer, J.P.: Teaching clinical reasoning: case-based and coached. Acad. Med. 85(7), 1118–1124 (2010); PubMed PMID: 20603909
2. Svensson, A., Lindberg, M., Meding, B., Sundberg, K., Stenberg, B.: Self-reported hand eczema: symptom-based reports do not increase the validity of diagnosis. British Journal of Dermatology 147, 281–284 (2002), doi:10.1046/j.1365-2133.2002.04799.x
3. Weisshaar, E., Kallen, U., Weiss, M.: 'The itching hand"- important differential diagnoses and treatment. J. Dtsch. Dermatol. Ges. 11(1), 31–42 (2013), doi:10.1111/j.1610-0387.2012.08002.x.
4. Jackson, S., Nesbitt, L.T.: Differential Diagnosis for the Dermatologist. Springer (2012) ISBN: 9783642280061
5. Pesut, D.J., Herman, J.: Metacognitive Skills in Diagnostic Reasoning: Making the Implicit Explicit. International Journal of Nursing Terminologies and Classifications 3, 148–154 (1992), doi:10.1111/j.1744-618X.1992.tb00530.x
6. Krause, P., Fox, J., O'Neil, M., Glowinski, A.: Can we formally specify a medical decision support system? IEEE Expert 8(3), 56–61 (1993), doi:10.1109/64.215223
7. Pandey, B., Mishra, R.B.: Knowledge and intelligent computing system in medicine. Comput. Biol. Med. 39(3), 215–230 (2009), doi:10.1016/j.compbiomed.2008.12.008
8. Davidson, E., Chiasson, M.: Contextual influences on technology use mediation: a comparative analysis of electronic medical record systems. Eur. J. Inf. Syst. 14, 6–18 (2005), doi:10.1057/palgrave.ejis.3000518
9. Ayala, F., Nino, M., Fabbrocini, G., Panariello, L., Balato, N., Foti, C., Tosti, A., Corazza, M., Valsecchi, R.H., Gola, M., Gallo, R., Guarneri, F., Pigatto, P.D., Cristaudo, A., Schena, D., Musumeci, M.L., Stingeni, L., Lisi, P.: Quality of life and contact dermatitis: a disease-specific questionnaire. Dermatitis 21(2), 84–90 (2010); PubMed PMID: 20233546
10. Weistenhöfer, W., Baumeister, T., Drexler, H., Kütting, B.: An Overview of Skin Scores Used for Quantifying Hand Eczema: A Critical Update According to the Criteria of Evidence-based Medicine. The British Journal of Dermatology 162(2), 239–250 (2010)
11. Eynard, D., Mazzola, L., Dattolo, A.: Exploiting tag similarities to discover synonyms and homonyms in folksonomies. In: Software: Practice and Experience. John Wiley & Sons, Ltd. (2012), doi: 10.1002/spe.2150

Ideal Mode Selection of a Cardiac Pacing System

Dominique Méry[1] and Neeraj Kumar Singh[2]

[1] Université de Lorraine, LORIA, BP 239, 54506 Vandœuvre-lès-Nancy, France
Dominique.Mery@loria.fr
[2] Department of Computer Science, University of York, United Kingdom
neeraj.singh@cs.york.ac.uk, Neerajkumar.Singh@loria.fr

Abstract. Mode transition in any inappropriate mode can be a common cause of any mishap in a complex health-care system. This paper presents an approach for formalizing and reasoning about optimal mode transition in a health-care system that uses several operating modes in various operating states. Modes are formalized and their relation to a state-based formalism is established through a refinement approach. The efficiency of this approach is presented by formalizing an ideal operating mode transition of a cardiac pacemaker case study. An incremental approach is used to develop the system and its detailed design is verified through a series of refinements. The consequence of this approach is to improve system structuring, elicitation of system assumptions and expected functionality, as well as requirement traceability using modes in state-based modeling. Models are expressed in EVENT B modeling language and validated by a model checker tool: ProB.

Keywords: Abstract model, Event-B, Proof-based development, Refinement, Modes, Pacemaker.

1 Introduction

The first permanent pacemaker was implanted in 1958 to a Swedish engineer at Karolinska Hospital, Sweden [9]. First generation of pacemaker focused on efficient performance and more programming modes to cover all kinds of pacemaker-dependent heart disease. For more than 50 years of research and development, there has been a wealth of different features incorporated into pacemaker design, including programmability, telemetry and different pacing modes.

Today, it is estimated that more than half a million people a year get pacemakers worldwide. Over the past 40 years the clinical indications for pacing have increased to include a large number of different cardiac arrhythmias. After several diagnosis tests and discussions, an ideal choice of pacemaker operating mode for an individual patient is considered that can provide the maximum benefits with as many features of normal sinus rhythm as possible [22].

Advanced technology pacemakers can automatically switch from one operating mode to other operating mode. Mode switching aims to achieve an appropriate ventricular rate during periods of atrial arrhythmias by the correct detection of premature atrial events and smooth transitions between atrial-tracking and non-tracking pacing modes [21].

V.G. Duffy (Ed.): DHM/HCII 2013, Part I, LNCS 8025, pp. 258–267, 2013.
© Springer-Verlag Berlin Heidelberg 2013

Optimal and alternative pacemaker operating modes are fixed for certain diagnosis. If a pacemaker operates in an inappropriate operating mode, then cardiac death is likely. In order to select an inappropriate operating mode, different kinds of complication are possible: pacemaker syndrome [4]; inappropriate atrial tracking of atrial tachyarrhythmias by a DDD or VDD [1]; additional ventricular block in a patient with sinus node dysfunction may not be easily detected initially [2]; lack of physiological heart rate response on exercise [6].

In this paper, we propose mode a transition methodology to structure system specification to facilitate rigorous design and to assure that the system will never switch in an undesirable state. We use term mode in the same sense as [13,7] : both as partitions of the state space, representing different working conditions of the system, and as a way to define control information, structuring system operation. An assessment of the proposed approach is given through a case study, relative to the formal development of an ideal operating mode transition for pacing to allow the pacemaker response to behave as physiologically as possible. We develop an incremental refinement-based formal model of mode selection and prove that the pacemaker will never switch in any undesirable operating mode. In case of any fault, pacemaker either use the preselected alternative operating mode or automatically switch in any alternative operating mode.

The formal specification of an ideal mode transition of the pacemaker is developed in the EVENT B modeling language which is supported by the RODIN platform [18] and generated proof obligations are proved using RODIN proof tools. The main idea is to start with a very abstract model of the system which includes all operating modes of the pacemaker. Details are gradually added to this first model by building a sequence of more concrete events. The relationship between two successive models in this sequence is *refinement* [3,5]. The formal specification must be validated to ensure that they meet the interdisciplinary requirements of mode transition of a pacemaker. Hence, formal specification validation is carried out by both formal modeling and domain experts. Moreover, we use the ProB tool [14] to animate formal specification of mode selection of the pacemaker for analyzing and validating each refinement.

The outline of the remaining paper is as follows: Section 2 presents related works. Section 3 represents formal definition of the model system and state the required properties. In Section 4, we explore the stepwise formal development of an ideal operating mode transition in the pacemaker. Finally, Section 5 concludes the paper along with directions for future work.

2 Related Work

A *modal system* is a system characterized by *operation modes*, which coordinates system operations. Many systems are *modal systems*, for instance, space and avionic systems, steam boiler control, transportation and space system and so on. Operational modes denote all the different functional behaviors according to system requirements. Operation modes help to reason about system behaviors by focusing on system properties observed under different situations. In this approach, a system is seen as a set of modes partitioning the system functionality over different operating conditions. The term *assumption* is used to denote different operating conditions and *guarantee* denotes the functionality ensured by the system under the corresponding assumption. A system may switch from one mode to another one in a number of ways characterized by mode transitions.

By analyzing requirements of pacemaker, we have found that the cardiac pacemaker system is also a *modal system* and it is based on *four-variable model* developed by Parnas and Madey [17]. According to the *four-variable model*, variables are continuous functions over the time and consist of *monitored* variables in the environment that the system responds to, *controlled* variables in the environment that the system is to control, *input* variables through which the software senses monitored variables, and *output* the variables through which the software changes the controlled variables. In the cardiac pacemaker system, *monitored* variables senses an intrinsic heart signal using pacemaker's sensors and *controlled* variables stimulate into the heart using pacemaker's actuator.

The use of operation modes is very common in real-time system. Every operation mode has specific time intervals for operating and modes are changing after a certain time bounds. Modecharts [13] focus on the specification of real-time properties of mode and mode switching. The authors have given the detailed information about the state space partition, various working conditions of the system and define the control information in large state machines. However, modecharts lacks adequate support to specifying and reasoning about functional properties. Some papers [19,10] have also addressed the problem of mode changing in real time system. Dotti et al. [7] have proposed both formalization and a refinement notion for *modal systems*, using existing support for the construction of *modal systems*.

H.D. Macedo, et al. [15] have developed a partial distributed real-time model of a cardiac pacing system using VDM. Gomes et al [11] have developed a formal specification of the pacemaker system using the Z modeling language. According to the paper, they have modelled the sequential model similar to H.D. Macedo et al. works [15]. Recently, a complete formal development of one and two-electrode pacemakers are presented in by D. Méry, et al. [16].

According to our literature survey, the cardiac pacemaker system is a *modal system* and none of the existing approaches for formalizing operating modes of the cardiac pacemaker system has used the refinement approach. We have used both formalization and refinement of a *modal system* for developing a formal specification of bradycardia operating modes of the cardiac pacemaker system using EVENT B modeling language.

3   Operation Modes

In multi-moded systems, the system consists of several operating modes. Each mode produces a different behavior, characterized by a set of functionalities that are carried out by different task sets. Using operating modes in multi-moded systems design offers two key advantages. First, it breaks up the complexity of a system into smaller pieces, making its specification easier. Second, an operating mode groups only those functions necessary in the actual situation. All other tasks are inactive in that mode. Different operating conditions are partitioning the set of modes of the system. Different operating conditions are used to represent *assumption* and *guarantee* denotes the functionality ensured by the system under the corresponding assumption. A system may switch from one mode to another in a number of ways characterised by *mode transition* [7].

A pair Γ/Δ is used to characterize a mode, where $\Gamma(\alpha)$ is an assumption predicate over the current system state and $\Delta(\alpha, \alpha')$ is a relation over the current and next states as the guarantee of the system. A set of variables α is characterising a system state and constrained by an invariant $I(\alpha)$. An invariant $I(\alpha)$ is to limit the possible states by excluding undesirable states. In this paper, we have assumed that a system is working in only in one mode at a time. We are not considering here multiple operating modes case such as mode overlapping and mode interference. It is an interesting challenge that cannot be sufficiently addressed in this paper due to space limitations. Following formal representation presents that mode assumptions (Γ) are mutually exclusive and exhaustive in respect to a model invariant. $\oplus$ is a set partitioning operator.

$$I(\alpha) = \Gamma_1(\alpha) \oplus \ldots \oplus \Gamma_n(\alpha) \tag{1}$$

A mode transition is an atomic step to switch from one mode to other mode. It is convenient to characterise a mode transition by a pair of assumptions. Assuming that mode is assigned an index, a mode transition from Γ_p/Δ_p to Γ_q/Δ_q is a relation on mode indices $p \rightsquigarrow q$. In general, a system has an initial transition $\top \rightsquigarrow r$ and it terminates by terminating transitions $t \rightsquigarrow \bot$ after switches into some system mode Γ_r/Δ_r. In mode transition system enters at least in one operation mode without switching $\top \rightsquigarrow \bot$.

There are restrictions on the way mode assumptions and guarantees are formulated. The states described by a guarantee must be wholly included into valid model states:

$$I(\alpha) \wedge \Gamma(\alpha) \wedge \Delta(\alpha, \alpha') \Rightarrow I(\alpha') \tag{2}$$

The assumption and guarantee of a mode must be noncontradictory. i.e. a mode should permit a concrete implementation:

$$\exists \alpha, \alpha'.(I(\alpha) \wedge \Gamma(\alpha) \Rightarrow \Delta(\alpha, \alpha')) \tag{3}$$

A system is characterised by a collection of modes and a vector of mode transitions:

$$\Gamma_1/\Delta_1, \ldots \Gamma_n/\Delta_n$$
$$p_1 \rightsquigarrow q_1, \ldots p_n \rightsquigarrow q_n \tag{4}$$

An operation mode (m, α) represents the state of a system, where m is an index of current operation mode and α is current system state. Above discussed system can be understand as follows: when system is operating in mode m the state of model variables changes so that the next state is any state α' satisfying both the corresponding guarantee $\Delta(\alpha, \alpha')$ and the modes assumption $\Gamma(\alpha')$:

$$\frac{\Gamma_m(\alpha) \wedge \Delta_m(\alpha, \alpha') \wedge \Gamma_m(\alpha')}{\langle m, \alpha \rangle \to \langle m, \alpha' \rangle} \tag{5}$$

Equation 6 represents that if there is a mode transition starting from a current mode, the transition could be enabled to switch the system into a new operation mode.

$$\frac{m \rightsquigarrow n \wedge \Gamma_m(\alpha) \wedge \Gamma_n(\alpha')}{\langle m, \alpha \rangle \to \langle n, \alpha' \rangle} \tag{6}$$

Above given two activities (5 and 6) compete with each other: a non-deterministic choice is made between the two activities and an initiating transition must find an initial state without referring to any previous state.

$$\frac{\top \rightsquigarrow k \wedge \Gamma_k(\alpha)}{\langle \top, undef \rangle \rightarrow \langle k, \alpha \rangle} \tag{7}$$

In equation 7, $undef$ represents a system state before to the execution of an initial transition. System termination is handled by the above given switching rule. All three rules (5,6,7) assume that an invariant holds in current and new states: $I(\alpha) \wedge I(\alpha')$. This is a consequence of given conditions 1 and 3. Refinement technique is used to build operation mode based model by introducing new modes and transitions of the system. A various kind of refinement techniques can be used to develop the concrete model.

4   Formal Analysis of Ideal Modes

This section presents a refinement based formal specification of an ideal operating mode transition to allow the pacemaker response to behave as physiologically as possible. A paper [20] presents a set of diagnoses and corresponding optimal, alternative and inappropriate operating modes of a cardiac pacemaker. The optimal mode of pacing should be considered for most patients. Alternative modes should be regarded as being less satisfactory, but acceptable in some group of patients - for example those who are disabled by another disease, those with very intermittent symptoms, or those who have short life of expectancy because of another disease [20]. The bradycardia operating modes(see Table-1 are prescribed by ACC/AHA/NASPE and BPEG working committee [22].

Table 1. Bradycardia operating modes of a cardiac pacemaker system

Category	Chambers Paced	Chambers Sensed	Response to Sensing	Rate Modulation
Letters	O-None	O-None	O-None	R-Rate Modulation
	A-Atrium	A-Atrium	T-Triggered	
	V-Ventricle	V-Ventricle	I-Inhibited	
	D-Dual(A+V)	D-Dual(A+V)	D-Dual(T+I)	

We begin by defining an EVENT B context in which we declare two new constants $Diagnosis$ and OP_Modes that represent an enumerated set of diagnoses and a set of possible operating modes, respectively. These constants are extracted from the articles [20,22].

```
axm1 : Diagnosis = {SND, AVB, SND_and_AVB, CAF_with_AVB, CSS, MVVS, NO_DISEASE}
axm2 : OP_Modes = {AAI, AAIR, VVI, VDD, DDD, DDI, DDDR, DDIR, VVIR, OOO}
```

Two new variables ($Diag\_OP$ and $diag$) are introduced in machine context. The variable $Diag\_OP$ is represented as a subset of optimal operating modes ($Diag\_OP \subseteq OP\_Modes$) and other variable $diag$ is represented as $diag \in Diagnosis$. Safety properties of the system are represented by two new invariants $(inv1, inv2)$. The first property states that when heart has not any disease then pacemaker operates in OOO operating mode. According to the Table-1, in OOO operating mode pacemaker is an ideal state. The next safety property states that if any diagnosis is member of $Diagnosis \setminus \{NO\_DISEASE\}$ then operating mode $(Diag\_OP)$ becomes a subset of all possible operating modes (OP_Modes).

Two significant events $(Heart\_OK$ and $Heart\_KO)$ are introduced in the abstract model. The event $Heart\_KO$ represents that the heart is not OK and heart has any diagnosis condition. Guard $(grd1)$ of event $Heart\_KO$ states that a variable $heart\_dig$ is a member of $Diagnosis \setminus \{NO\_DISEASE\}$, then set of operating modes (OP_Modes) and heart diagnosis $(heart\_dig)$ are assigned in an atomic step to the variables $Diag\_OP$ and $diag$, respectively. The detection of a diagnosis and corresponding operating modes are made more specific in the refined layers. $Heart\_OK$ event models the non-detection of any diagnosis in the heart. The $Heart\_KO$ and $Heart\_OK$ events should be viewed together are modeling the possible outcome of a diagnosis which indicates either selection of required optimal operating modes or heart is OK.

$inv1 : diag = NO\_DISEASE \wedge$ $\quad Diag\_OP \neq \varnothing$ $\Rightarrow$ $\quad Diag\_OP = \{OOO\}$ $inv2 : diag \in Diagnosis$ $\quad \setminus \{NO\_DISEASE\}$ $\Rightarrow$ $\quad Diag\_OP \subseteq OP\_Modes$	**EVENT Heart_KO** **ANY** $heart\_dig$ **WHERE** $\quad grd1 : heart\_dig \in diagnosis$ $\qquad \setminus \{NO\_DISEASE\}$ **THEN** $\quad act1 : Diag\_OP : |Diag\_OP'$ $\qquad \subseteq OP\_Modes$ $\quad act2 : diag := heart\_dig$ **END**	**EVENT Heart_OK** **ANY** $heart\_dig$ **WHERE** $\quad grd1 : heart\_dig \notin diagnosis$ $\qquad \setminus \{NO\_DISEASE\}$ **THEN** $\quad act1 : Diag\_OP := \{OOO\}$ $\quad act2 : diag := heart\_dig$ **END**

4.1   First Refinement

In the abstract model, we have seen that diagnosis is detected in a single atomic step. This refinement level presents CSS and $MVVS$ diagnoses. A new event $Heart\_CSS\_MVVS$ is introducing in this refinement. The $Heart\_CSS\_MVVS$ event is a refinement of the abstract $Heart\_KO$ event and represents successful detection of CSS and $MVVS$ diagnoses. First invariant $(inv1)$ represents an optimal operating modes on the successful detection of CSS and $MVVS$ diagnoses. Second invariant $(inv2)$ states that the diagnoses $MVVS$ and CSS guarantees never select any inappropriate operating modes.

$inv1 : diag \in \{MVVS, CSS\} \wedge Diag\_OP \neq \varnothing$ $\Rightarrow$ $\quad Diag\_OP = \{DDI\}$ $inv2 : diag \in \{MVVS, CSS\} \wedge Diag\_OP \neq \varnothing$ $\Rightarrow$ $\quad Diag\_OP \nsubseteq \{AAI, VDD, VVI\}$	**EVENT Heart_CSS_MVVS** **REF** $Heart\_KO$ **ANY** $heart\_dig$ **WHERE** $\quad grd1 : heart\_dig \in \{CSS, MVVS\}$ **THEN** $\quad act1 : Diag\_OP := \{DDI\}$ $\quad act2 : diag := heart\_dig$ **END**

4.2   Second Refinement

In the second refinement, two events $Heart\_MVVS$ and $Heart\_CSS$ represent a refinement of $Heart\_CSS\_MVVS$ event. This refinement level presents CSS and $MVVS$ diagnoses separately as a result of final detection of CSS and $MVVS$

diagnoses and their optimal operating modes. Other two events $Heart\_AVB$ and $Heart\_SND$ are also introduced in this level as refinement of $Heart\_KO$ event. We have given an example of a refined event $Heart\_SND$. Other event ($Heart\_AVB$) is also refined in a similar way. A set of new invariants ($inv1 - inv8$) are introduced as safety properties. These invariants state that the pacemaker uses optimal operating modes according to the diagnoses(CSS, MVVS, SND, AVB) and never switch in any inappropriate mode.

$inv1 : diag = CSS \wedge Diag\_OP \neq \varnothing \Rightarrow Diag\_OP = \{DDI\}$
$inv3 : diag = CSS \wedge Diag\_OP \neq \varnothing \Rightarrow Diag\_OP \nsubseteq \{AAI, VDD\}$
$inv4 : diag = MVVS \wedge Diag\_OP \neq \varnothing \Rightarrow Diag\_OP = \{DDI\}$
$inv2 : diag = MVVS \wedge Diag\_OP \neq \varnothing \Rightarrow Diag\_OP \nsubseteq \{AAI, VDD, VVI\}$
$inv5 : diag = SND \wedge Diag\_OP \neq \varnothing \Rightarrow Diag\_OP = \{AAIR\}$
$inv6 : diag = SND \wedge Diag\_OP \neq \varnothing \Rightarrow Diag\_OP \nsubseteq \{VVI, VDD\}$
$inv7 : diag = AVB \wedge Diag\_OP \neq \varnothing \Rightarrow Diag\_OP = \{DDD\}$
$inv8 : diag = AVB \wedge Diag\_OP \neq \varnothing \Rightarrow Diag\_OP \nsubseteq \{AAI, DDI\}$

EVENT Heart_SND
REF $Heart\_KO$
ANY $heart\_dig$
WHERE
  $grd1 : heart\_dig = SND$
THEN
  $act1 : Diag\_OP := \{AAIR\}$
  $act2 : diag := heart\_dig$
END

4.3 Third Refinement

This refinement level presents as similar to the previous two refinements. Two events $Heart\_Cr\_AF\_with\_AVB$ and $Heart\_SND\_and\_AVB$ are introduced as a refinement of the event $Heart\_KO$, which are used to detect the CAF_with_AVB and SND_with_AVB diagnoses. Some new invariants ($inv1 - inv4$) are introduced as safety properties. These invariants state that the diagnosis SND_with_AVB and CAF_with_AVB are used always optimal operating modes and never operate in any inappropriate modes.

$inv1 : diag = SND\_and\_AVB \wedge Diag\_OP \neq \varnothing \Rightarrow Diag\_OP = \{DDDR, DDIR\}$
$inv2 : diag = SND\_and\_AVB \wedge Diag\_OP \neq \varnothing \Rightarrow Diag\_OP \nsubseteq \{AAI, VVI\}$
$inv3 : diag = CAF\_with\_AVB \wedge Diag\_OP \neq \varnothing \Rightarrow Diag\_OP = \{VVIR\}$
$inv4 : diag = CAF\_with\_AVB \wedge Diag\_OP \neq \varnothing \Rightarrow Diag\_OP \nsubseteq \{AAI, DDD, VDD\}$

4.4 Fourth Refinement

This is the final refinement of the system. A new variable alternative operating modes ($Diag\_OP\_Alter$) is defined as a subset of bradicardia operating modes in $inv1$. We introduce the alternative operating modes [20] in all events for each diagnosis. New guards and actions are introduced for modeling alternative operating modes in all events of the last refinement. No any new events are introduced in this refinement level. A set of new invariants ($inv2 - inv7$) is introduced for checking desired behavior of the optimal and alternative operating modes transition. New introduced invariants generate proof obligations. Generated proof obligations are discharged by RODIN proof tool and state that the pacemaker system never use any inappropriate mode for all given diagnoses.

$inv1 : Diag\_OP\_Alter \subseteq OP\_Modes$
$inv2 : diag = SND \wedge Diag\_OP \neq \varnothing \Rightarrow (Diag\_OP = \{AAIR\} \wedge$
  $Diag\_OP\_Alter = \{AAI\} \wedge Diag\_OP \nsubseteq \{VVI, VDD\} \wedge Diag\_OP\_Alter \nsubseteq \{VVI, VDD\})$
$inv3 : diag = AVB \wedge Diag\_OP \neq \varnothing \Rightarrow (Diag\_OP = \{DDD\} \wedge$
  $Diag\_OP\_Alter = \{VDD\} \wedge Diag\_OP \nsubseteq \{AAI, DDI\} \wedge Diag\_OP\_Alter \nsubseteq \{AAI, DDI\})$
$inv4 : diag = SND\_and\_AVB \wedge Diag\_OP \neq \varnothing \Rightarrow (Diag\_OP = \{DDDR, DDIR\} \wedge$
  $Diag\_OP\_Alter = \{DDD, DDI\} \wedge Diag\_OP \nsubseteq \{AAI, VVI\} \wedge Diag\_OP\_Alter \nsubseteq \{AAI, VVI\})$
$inv5 : diag = CAF\_with\_AVB \wedge Diag\_OP \neq \varnothing \Rightarrow (Diag\_OP = \{VVIR\} \wedge Diag\_OP\_Alter = \{VVI\} \wedge$
  $Diag\_OP \nsubseteq \{AAI, DDD, VDD\})$
$inv6 : diag = CSS \wedge Diag\_OP \neq \varnothing \Rightarrow (Diag\_OP = \{DDI\} \wedge Diag\_OP\_Alter = \{DDD, VVI\} \wedge$
  $Diag\_OP \nsubseteq \{AAI, VDD\} \wedge Diag\_OP\_Alter \nsubseteq \{AAI, VDD\})$
$inv7 : diag = MVVS \wedge Diag\_OP \neq \varnothing \Rightarrow (Diag\_OP = \{DDI\} \wedge Diag\_OP\_Alter = \{DDD\} \wedge$
  $Diag\_OP \nsubseteq \{AAI, VVI, VDD\} \wedge Diag\_OP\_Alter \nsubseteq \{AAI, VVI, VDD\})$

We have described here only summary informations about each refinement in form of very basic description of the operation mode handling of a cardiac pacemaker using incremental refinement-based approach and omit detailed formalisation of events and proof details due to limited space. To find complete formal representation of an ideal operating mode transition in the cardiac pacemaker see[1].

4.5   Validation of Models

There are two main validation activities in EVENT B ; *consistency checking* and *model analysis*. Both are complementary for designing a consistent system. This section conveys the validity of the model by using a ProB tool [14] and Proof Statistics. "Validation" refers to the activity of gaining confidence that the developed formal models are consistent with the requirements, which have been extracted from the articles [20,22]. We have used the ProB tool [14] that supports *automated consistency checking* of EVENT B machines via model checking [8] and constraint-based checking [12]. Animation using ProB worked very well and we have then used ProB to validate the EVENT B formal specification according to the desired behavior of the system. We have validated the complete formal specification of an ideal operating mode transition in the pacemaker.

The Table-2 is expressing the proof statistics of the development in the RODIN tool. These statistics measure the size of the model, the proof obligations generated and discharged by the RODIN prover, and those are interactively proved.

Table 2. Proof Statistics

Model	Total number of POs	Automatic Proof	Interactive Proof
Abstract Model	8	8(100%)	0(0%)
First Refinement	10	6(60%)	4(40%)
Second Refinement	61	60(98%)	1(2%)
Third Refinement	34	33(97%)	1(3%)
Fourth Refinement	48	37(77%)	11(23%)
Total	161	144(89%)	17(11%)

The complete development of an ideal operating mode selection or automatic mode transition in the pacemaker system results in 161(100%) proof obligations, in which 144(89%) are proved automatically by the RODIN tool. The remaining 17(11%) proof obligations are proved interactively using RODIN tool. In order to guarantee the correctness of the system, we have established various invariants in stepwise refinement. Most of the proofs are automatically discharged. It should be noted that the manual proofs were not difficult. Proofs are quite simple, and achieved with the help of a simple *click* operation. The stepwise refinement of the system helps to achieve a high degree of automatic proof.

5   Conclusion and Future Works

In this paper the notions of modes transition are formally defined. These notions allow explicit characterization of various system conditions, through expressing assumptions,

---

[1] Available at
http://www.loria.fr/~singhnne/
mywork/opmode/OpModePacemaker.pdf

and the properties of the system working under such conditions, through the use of guarantees. The complexity of design is reduced by structuring systems using modes and by detailing this design using refinement. This approach makes it easier for the developers to map requirements to models and to trace requirements. For quick understanding, we have applied this mode transition methodology for formalizing and reasoning about optimal mode transition using a cardiac pacemaker case study. The formal model has covered the general diagnoses and their optimal and alternative operating modes [20,22] of the pacemaker system. This case study indicates that inappropriate mode transition can be cause of many problems (see Section 1). It also suggests that such an approach can yield a viable model that can be useful for validation and correct selection of optimal modes for any diagnosis. More precisely, we have presented a formal development of optimal mode transition and prove it that it will never switch in any inappropriate operating mode. This proposed technique intend to assist in the design process of system where correctness and safety are important issues.

We have outlined how an incremental refinement approach to the ideal mode transition system allows us to achieve a very high degree of automatic proofs using RODIN tool. The approach we have taken is not specific to Event-B. We believe a similar approach could be taken using other state-based notations such as ASM, TLA or Z. RODIN proof tool was used to generate the hundreds of proof obligations and to discharge those obligations automatically and interactively. Another key role of the tool was in helping us to discover appropriate gluing invariants to prove the refinements. Without this level of automated support, making the changes to the refinement chain that we did make would have been far too tedious. In summary some key lessons are that incremental development with small refinement steps, appropriate abstractions at each level and powerful tool support are all invaluable in this kind of formal development. Finally, we have validated the mode selection system using the ProB model checker as validation tool and verified the correctness of desired behavior of the system according the medical domain experts.

In the future, we have planned to extend this mode transition methodology for real time system and apply on very high sensitive hybrid systems: avionic, cruise control, atomic plants, medical devices and so on. All kind of hybrid systems use several operating modes in real time where an inappropriate mode transition is a very common cause of mishap.

Acknowledgement. Neeraj Kumar Singh was supported by grant awarded by the Ministry of University and Research.

References

1. Castellanos Jr., A., Lemberg, L., Rodriguez-Tocker, L., Berkovits, B.V.: Atrial synchronized pacemaker arrhythmias: revisited. Am. Heart, Pub. Med. 2, 199–208 (1968)
2. Steinbach, K., Forohner, K., Meisl, F.: Atrial stimulation. In: Perez Gomez, F. (ed.) Cardiac Pacing, p. 629 (1985)
3. Abrial, J.-R.: Modeling in Event-B: System and Software Engineering. Cambridge University Press (2009) (forthcoming book)
4. Ausubel, K., Furman, S.: The Pacemaker Syndrome. Annals of Internal Medicine 103(3), 420–429 (1985)

5. Back, R.: On correct refinement of programs. Journal of Computer and System Sciences 23(1), 49–68 (1979)
6. Allen, A., Clarke, M.: Rate responsive atrial pacing resulting in pacemaker syndrome. PACE 10, 1209 (1987)
7. Dotti, F.L., Iliasov, A., Ribeiro, L., Romanovsky, A.: Modal systems: Specification, refinement and realisation. In: Breitman, K., Cavalcanti, A. (eds.) ICFEM 2009. LNCS, vol. 5885, pp. 601–619. Springer, Heidelberg (2009)
8. Grumberg, O., Clarke, E.M., Peled, D.: Model Checking. MIT Press (1999) ISBN 978-0262032704
9. Elmqvist Rune, S.A.: An implantable pacemaker for the heart. In: Medical Electronics. International Conference on Medical Electronics, vol. 2, pp. 253–254. Iliffe, London (1959)
10. Fohler, G.: Realizing changes of operational modes with a pre run-time scheduled hard real-time system. In: Proceedings of the Second International Workshop on Responsive Computer Systems, pp. 287–300. Springer (1992)
11. Gomes, A.O., Oliveira, M.V.M.: Formal specification of a cardiac pacing system. In: Cavalcanti, A., Dams, D.R. (eds.) FM 2009. LNCS, vol. 5850, pp. 692–707. Springer, Heidelberg (2009)
12. Jackson, D.: Alloy: a lightweight object modelling notation. ACM Trans. Softw. Eng. Methodol. 11(2), 256–290 (2002)
13. Jahanian, F., Mok, A.K.: Modechart: A specification language for real-time systems. IEEE Trans. Softw. Eng. 20(12), 933–947 (1994)
14. Leuschel, M., Butler, M.: Michael Leuschel and Michael Butler. In: Araki, K., Gnesi, S., Mandrioli, D. (eds.) FME 2003. LNCS, vol. 2805, pp. 855–874. Springer, Heidelberg (2003)
15. Macedo, H.D., Larsen, P.G., Fitzgerald, J.S.: Incremental Development of a Distributed Real-Time Model of a Cardiac Pacing System Using VDM. In: Cuellar, J., Sere, K. (eds.) FM 2008. LNCS, vol. 5014, pp. 181–197. Springer, Heidelberg (2008)
16. Méry, D., Singh, N.K.: Functional behavior of a cardiac pacing system. International Journal of Discrete Event Control Systems 1 (2010) (in Press)
17. Parnas, D.L., Madey, J.: Functional documents for computer systems. Sci. Comput. Program. 25(1), 41–61 (1995)
18. Project RODIN. Rigorous open development environment for complex systems (2004), http://rodin-b-sharp.sourceforge.net/
19. Real, J., Crespo, A.: Mode change protocols for real-time systems: A survey and a new proposal. Real-Time Syst. 26(2), 161–197 (2004)
20. Report. Recommendations for pacemaker prescription for symptomatic bradycardia. British Heart Journal 66(2),185–189 (1991)
21. Sutton, R., Stack, Z., Heaven, D., Ingram, A.: Mode switching for atrial tachyarrhythmias. The American Journal of Cardiology 83(5, suppl. 2), 202–210 (1999)
22. Epstein, A.E., DiMarco, J.P., Ellenbogen, K.A., Estes III, N.A.M., Freedman, R.A., Gettes, L.S., Gillinov, A.M., Gregoratos, G., Hammill, S.C., Hayes, D.L., Hlatky, M.A., Newby, L.K., Page, R.L., Schoenfeld, M.H., Silka, M.J., Stevenson, L.W., Sweeney, M.O.: ACC/AHA/HRS 2008 Guidelines for Device-Based Therapy of Cardiac Rhythm Abnormalities. Circulation, 117(21):2820–2840 (2008)

Development of a Measurement and Evaluation System for Bed-Making Activity for Self-training

Ayanori Nagata[1], Zhifeng Huang[1], Masako Kanai-Pak[2], Jukai Maeda[2],
Yasuko Kitajima[2], Mitsuhiro Nakamura[2], Kyoko Aida[2], Noriaki Kuwahara[3],
Taiki Ogata[1], and Jun Ota[1]

[1] Research into Artifacts Center for Engineering (RACE), The University of Tokyo,
5-1-5 Kashiwanoha, Kashiwa-shi, Chiba 277-8568, Japan
{nagata,zhifeng,ogata,ota}@race.u-tokyo.ac.jp
[2] Faculty of Nursing, Tokyo Ariake University of Medical and Health Science,
2-9-1 Ariake, Koto-ku, Tokyo 135-0063, Japan
{p-kanai,jukai,kitajima,m-nakamura,k-aida}@tau.ac.jp
[3] Department of Advanced Fibro-Science, Kyoto Institute of Technology,
Matsugasaki, Sakyo-ku, Kyoto 606-8585, Japan
nkuwahar@kit.ac.jp

Abstract. This study proposes a method to automatically measure multiple objects by image processing for constructing a system for nursing trainees of self-training in the skill of bed making. In a previous study, we constructed a system to measure and evaluate trainee performance using three RGB-D (RGB color and depth) sensors. Our previous system had a problem with recognition of equipment such as the bed pad and the sheet because of color change by the light condition, the automatic color correction by the sensors and color variability in one object. In this paper, we used color reduction and cluster selection for equipment recognition. The system reduced the color in images by using k-means clustering and recognized the clusters as separate objects by predetermined thresholds. Compared with the previous method, the recognition accuracy was higher and the accuracy achieved was 70%.

Keywords: image processing, self-training support system.

1 Introduction

With the population aging, the need for well-trained nurses is increasing. It is very important for nursing trainees to learn accurate nursing skills, such as wheelchair transfer and bed making, because performing heavy tasks can cause fatigue or injury not only for patients but also for nurses [1–3]. For efficient and adequate learning, trainees need to practice the skills repeatedly with evaluation and feedback from nursing teachers to correct improper movement. However, nursing trainees are hindered from efficiently learning nursing skills because nursing teachers and instruction time are limited.

V.G. Duffy (Ed.): DHM/HCII 2013, Part I, LNCS 8025, pp. 268–275, 2013.

To overcome this problem, a number of studies have tried to construct a system of self-learning for certain nursing skills [4–8]. Itami *et al.* constructed a system that evaluated the body mechanics of trainees during bed making with angle sensors, goniometers and electromyographs attached on the trainees' body [5]. This system could measure the posture of trainees and could provide them with feedback, showing images of their posture and data from sensors. The authors found some improvement in the trainees' skills by using this system. However, this study focused only on the trainees' movements and not on the objects they manipulated, such as the bed, the sheet, etc. In addition, sensors attached on the trainee's body could hinder the natural and smooth procedure of nursing skills.

Yonetsuji *et al.* constructed a system that evaluated the skill of transferring patients from bed to wheelchair using cameras and markers on the trainee [6]. This system could measure and recognize the states of the trainee, patient and the wheelchair. Matsumura *et al.* constructed a system that measured the movement in transferring patients from bed to wheelchair [7]. This system used RGB-D (RGB color and depth) sensors for the measurement of posture. Using this system, the authors quantified the differences in operation by trainees and teachers.

From the viewpoint of self-training, the previous systems had one problem that has yet to be overcome, namely the automatic evaluation of trainee performance, which should be assessed in the same way as when human teachers do.

Therefore, we developed a system that could automatically measure and evaluate trainee performance by using image processing, focusing on the bed-making procedure [8]. The system was equipped with three RGB-D sensors to automatically recognize the trainees' movements and the state of multiple objects, such as the bed, the bed pad and the sheet. In addition, through consulting nursing teachers and a textbook [9] used in nursing university courses, we determined the criteria to evaluate the trainees' skills involved in bed making, such as body movement and the state of the bed and the sheet. Using these criteria, the system could automatically evaluate trainee performance.

However, in our previous study, a problem arose in recognizing multiple objects, i.e., the bed, the bed pad and the sheet. This low recognition led to low evaluation accuracy of trainee performance. This problem was caused by the lack of stability in color recognition from changes in light conditions and the auto correction of color by the sensors in addition to the color variability in one object. Because the previous system recognized respective objects by predetermined color thresholds for each object, the whole color change of images led to false recognition. Therefore, in this paper, we propose an image processing method to solve the recognition problem. To construct a system that is robust to color change, we used the color reduction method using k-means clustering.

2   Automatic Measurement of Bed-Making Skills

2.1   Skills for Bed Making and Evaluation Points of the Skills

The bed-making procedure was divided into the following skills (Fig. 1) [8]. 1) Place the bed pad on the top right-hand side of the bed (Fig. 1 (a)). 2) Spread the bed pad on the mattress (Fig. 1 (b)). 3) Place a sheet on the top right-hand side of the bed and spread it out in the same way as the bed pad (Fig. 1 (c)). 4) The part of the sheet hanging from the bed is then tucked under the mattress. At this point, the nurse takes the portion of sheet hanging from the corner of the bed and folds it into two triangles (Fig. 1 (d) and (e)). The top point of the triangle should lie on top of the bed, and the bottom of the triangle should extend down the side of the bed. The bottom of the triangle is tucked tightly under the mattress (Fig. 1 (f)) and the top point of the triangle is then turned under the mattress (Fig. 1 (g)). The same procedure (Fig. 1 (f) and (g)) is repeated for the parts of the sheet hanging from the other three corners of the bed. 5) Finally, the edges of the sheet hanging between the corners are tucked tightly under the mattress (Fig. 1 (h)). When working with the sheet, it is important that the nurses keep their feet wide apart and bend their knees to prevent low back pain (Fig. 1 (i)). In addition, to avoid injury from the bed frame, the nurses should keep their palms facing downward while tucking the sheet under the mattress.

To evaluate these skills, we defined eight evaluation points for each skill [8]. The evaluation points are shown in Table 1.

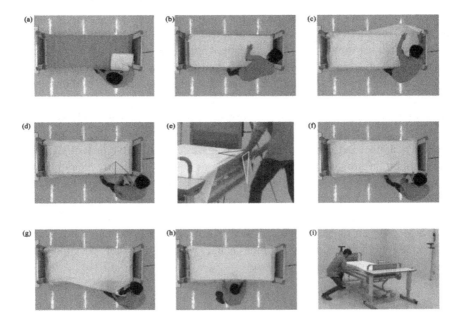

Fig. 1. Bed-making operation

Table 1. Evaluation points. The first two items are related directly to recognition of the bed, the bed pad and the sheet.

ID	Evaluation Points
1	Position of the bed pad and the sheet before spreading them
2	Spreading the sheet on the bed
3	Order of operation used on the sections of sheet hanging from the four corners of the bed
4	Manner of holding the mattress and sheet while manipulating the edge of the sheet
5	Direction of the palms while tucking the edge of the sheet edge under the mattress
6	Direction of pulling the final corner of the sheet
7	Posture while tucking the sheet edge under the mattress
8	Number of creases remaining after completion of the task

2.2 A System for Measuring Bed-Making Skills and a Method of Image Processing

To measure the evaluation points by image processing [8], we decided on measurement items corresponding to each evaluation point. The measurement items were classified into two types: the posture of the nurse and the position and state of the equipment, i.e., the bed pad, the sheet and the bed.

To recognize trainees and objects, we constructed a measurement system including three RGB-D sensors (Kinect; Microsoft) [8] (Fig. 2). A Kinect was hung vertically from the ceiling above the bed to measure the position and the state of the bed pad, sheet, bed and trainee. Two Kinects were placed horizontally to measure the trainee's posture. In addition, to measure the palm direction with the Kinects, the trainees wore two black marks on the inner side of their forearm. The marks were made by black stickers that could be detected by the Kinects.

We used three methods to measure the evaluated items: i) classification of the region of each image, corresponding to the evaluation points by using distance information and color recognition; ii) quantification of trainees' posture using skeleton information from trainees' bodies, provided by the Kinects; and iii) line detection using Hough transform for measuring the number of creases in the sheet.

To evaluate each item, it was necessary to automatically extract specific operations from the whole image. However, the order of some operations in bed making was not fixed. Therefore, we first divided the operations involved into three segments: segmentation I) putting on the bed pad, spreading the sheet; segmentation II) handling the edges of the sheet; and segmentation III) after smoothing the sheet. The order of these segments was fixed.

When the bed pad was recognized but not the sheet, the image was included in segmentation I. When the sheet was recognized and the area of the sheet was smaller than the area of the bed, the image was categorized as segmentation II. When the sheet was recognized and the area of the sheet was larger than the area of the bed, the image was classified as segmentation III.

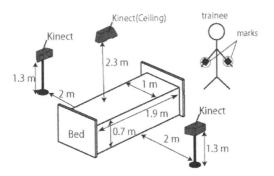

Fig. 2. The measurement system: a set of three Kinects positioned depending on the objects being measured and the range that the sensors can observe

2.3   Improvement in Equipment Recognition

In our previous study [8], we had problems with the color thresholds. These thresholds were used to recognize separately objects such as the bed, the bed pad and the sheet. In the previous study, the thresholds were set manually before the experiment. However, changes in light conditions and color correction by Kinect led to a decrease in recognition rate. In particular, the decrease in the recognition rate of the bed pad and the sheet led to the decrease in the recognition rate of the other evaluation items because the recognition of the bed pad and sheet was related to the division between the three segments. To solve this problem, we developed a new recognition method as follows.

In the first stage, by using depth information from the Kinect on the ceiling, the area of the bed was recognized, which was achieved in the following manner. First, an area within a depth of ± 30 cm of the center of the image was recognized. The center of the image was always included in the area of the bed. Then, based on the four points on the bounds of the area—the highest, lowest, rightmost and leftmost points of the bounds in the image—a rectangular area was created. Finally, 30 pixels were cut off the left, right, top and bottom sides of the rectangular area. The residual area was recognized as the bed area.

In the second stage, the number of colors used for image processing was reduced from 16,777,216 to 16 by k-means clustering. Then, the distance in color space between the color of each cluster and the colors, which was determined in advance manually for the bed pad and the sheet, was calculated. The cluster with the color distance that was nearest to the predetermined color for each object was recognized as the respective object. In addition, the next nearest cluster was also recognized as the object if the distance of the first and second nearest clusters was smaller than the predetermined thresholds. This cluster addition was continued until the distance between the neighboring clusters became larger than the threshold. In addition, to reduce calculation time, the size of each image was reduced from 640×480 to 80×60.

3   Experiment

To examine the validity of the proposed method, we applied the previous [8] and the proposed methods to images of 33 bed-making trials by five nursing students and five caregivers who had not worked as professionals for several years.

In this experiment, we investigated the recognition accuracy of the following four steps of the bed-making process: A) the trainee places the bed pad on the bed (Fig. 3(a)); B) the trainee spreads the pad (Fig. 3(b)); C) the trainee places the sheet on the bed (Fig. 3(c)); and D) the trainee spreads the sheet (Fig. 3(d)). The first and third steps correspond to the first point in Table 1. The second step is set to change the threshold from that of the bed pad to that of the sheet. With the fourth step, the system evaluates item 2 in Table 1.

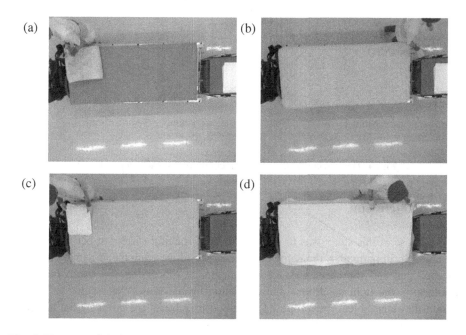

Fig. 3. The state of the bed-making process includes the following steps: (a) The trainee places the bed pad on the bed. (b) The trainee spreads the bed pad. (c) The trainee places the sheet on the bed. (d) The trainee spreads the sheet.

4   Results and Discussion

Figure 4 shows the recognition accuracy of the four steps related to the recognition of the bed, the bed pad and the sheet when using the previous method [8] and the proposed method. For all four steps, the recognition accuracy improved with the proposed method. In particular, the percentage of recognition accuracy of steps 4, spreading the sheet, improved to 78% (from 10% with the previous method) with the proposed method.

This result shows that the proposed method was robust enough to color changes by light conditions and correction by the sensors and to color variability in the area of the equipment.

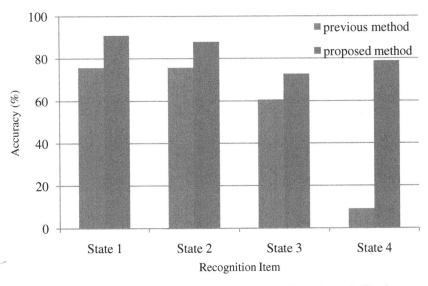

Fig. 4. The percentage of accurate recognition for each step in Fig. 3

5   Conclusion

The purpose of this study was to improve the self-training system of bed making for trainees [8]. In particular, the recognition accuracy of the equipment, namely the bed, the bed pad and the sheet was focused on image processing. To overcome color changes by the light conditions and correction by the sensors and color variability within the same object, we proposed a method to subtract the color by the k-means clustering method and to recognize the clusters as each of the objects by predetermined thresholds. The results show that the recognition accuracy of the proposed method was overall higher than the previous method with an accuracy of over 70%.

Acknowledgment. This work was supported by MEXT/JSPS KAKENHI (23593194, 24300079).

References

1. Kokubo, Y., Maezawa, Y., Furusawa, N., Uchida, K., Baba, H.: Kango shokuin no youtu anketo chousa kara mita youtu no yobo to taisaku (Management and Prevention of Low Back Pain in Nursing Personals). Report of Questionnaire Analysis. J. Lumbar Spine Disord 6(1), 52–55 (2000) (in Japanese)
2. Matsui, T., Kobayashi, M., Okagawa, S.: Kindenzu to eizo bunseki kara mita kaijo dousa no tokuchou –taii henkan dousa to kurumaisu ijo dousa ni tuite (Characteristics of Nursing-Care Motion in Terms of Electromyographic and Motion Analysis during Lifting and Posture Changing on Bed, and Transferring from Bed to Wheelchair). Journal of Social and Information Sciences 11(1), 1–14 (2008) (in Japanese)
3. Tong, H., Toyoshima, S., Hoshikawa, T., Kawabata, A.: Kurumaisu eno ijokaigodousa ni kansuru undogakuteki bunsekikenkyu (Kinematic Analysis of Transferring Motion during Carrying a Subject from the Bed to the Wheelchair). Journal of SOBIM Japan 27(9), 37–42 (2003) (in Japanese)
4. Han, J., With, P.H.N., Merien, A., Oei, G.: Intelligent Trainee Behavior Assessment System for Medical Training Employing Video Analysis. Pattern Recognition Lett. 33, 453–461 (2012)
5. Itami, K., Yasuda, T., Otsuki, Y., Ishibashi, M.: Beddomeikingu dousa niokeru zenkei kakudo ni chakumoku sita bodei mekanikusu chekku sisutemu no kaihatsu (Development of a Checking System for Body Mechanics Focusing on the Angle of Forward Leaning During Bedmaking). Japan Journal of Educational Technology 33(1), 1–9 (2009) (in Japanese)
6. Yonetsuji, T., Takebe, Y., Kanai-Pak, M., Maeda, J., Hirata, M., Kitajima, Y., Nakamura, M., Aida, K., Takabatake, Y., Kuwahara, N., Ota, J.: A Measurement and Evaluation Method of a Support System to Teach How to Improve Transferring Patients. In: Proceedings of the 2011 IEEE International Conference on Robotics and Biomimetics, vol. 151, pp. 908–913 (2011)
7. Matsumura, M., Izumi, M., Majima, Y., Maekawa, Y.: Beddo kurumaisu ijo dousa niokeru jukutatusha to syosinsya no sai chusyutsu (Difference Between Skilled Workers and Beginners on Patient Transfer Work from Bed to Wheelchair). Papers of the Technical Meeting on Information System, IEE Japan 2011, vol. (29), pp. 97–102 (2011) (in Japanese)
8. Nagata, A., Huang, Z., Kanai-Pak, M., Maeda, J., Kitajima, Y., Nakamura, M., Aida, K., Kuwahara, N., Ogata, T., Ota, J.: Supporting System for Self Training of Bed making Using Image Processing with Color and Distance Information. In: 2012 IEEE International Conference on Robotics and Biomimetics (ROBIO 2012), Guangzhou (2012)
9. Yoshida, M., Honjo, K.: Shasin de wakaru jisshu de tukaeru kango gijutu (Nursing skills seen in the photos, for practical training). Intermedica, Japan (2010)

Usability Problems in Patient- and Clinician-Oriented Health Information Systems: What Are They and How Do They Differ?

Dinara Saparova[1,*], Josipa Basic[1], Yunhui Lu[1], Francis Kibaru[1],
Yanfei Ma[1], and Borchuluun Yadamsuren[2]

[1] School of Information Science and Learning Technologies,
University of Missouri, Columbia, MO
{ds754,jbyv7,yl55f,fk4k3,ymyp6}@mail.missouri.edu
[2] School of Information Science and Learning Technologies,
University of Missouri, Columbia, MO
YadamsurenB@missouri.edu

Abstract. This study aimed to identify the usability problems in the eVisits based on the interaction experience of the three target user groups and compare their preferences for usability features. We used think aloud usability sessions with 5 patients, 5 nurses and 5 physicians in a laboratory setting to examine users' interaction with the eVisits. Nielsen's usability heuristic principles were applied to analyze the recorded usability sessions in Morae. Usability feature preferences among three groups were overlapped in the four heuristics. However, each user group had their own perceptions of these criteria specific to their unique needs. Clinicians tended to emphasize the importance of features relevant to their professional activity. Error prevention and aesthetic/minimalist design heuristics were brought up in the comments of physicians while two other groups did not mention anything related to these criteria. Only patients expected the features related to help and documentation heuristic.

Keywords: usability, e-visit, electronic visit system, health information system.

1   Introduction

Health information systems (HIS), which are computer based information systems used in healthcare settings, are represented by patient centered information systems, administrative information systems, clinical and laboratory information systems, and other types (see overview of HIS in [1]). HIS are designed for storing and processing health information, which later can be communicated by and presented to either health care professionals or patients in the context of inpatient or outpatient care [2].

Electronic visit systems (also known as eVisits) have been a recent innovation developed in an effort to provide health care available in many forms and whenever

---

* Corresponding author.

V.G. Duffy (Ed.): DHM/HCII 2013, Part I, LNCS 8025, pp. 276–285, 2013.

needed [3]. According to the American Academy of Family Physicians (AAFP) definition, e-visit is an evaluation and management service provided by a physician or other qualified health professional to an established patient using a web-based or similar electronic-based communication network for a single patient encounter. eVisits are typically offered to treat routine illnesses (nasal allergies, urinary tract infections, sinus infections, stomach flu, sore throat, pink eye, high blood pressure) and other health conditions (weight management, contraception, insomnia, back pain, and gastroesophageal reflux disease). Several parties can benefit from eVisits. Hospitals benefit from reducing bed occupancy in favor of those patients with greater need for them. Physicians benefit by saving in-office time spent with a patient [4] and allowing asynchronous care. Patients benefit from eVisits because they get faster, convenient (e.g., even when travelling and 24/7), and affordable access to healthcare. Additionally, parents of young children and adult children of aging parents can request health care on behalf of their dependents. Success of an eVisit greatly depends on the effectiveness/efficiency of the individuals involved and the cooperative efforts of the main actors involved in the process.

With the increasing demand for HIS utilization in healthcare, usability of such systems, as eVisits, is crucial to improve their usefulness, ease of use, and user satisfaction [5]. A substantial body of research has been reported on the usability problems of HIS [6–8] and the most suitable methodologies for revealing them [9, 10]. However, there is a lack of research that addresses the differences in the preferences for system usability features by the various user groups who are involved in interaction through the system. Learning about the differences in usability expectations from the main user groups of e-Visits system would help the system designers and developers improve these health care systems.

2   Purpose of Study

For this study we selected an eVisits that was under development by an international health care information technology corporation that specializes in providing/supplying complete systems for hospitals and other medical organizations. Prior to its launch, eVisits went through rigorous evaluations with three different user groups: patients, nurses, and physicians.

The main goal of this study was to identify the potential usability problems in eVisits based on the interaction experience of the main target user groups of the system.

Specifically, we pursued the following research questions:

1. What types of usability problems did patients and clinicians experience when completing an eVisits and interacting with the system?
2. What were the differences, if any, in feature preferences reported by patients and clinicians when interacting with an eVisits?

Methodology

2.1   Participants

Participants of the study represented three user groups: patients (n=5), nurses (n=5), and physicians (n=5). We recruited local community people in the roles of patients and the practicing clinicians at a large Midwestern university in the roles of nurses and physicians on the voluntary basis. Participants represented the convenient sample of users and received the monetary compensation, in the form of gift cards, for their participation.

2.2   Procedures

Data was collected through usability testing, which allowed for examination of how each user group performed on a list of specifically developed tasks, for which the system was designed in a controlled lab setting [11]. These tasks were representative of the naturalistic scenarios that each user group would be performing in a fully functional eVisits (Table 1).

During a usability testing session, each participant worked on task completion individually and was asked to verbalize his/her thoughts and actions. The sessions took place in a laboratory setting, lasting approximately 45-60 minutes, and were recorded with the Morae 3.2.1 software. Upon completion of each task, participants were asked to rate their perceived level of satisfaction with the ease of completing each task and the amount of time it took them to complete each task on a 7-point Likert scale. At the end of the session, participants were invited to participate in a semi-structured interview to share their overall thoughts of their interactions with the system and its usability. For the purpose of data triangulation, participants' self-reported feedback was coupled with facilitator observations. This procedure allowed us to capture the characteristics of user interactions with the system not reported by participants per se.

Table 1. Examples of tasks

	Patients	Physicians	Nurses
Task 1	Start a sore throat eVisit with the Northline Clinic	Locate eVisit in provider's queue	Locate a new sore throat eVisit in triage queue
Task 2	Start a pink eye eVisit with the Northline Clinic	Locate newly assigned eVisit in provider's queue	Locate an eVisit that needs to be reassigned in the triage queue
Task 3	Start a stomach flu eVisit with the Northline Clinic	Review summary	Locate a new pink eye eVisit in triage queue
Task 4	Start a nasal allergy eVisit with the Northline Clinic.	n/a	Locate a specific patient case

2.3   Data Analysis Approach

Data analysis included reviewing the recorded sessions and coding their content for occurring themes of usability problems, based on ten usability heuristics proposed by Jacob Nielsen [12]. We chose this approach for data analysis because all ten heuristics relate to criteria that affect product/system/website usability,[1] especially since usability heuristics has been previously applied to evaluation of health systems in several studies [12, 13]. To draw a bigger picture of users' preferences for usability criteria among different user groups, we also employed an inductive approach by being open to new occurring themes.

3   Results

3.1   Participants

Patients. The patients user group was represented by females (n=5) between 30 – 69 years old. The developers of eVisits requested the selection of this specific age group and gender for patients' group. In terms of education level, all but one user had graduate degrees. All five representatives of the patient user group reported that they use computer on a daily basis and considered themselves as proficient computer users. Only one person reported having used an eVisits previously.

Nurses. The nurses user group was represented by females (n=5) between 20 – 49 years old. Three participants were registered nurses, one was an education nurse, and one was a nurse practitioner. Their years of experience varied between 3 and 26 years. Three nurses had bachelor's degree, and two nurses master's degrees. All nurses reported that they use computer on a daily basis and considered themselves as proficient computer users. Four nurses had five or fewer years of using EMR, and none of them had used an eVisits before.

Physicians. The physicians user group was represented by males (n=3) and females (n=2) between ages 30 – 69 years old. The sample included four practicing family physicians and one dermatologist. Two physicians had less than 15 years of experience, while the other three had been practicing for over 30 years. The highest level of education among physicians was a doctorate in medicine. All physicians reported using a computer on a daily basis and considered themselves proficient in computer use. Two physicians reported using an EMR system for less than 10 years, while the other three said between 11 and 15 years. One physician had used an eVisits in the past.

---

[1] The ten usability heuristics include (1) Visibility of system status, (2) Match between system and the real world, (3) User control and freedom, (4) Consistency and standards, (5) Error prevention, (6) Recognition rather than recall, (7) Flexibility and efficiency of use, (8) Aesthetic and minimalistic design, (9) Help users recognize, diagnose, and recover from errors, (10) Help and documentation [12].

3.2   Research Question 1

What types of usability problems did patients and clinicians experience when completing an eVisit and interacting with the system?

Patients. Analysis indicates that patients expected to have six out of ten heuristics to be applied to the eVisits. They preferred more user control and freedom. For example, when initiating an eVisit and completing the form, they wanted to be able to provide more comments to further describe the symptom for their visit, to move freely between the questions, to change their answers, and to choose from readily available information instead of trying to come up with information on their own, such as the name of the pharmacy. They also wanted to be guided and provided with examples of how to fill out the form correctly. This part could serve as an indication of preference for better help and documentation about the system. In terms of system flexibility and efficiency of use, patients expected the system to change the requirements automatically for completing an eVisit based on the patient's physical condition. For example, if patients reported high fever or severe vomiting, they expected the system to reduce the number of questions they needed to answer due to the inability to spend a significant amount of time in front of the computer. Alternatively, if patients were not eligible for an eVisit, they expected to see such a message early on in the process of completing the form. Upon completing an eVisit, patients also wanted to have clear indication about the next step from the system, such as when and how they would be contacted regarding their visit. In terms of matches between system and the real world, patients thought that some symptoms overlapped, e.g., watery eyes and discharge from the eye, and some terms that described pain could be confusing for ordinary users. The average perceived satisfaction score (1=strongly disagree; 7=strongly agree) with the ease of completing tasks and the amount of time spent on task completion are reported in Table 2.

Table 2. Participant satisfaction scores (patients)

	Task 1	Task 2	Task 3	Task 4
Ease of completing tasks	5.8	6.4	5.8	6.2
Time spent on completing tasks	6.4	6.6	5.8	6.4

Physicians. The findings of this study suggest that physicians addressed eight out of ten heuristics during their interaction with the system. Particularly, they wanted the system to suggest a narrowed down list of medications based on the entered diagnosis and to generate a list of their preferred medications. When working on an eVisit physicians expressed the preference for system-generated information feed features, such as pre-set wording for description for certain medical conditions, and automatic calculation of the quantity of pills based on the medication dosage and duration. Physicians liked a system-generated diagnosis based on the symptoms described by patient. This feature allowed them to compare their own diagnosis with those ones generated by the system. They stated that spell checking option in the text entries would be beneficial. They appreciated the error prevention feature that stopped them from printing or sending prescription to a patient without previewing it first. As for visibility of system status, physicians wanted to be aware of the number of pending eVisits in their queue, and they expected to be able to see the latest eVisit first because such information presentation was consistent with other applications they have used before. Physicians also wanted to know patient's expectations before starting an eVisit, e.g., whether a patient initiated an eVisit because s/he simply needed an advice or a professional opinion or a prescription for medication. They also expected to have a confirmation whether patients' previous eVisits were completed. They wanted to see confirmation that they did not miss any unattended eVisits in the system. While working on an eVisit, physicians expressed their concerns about the credibility of information entered by the patient. Therefore, they wanted to know where patient history was coming from, i.e., from a patient or from EHR. Additionally, when writing a message to a patient, they did not like to be limited by the number of characters as it happened during the testing. They also expressed that they expect to see confirmation if a patient received their message. In terms of consistency and standards, physicians indicated that they were not familiar with some non-conventional abbreviations, e.g., 'pat' for 'patient', did not know the difference between 'new' and 'in triage', and preferred using medical vocabulary from the Intelligent Medication Objects (IMO). Finally, physicians did not like the fact that it was their responsibility to cancel an eVisit, especially if they had not yet started to work on it. Finally, a number of physicians were not satisfied with the look and placement of certain design elements, e.g., cancel and send buttons were hidden behind the text and were therefore effectively invisible. The average perceived satisfaction scores (1=strongly disagree; 7=strongly agree) with the ease of completing tasks and the amount of time spent on task completion are reported in Table 3.

Table 3. Participant satisfaction scores (physicians)

	Task 1	Task 2	Task 3
Ease of completing tasks	4.4	4.8	4.6
Time spent on completing tasks	4.6	5	4.8

Nurses. The findings of this study indicate that nurses addressed five out of ten usability heuristics. They emphasized the importance of visibility of system status. For example, they wanted to be informed when the system was down. Additionally, they wanted to receive confirmation of their actions, such as successful cancellation of an eVisit or re-assignment of a patient to another physician. In terms of system flexibility and efficiency of use criteria, nurses wanted to be able to locate necessary information, such as the number of patients that had been assigned to a particular physician, certain patients, and specifics about their labs in a timely manner. In doing so, nurses wanted to utilize a search function instead of browsing content. In terms of match between system and the real world criteria, nurses wanted patients' lab results to be displayed with the latest results on top part of the list, accompanied by time stamp (time/month/date/year). Nurses also expressed their preference for conventional terminology, e.g., 'patient' vs. 'pat', or 'min' vs. 'm'. In some cases, they were confused with the meaning of 'in triage' because this expression did not indicate whether the patient returned to triage and needed to be reassigned or whether it was a new patient. When asked about the purpose and the content of a note, a few nurses were unclear about its purpose and who it should be addressed to. The average perceived satisfaction scores (1=strongly disagree; 7=strongly agree) with the ease of completing tasks and the amount of time spent on task completion are reported in Table 4.[2]

Table 4. Participant satisfaction scores (nurses)

	Task 1	Task 2	Task 3	Task 4
Ease of completing tasks	3.25	4.5	5.5	5.5
Time spent on completing tasks	4.5	4.5	5.25	5.25

3.3   Research Question 2

What were the differences, if any, in feature preferences reported by patients and clinicians when interacting with an eVisit system?

Analysis of usability problem types by user groups revealed that representatives of three user groups emphasized the importance of different system features (Table 5).

Usability feature preferences among three groups were overlapped in the following four heuristics: match between system and the real world, consistency and standards, recognition rather than recall, and flexibility and efficiency of use. They wanted the system to support and improve their performance, to exclude the use of any unfamiliar words and terminology, to present information in the order of urgency and in the format they were accustomed to, and to include an automatic feed of already available information to avoid information re-entry, e.g., pharmacy name, a preferred medication list, patient search. Nurses and physicians brought up the features related to visibility of system status. Nurses expected to see the clear indications in the system to be informed whether the system was down, messages to the patients were sent, or an eVisit was cancelled. Physicians wanted to be able to see the most current eVisit information on top part of the screen and have visual cue for the number of pending eVisits. Both patients and physicians wanted to have more user control and freedom during completing an eVisit – patients were willing to provide more specific information than asked in the form, and physicians wanted to tailor the repetitive actions in the system. Physicians liked that the system demonstrated error prevention functionality, which made them to preview the prescribed medication to proceed further. In

---

[2] One of the nurses was unable to provide ratings of her satisfaction with the task performance due to a technical problem. Therefore, we reported the average score of four participants only.

addition to this function, they expected having spell checker and automatic calculation of medication quantity based on suggested dosage and duration. Physicians also noted that the icons and buttons should stand out from the background color to be easily noticeable.

Table 5. Comparison of system feature preferences among the three user groups

Heuristics/User groups	Patients	Physicians	Nurses
(1) Visibility of system status		+	+
(2) Match between system and the real world	+	+	+
(3) User control and freedom	+	+	
(4) Consistency and standards	+	+	+
(5) Error prevention		+	
(6) Recognition rather than recall	+	+	+
(7) Flexibility and efficiency of use	+	+	+
(8) Aesthetic and minimalist design		+	
(9) Help users recognize, diagnose, and recover from errors			
(10) Help and Documentation	+		
Total n of heuristics addressed:	6	8	5

Error prevention and aesthetic/minimalist design heuristics were brought up in the comments of physicians while two other groups did not mention anything related to these criteria. Only patients emphasized about the importance of features related to the help and documentation heuristic.

4   Conclusion

This paper sought to investigate the specifics of user interaction with an eVisits – an interactive web-based system capable of offering medical care to a patient by a medical institution that can replace regular face-to-face visits. We aimed to explore if there are any differences in the types of usability problems encountered by the three different user groups (physicians, nurses, patients) when they interacted with eVisits. We applied Nielsen's usability heuristic principles in our data analysis.

The findings of our study revealed that clinicians tended to emphasize the importance of features relevant to their professional activity. Physicians pointed out eVisits features that would support their performance and allow them to be efficient in their work (e.g., error prevention and minimalist design) by overcoming cognitive and information overload (e.g., recognition rather than recall, user control and freedom, flexibility and efficiency of use) and spending minimum time on learning system features (e.g., aesthetic and minimalist design). Nurses, as an intermediary between patients and physicians, emphasized the importance of usability features that would assist them with more efficient work coordination (e.g., recognition rather than recall) and overall control of an eVisits process (e.g., visibility of system status).

All three user groups expected the system to demonstrate a match between system and the real world, consistency and standards, recognition rather than recall, and flexibility and efficiency of use heuristic criteria. However, each user group had their own perceptions of these criteria specific to their unique needs. Only patients emphasized the importance of features related to the help and documentation heuristic. They reported perceived difficulties to interact with eVisits. A well-designed and built-in help feature in the system would help patients to interact with the system more easily.

Obvious differences in feature preferences for eVisits between patients and clinicians might be related to the fact they interacted with the interfaces designed with slight differences for their specific needs. However, the findings of the present study demonstrate the general trends for user interface design features and functionalities that should be incorporated in e-Visits type of health information systems for patients and clinicians. Revealing the distinct needs for various user groups as well as the system flaws and successes through usability testing can contribute to successful system design and its further implementation, adoption, and use.

References

1. Yusof, M.M., Papazafeiropoulou, A., Paul, R.J., Stergioulas, L.K.: Investigating evaluation frameworks for health information systems. International Journal of Medical Informatics 77, 377–385 (2008)
2. Ammenwerth, E., De Keizer, N.: An Inventory of Evaluation Studies of Information Technology in Health Care, pp. 44–56 (2005)
3. Institute of Medicine. Crossing the Quality Chasm: A New Health System for the 21st Century (2001)
4. Rosen, P., Kwoh, C.K.: Patient-physician e-mail: an opportunity to transform pediatric health care delivery. Pediatrics 120, 701–706 (2007)
5. Zhang, J., Walji, M.F.: TURF: toward a unified framework of EHR usability. Journal of Biomedical Informatics 44, 1056–1067 (2011)
6. Segall, N., Saville, J.G., L'Engle, P., Carlson, B., Wright, M.C., Schulman, K., Tcheng, J.E.: Usability evaluation of a personal health record. In: AMIA.. Annual Symposium Proceedings / AMIA Symposium, AMIA Symposium 2011, pp. 1233–1242 (2011)
7. Bartlett, Y.K., Selby, D.L., Newsham, A., Keding, A., Forman, D., Brown, J., Velikova, G., Wright, P.: Developing a useful, user-friendly website for cancer patient follow-up: users' perspectives on ease of access and usefulness. European Journal of Cancer Care 21, 747–757 (2012)
8. Brewer, N.T., Gilkey, M.B., Lillie, S.E., Hesse, B.W., Sheridan, S.L.: Tables or bar graphs? Presenting test results in electronic medical records. Medical Decision Making: an International Journal of the Society for Medical Decision Making 32, 545–553 (2012)

9. Yen, P.Y., Bakken, S.: Review of health information technology usability study methodologies. Journal of the American Medical Informatics Association: JAMIA 19, 413–422 (2012)
10. Jaspers, M.W.: A comparison of usability methods for testing interactive health technologies: methodological aspects and empirical evidence. International Journal of Medical Informatics 78, 340–353 (2009)
11. Nielsen, J.: Usability Engineering. Morgan Kaufman, San Diego (1993)
12. Zhang, J., Johnson, T.R., Patel, V.L., Paige, D.L., Kubose, T.: Using usability heuristics to evaluate patient safety of medical devices. Journal of Biomedical Informatics 36, 23–30 (2003)
13. Liu, L.S., Hayes, G.R.: Heuristic Evaluation of Personal Health Records Systems. In: Workshop on Interactive Systems for Health at CHI 2010 (2010)

Part III
Safety of the Human Environment

AmI-Technology at Work – A Sociological Perspective Covering Aspects of Occupational Safety and Health (OSH)

Michael Bretschneider-Hagemes

IFA - Institute for Occupational Safety and Health of the German Social Accident Insurance
Alte Heerstraße 111, 53757 Sankt Augustin, Germany
michael.bretschneider-hagemes@dguv.de

Abstract. Ambient Intelligence (AmI) technologies are becoming increasingly widespread in working life. Some of these are specific applications already integrated in the workflow, while others are ambitious strategies on the verge of immediate industrial implementation. However different they may be, they are commonly discussed under the shared term of "ambient intelligence" as a conceptual catch-all. In the present article, the author reflects on this somewhat simple definition and, with the aid of technology-centred definitions on the one hand and issues of the sociology of work relating to human-centricity on the other, he facilitates more instructive access to the responsible application of AmI technologies in the world of work.

Keywords: ambient intelligence, mobile ICT, mental stresses, alienation, surveillance.

1   Introduction

Ambient Intelligence (AmI) is a much-discussed term. Intelligent houses are inhabited by smart objects and the human carriers of these technical artefacts. Intelligent cars with smart tyres and computers provide increasing assistance in the transportation of their occupants to their destinations and intelligent factories support the employees there with a multitude of assistance systems. While the fields of application of AmI are manifold, how AmI is viewed is one-sided. The star of interactivity is all too often hailed with blind faith in technology and progress, without a judicious pause to estimate the consequences in good time. The present first attempt at an account of AmI from the point of view of the philosophy and sociology of work aims to give pointers to ways of remedying this deficit in industrial applications of AmI.

To afford simple and clearly structured access to the subject, I shall start with a technology-centred attempt at a definition and with the concept of "smartness". By analogy with Taylor and Focault, I shall outline, in propositions, the typical characteristics of AmI in the following. A resultant performance specification for the application of AmI technologies will follow at a later date.

V.G. Duffy (Ed.): DHM/HCII 2013, Part I, LNCS 8025, pp. 289–296, 2013.

2   The Delimitation of Technical Artefacts – What Counts as AmI?

A noteworthy problem in the debate on Ambient Intelligence is the remarkable confusion surrounding the definition of what AmI is. What is usually encountered is a whole potpourri of technical concepts, actual/potential applications and scenarios. As usual for a theme from the realm of social megatrends, the situation is acerbated by the fact that, for economic and/or political reasons, all manner of activists jump onto the bandwagon in a bid for their share of the cake in terms of funding and market access. Any discussion of this topic worth taking seriously ought to make a determined effort to conceptually demarcate the subject-matter beforehand. This demarcation derives its value not so much from a watertight and eternal definition, but rather from the exclusion of what falls outside its conceptual bounds. With this in mind, I have attempted in the following a thematic delimitation based on the technical artefact and on the rough architecture of the artefacts involved in interaction. In the following, a more abstract discussion of the sociology and implications for the philosophy of work should be able to dock onto this construct. Point of departure for a definition:

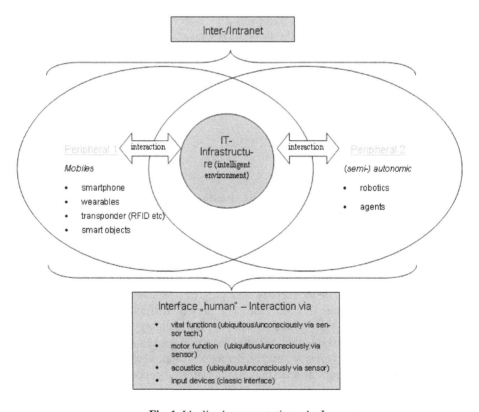

Fig. 1. Idealized representation - AmI

AmI designates an IT-networked environment (room, truck or the like) that, with the aid of mobile information and communication terminals and/or acoustic, motor and other signals, is usually intuitively usable, often processing information autonomously with the aid of sensors, and is usually constantly switched on (see Fig. 1). The purpose of its practical applications can currently be found in the assistance (e.g. data glasses, driving assistants, data mirrors etc.) of a huge range of work actions, the collection/processing of information (warehouse inventories, logistics, tracking etc.) and the (partial) automation of processes.

The figure clearly shows that AmI is by no means a single technical artefact such as data glasses or a smartphone, but always involves a complex interplay of a central and networked IT infrastructure with computer units, peripheral and on the whole passive artefacts such as smartphones and transponders (see Figure 1, Peripheral 1), peripherally active artefacts such as software agents and robotics applications (see Figure 1, Peripheral 2), an Inter/intranet access for data sourcing and an often extremely elaborate human interface.

It should be borne in mind here that the examples are equivalents that do not all have to be present to satisfy the definition of Ami.

2.1   Smart or Not Smart?

In the AmI debate, one term is conspicuous through its omnipresence: smart.

The idea is that "smart" objects should stand apart from existing technologies thanks to such attributes as user-centred assistance, intelligence and autonomy and thus enrich the lives of the people who use them. At the same time, frequently cited examples of smartness give rise to considerable doubts about the mentioned properties:

"Examples of smart objects are car tires that tell the driver when the air pressure is decreasing." [1].

This dilution of the definition of smart leads to confusion about the subject of discussion. The artefact in the cited example (car tire) is anything but smart. It is a trivial machine:

"A trivial machine is characterized by a clear relationship between its 'input' (stimulus, cause) and its 'output' (reaction, effect). This invariant relationship is the 'machine'. Since this relationship is fixed for all time, it is a deterministic system; and since an output once observed for a certain input will be the same for the same input at a later date, it is also a predictable system" [2].

In terms of the tire, this means that precisely whenever a certain minimum pressure is reached, a warning signal is issued. This function couldn't be more trivial. Such artefacts are explicitly disregarded here. The world is familiar with them in myriad guises and knows more or less how to respond to them and how to deal with them. Complex machines, on the other hand, operate entirely differently:

"The so-called 'non-trivial' machine is (...) in a sense trivial in that it – like the 'trivial machine' – is a machine, i.e. conforms to a precisely defined rule. An observer who is unfamiliar with the mechanism and therefore has a black box in front of him has very poor chances of uncovering the logic of a 'non-trivial machine' by experimentation, for instance" [2].

Complex machines therefore become black boxes in that they change their inherent internal operative state. They perform different functions in relation to their experience and/or, in practical terms, through supplementary dynamic information from an external source like the Internet that is integrated into the operative process in specific situations. The results of their action are not therefore predictable for an outside observer.

Example: To stay with our tyre, we can imagine the following situation. A tyre suddenly loses pressure. Thanks to its sensors, the car computer recognises the state, knows on the basis of its experience (fatigue recognition sensors) about the driver's reactions (slow in this case), also has via an Internet link current details of approaching road works and decides not to an issue a signal to the driver, but to autonomously initiate a braking process.

An outside observer would not be able to understand why one vehicle suddenly brakes (driver tired) and another, identical one doesn't (driver alert). The technology has the quality of a black box and is smart. In the following, only technologies that through interaction are smart in this sense are to be subsumed under the term "ambient intelligence". In addition, there is also mention in the following of industrial applications of AmI, in which it, like every technology, is given a context-dependent quality.

3   Assessment of the Ascribed Attributes of AmI

3.1   AmI Is Human-Centric

Whenever there is mention of AmI in public discussion and in popular scientific media, it is commonly assumed to be fundamentally different from conventional technologies. Technology is no longer a cumbersome, physically graspable thing that often hinders people with its shortcomings, but a universally available resource that has now assumed objective form (cf.[3]).

"Whereas in the age of the mainframe and PCs computing capacity was still a scarce resource, new technologies and continuing progress in the field of information and communication technologies promise the omnipresent availability of information and services. At the centre of this is no longer the machine with its technical capacities and limitations, but the human being with his/her personal needs and wishes. The computer now only operates in the background as an unobtrusive but constantly available electronic assistant." [1].

What we see here is the romantic interpretation of a technical revelation. This should be treated with distrust. The question of what is human-centric about AmI can be quickly investigated and explained on the basis of examples of scenarios (partly real, partly invented):

Example I - AmI-supported order-picking:
The production line workers of a car maker are supplied with the components they need by workmates known as pickers. The components are stored in a neighbouring racking bay, which is fully computer-controlled. The central computer is informed a short time in advance of the vehicle variants being assembled. Via a head-mounted display (HMD) linked to the central computer, the pickers are informed according to the context in which rack the parts needed by production line workers can be found.

Example II - AmI-supported light control:
The office workplaces of a leading insurance company are equipped with eye-blink sensors and other sensors to monitor employees' vital data. By cleverly processing the sensor information in the central computer, the system is aware of the onset of employees' fatigue and lack of concentration in the course of the day. As a result, the light colour is reduced to 17,000 kelvin, a bluish light that has a performance-enhancing effect on the hormone balance.

Taylorism-Critical Assessment. By means of the examples given above, real application scenarios and the technically possible illustrate the kind of human-centricity implicit in AmI. It serves mainly as an elevation of scientific management, a Taylorisation of the workplace (cf. [4] [11]), to a new, unprecedented level.

Proposition: AmI potentially separates mental work from physical labour and results in knowledge expropriation, the downskilling of the affected groups of employees, and thus to a casualisation of their work.
    Typical of AmI is the central storage of experiential knowledge and expert knowledge in a central database. Order picking is a good example for explaining this: the computer management of storage locations, walking routes and current production/parts needs means the provision of a great deal of experiential knowledge. Before AmI technologies (and their forerunners) were introduced, experienced skilled workers were needed to flawlessly handle the complex tasks associated with the frequent product changes on the production line. This knowledge is now centrally stored and made available to the unskilled labourers via their displays. The knowledge is now exclusive, with the expected consequence that workers become increasingly dependent and their work becomes increasingly casual. The separation of work from personal skills and from a comprehensive work experience will result in considerable mental stress as a result of the experience of alienation.

3.2   AmI Is Ubiquitous

The ubiquitous computing accompanying AmI technology refers to the form of computing that is becoming characteristic of the 21st century (cf. [3]). Its essence lies in the omnipresence of information technology owing to wireless and wide-area networking, and in the seamless and invisible integration of this networking into everyday (working) life. At present, mobile workers can still be recognized as such by the notebooks or tablet PCs perched on their knees. By contrast, ubiquitous computing refers to the inconspicuous integration in the background of mobile IT terminal devices which provide access to the ubiquitous IT infrastructure. Wearables of various types are already available on the market. Rather than themselves being the direct focus of human attention as is currently the case, they are instead to form a natural component of a partly virtual objectivity enhanced by IT, which the subject must deal with either consciously or unconsciously. The environment itself becomes the interface. This property, too, is interpreted by the digital avant-garde as a starry-eyed prophecy:

"There is more information available at our fingertips during a walk in the woods than in any computer system, yet people find a walk among trees relaxing and computers frustrating. Machines that fit the human environment, instead of forcing humans to enter theirs, will make using a computer as refreshing as taking a walk in the woods." (cf. [3]).

This assessment is notable for its naive carefreeness, which has more in common with science-fiction fantasies than with the human environment and in particular the working environment in the prevailing power structures. The following digression is intended to describe an essential problem of this assessment, the panoptic nature of AmI:

The panopticum is a concept devised by the philosopher Jeremy Bentham (cf. [5]) for the design of factory workplaces, schools and prisons and which enables a single observer to oversee a large number of people simultaneously. A typical characteristic of a panoptic building was and continues to be the facility for observing persons from a central location. Some traditional factories featuring a raised observation point which cannot be looked into from the workers' workplaces are an example. Common prison buildings feature a central observation tower, from which the cell wings branch outwards. This architectural arrangement enables a guard to observe areas without himself being visible by those he is observing. As a result, not only may fewer guards suffice, which is desirable for economic reasons; it may even be possible to dispense with the guards altogether, either temporarily or permanently. Ignorance of whether or not one is under observation at a given time leads to internalization of surveillance and thereby to an exceptionally economic means of imposing discipline (cf. [6]). Bentham, like other utilitarians after him, believed himself to be on the moral high ground. Michel Foucault later recognized this principle of discipline as an essential aspect of modern society (cf. [7]). Pointedly, the proposition is as follows:

AmI risks becoming the digital equivalent of the panopticum.
As already established, environments become intelligent when they feature a range of sensor equipment which is interconnected and delivers information for interpretation at a central point. In work scenarios, the sensors may register not only the position of the workers, but also their vital data, implicit communication such as facial expressions, and of course periods of time. The worker is thus continually under omnipresent digital eyes, the presence of which he is conscious of to a greater or lesser degree. Mobile IT-supported work involving smartphones, notebooks and similar devices already gives workers grounds to fear that their every step is being monitored and that movement profiles are being generated; this fear sadly is often not unfounded [8]. Whereas a smartphone could at least be switched off (albeit requiring justification later) and an e-mail left unanswered until the next break, the invisibility

and potential ubiquity of AmI leads to a total loss of control over the technical artefacts. Unless restrictions are consciously imposed, human beings are entirely at the mercy of AmI and produce data at every step by their mere being. In the opinion of BEIGEWUM, the Austrian Advisory Council for Society, Economic and Environmental Alternatives, the consequence that is to be feared is that the active subject will be degraded to a *forced consumer or occupant of AmI* (cf. [9]). Zygmunt Bauman goes as far as to see in the digitalized post-modern world a postpanoptic system of surveillance and discipline (cf. [10]). This world, he argues, is characterized by the fact that its key equivalents are not directly physically tangible in form (the central server as opposed to the watchtower) and will also not necessarily be tied to a particular location. AmI technologies satisfy these criteria, and could potentially be the digital equivalent of the panopticum in the postmodern world, implementing it by ubiquitous surveillance technologies, the objectivity of which can no longer be observed and the transparency of which progressively decreases.

4   Performance Specification for the Use of AmI Technologies

The formulated proposition and its discussion have revealed a significant risk and the negative potential of AmI technology. At the present time, these technologies are becoming gradually but increasingly widespread in the home and in industrial fields of application. There is still time for governments to act in consciously shaping this technology. In an ethical performance specification, the formulated problems are set against criteria that attempt to solve or prevent them arising. The performance specification is in preparation and can be made available on request even in advance of publication.

References

1. Mattern, M.: Acht Thesen zur Informatisierung des Alltags, Institut für Pervasive Computing. ETH Zürich (2007)
2. von Foerster, H.: Wissen und Gewissen, in: Zukunft der Wahrnehmung: Wahrnehmung der Zukunft. Suhrkamp-Verlag, Frankfurt (1993)
3. Weiser, M.: The Computer for the 21st Century. Scientific American Ubicomp Paper (1991)
4. Kurz, R.: Schwarzbuch Kapitalismus – Ein Abgesang auf die Marktwirtschaft. Ullstein-Verlag, München (2002)
5. Bentham, J.: The Works of Jeremy Bentham, published under the Superintendence of Executor. In: Bowring, J. (ed.) Proposal for a New and Less Expensive Mode for Employing and Reforming Convicts, vol. 11. William Tait, Edinburgh (1843), http://oll.libertyfund.org/title/2234/210578 (accessed on August 20, 2012)
6. Fink-Eitel, H.: Michel Foucault – Zur Einführung. Junius Verlag, Hamburg (2002)
7. Foucault, M.: Überwachen und Strafen – Die Geburt des Gefängnisses. Suhrkamp, Frankfurt a.M (1992)

8. Bretschneider-Hagemes, M., Kohn, M.: Ganzheitlicher Arbeitsschutz bei mobiler IT-gestützter Arbeit. In: Brandt, et al. (eds.) PaPsD – Arbeitsschutz und Arbeitsgestaltung von Mobiler Arbeit. Ver.di, Berlin (2010)
9. Crutzen, C.: Das Unsichtbare und das Sichtbare des artifiziellen Handelns im täglichen Leben. In: Kurswechsel 3/2007, Zeitschrift des Beirats für gesellschafts-, wirtschafts- und umweltpolitische Alternativen, Wien (2007)
10. Bauman, Z.: Flüchtige Moderne, Edition Suhrkamp, Frankfurt/M (2003)
11. Taylor, F.W.: The principles of scientific management. Cosimo, New York (2006) (Neuauflage des Originals von 1911)

List of Figures

Figure 1: Idealised representation of ambient intelligent ICT
(our own depiction)

Bayesian Affordance-Based Agent Model for Wayfinding Behaviors in Evacuation Problems

Moise Busogi[1], Namhun Kim[1], Dongmin Shin[2], Hokyoung Blake Ryu[2], Arm Yoo[1], and Dongchul Kim[3]

[1] Ulsan National Institute of Science and Technology, UNIST-gil 50, Ulsan 689-798, Republic of Korea
{busogi,nhkim,yoodkfmal}@unist.ac.kr
[2] Hanyang University, 222 Wangsimini-ro, Seongdong, Seoul 133-791, Republic of Korea
{dmshin,hryu}@hanyang.ac.kr
[3] ITSTAR, 1327-6 Dal-dong, Nam-gu Ulsan, Republic of Korea
4659issac@hanmail.net

Abstract. In this paper, we propose a modeling framework of rational human actions in human-environment systems by evaluating probable human actions in physical and psychological dimensions. In the affordance theoretic perspective, an environment offers certain physical and psychological limitations to filter a finite number of feasible human actions that lead to desired system states in a spatio-temporal dimension. By integrating physical and psychological constraints in human decision making processes, a value-based Bayesian-affordance model is proposed using Markov Decision Model. To this ends, two different types of filters, '*F1*' and '*F2*' are proposed, where '*F1*' is a preference-based numerical filter conceived at the planning level for psychological constraints and '*F2*' an affordance-based numerical filter at the execution level in which agent's perception of physical action availability plays a big role. Finally, a simple example based on the proposed model is illustrated to verify the proposed framework and the analysis results are discussed.

Keywords: Affordance, way-finding, dynamic programming, Markov Decision Process.

1 Introduction

Predicting human action is a challenging task, if not impossible due to many uncertain factors involving decision making of an agent [1]. However, the degree of difficulty can be tremendously reduced by acquiring more related information on the agent's perceptions and understanding of environments, such as its belief, its purpose as well as its environment [2].

According to Daniel Dennett, in his theory of intentional stance, predicting a rational agent is not somehow impossible task [2]. Predicting human action offers a boost in simulating human actions in space and time dimensions, which in turn provides a necessary tool to understand human-environment interactions. Gimblett *et al.* 1997

V.G. Duffy (Ed.): DHM/HCII 2013, Part I, LNCS 8025, pp. 297–306, 2013.

explains how human action simulation not only allows examining but also testing different observation of a system behavior [3].

Despite many theories suggesting the unpredictability of human action, within a given space and time, the environment tend to offer plenty of constraints that give less and less options and choices to the agent, therefore making it easier to predict probable human actions to reach his/her goal. In some of human-environment interactions such as way-findings, there is a clear and a stable goal and human tend to perceive action opportunities and different cues in a somehow a consistent way. In this paper, action opportunities and constraints are modeled using the theory of affordance [4, 5] which will be discussed further in detail in section 2.

Way-finding can be seen as a combination of human factors and environment factors where a human decision making is led by his or her perception of the environment. Arthur and Passini define wayfinding process as the combination of Decision making, Decision executing, and Information processing [6]. The wayfinding is heavily affected by the agent perceptual capabilities, fundamental information-processing capabilities, previously acquired knowledge, and motor capabilities [7].

This research intend to assist designers or modelers of human-involved systems in understanding and mapping human decision process with respect to the environmental affordances therefore helping them to create effective and efficient cues to guide human in making appropriate decision. Furthermore, due to limitations of human experimentation, the resulting agent will be very useful tool in simulating human behavior in an environment that was otherwise impossible or inappropriate for real human experimentation.

The rest of paper is composed as follows; in section 2,related works are briefly reviewed; in section 3, we present our model framework; in section 4, an example is given to illustrate the proposed framework; finally, a brief conclusion follows to wrap up the discussion.

2   Related Works

2.1   Affordance Theory and Human Decision Modeling

The word affordance was first introduced by Gibson in 1979 to refer to the environment property that provides or furnishes the animal to take an action, either for the good or ill of the system [4]. Since its introduction, the affordance theory got a lot of attention from researchers in various field such as artificial intelligent, usability, etc. [8-10], however, less has been done to incorporate it in human decision modeling. Joo *et al.* developed Conceptual Framework for Affordance-Based Simulation of Human Behavior using Finite State Automata (FSA) [11]. Whereas Joo *et al.* deeply consider the agent-environment interaction; there is no much focus on the agent abilities and preferences, therefore leading every agent in making exactly same choice. Chris *et al.* presented a Bayesian goal inference model, in which a Markov decision process was used to approximate action probabilities [12], however, among others, a systematic description of agent and environment interaction was given little attention.

3   Modeling Framework

Rational agent are assumed to choose the most cost effective way to achieve a goal; however, limited information and different uncertainties within the agent environment makes it harder for the agent to effectively choose the optimal path to reach the intended goal. Due to these uncertainties, the agent makes a decision using the available information and updates his/her choices along the execution process when new information is revealed along the process [13].

To further understand, let's consider a system that consists of a human in a multistory building. In this system, we consider the floors as states of the system from which a human transit to another state (floor) by taking series of relevant actions. The actions can include: walking, running, taking an elevator, taking an escalator, jump, use a rope and so on. A rational agent choice of action usually correlates with the cost-effective way of reaching the goal. Agents encounter different types of costs while trying to reach a goal [14]. The computational model for representation of rational human agents should include the formal process of incurring a goal-directed and perception-based action as shown in Fig 1.

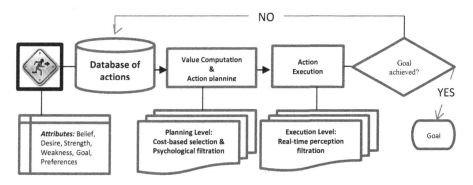

Fig. 1. Action selection process frameworkAction Selection- Physical Domain

We define an environment as anything not intrinsic to the agent, within the system. Within the system, there is an interaction between an agent and an environment. According to theory of affordance, this interaction is the essence of action and result in the changing of the agent's state. Agents are believed to have belief and desires [2]. These beliefs and desires differentiate one agent to another, and they do not only determine the agent's goal (g) but also its inner resources that lead the agent to choosing an action. As it is defined in the Markov decision process; our agent gets a reward r(t) for performing action a(t) and reaching state s(t+1) from state s(t). C(a) is the cost it takes an agent to take action a.

Using dynamic programming we assign optimal value to each state based on the optimal policy. A policy is a mapping of action to state. Since the agents are assumed to be rational, the probability of choosing an action is proportional to Q, the expected value of taking the action. In the proposed model, the agents make a finite number of steps to reach the goal. Let π be the best policy to reach the goal with the maximum total reward $r.\pi$ maps the series of actions that minimize total cost from the current state to the goal state, $\pi: s \in S \rightarrow \pi(s) \in A$, where S denotes the set of states of the system, and A denotes the set of available actions. By following the optimum policy the value of state s will be

$$V_N^\pi(s) = \sum_{t=0}^{t=N-1} E^\pi[r(s_t, a_t | s_0 = s, g, w)]$$

, where:

$V_N^\pi(s)$: The expected value of state s given that he executes policy π,

s_t: State at time t,

g: Agent's goal,

w: Environment state,

a_t: Agent action at time t, and

N: Finite number of steps to reach the goal.

While in state s, an agent can choose any available action within the state. To better understand the value of action a in state s, $Q^\pi(s, a | g, w)$ is defined, which is the expected value when starting from s executing action a and then follow policy π afterwards. $Q^\pi(s, a | g, w) = r(s, a) + \sum_{s_t} p(s_t | s, a, g, w) V^\pi(s_t)$. Since we consider our agents to be rational at a given degree, the probability P (a) to choose a given action in a given state will be proportional to its action-value of $Q^\pi(s, a | g, w)$ [15].

3.1   Action Selection-Psychological Domain

In 1956, Simon argued that people are satisfied with a good enough solution that approximate the accuracy of optimal algorithms without placing too heavy demand on the cognitive system [16], which mainly refers to the effect of psychological cost on human decision making. After rating different actions based on physical cost, the proposed model employs the psychological factors of preference as filters in the proposed framework of human action selection model. These filters use the subjective perception and interpretation of environmental affordances as well as the effectivity of the agent, not only in the planning level but also at the execution process.

Planning Level. The planning level filtration is an expected affordance-based psychological filtration of activities required to create a desired goal on some scale. By considering each action in the database of actions, each action is given a binary score i with respect to both affordance and effectivities. For example, for an agent considering climbing stairs, his binary score on effectivity is 1 if he has physical ability to climb and the affordance score is 1 if there are stairs on which climbing is possible. If the stairs had missing steps, that makes it impossible for an agent to climb, the rating score would be 0 instead 1 for the affordance. It is important to understand that at the planning level, both affordance and effectivities are imaginary and approximated through different cues and prior experiences without a direct perception.

Among the possible actions, some are more affordable than others due to not only the energy or time spent performing these actions but also to different level of meditation [16]. In this sense, the meditation level is applied to model a function of stress, attention, or any other mental or emotional cost associated with taking any given action. Using the expected meditation level, the agent filters the available action using F_1, which is a numerical filter representing possibility to choose an action at the planning level. Let p_1 be a numerical score to denote the complexity of performing a given action a in a given environment. In other words, p_1 denote how mentally easy to perform a given action in a given environment within a given state. In the proposed model, p_1 takes a continuous value from 0 to 1. Thus, more mentally challenging actions get relatively lower rating. The lower the stress, the higher the value of p, thus a stress-free state would mean p valued nearly to 1. As specified earlier, F_1 is a product of not only the environment score but also the agent score with respect to a given action. In our model the agent score is denoted by q_1. q_1 denotes the agent relative level of expertise, skill, risk taking behavior and other   subjective advantage or disadvantage in terms of taking a given action in a given state and a given environment state. Before determining the value of q_1 a reference agent should be determined by which other agents must be compared to. The reference agent should be a typical agent with characteristics of an average agent and its q_1 value should be 0.5.

$$F_1 = i.p_1.q_1, \text{where} \qquad (1)$$

$$i = \begin{cases} 1 \text{ if the action is possible wrt to affordance Effectivities} \\ 0 \qquad\qquad\qquad\qquad\qquad\qquad\qquad\qquad\quad otherwise \end{cases}, \text{ and}$$

$$q_1, p_1 \in [0,1].$$

Incorporating the filter into the cost based selection gives us the new action probability.

$$P(a)=P1.F1 \qquad (2)$$

Execution Level. An agent does not necessarily follow the path conceived in the planning level; instead, he/she may adapt to the real situation by updating his/her decision based on updated information. In the planning level, human agents expect specific action opportunities that might help them to reach the goal state in the imaginary spatial-temporal dimension. However, a real action opportunity of the affordance-effectivity dual is only available in a certain space and time. The expected environmental situation can change and it inevitably makes the agent change the plan to reach the goal state frequently. To account the change between the expected environment and the real environment, the agent applies the second filter 'F_2', which incorporates the agent's real-time perception of environmental affordance as opposed to the expected affordance in the planning level. When the expected action opportunity conceived at the planning level matches the real time affordance, the agent should stick to the decision made in the planning level. Therefore F_2 must penalize any action for which the existence of affordance-effectivity dual is less probable than expected. Also, F_2 must promote the actions for which the affordance-effectivity duals are more probable than expected. Similarly, F_2 is defined as follow:

$$F2 = i.p_2.\frac{p_2}{p_1} \text{ , where} \qquad (5)$$

$$i = \begin{cases} 1 \ if \ the \ action \ is \ possible \ wrt \ to \ affordance \ \ Effectivities \\ 0 \qquad\qquad\qquad\qquad\qquad\qquad\qquad\qquad\qquad otherwise \end{cases},$$

$p_2 = real \ affordance \ rating$, and

$q_2 = real \ effectivity \ rating$.

Let $P(a)$ denote the probability of a given action at the planning level. $P'(a) {\sim} P(a).F_2$, where $P'(a)$ is the action probability at the execution level.

4   An Illustrative Example

For verification of the proposed model, we illustrate two different environment states separately in the analysis of the multi-story building.

4.1   Optimum Policy

In this illustration we consider a policy as any combination of action-state that result in reaching the goal. For example, for an agent in 4th floor whose goal is to exit the building, taking an elevator to the first floor and then exit the building can be considered as one of the policies. Fig 2 illustrates few possible policies. A policy is optimal if and only if it reaches the goal while maximizing total rewards; in our case, minimizing the total cost of reaching the goal.

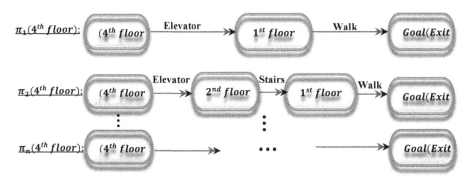

Fig. 2. Policy options

For each policy $\pi_i(s)$ there is an associated value $V^\pi(s)$ which is the function of rewards collected throughout the process to reach the goal. In this illustration we express the rewards in function of the total cost of reaching the goal following cy $\pi_i(s)$. $V^\pi(s)$ is inversely proportional to the cost function. Let c_i be the cost of reaching the goal following the policy $\pi_i(s)$. $\pi_i(s) = \pi_{optimal}(s)$ if and only if $c_{opt} = Min \ (\ c_i)$ for all i. In this stage, dynamic programing algorithm is used to assign the optimal policy to each state as well as the associated values. Based on the optimal values of each state obtained following a given policy, the agent compute

$Q^\pi(s, a|g, w)$ which is the expected value when starting from state, s, executing action a and then follow policy $\pi_i(s')$ afterwards.

4.2   Normal Working Environment

We consider the building floors as state of the system and the exit being the final state which is the goal in this case. First of all, we compute the cost of taking a given action from a given state in a given environment. Only three states are considered in this example: 5th floor, 1st floor and goal which is to exit the building. The following table shows the energy cost as well as the time required to perform a given action from 5th floor. It was computed based on little references[1]and intuition.

Table 1. Cost of action

Action	Time	Energy	Cost	$p(s'\ /\ s, a)$	$P1(a/g, s, w)$
Take stairs	1min	10 Cal	2	1	0.089766607
Take elevator	30sec	1 Cal	0.1	1	0.897666068
jump	5 sec	1 Cal	0.016667	0.001	0.010771993
Use a rope	2min	200 Cal	80	0.8	0.001795332

Since time and energy have different units, it is hard to add up the total cost in order to compare different actions. A clear research on agent indifference curve for time and energy is needed to better decide their weight in the cost function. In this illustration, the cost is the product of both time and energy where 30 seconds of time and 10 calories of energy are both equivalent to one unit of cost. Using the cost value we compute the Q^π value of every available action. The reward of performing an action is proportional to the probability of reaching the next state and inversely proportionally to the cost. The action probabilities based on the physical cost of performing the action are stored in Table 1. As discussed earlier, psychological cost also play a major role in this probability distribution, as shown in Table 2.

Table 2. Psychological filters –Normal environment

Action	p1	i	q1	F1
Take elevator	0.9	1	0.5	0.4
Walk Stairs	0.8	1	0.5	0.45
Jump	0.01	1	0.5	0.005
Use a rope	0.3	1	0.5	0.15

Recall that p1 denotes how mentally easy to perform a given action in a given environment whereas q1 denote the agent relative level of expertise, skill, risk taking behavior and other subjective advantage or disadvantage in terms of taking a given action in a given state and a given environment state. Note that the ratings given in

---

[1] http://www.healthstatus.com/calculate/cbc

Table 2 are for a reference agent. The ratings are intuitive in this illustrative example. By using our model framework, the action probabilities are depicted in the chart below. Despite being hard to know the real probability in real life situation, it is still understandable to assume that more than 90 percent of people in 5th floor will plan to take an elevator when they are trying to exit the building. At the execution level, the probability may change depending on the real situation. For example if there are many people waiting for the elevator, some people may opt to take stairs instead of waiting for the elevator. Similarly, in case of unexpected emergency like fire, F2 must be used to adjust the new and real situation as discussed in the next section.

4.3   Evacuation in Emergency

In case of fire emergency, an agent must figure out the right action given the urgent and dangerous environment. While taking an elevator was safe in the normal situation, in case of emergency, taking an elevator, becomes more risky, which explains why $F1$ in both environment must differ as shown in Table 3, since the underlying psychological cost is different.

Table 3. Psychological filters –Fire emergency

Action	$p1$	i	$q1$	$F1$
walk the stairs	0.8	1	0.5	0.4
take an elevator	0.2	1	0.5	0.1
jump	0.1	1	0.5	0.05
Use a rope	0.4	1	0.5	0.2

As shown in Fig 3, in case of fire emergency, the majority of people obviously use the stairs as expected. In emergency situation $F2$ plays a major role since there is a big gap between information available to the agent at the planning level and the real-time information. For example, the location of the fire and its propagation speed will certainly affect the agent action selection and $F2$ ensures that the real-time information is incorporated into the proposed model. $F2$

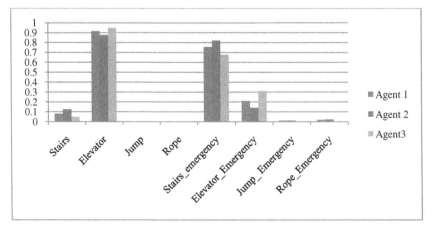

Fig. 3. Action probability

5   Conclusion

Although affordance theory has explained much of goal-directed and perception-based human actions within environments, it has been a different story to build a computational model based on the theory of affordance to represent human behavior in the system. Thus, in this paper, we propose a Bayesian affordance-based model for human decision making behavior for representation of a rational agent. The model uses MDP to estimate action-state values for the optimal policy while different affordance-based filters are used to capture the possible actions at the planning level as well as the execution level. In the execution level of the action taking/decision making process of the human agent model, the state transitions (human actions) are probabilistically occurred based on the state values as well as series of affordance-based numerical filters which are a preference-based numerical filter of $F1$ in planning level and physical filter of $F2$ in the execution level. The model is expected to mimic rational human behaviors and to be used for agent-based modeling and simulation of human-included complex systems. From the planning level to the execution level, the proposed framework covers dynamic decision making processes with consideration of MDP for planning level and affordance-based model for execution level. We adopt the probability based action selection model to present the uncertainty of human actions within the dynamic environments.

A simple numerical illustration has been used to explain our model. The illustrative example shows how the proposed framework can work with MDP and affordance concept in the planning and execution levels. We confess that the model has not been validated and tested in real situation. However, we still think that the proposed model can be used to investigate the influence of human-involvement into the system and show the effect of interactions among the system and human agents under dynamic and uncertain situations. In this regard, we are planning to build a more sophisticated illustrative example using agent-based simulation, and validate it to the real life situation (e.g., building evacuation under fire) in the future.

Acknowledgement. This research was supported by Basic Science Research Program through the National Research Foundation of Korea (NRF) funded by the Ministry of Education, Science and Technology (No 2012-0003593 and No. 2012-047663).

References

1. Whitely, S.E.: Individual inconsistency: Implications for test reliability and behavioral predictability. Applied Psychological Measurement 2(4), 571–579 (1978)
2. Dennett, D.C.: The Intentional Stance (6th printing). MIT Press, Cambridge (1996)
3. Gimblett, H., Itami, R., Durnota, D.: Some Practical Issues in Designing and Calibrating Artificial Human-Recreator Agents in GIS-based SimulatedWorlds. Complexity International 3 (1996)
4. Gibson, J.J.: The Ecological Approach to Visual Perception. Houghton Mifflin, Boston (1979)

5. McGrenere, J., Ho, W.: Affordances: Clarifying and Evolving a Concept. In: Proceedings of Graphics Interface Montreal, Quebec, Canada, pp. 179–186 (2000)
6. Passini, R.: Wayfinding: A conceptual framework. Urban Ecology 5(1), 17–31 (1981)
7. Allen, G.L.: Spatial abilities, cognitive maps, and wayfinding: Bases for individual differences in spatial cognition and behavior, pp. 46–80. Johns Hopkins University Press, Baltimore (1999)
8. Arkin, R.C.: Behavior-based robotics. MIT Press, Cambridge (1998)
9. Kirlik, A., Miller, R.A., Jagacinski, R.J.: Supervisory control in a dynamic uncertain environment: A process model of skilled human-environment interaction. IEEE Transactions on Systems, Man, and Cybernetics 23(4), 929–952 (1993)
10. Kim, N., Shin, D., Wysk, R., Rothrock, L.: Using finite state automata (FSA) for formal modeling of affordances in human-machine cooperative manufacturing systems. International Journal of Production Research 48(5), 1303–1320 (2010)
11. Joo, J., Kim, N., Wysk, R., Rothrock, L., Son, Y., Oh, Y., Lee, S.: Agent-based simulation of affordance-based human behaviors in emergency evacuation. Simulation Modeling Practice and Theory 32, 99–115 (2013)
12. Baker, C.L., Tenenbaum, J.B., Saxe, R.R.: Goal inference as inverse planning. In: Proceedings of the Twenty Ninth Annual Conference of the Cognitive Science Societ (2007)
13. Ariely, D.: Controlling the Information Flow: Effects on Consumers' Decision Making and Preferences. Journal of Consumer Research 27(2), 233–248 (2000)
14. Dubberly, H., Maupin, C.J., Pangaro, P.: Bio-cost: An Economics of Human Behavior. Guest Column in ASC / Cybernetics of Human Knowing (2010)
15. Sigaud, O., Buffet, O.: Markov Decision Processes in Artificial intelligent. John Wiley &Sons, Inc., Hoboken (2010)
16. Simon, H.A.: Rational choice and the structure of environments. Psychological Review 63, 129–138 (1956)

A Sustainable Human Centered Design Framework Based on Human Factors

H. Onan Demirel[1] and Vincent G. Duffy[1,2,3]

[1] School of Industrial Engineering
[2] School of Agriculture and Biological Engineering
[3] Regenstrief Center for Healthcare Engineering
Purdue University
47907 West Lafayette, IN, USA
{hdemirel,duffy}@purdue.edu

Abstract. Since humans are creators and users of artifacts and processes, and are constrained by limited resources, a sustainable approach with human element in the center of the development cycle is vital today. Managing and understanding technical and analytical issues about human element in design process is a core challenge for practitioners to develop and improve design strategies that serves to accommodate human needs, abilities and limitations. Although attention has increased in recent decades, direct progress towards a sustainable product development is still not apparent. Methods for sustainability are mostly applied as post-processing activities to safeguard nature, however a pro-active approach is necessary. A sustainable Human Centered Design platform provides an alternative approach to deal with the degeneration of the ecology while providing alternative criteria for considering customer requirements. This paper focuses on improving product design by considering Human Factors as a medium to integrate Sustainability and Human Centered Design strategies. The emphasis in this framework is to introduce Human Factors aspects of product design early in the concept generation phase, provide a modular platform to allow integration of domain knowledge and technologies and to enhance the product development, and overall well being of human element in design cycle.

Keywords: Human Centered Design, Sustainability, Human Factors, Product Design, Digital Human Modeling, Ergonomics.

1 Introduction

The design field is regarded as an activity or a process domain rather than a scientific discipline. It is the convergence of scientific, non-technical and social processes. In daily communication, the term design is mostly associated with crafting and/or constructing artifacts, however it is actually a thought process for creating tangible and intangible products, services and processes. Depending on the field of interest there are prominent differences at the extremes [1,2]. Design may encompass vast variety of context, knowledge and experiences from different domains. Design outcomes may range from vehicles, machines, consumer products and artistic items at the one end of

V.G. Duffy (Ed.): DHM/HCII 2013, Part I, LNCS 8025, pp. 307–315, 2013.

the spectrum, to software, interactive systems and thought processes at the other end. This broad perspective brings the need of considering both technical and non-technical aspects, which includes; form and functionality, as well as means of integration with advancements in technology, engineering, artistic trends, sciences, society, policy making, education, sustainability, business and education (Fig.1).

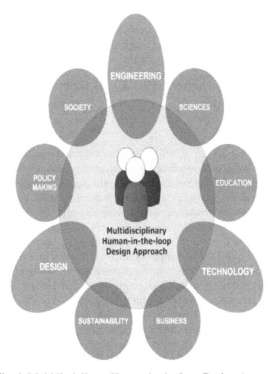

Fig. 1. Multidisciplinary Human-in-the-loop Design Approach

Global marketing competition and rapidly changing customer demands require innovative design, manufacturing and maintenance techniques to provide high level customer appreciation and safety for the end user [3]. The need for optimizing trade-offs among changing consumer attributes (customization, variety of options), convergence of new technologies (nanotechnology, biotechnology), ecological awareness (green design, recycling), financial concerns has challenged designers and motivated design industry to seek alternative methods. There are many methods introduced, however the majority of these methods focus on the specific parts and/or elements of the design process rather than offering a holistic approach. This paper provides a brief introduction to a holistic framework based on Human Factors, which integrates different domains and design elements to form a sketch-to-analysis type design process.

2   Human Element and Sustainability in Product Design

Human element is the core of any design process. Since humans are the creators and users of artifacts and processes, and are constrained by limited resources, a sustainable approach with the human element in the center of the development cycle is vital today. It is challenging to find an optimum in such a diverse, complex and dynamic system, which encompasses human and nature. However understanding common elements and starting to develop a product design process around these elements have potential to build a robust design platform. A sustainable Human Centered Design platform provides an alternative approach to deal with the degeneration of the ecology while providing alternative criteria for considering customer requirements [4,5].

2.1   Human Centered Design

Introducing a new product to market comes with high risks. A product with technology innovation may result in market failure, if it does not follow customer requirements [6,7]. Understanding customer attributes and following consumer trends have became major success drivers between products. Designers in quest to find versatile strategies to deliver innovative products in high volumes with short lead times at a reasonably low cost, while satisfying customer wants and meeting environmental rules and regulations. This beneficial, yet hard to achieve goal brought challenges for product design [6,7,8].

Human Centered Design integrates different technical and social fields of expertise to enhance well-being of people by improving product-user interaction, increasing usability, safety and efficiency. Definition of Human Centered Design may differ depending on the context, however the approach involves techniques which communicate, interact and stimulate people involved in product interaction and continuously improve the product characteristics depending on needs, abilities and limitations of users [9,10]. Although above definition is very similar to Human Factors, Human Centered Design is not a scientific domain but a design methodology, which captures variability between users and accommodates these differences efficiently in product design, which would satisfy users from different physical and cognitive perspectives. Managing and understanding technical and analytical issues about the human element in the design process is a core challenge for practitioners to develop and improve design strategies that serves to accommodate human needs, abilities and limitations [11].

2.2   Sustainability

The definition of sustainability may vary, depending on the context, the domain and practitioner/author's point of view. Topics in media regarding sustainability focus on protection, preservation and conservation of environment and nature. However, in theory and application sustainability has a much larger coverage and impact area in daily living and should not be solely regarded as a post-process activity to safeguard ecology. Sustainability is a pro-active approach for increasing the quality of living, which considers wide range of different context and domain knowledge. According to World Commission on Environment and Development sustainability can be defined as *"meeting the current needs without compromising ability of future generations to meet their own needs"* [12]. Also The Rio Declaration on Environment and Development's first principle is that *"human beings are at the center of concerns for sustainable development. They are [entitled] to a healthy and productive life in harmony with nature"* [12].

Above definitions clearly show that the core activity and focus of the sustainability is the human element and it requires a pro-active approach, which would improve quality of human life by considering every aspect of life that would have inner, inter and trans-disciplinary relationships with the human element. Today, earth's population consumes natural resources faster than the Earth replenishes them [12]. Methods for sustainability are mostly applied as post-processing activities to safeguard nature, however a pro-active approach is necessary. Although attention has increased in past decades, a direct progress towards a sustainable development is still not evident. In the near future, the convergence of new technologies will force the replenishment rate and increase the scarcity of resources, especially in energy, food and water, which will affect every facet of the community [13]. Therefore, sustainability is a key approach towards dealing with the changing dynamics of the human element, society and ecology. Design domain must incorporate the sustainability approach into design process of artifacts and systems in order to provide a positive-pull to society, which would create a well-maintained and or ongoing (self-sustained) system that does not degenerate resources of future generations while providing good quality of living to present generation [13].

3   Human Factors in Product Design

3.1   Human Factors

The main focus of Human Factors is design of optimal products and systems. This involves developing both research and application framework to build a knowledge base about human needs, abilities and limitations, then apply this knowledge to the design of human-machine system products or services. Human Factors domain utilizes the knowledge gained from different disciplines and utilize this knowledge for design and evaluation products, services, tasks, environments and systems which consider human needs, abilities and limitations. Therefore Human Factors is both a theoretical and an applied science and strongly associated with engineering due to its design focus [10,14].

Different range of requirements must be satisfied for a compatible human-artifact systems. Therefore Human Factors design can be defined as mapping from human-artifact systems compatibility (including capabilities and limitations) to system requirements (including ecology, cost, time, safety). Human Factors design practices must consider human capabilities and limitations with the artifact systems while satisfying design constraints such as environmental awareness, cost, time, safety and regulations [10]. This would extend the scope of Human Factors from contemporary design to a more hybrid form of a design, which would bring a more holistic approach to design of products and systems [10,14].

3.2   Importance of Human Factors in Design Domain

Literature review reveals that most of the designers do not regard Human Factors Engineering (HFE) principals during design of products [3,10,15]. Also, not enough fundamental interest is paid to HFE principles comparing to mechanical engineering or software programming. However, if designers employ a better design practice through HFE and follow a Human Centered Design approach, failures due to poor design practice would decrease [16]. Only two percent of decisions during design process were logical, and the rest 98% were decisions based on past experience and intuition. This case-based trial-and-error procedure and requires modification design slightly and evaluate results to see any progress is made. During this associative and negotiating cognitive work, human needs, abilities and limitations are omitted or not get sufficient attention [10,14]. It is possible to put many human characteristics or outcomes (such as comfort, fatigue) into a systematic and a structured order. This may eliminate some of the irrational nature in conceptual design and product innovation and keep important "measurable" human design elements within attention throughout the product development cycle [10,14].

4   Human Factors to Assist Sustainability and Human Centered Design

Information provided in above sections demonstrates that there are many commonalities between Sustainability and Human Centered Design and that both can be considered within the Human Factors domain. Each focuses on the well-being of human and attempts to improve product design and user outcomes. Therefore, it is natural for Human factors engineers to encompass ecological issues during design process and a must for consideration of safe, comfortable and sustained interaction with individuals and other elements of the system [17]. Human factors engineers are also prepared to understand, theorize and implement sustainability concepts in the design process [17]. It is suggested that Human Factors might provide a holistic approach to product design and assist in integrating Sustainability concepts with Human Centered Design [12].

4.1   A Sustainable Human Centered Design Framework Based on Human Factors

The proposed design framework not only integrates Design, Engineering and Technology, it also provides a more systematic understanding of human element and a related domain, Sustainability, within the product development process. This multidisciplinary approach also allows a modular integration to second and third party domains (including Sustainability and Education) that can provide a knowledgebase and methods to support product development. The emphasis in this framework is to introduce Human Factors aspects of product design early in the concept generation phase, provide a modular platform to allow integration of new technologies and to enhance the form, functionality, safety, usability, sustainability and marketing of products. Digital Human Modeling (DHM) is proposed as a middle-ware, which would establish a design medium between these domains. The key contribution of this framework in the context of the Human Factors literature is that DHM is used here as a design medium between related domains rather than solely as an ergonomics evaluation tool. The quantitative nature of DHM and its flexibility in integration with digital design tools and platforms make DHM a unique design tool, which could provide a seamless integration with concurrent engineering platforms and form a linkage between technical and non-technical aspects of concept product development.

4.2   Digital Human Modeling

The complex functions of the human body, both physical and cognitive, can be digitally represented, simulated and/or analyzed through DHM tools [18]. DHM uses digital humans as representations of workers inserted into a simulation or virtual environment to facilitate the prediction of performance and/or safety. Also, it includes visualizations of the human with the math and science in the background [19,20]. DHM helps organizations design safer and efficient products while optimizing the productivity and cost [21]. Engineering design practices that utilize DHM have the potential to enable engineers to incorporate human factors engineering principles earlier in the design process [3,22]. Traditionally, DHM applications have been utilized by manufacturing and design industry. One of the first digital human modeling applications was implemented by the U.S. military for cockpit design in which virtual drivers were used to assess the safety and the performance of the prototyped vehicles. This minimized the need of expensive and bulky physical mockups [3,18].

4.3   A Brief Introduction to Framework

Above integration provides a platform for integrating Human Factors in early phases of the design process, and acts as a medium to provide a bridge between a wide range of technical and non-technical domains. In the core of the framework DHM is used as both an analytical design/analysis tool as well as a communication medium between contributors in each different stage of the design. The Human Centered product development in this study keeps user needs, abilities and limitations in focus and Human Factors methods and tools encompass different domains related to design process integrated within the framework. The variations and combinations of methods and technologies inside the framework depend on the nature of the product in design. Sustainability, in this case, can be added to the design cycle as a sub-category of the Human Factors domain (Fig.2). Digital Human Modeling makes this integration possible. Ecology-human related components of the design content can be carried into the design cycle by using Digital Human Modeling tools and methods.

The framework discussed in above is demonstrated with a brief study in vehicle design domain. Figure 3 demonstrates how a concept Formul-1 race car was developed from scratch. The product development started with 2D digitalized sketching and then 3D models were generated. At Stage 2 (Human Factors), DHM tools were utilized to check driver's posture and biomechanics assessment was run to generate comfort study. Meanwhile, materials used in this process (recycled materials or materials coming from energy efficient process/factories) were integrated to the sustainable development process. After defining acceptable cockpit geometry and driver posture, engineering analyses were applied to check structural integrity of the cockpit and chassis as well as control systems. At the very end stage a digital prototype of was rendered (Fig.3).

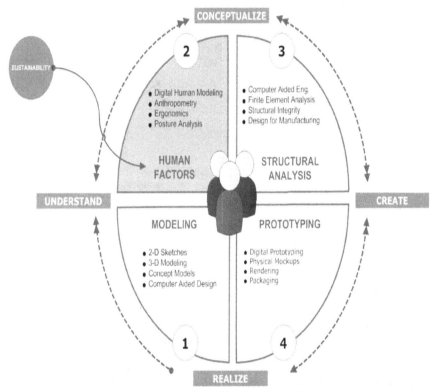

Fig. 2. The Nature of Design (Overall)

In this introductory case example which was considered after actual design, there was no effective means of real integration in terms of Sustainability (green materials) with the actual design process. Parts of this case are included in order to demonstrate the potential of the framework to support Sustainable Human Centered Design process. It is authors' belief that a real holistic integration based on the framework is possible and the use of Human Factors tools and methods would form an ideal platform for future design challenges.

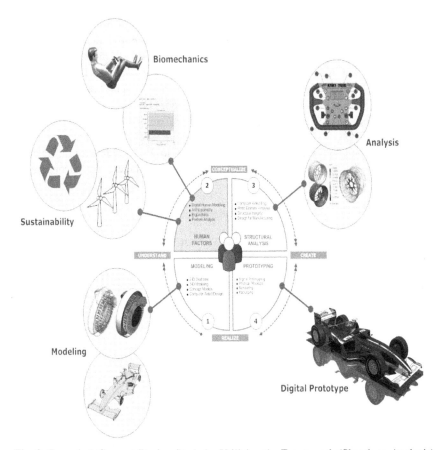

Fig. 3. Formula 1 Concept Design Study by Utilizing the Framework (Sketch-to-Analysis)

References

1. Raymer, D.P.: A Conceptual Approach. In: Raymer, D.P. (ed.) Design - A Seperate Discipline, pp. 1–10. American Institute of Aeronautics and Astronautics (1989)
2. Holmes, W.P., Azam, M.A., Hills, P.C.: A Preliminary Study of the Relationship Between Industrial Design and Engineering Design. In: Proceedings of the 1st Conference on Designing Interactive Systems: Process, Practices, Methods, & Techniques, pp. 105–114. ACM, New York (1995)
3. Chaffin, D.B.: Digital Human Modeling for Vehicle and Workplace Design. Society of Automotive Engineers, Warrendale (2001)
4. Thatcher, A.: Green Ergonomics: Definition and Scope, pp. 1–11 (August 2012) (published online), doi:10.1080/00140139.2012.718371
5. Dekker, S.W., Hancock, P.A., Wilkin, P.: Ergonomics and Sustainability: Towards an Embrace of Complexity and Emergence. Ergonomics, 1–8 (September 2012) (published online), doi:10.1080/00140139.2012.718799
6. Tseng, M.M., Du, X.: Design by Customers for Mass Customization Products. The International Academy for Production Engineering 47(1), 103–106 (1998)

7. Silveira, G., Borenstein, D., Fogliatto, F.S.: Mass Customization: Literature Review and Research Directions. International Journal of Production Economics 1(13), 1–13 (2001)
8. Wickman, C., Soderberg, R.: Increased Concurrency Between Industrial and Engineering Design using CAT Technology Combined with Virtual Reality. Journal of Concurrent Engineering 11(1), 7–15 (2003)
9. Helander, M.G.: The Human Factors Profession. In: Salvendy, G. (ed.) Handbook of Human Factors and Engineering, 2nd edn., pp. 3–16. Wiley (1997)
10. Karwowski, W.: The Discipline of Ergonomics and Human Factors. In: Salvendy, G. (ed.) Handbook of Human Factors and Ergonomics, 3rd edn., pp. 3–31. Wiley (2006)
11. Nemeth, C.P.: Human Factors Methods for Design: Making Systems Human-Centered. CRC Press (2004)
12. Martin, K., Legg, S., Brown, C.: Designing for sustainability: ergonomics - carpe diem. Ergonomics, 37–41 (October 2012), doi:10.1080/00140139.2012.718368.
13. Karwowski, W.: Building Sustainable Human-Centered Systems: A Grand Challenge for the Human Factors and Ergonomics Discipline in the Conceptual Age. In: Corporate Sustainability as a Challenge for Comprehensive Management, pp. 117–128 (2008)
14. Czaja, S.J., Nair, S.N.: Human Factors Engineering and Systems Design. In: Salvendy, G. (ed.) Handbook of Human Factors and Ergonomics, 3rd edn., pp. 32–49. Wiley (2006)
15. Daams, B.J.: Force Exertion in User Product Interaction. In: Karwowski, W., Marras, W.S. (eds.) The Occupational Ergonomics Handbook, pp. 421–435. CRC Press LLC, Boca Raton (2000)
16. Clarkson, J., Ward, J.: Human Factors Engineering and the Design of Medical Devices. In: Carayon, P. (ed.) Handbook of Human Factors and Ergonomics in Health Care and Patient Safety, pp. 367–383. Routledge, Boca Raton (2006)
17. Marano, A., Di, G., Rossi, E.: Strategies and Arguments of Ergonomic Design for Sustainability, Work. A Journal of Prevention, Assessment and Rehabilitation 41, 3869–3873 (2012), doi:10.3233/WOR-2012-0053-3869.
18. Sundin, A., Örtengren, R.: Digital Human Modeling for CAE Applications. In: Salvendy, G. (ed.) Handbook of Human Factors and Ergonomics, pp. 1053–1078. John Wiley & Sons Inc. (2006)
19. Demirel, H.O., Duffy, V.G.: Application of Digital Human Modeling in Industry. In: Duffy, V.G. (ed.) Digital Human Modeling, HCII 2007. LNCS, vol. 4561, pp. 824–832. Springer, Heidelberg (2007)
20. Demirel, H.O., Duffy, V.G.: Digital Human Modeling for Product Lifecycle Management. In: Duffy, V.G. (ed.) Digital Human Modeling, HCII 2007. LNCS, vol. 4561, pp. 372–381. Springer, Heidelberg (2007)
21. Yang, J., Abdel-Malek, K., Farrell, K.: The IOWA Interactive Digital Human Modeling Virtual Environment. In: Proceedings of IMECE 2004, ASME International Engineering Congress, The 3rd Symposium on Virtual Manufacturing and Application, Anaheim, CA, pp. 1059–1067 (2004)
22. Demirel, H.O.: Sensory Feedback Mechanism for Virtual Build Methodolgy. Thesis: Unpublished Manuscript. Purdue University, West Lafayette (2008)
23. Porter, J.M., Keith, C., Freer, M.T.: Computer-Aided Design and Human Models. In: Karwowski, W., Marras, W.S. (eds.) Occupational Ergonomics: Principles of Work Design, pp. 479–499. CRC Press (2003)

Putting in Perspective Human-Machine System Theory and Modeling: From Theoretical Biology to Artifacts Integrative Design and Organization

"Artem Augmented Human Project"

Didier Fass

ICN Business School, Mosel Loria UMR CNRS 7503, Université de Lorraine
Didier.fass@loria.fr

Abstract. Thinking about human systems integration is thinking human, system and human-system for designing and organizing system of systems from human-machine level to socio-technological level. For critical human in-the-loop systems there is a strong need of reliability and consistency from modeling, development and life cycle systems. A main epistemic issue rises: does it exist a conceptual framework, both theoretical and experimental, that ensures reliability and consistency of human system integration design and organization? According to the Italian Renaissance painting perspective principles invention, our paper puts in perspective human systems integrations from theoretical biology to systems sciences, and it presents an isomorphic framework for modeling human systems integration especially adapted at the human machine level, for medicine, defense and aerospace.

Keywords: human systems integration, human-machine, theoretical biology, systems theory, isomorphic framework, perspective, modeling.

1   Introduction

"The field of Human Factors and its many descendants - Cognitive Engineering, Human-Computer Interaction, Cognitive Ergonomics, Human-Systems Integration, ...—has made numerous, wonderful advances in the many decades since the enterprise began. But the discipline still serves many to rescue rather than to create. It is time for a change." Don Norman [1]

Reliable design and correctness by construction systems are two main issues for human systems integration and organization from human-machine systems to socio-technical systems especially for safety and life critical systems. With current interactive systems, from smartphone, airplane cockpit devices and bedside monitor in intensive care, to teleoperation systems, boundaries between human and artifact are fading. Within converging technologies (nano-bio-info-cogno or NBIC) [2] [3] that dynamics develops.

That disappearance of boundaries between a biological and social human and its interactive physical and information processing artifacts challenges engineering methodologies and ergonomics of systems design.

V.G. Duffy (Ed.): DHM/HCII 2013, Part I, LNCS 8025, pp. 316–325, 2013.
© Springer-Verlag Berlin Heidelberg 2013

Current and future technical developments for enhancing human skills and capabilities or medical care and implantable devices challenge new scientific and technical knowledge and development methods. Understanding that synthetic hybridization requires an original conceptual and knowledge framework, that allows to think and model *"enhanced or augmented human"* as an integrated dynamic, structural and functional whole [4].

1.1   Human System Integration (HIS)

Originally as technical and managerial concept [5], human systems integration (HIS) was defined in the middle of the eighties by the US defense department. It is used in acquisition programs requirements definition of total system design and organization. It aims to maximize the overall system performance while ensuring a safe, efficient, and enhanced interaction between the user and the technical system [6]. Defining a system more broadly than hardware and software refer to human centered design [7] in contrast with automation and machine centered design [8].

That methodology [9] is concerned with the integration of human capabilities and performances, from individual to social level [10] into the design of complex human-machine systems supporting safe, efficient operations; there is also the question of reliability. That issue requires thinking human as an element of the system and translating it qualitatively throughout design, development and testing process [11].

Human systems integration also involves augmented human design with the objectives of enhancing human capabilities and improving human performance [12] using interactive technologies at the level of human-machine system and human machine symbiosis [13].

Today HIS refers to systems that require human interactions -human in-the-loop systems, but new automated technologies are emerging more and more integrated on the human body from wearable to implementable. The human automated machine is closer. The concept of human system integration must be revised!

1.2   Scientific and Technical Context

Human machine is currently both a techno-scientific research and development topic and a philosophical and anthropologic theme of discussion. From one side, reductionism postulates reducing the human organism to an intelligent machine and its physical (mechanical) and computational properties. On another side, some one claims for a metaphysical and transcendental humanistic ideal inherited from Italian Renaissance and Vitruvius.

Between Human, with a capital H, as a philosophical ideal and human as an abstract category of a biological system, there is life, multidimensional reality and death. Therefore, how understanding and conceiving human and human-artifact or machine nature and their scientific principles theoretically?

That question highlights some scientific and technological interdisciplinary questions:

— What does human systems integration really mean from systems sciences or general systems theory to theoretical biology and integrative physiology applied to human systems engineering?
— What is a good epistemic framework for human-machines modeling? Which system and theory of knowledge is relevant? Which ethical reasoning? Which logics?
— What is the validated scientific grounding for safety critical automation design and human systems integration?
— What is a good and reliable model of automation and integrated human machine "physiology" and behavior?
— Which are the formal and experimental method for ensuring modeling, validation and certification of human-machine system design and organization?

1.3   Epistemology and Modeling

Epistemology and modeling are causally linked. The epistemic framework structures model. They are related to knowing and representing knowledge, not only for understanding the natural or artificial world, but also for designing and organizing technologies. According its internal – logic, and external – experimental, validity that framework ensure consistency and practical validity of the model. Different epistemic frameworks might provide different models of the same object or system with a wide range of robustness and predictability. The most general is the grounding epistemic framework; the most predictable and robust is the model. It is not a metaphysical contingency but a realistic and naturalistic necessity.

It is a main issue for safety and sustainability of automation design and human system integration.

2   Historical Perspective

The way we think and conceptualize the world and the relation between its elements within its related level of organization influences our capabilities of representation, modeling, designing and organizing artifacts from human-machine to socio-technical systems.

HIS safety and predictive modeling and design need a new insight and an adapted conceptual framework.

We need a shift from an analytical and reductionist framework, based on mechanism and linear causality in witch human machine design is reduced to interactions design as an informational and computational processing to a systemic and organismic conceptual framework based on theoretical biology and general system theory.

2.1   The HSI Founding Experiment: "La tavoletta di Brunelleschi"

The general problem of human systems integration is not recent. In 1415 for helping other people being aware of the artificial perspective principles of representation as he was, Filippo Brunelleschi, a self-taught architect and certainly the central perspective inventor, made-up a special device, "la tavoletta", (Fig. 1.). The Tavoletta is the combination by two technical parts: a painted tablet and a looking-glass. The tablet is painted on its intrados with the Duomo Baptistery realistic representation according perspective principles of drawing (central point of view, skylines and converging lines). Holding the tablet and the mirror, the user was looking on the virtual reflected image trough the tablet opening trying to superimpose the virtual image on the real monument. Brunelleschi's Tavoletta is the ancestor of virtual reality and augmented reality.

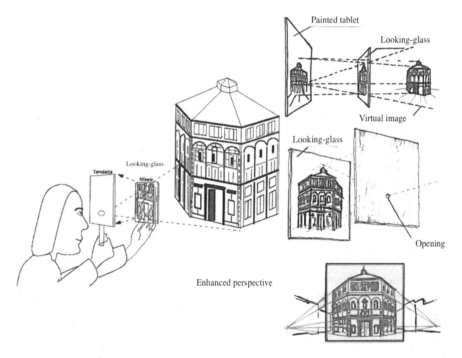

Fig. 1. Performed in the early Italian Renaissance (1415) in Florence, Filippo Brunelleschi's Tavoletta experience is the founding experiment for human systems integration and augmented reality. It demonstrated the geometrical framework of perspective conceptualization and representation.

It summarizes the modern aims of human system integration design and organization. The success of that experience depends on:

1. Designer skills for conceiving relevant abstraction of a part of reality and developing an artificial representation using artifice;

2. Formal and experimental representational medium;
3. Device shaping in relation to the required function, its design;
4. The acknowledgement of usage context or operating context;
5. Physical ergonomics of the device, its ability to induce and facilitate its handling situation (without injury);
6. The ability of the device to stimulate cognitive, imaginative and action capabilities of an operator (affordance [14])… who must understand and operate the device to realize the experience;
7. Skills and training of the user.

2.2   Cybernetics and Human Machine Systems

Cybernetics, defined by Wiener [15] as "the science of control and communication in the animal and the machine", had and has a great influence on automation design and human-machine systems concepts and development. It deals with information theory, automatic control theory, algorithm theory, regulation, stability, and homeostasis. Cybernetics is about regulation and control of a mechanical system behavior [16] and human-machine problem have been viewed as an exchange of information between the operator and the controlled object. It is concerned with the processing by a decision-making algorithm of input information into control signals, a command [17], this independently of the nature of the machine (biological, mechanical, electronic...) [18]. In that context, every good regulator of system must be a model of that system or must be isomorphic with the system being regulated [19]. Despite this theorem, cybernetics remains behaviorist and computational, i.e., postulating that information processing and computing are fundamental basis of decision-making function or knowledge the same as cognitive. But human as biological system, is not a computational or state machine [20].

2.3   Theoretical Biology and General Systems Theory

Designing and developing human machines systems using interactive and artificial technologies requires integrating artificial elements and structural design usually by artificial or artifactual functional interactions and its dynamics.

In this scientific framework, the question becomes: how to integrate the technical and human needs and requirements, biological peculiarities, into specifications of a technological system (physical and informational) design able to be used by a human (biological system) or integrated or coupled to the human body? Requiring that design and organization might ensure stability and consistency of the overall system (integrated human machine system) function and behavior in space and time?

Behind this in mind, it is necessary to develop theoretical principles of human systems integration, based on a continuous approach between biology and anthropology [15] [16] [17], taking into account the isomorphic and proven principles of general systems theory [18], and of theoretical biology and integrative physiology theory [19].

Human nature cannot be reduced to a metaphoric "model" of any kind of machine or computation even it is heuristic. Engineered artifacts have their own technical and physical requirement. The question of nature of human-machine systems is an issue of integrative design and organization.

3   Human System Integration and Modeling

"Experience without theory is blind, but theory without experience is mere intellectual play." Emmanuel Kant. According that kant's sentence we have developed a

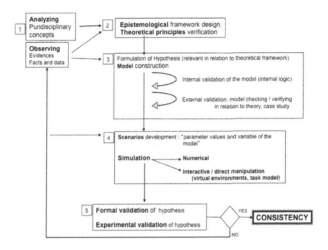

Fig. 2. Our approach associates formal and experimental methods for validating human-machine model consistency. It is first to state an multidisciplinary epistemological framework after analyzing existing multidisciplinary concepts and validate their relevance using model checking and realistic case study; secondly to validate the relevance of this epistemological framework and its ability to generate a safe and integrated modeling method, validating overhang the intrinsic quality of formal models and extrinsic validity by simulation and experimentally by comparison to reality by expert analysis and expert feedback.

HIS needs the production of a new body of knowledge and a general and reliable framework for designing, i.e., theoretical principles proven and validated description or modeling of human machine system. The purpose of the production of this new epistemological apparatus is to provide a scientific and technical framework for predictive integrative and safe modeling of human-machine systems. The challenge is to prefigure or provide a tool for designing and organizing an hybrid system from which nature is to be defined.

4   A Theoretical Framework

"The ultimate model of a cat is of course another cat, whether it be born of still another cat or synthetized in laboratory" Arturo Rosenblueth, Norbert Wiener and Julian Bigelow, January 1943.

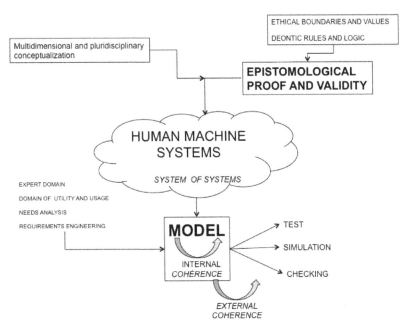

Fig. 3. Challenging human-machine system design and organization is modeling an heterogeneous system of systems (different by nature). That requires a proven and validate epistemic framework fitted to hybrid system, challenging the question of human machine system nature and ensuring human systems integration reliability.

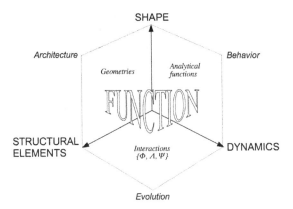

Fig. 4. Our isomorphic epistemic framework for human-machine systems integrative design and organization

4.1   Classical Epistemic Framework

From General systems theory and Cybernetics, some previous works in systems sciences and modeling have demonstrated the relation between system theory, modeling and epistemology. Some attempt to define invariant category conceptual element of general system have done, i.e., Pierre Delattre have done an epistemic analysis showing tree main categories of systems invariance: structure, function and evolution [26].

Previously, according system engineering and classical system epistemology, we have proposed to ground our modeling method of human-machine system on the concepts of structure, function and dynamics. We have defined the relation of three pair of invariant as Architecture{structure, function}; Behavior{Function, Evoution} and Evolution{Structure, Dynamics}. We have considered these three relation as three plane of an Euclidian space [27], were each invariant was a structuring axis for a system model. Nevertheless that epistemic framework of invariants was a mistake because structure and architecture are equal and function, as an issue of purpose and teleology, is not realy existing *per se*, it is related to a structural shape (a Gestalt) and the dynamic of the system. By consequences we are suggestion a new epistemic framework for modeling human-machine systems.

4.2   Our Isomorphic Epistemic Framework

For modeling human-machine systems, we have grounded our new epistemic framework on isomorphism. We have found new general categories of system elements that allow the same representation framework for integrating two systems different by nature. Our isomorphic epistemic framework is composed by three main isomorphic categories of interlocked elements: structural element, shape and dynamic.

As previously we were able to define three pair of isomorphic relation: Architecture{structural elements, shape}, Behavior{shape, dynamics} and Evolution{structural elements, dynamics}. Thus architecture is describable by a set of possible geometries, from Euclidian to no-Euclidian and other, behavior is describable by a set of functional analysis and algorithm, and evolution is describable by a set of modal interactions where each interaction might be compose on three modal parameters: physical, logical and physiological or behavioral dimensions according to Chauvet's theoretical integrative physiology [25]. It has been experimentally validated [3].

5   Conclusion and Perspective

Just like the drawing of perspective, where the correctness construction is formally ensure by structuring lines and point of view principles, human-machine system modeling must be ensure by an isomorphic framework of epistemic principal proven and validated experimentally and formally. It will be a necessary condition to the future development of human-machines systems. But it is not sufficient, future development needs also intuition, how-know, expertise and ethics.

References

1. Roco, M.C., Bainbridge, W.S.: Converging technologies for improving human performance-nanotechnology, biotechnology, information technology and cognitive science. Technical report, National ScienceFoundation (2002), http://www.wtec.org/ConvergingTechnologies/Report/NBIC_report.pdf
2. Nordmann, A.: Converging technologies - Shaping the future of european societies. Technical report, European Communities (2004)
3. Fass, D.: Augmented human engineering: a theoretical and experimental approach to human system integration. In: Cogan, B. (ed.) System Engineering – Practice and Theory, Intech, pp. 257–276. Open Access Publisher, Rijeka (2012)
4. Norman, D.: Why Human Systems Integration Fails (And Why the University Is the Problem), invited talk for the 30th anniversary of the Human-Systems Integration Board of the National Research Council. The National Academies, Washington, DC (December 2, 2010), http://www.jnd.org/dn.mss/why_human_systems_in.html
5. Haskins, C. (ed.): Systems Engineering Handbook: a guide for processes and activities. International Council on Systems Engineering (INCOSE) (2010)
6. Defense Acquisition Guidebook. Department of Defense (2012), https://dag.dau.mil
7. Ehrhart, L.E., Sage, A.P.: Handbook of human systems integration, chapter User-centrerd systems engineering framework. Series in Systems Engineering and Management, pp. 295–373. Wiley (2003)
8. Amalberti, R.: Les facteurs humains à l'aube de l'an 2000, pp. 5–12. Phoebus (1998)
9. Pew, R.W., Mavor, A.S. (ed.) Human-System Integration in the System Development Process: A New Look. The National Academies Press, committee on human-system design support for changing technology, commit- tee on human factors, national research council, national research council edition (2007), http://www.nap.edu/openbook.php?recordid=11893
10. Rousse, W.B., Boff, K.R.: Organizational Simulation. Wiley Series in Systems Engineering and Management (2005)
11. Booher, H.: Handbook of human systems integration, Introduction: Human Systems Integration. Series in Systems Engineering and Management, pp. 1–30. Wiley (2003)
12. Engelbart, D.C.: Augmenting human intellect: a conceptual framework, AFOSR-3233 Summary Report, Stanford Research Institute, Menlo Park, California 94025, USA (October 1962), http://www.dougengelbart.org/
13. Licklider, J.C.R.: Man-Computer Symbiosis. IRE Transactions on Human Factors in Electronics HFE-1, 4–11 (1960) ISSN: 0096-249X
14. Gibson, J.J.: The theory of affordance. In: Shaw, R.E., Bransford, J. (eds.) Perceiving, Acting and Knowing, pp. 67–82. Lauwrence Erlbaum Associates, Hillsdale (1997)
15. Wiener, N.: Cybernetics. John Wiley & Sons, New York (1948)
16. Parin, V.V., Bayevskiy, R.M.: Introduction to medical cybernetics, Translation of "Vvedeniye v meditsinskuyu kibernetiku."Izdatel'stvo "Meditsina," Moscow, 1966. NASA Technical Translation F-459, Washington, D. C. (1967)
17. Rosenblueth, A., Wiener, N., Bigelow, J.: Behavior, Purpose and Teleology. Philosophy of Science 10(1), 18–24 (1943)
18. Ashby, R.: An introduction to cybernetics. Chapman & Hall, London (1957)
19. Conant, R., Ashby, R.: Every good regulator of a system must be a model of that system, Int. J. Int. J. Systems Sci. 1(2), 89–97 (1970)

20. Kováč, L.: Inforamtion and knowledge in biology : time for reappraisal (2). Plant Signalling & Behavior 2, 65–73 (2007)
21. Lorenz, K.: L'envers du miroir: Une histoire naturelle de la connaissance (Behind the Mirror: A Search for a Natural History of Human Knowledge). Flammarion, Champs Sciences (1973)
22. Lyon, P.: The biogenic approach to cognition. Cognitive Processing 7(1), 11–29 (2006)
23. Edelman, G.M.: Second nature. Brain science and human knowledge. Yale University Press, New Haven and London (2006)
24. von Bertalanffy, K.L.: General System theory: Foundations, Development, Applications. George Braziller, New York (1968) (revised edition 1976)
25. Chauvet, G.: Hierarchical functional organization of formal biological systems: a dynamical approach. I, II and III. Phil. Trans. Roy. Soc. London B 3, 1471–2970 (1993) ISSN: 1471-2970
26. Delattre, P.: Système, structure, fonction, évolution - Essai d'analyse systémique, Maloine (1985)
27. Lieber, R., Fass, D.: Human Systems Integration Design: Which Generalized Rationale? In: Kurosu, M. (ed.) HCD 2011. LNCS, vol. 6776, pp. 101–109. Springer, Heidelberg (2011)

Friction Measurements in a Hand Tool Factory

Kai Way Li[1,*], Ching Chung Chen[2], Liwen Liu[3], and Chih-Yong Chen[3]

[1] Department of Industrial Management, Chung-Hua University, Hsin-Chu 300, Taiwan
[2] Department of Information Management, Hsing Wu University of Science & Technology,
New Taipei, Taiwan
[3] Institute of Occupational Safety and Health, New Taipei, Taiwan
kai@chu.edu.tw

Abstract. Floor slipperiness has been identified as one of the major risk factors affecting the occurrence of slipping and falling on workplaces. Floor slipperiness assessment was conducted in a factory manufacturing hand tools in Taiwan. Three areas in the machine shop factory were measured. The friction measurements were conducted using the Brungraber Mark II slipmeter. A total of 96 measurements of the coefficient of friction on the floor were conducted. In addition, six employees were interviewed concerning their experiences of slipping and falling in the sector and their perception of floor slipperiness. The results showed that the floor in the sink area had significantly ($p<0.0001$) lower COF values than the other two areas. The COF values in the sink area were all less than 0.5, a safety standard commonly adopted in the USA. Six of the employees in the factory were interviewed concerning their perception of floor slipperiness and their experiences of slipping & falling in the working areas. The results were discussed.

Keywords: slip & fall, floor slipperiness, coefficient of friction, field measurement.

1   Introduction

Slipping and falling create serious occupational safety burdens worldwide [1-2]. The Labor Inspection Annual Report [3], publish by the Council for Labor Affairs annually, indicates that there were 1,835 fall incidences in 2011 in Taiwan. This accounted for 15.97% of all occupational incidences. This means that there was one occupational incidence in every 6.26 incidences. Falling, only next to being caught in or compressed by, was the number two leading cause of occupational incidence. It is a common belief that the risk of slip and fall is floor slipperiness dependent [4-9]. The coefficient of friction (COF) on the floor has been adopted to indicate floor slipperiness [8-13]. The COF on the floor may be measured using a friction measurement device [13-18]. A measured static COF of 0.5 has been adopted as a safety guideline in the USA [19].

---

* Corresponding author.

V.G. Duffy (Ed.): DHM/HCII 2013, Part I, LNCS 8025, pp. 326–331, 2013.

There are many factors affecting the COF on the floor. Floor contamination is probably one of the most commonly discussed issues in practice. Water contamination is not uncommon. It is a common belief that wet and oily floors are more slippery than the dry ones. This belief has been supported by both scientific theory and empirical studies. The squeeze film theory [20] is probably the most frequent adopted scientific basis describing the effects of liquid on the friction on a floor.

Field studies on floor slipperiness measurements are common. However, most friction measurements in the field were focused on restaurant, dining services, and college campus [21-25]. Friction measurements on hand tool manufacturing are rare in the literature. In this study, a field measurement of floor slipperiness in a food manufacturing factory was conducted. The objectives of such measurement was to assess the risk of slipping & falling in a real working environment and to compare the measurement results with those reported by the workers in the same locations.

2   Method

A hand tool manufacturing factory in central Taiwan was selected for study. This factory produces wrench of different specification. The manufacturing process includes heating, cutting, punch, polishing, electroplating, and so on. Upon arrival at the factory, the research personnel took a walk through tour in the factory to visually check the floor conditions in each sector. Three areas were selected for measurement upon mutual agreement between the research personnel and the factory manager. One area was in a machine shop area (see Fig. 1 (a)). The second area was a storage room for tools waiting for maintenance and repairs (see Fig. 1 (b)). The third area was in the sink area adjacent to a laboratory (see Fig. 1 (c)). The floor in the machine shop is concrete floor with epoxy payment. The floor in the storage room is concrete floor. Both the floors in the machine shop and storage room were dry but covered with sticky oil. The floor in the sink area is flat ceramic tile. The workers in the areas need to wash their hands before they can answer a cell phone call or to take a break as their hands were dirty with machine oil most of the time during the day. There are no hand drier and paper towels in this area. The floor in this area was wet and greasy as workers came to wash their hands frequently and dripping on the floor after hand washing. There is no floor cleaning during the day.

The Brungraber Mark II (BMII) slipmeter was used in the friction measurements. This slipmeter is commonly used in the USA for field study involved slipping & falling incidences. The standard test method of using the BM II is published by the American Society for Testing and Materials (ASTM) [26]. The measurement protocol by Chang [27] was adopted. A flat Neolite footwear pad was used.   The temperature and humidity in the popcorn sector at the time of measurement were 33 $^{\circ}$C and 62%, respectively. For each of the three areas, eight points on the floor were measurement.

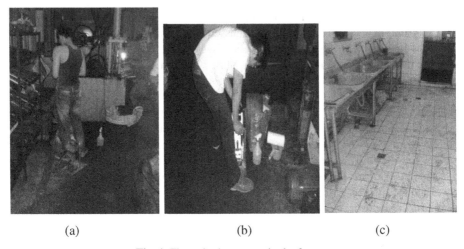

(a)   (b)   (c)

Fig. 1. Floors in three areas in the factory

The measured points were on the walking path in each area and were separated for approximately 30 cm for the adjacent points. Four measurements were collected on each point. There were a total of 96 measurements (8*3*4).

In addition to the friction measurements, six employees were interviewed concerning their experience of slipping & falling in these areas and their perception of floor slipperiness in these areas. The age of these interviewees was 31.33 (±8.73) yrs. Three of the interviewees were males and the others were females. The age of the male interviewees was 38 (±8.88) yrs. The age of the female interviewees was 24.6 (±4.04) yrs. A rating scale, from 1 (extremely slippery) to 5 (not slippery), was adopted for subjective slipperiness measurements. The interviewees were interviewed on one-on-one basis. The interviewees were also requested to report their experiences of slipping & falling in the working areas in the past twelve months. In addition, they reported their witnesses on the slipping and falling of their peers.

Descriptive statistics and analysis of variance (ANOVA), and Duncan's multiple range tests were performed. Kruskal-Wallis test was performed for the subjective rating of floor slipperiness.

3   Results and Discussion

The hand tool factory visited was belonged to a traditional manufacturing company. Such a company is normally regarded as having poor working environments as far as safety & health are concerned. Table 1 shows the mean COF values for each sampling point on the floor in each area. It was found that all the readings of the COF in the sink area were lower than 0.5, a safety standard proposed by the US industries [19], while all the readings in the other two areas had relative high COF values.

Table 1. Mean COF values on each

Machine shop	COF	Sink	COF	Storage area	COF
1	0.83	1	0.22	1	0.59
2	0.77	2	0.19	2	0.65
3	0.69	3	0.16	3	0.65
4	0.66	4	0.16	4	0.61
5	0.81	5	0.17	5	0.61
6	0.80	6	0.16	6	0.67
7	0.79	7	0.14	7	0.70
8	0.78	8	0.14	8	0.67

The ANOVA results on the COF data for the three areas were statistically significant. Duncan's multiple range test results showed that The COF in the machine shop (0.76 ±0.06) was significantly ($p<0.05$) higher than those of the storage room (0.64± 0.05) and sink area (0.17±0.03). The COF in the storage room was significantly ($p<0.05$) higher than that of the sink area. Engineer oils and other machining liquids are routinely used in the machine shop. The floors in both the machine shop and storage areas look greasy. However, the grease on the floor was sticky. The COF readings in these two areas were higher than we expected. This might be attributed to the facts that the sticky grease was solid instead of liquid. There was no squeeze film effects on floors contaminated with this type of contaminants.

The employees interviewed showed that three out of six employees had the experiences of slipping without falling in a year. Two of them slipped in the storage rooms and the third one slipped in the sink area. The reasons of the slipping without falling were grease on the floors. For the witness of slipping & falling of others, only one slipping and falling was reported. This case occurred in the metal cutting operating area where the floor was contaminated with grease. The Kruskal-Wallis test results indicated that the subjective ratings of floor slipperiness in the three areas were not statistically significantly. The rating for the machine shop, storage room, and sink area were 4.67 (±0.52), 4.5 (±0.55), and 2.38 (±0.98), respectively. The sink area had the lowest floor slipperiness score even though it was not significantly lower than the other two locations.

There are over 30 workers in the machine shop. However, most of them could not stop their work for an interview upon our visit. The small sample size of the worker interview created one of our limitations of the study. In addition, we could conduct friction measurements only on those floors that would not interfered with the traffic and operations of the workers. Some of the floors may possess low floor slipperiness but were not measurable due to safety concerns of the research personnel.

4   Conclusion

A friction measurement study was conducted in a hand tool factory. Six of the workers were interviewed concerning their perception of floor slipperiness in the working areas and their experiences slipping & falling for their self and their peer. The results found that the floors in the sink areas, where workers wash their hands frequently, had significantly the lowest COF values than the other two areas. The work interview results also indicated that the sink was the most slippery area even though the subjective score of this area was not significantly lower than the other two areas.

Acknowledgments. This research was financially supported by the Institute for Occupational Safety & Health (IOSH), Council of Labor Affairs, ROC, under grant #101-H320.

References

1. Leamon, T.B., Murphy, P.L.: Occupational slips and falls: more than a trivial problem. Ergonomics 38(3), 487–498 (1995)
2. Leamon, T.B., Li, K.W.: Microslip Length and The Perception of Slipping. In: Proceedings of 23rd International Congress on Occupational Heath, Montreal, Canada, p. 17 (1990)
3. Labor Inspection Annual Report, Council of Labor Affairs of ROC, Taipei (2012) (in Chinese)
4. Chang, W.R., Cotnam, J.P., Matz, S.: Field evaluation of two commonly used slipmeters. Applied Ergonomics 34(1), 51–60 (2003)
5. Andres, R.O., Chaffin, D.B.: Ergonomic analysis of slip-resistance measurement device. Ergonomics 28, 1065–1079 (1985)
6. Perkins, P.J.: Measurement of Slip Between the Shoe and Ground During Walking, Walkway Surfaces: Measurement of Slip Resistance, ASTM STP 649. In: Anderson, C., Senne, J. (eds.) American Society for Testing and Materials, pp. 71–87 (1978)
7. Perkins, P.J., Wilson, M.P.: Slip Resistance Testing of Shoes New Development. Ergonomics 26(1), 73–82 (1983)
8. Bunterngchit, Y.: Measurement of Dynamics Friction Available between Shoes and Floors Appropriate to Friction Demand in Walking. Unpublished Ph.D. Dissertation, University of New South Wales, Austrial (1990)
9. Grönqvist, R., Chang, W.R., Courtney, T.K., Leamon, T.B., Redfern, M.S., Strandberg, L.: Measurement of slipperiness: fundamental concepts and definition. Ergonomics 44(13), 1102–1117 (2001)
10. Liu, L., Li, K.W., Lee, Y.-H., Chen, C.C., Chen, C.-Y.: Friction measurements on "anti-slip" floors under shoe sole, contamination, and inclination conditions. Safety Science 48, 1321–1326 (2010)
11. Chang, W.-R., Grönqvist, R., Leclercq, S., Myung, R., Makkonen, L., Strandberg, L., Brungraber, R.J., Mattke, U., Thorpe, S.C.: The role of friction in the measurement of slipperiness, Part 1: friction mechanisms and definition of test conditions. Ergonomics 44(13), 1217–1232 (2001)

12. Chang, W.R., Grönqvist, G., Leclercq, S., Brungraber, R.J., Mattke, U., Strandberg, L., Thorpe, S.C., Myung, R., Makkonen, L., Courtney, T.K.: The role of friction in the measurement of Slipperiness, Part 2: Survey of friction measurement devices. Ergonomics 44(13), 1233–1261 (2001)
13. Li, K.W., Chang, W.-R., Leamon, T.B., Chen, C.J.: Floor slipperiness measurement: friction coefficient, roughness of floors, and subjective perception under spillage conditions. Safety Science 42, 547–565 (2004)
14. Hanson, J.P., Redfern, M.S., Mazumdar, M.: Predicting slips and falls considering required and available friction. Ergonomics 42(12), 1619–1633 (1999)
15. Chang, W.R., Matz, S.: The slip resistance of common footwear materials measured with two slipmeters. Applied Ergonomics 32, 540–558 (2001)
16. Grönqvist, R., Roine, J., Järviinen, E., Korhonen, E.: An Apparatus and a Method for Determining the Slip Resistance of Shoe and Floor by Simulation of Human Foot Motions. Ergonomics 32(8), 979–995 (1989)
17. Grönqvist, R., Hirvonen, M., Tohv, A.: Evaluation of three portable floor slipperiness testers. International Journal of Industrial Ergonomics 25, 85–95 (1999)
18. Li, K.W., Chang, W.R., Chang, C.-C.: Evaluation of Two Models of a Slipmeter. Safety Science 47, 1434–1439 (2009)
19. Miller, J.M.: "Slippery" work surface: Toward a performance definition and quantitative coefficient of friction criteria. Journal of Safety Research 14, 145–158 (1983)
20. Moore, D.F.: The friction and lubrication of elastomers. In: Vaynor, G.V. (ed.) International Series of Monographs on Material Science and Technology, vol. 9, Pergamon Press, Oxford (1972)
21. Chang, W.R., Li, K.W., Huang, Y.H., Filiaggi, A., Courtney, T.K.: Assessing floor slipperiness in fast-food restaurants in Taiwan using objective and subjective measures. Appl. Ergon. 35, 401–408 (2004)
22. Chang, W.R., Li, K., Huang, Y.H., Filiaggi, A., Courtney, T.K.: Objective and subjective measurements of slipperiness in fast-food restaurants in the USA and their comparison with the previous results obtained in Taiwan. Safety Science 44, 891–903 (2006)
23. Chang, W.R., Li, K.W., Filiaggi, A., Huang, Y.H., Courtney, T.K.: Friction Variations in Common Working Areas of Fast-Food Restaurants. Ergonomics 51(12), 1998–2012 (2008)
24. Li, K.W., Hsu, Y.-W., Chang, W.-R., Lin, C.-H.: Friction Measurements on Three Commonly used Floors on a College Campus Under Dry, Wet, and Sand-Covered Conditions. Safety Science 45, 980–992 (2007)
25. Hsu, Y.-W., Li, K.W.: A field assessment of floor slipperiness in a fish market in Taiwan. Saf. Sci. 48, 556–561 (2010)
26. American Society for Testing and Materials, F-1677-96: Standard method of test for using a portable inclinable articulated strut slip tester (PIAST), Annual Book of ASTM Standards. vol. 15.07. West Conshohochen, PA, American Society for Testing and Materials (2004)
27. Chang, W.R.: The effects of slip criteria and time on friction measurements. Safety Science 40, 593–611 (2002)

Development of Human Balance Assessment System with Continuous Center of Gravity Tracking

Ben-Yi Liau[1], Chi-Wen Lung[2], and Yih-Kuen Jan[3]

[1] Department of Biomedical Engineering, Hungkuang University, Taichung, Taiwan, ROC
[2] Department of Creative Product Design, Asia University, Taichung, Taiwan, ROC
[3] Departments of Kinesiology & Community Health and Computational Science & Engineering,
University of Illinois at Urbana-Champaign, Champaign, IL, USA
byliau@sunrise.hk.edu.tw

Abstract. Fall is the second leading cause of injures for older adults in Taiwan. If fall risk can be prevented or decreased, fall and its complications could be reduced effectively. The purpose of this study is to develop the human balance assessment system with LabVIEW program interface. 10 healthy adults were enrolled in this study. They were evaluated under four kinds of postures while standing on a 2-axis force platform for 20 seconds. The results showed the displacements in both X and Y directions were smaller during stand with two legs and open eyes ($p<0.05$). Balance index results also revealed balance ability become lower while standing with one leg and closed eyes ($p<0.05$) In conclusion, different postures would affect balance. These differences can be assessed by this system. It is hope fall can be prevented in advanced and decrease the medical burden in older adults by the system in the future.

Keywords: fall risk, balance, force platform.

1 Introduction

With the progress of modern medical technology, life of human becomes longer and longer. However, healthy problems and nursing would be a huge burden with aging population. One of important topic in older people is "fall". Fall is the second leading cause of injures for older adults in Taiwan. In 1987, the definition of a fall was provided by Kellogg International Working Group. Fall is "unintentionally coming to the ground or some lower level and other than as a consequence of sustaining a violent blow, loss of consciousness, sudden onset of paralysis as in stroke or an epileptic seizure" [1]. Fracture is one of the serious complications resulted from fall. Injures of fall in older adults might be not only the high prevalence but also the high susceptibility to injury and co-morbid disease. It makes mild fall lead to serious condition. Lacking strength of lower extremity, difficult gait and balance would increase fall risk. Injure of fall would make limb can not be controlled properly and self-care would be more difficult. Therefore, they might need long term care or rehabilitation. All of them can be a huge burden for medical resource. Fall could be fatal in the healthy of older adults. For these reasons, if fall risk can be prevented or decreased, fall and its complications could be reduced effectively. Falls are a major threat to the health of older persons. In 1996, Nevitt et al. evaluated potential risk factors for falls. They found

V.G. Duffy (Ed.): DHM/HCII 2013, Part I, LNCS 8025, pp. 332–337, 2013.

the proportion of subjects with two or more falls per year increased from 0.10 for those with none or one of these risk factors to 0.69 for those with four or more risk factors. Among older persons with a history of a recent fall, the risk of multiple non-syncopal falls can be predicted from a few simple questions and examinations [2]. Previous studies also applied some gravity sensor to develop assessment system [3-4]. Recently, Wii balance board was adopted to evaluate balance ability [5]. Also, several physical approaches were compared and used to assess balance [6]. Due to fall risk is highly related to balance ability [7-9]. Therefore, the purpose of this study is to develop a multi-parameters balance assessment system with applying average center location, balance index, base area, and center location displacement for evaluating the human balance ability with LabVIEW program interface. Average center of gravity location can indicate the final displacement during the period of standing. Balance index may evaluate balance ability according to the change of center of gravity. Base area can calculate the region of total track. Center location displacement can indicate the displacement of center of gravity in both 2-axis. Integrate these results, it is expected that a noninvasive, low cost, reliable, simple and quantitative biomedical signal assessment system can be developed in this research for effective assessment and prevention of fall in older adults.

2   Methods

2.1   Participants

There are 10 healthy adults were enrolled in this study. They were evaluated under four kinds of postures (stand with two legs and open eyes, stand with two legs with closed eyes, stand with one leg and open eyes, stand with one leg and closed eyes) while standing on a 2-axis force platform (PASCO PS-2142) for 20 seconds. The data sampling rate were set to be 250 Hz.

2.2   Balance Signal Measurement

The balance system was based on the 2-axis force platform (PASPORT, PS-2142, USA). The force platform continuously measures force applied to it in two separate directions: normal to its surface (up to 4400 N) and along an axis parallel to its surface (up to 1100 N). Each of the four feet is connected to a beam with a strain gauge, through which the platform's electronics measure the force. As well as the sum of the normal forces applied to the four beams, the platform can be set to output the separate normal force measured by each beam. The size of the platform is 29 x 29 cm as shown in figure 1.

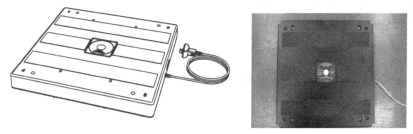

Fig. 1. The force platform was used to collect the normal force signals while standing

2.3   Data Analysis and Interface

ASCII files with data from the four sensors were processed by LabVIEW codes to estimate balance parameters. The force was determined in a defined area [29 ×29 cm^2] around the sensors. A average location of gravity center on the force platform may be calculated by the signals of normal forces. The location of gravity center is estimated as equation (1).

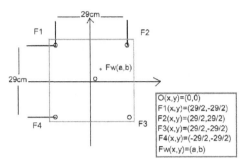

$$F_1 + F_2 + F_3 + F_4 = F_w$$

$$a = \frac{14.5(-F_1 + F_2 + F_3 - F_4)}{F_w}, \quad b = \frac{14.5(F_1 + F_2 - F_3 - F_4)}{F_w} \tag{1}$$

Where $F_1 \sim F_4$ is the force in each sensors, F_w is sum of normal forces, a and b is coordinates in x-axis and y-axis.

Balance Index (BI) can quantify the balance ability of human body. The value of balance index is estimated as equation (2). Due to larger value means far away more from aver age center of gravity, larger BI value, less balance ability [10].

$$BI = \sqrt{\frac{(\sum(O_x - X)^2 + \sum(O_y - Y)^2)}{N}}, \quad N \text{ is sample size} \tag{2}$$

Where O_x and O_y is the continuous coordinates of gravity center in time domain. X and Y is the average center of gravity. N is sample size.

3   Results and Discussion

The operation interface of this assessment system programmed by LabVIEW can show the track of center of gravity (COG), average position of COG, balance index and other parameters as showed in figure 2.

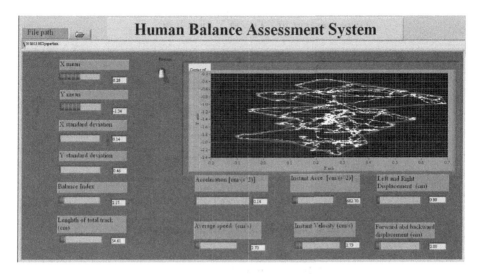

Fig. 2. The interface of human balance assessment system

Fig. 3 and 4 showed the displacements in both X and Y directions were smaller during stand with two legs and open eyes (p<0.05). Balance index results also revealed balance ability also become lower while standing with one leg and closed eyes (p<0.05) as showed in Fig. 5. Integrate these results, it indicated human balance ability was better during stand with two legs and open eyes (p<0.05) according to these comparison of parameters. On the other hand, stand with one leg and closed eyes will decrease balance ability.

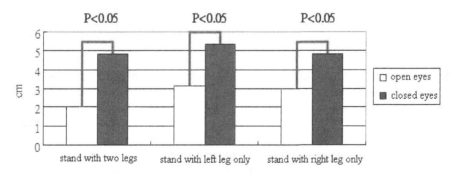

Fig. 3. Displacement of COG in X direction

Displacement of COG in Y direction

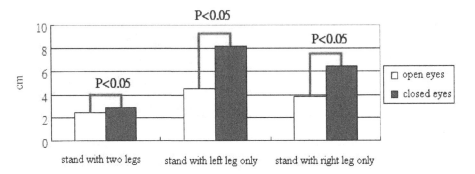

Fig. 4. Displacement of COG in Y direction

Balance Index (BI)

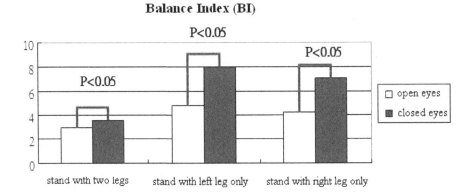

Fig. 5. Balance index (BI) results

4   Conclusions

According to the results, different posture would affect balance sense and ability. It can be assessed by this system with these parameters. Therefore, this system with easy test can provide fast and effective evaluation and these parameters can be adopted to assess fall risk, too. It is hope fall can be prevented in advanced and decrease the medical burden in older adults by the system in the future.

Acknowledgements. The authors would like to thank the National Science Council, Taiwan, and Hungkuang University for supporting this research under Contract No. NSC 101-2221-E-241 -009 and HK-CCGH-100-06.

References

1. Gibson, M.J.S., Andres, R.O., Kennedy, T.E., Coppard, L.C., et al.: Kellogg International Work Group on the Prevention of Falls by the Elderly, The prevention of falls in later life: a report of the Kellogg International Work Group on the Prevention of Falls by the Elderly (1987)
2. Northridge, M.E., Nevitt, M.C., Kelsey, J.L.: Non-syncopal falls in the elderly in relation to home environments. Osteoporosis International 6(3), 249–255 (1996)
3. Persson, L., Karberg, M., Magnusson, M.: "Effect of different treatment on postural performance in patients with cervical root compression. Journal of Vestibular Research 6(6), 439–453 (1996)
4. Uimonen, S., Sorri, M., Laitakari, K., Jamsa, T.: A comparsion of three vibratiors in static posturography: the effect of vibration amplitude. Medical and Enginering Physics 18(5), 405–409 (1996)
5. Clark, R.A., Bryant, A.L., Pua, Y., McCrory, P., Bennell, K., Hunt, M.: Validity and relability of the Nintendo Wii Balance Board for assessment of standing balance. Gait & Posture 31(3), 307–310 (2010)
6. Lafond, D., Duarte, M., Prince, F.: Comparison of three methods to estimate the center of mass during balance assessment. Journal of Biomechanics 37(9), 1421–1426 (2004)
7. Rubenstein, L.Z.: Falls in older people: epidemiology, risk factors and strategies for prevention. Age and Ageing 35(2), i137–i141 (2006)
8. Fuller, G.F.: Falls in the elderly. American Family Physician 61(7), 2159–2168 (2000)
9. Salminen, M., Vahlberg, T., Sihvonen, S., Sjosten, N., Piirtola, M., Isoaho, R., Aarnio, P., Kivela, S.-L.: Effects of risk-based multifactorial fall prevention on postural balance in the community-dwelling aged: A randomized controlled trial. Archives of Gerontology and Geriatrics 48(1), 22–27 (2009)
10. Lin, B.C., et al.: Sports Biomechanics. Wagner Publishing Co., Taiwan (2008)

Constructing Ergonomic Safety Modelling for Evaluating New Designs of Child Car Seats

Che-Yu Lu and Hsin-Hsi Lai

Department of Industrial Design, National Cheng Kung University,
No. 1, Ta-Hsie Rd. Tainan, Taiwan 70701, ROC
Joeylu0627@gmail.com, Hsinhsi@mail.ncku.edu.tw

Abstract. The safety and ergonomic compatibility are the most important parts for designing child car seats. Since the children, especially the infants, cannot objectively express their aptitudes of safety, comfort and opinions very well, they cannot be suitable subjects for ergonomic design experiments. Applying computers to simulate human motions for solving ergonomic design problems has been explored for many years, especially in substituting real human engaging in high risking tasks. However, in some specific fields of product design, intelligent man-machine (abbreviated as IMM) models suitable for designers are scarcely studied. The main purpose of this paper is trying to construct a totally new IMM model to aid designers of child car seats in the process of evaluating their new design concepts. The new computerized child model with self-adjusting functions can be fitted to car seat designed by any designers. The designer can maneuver the model to understand the potential design risks and ergonomic compatibility, and then improve his design.

Keywords: Child, belt design, solidwork.

1 Introduction

One goal of artificial intelligent research in design is to try to characterize the design process in enough detail that systems can be built more easily, that design knowledge can be acquired more easily, and that design tools can be matched to design problems (Chen et. al., 2006)[1]. Many people would agree that the general flow of design could be characterized by requirements formulation, analysis synthesis, ideation and evaluation (Lai, 2009)[2]. Design in any domain requires evaluation. If we can describe the essential characteristics of this reasoning skill, including the knowledge used and the process, then this can be more easily implemented for any domain (Gero and Sanders, 2009)[3]. Design evaluation can be more effective and more accurate by building useful Intelligent Computer-Aided Design (IntCAD) systems (Brown, 2007; 2009)[4,5]. Systems can range from autonomous design tools, that when given requirements will produce designs, to design aids that interact with a human designer (or designers) to support the design activity (Liu and Brown, 2009)[6]. According to the above previous studies, this paper is focused on searching for an intelligent man-machine model system to assist the child car seat designers to evaluate their new

V.G. Duffy (Ed.): DHM/HCII 2013, Part I, LNCS 8025, pp. 338–347, 2013.
© Springer-Verlag Berlin Heidelberg 2013

designs more accurately and more effectively by integrating the knowledge of artificial intelligence, design methodology and ergonomics.

There have been many computerized human models for the use of product designers. But most of these are two-dimensional models for adults that cannot be used for the specific use of child car seat designers to evaluate the safety and ergonomic compatibility of their new design concepts (Frank and Marach, 2008;)[7]. The related studies on man-machine models to evaluate the spatial layouts and ergonomic safeties, which may need to employ the knowledge of artificial intelligence, are just in the stage of starting point (Joseph, 1999)[8]. Therefore, this paper aims at applying the knowledge of artificial intelligent techniques; design methodology and anthropometrical engineering to create a new man-machine model that can intelligently evaluate the new design concepts, which is a rather essential design activity for the child car seat designers (Miller, 1998)[9]. This new intelligent model should be operated friendly for the future designers to achieve the final goal of seeking most efficient and effective design functions for the whole man-machine system.

In the current study, the intelligent new model is tried to simulate the designers' behavior to evaluate new design concepts of child car seat efficiently and effectively. Therefore, main purposes of the new model should include the following:

According to the present anthropometrical data of domestic children to build standard child models for observing and simulating child's restrictions and ranges of activity in the car seats, and to provide the designers the principles, standards and suggestions of ergonomic design.

According to the constructing types of present child car seats in use to build standard child car seat models. Due to the domestic makers still don't have the car seats specifically made for Taiwan children, the seat models are built from abroad.

Using the method of computer simulation to build an intelligent man-machine (abbreviated as IMM) model for the study of man-machine interface, and to provide designers to observe the child's static visibility, motion range simulation and dimensional restrictions in the car seat, and then to assess the ergonomic compatibility of their new designs and to revise them accordingly.

Realizing the above main purposes, research procedures of this study can be depicted to study the basic anthropometrical data of children, and then to build standard child models accordingly, to study the typical constructing components of child car seat, and then to build standard safe seat models accordingly, to explore the conventional computer simulation models and to assess them carefully, to construct a new computer program for the IMM model to simulate the evaluating behavior of child car seat designers and operating the new developed intelligent model by potential model users and improving it afterward.

2   Basic Study

2.1   Analysis of the Anthropometrical Data for Children

The construction of human model for child safety seats involves extensive anthropometrical data, including physiological developing characteristics, static body measurements and dynamic body measurements of child. This part of anthropometrical data had been finished by the author in 1999(Lai and Chang, 2007; 2009)[10,11]. The data used in this study are the children aged ranging from one-year to three-year.

2.2   Analysis of Safety Seat Components for Children

The child car seats, also called as child restraint device for automobiles, are suitable for the use of children to avoid or reduce the injuries during car accidents. This study is focused on representing the relationship between man and machine models, and the interference with each other. Thus, in order to build the man-machine model, the understandings of individual components and functions are needed. Figure 2 shows the individual components of a typical child car seat, which conforms to the standard classifications of China National Standard (CNS 11497). Functions and individual components are defined as the following:

1. Child safety belt: It is composed of weaving belt, buckle and length adjuster to restrain the child, and is a part of protection devices.
2. Assistant safety belt: It is to protect the child car seat from sliding and to make the protection device more stable by adding a fixed safety belt from the back support of the seat.
3. Buttock support: It is one part of protection device to support the child's buttock.
4. Back support: It is also one part of protection device to support the child's back and head.
5. Lateral support: It is a part of back support to protect the head against moving horizontally.
6. Contact surface: While fitting up the child model to the protection device, the entire surfaces surround the head and human body of child model.
7. Top slots: These are the slots to make the safety belt to go through the rear side of car seat.
8. Bottom slots: Functions are the same as top slots. Children can use different height of slots in accordance with their stature.
9. Shoulder straps: These are safety straps, which mount the shoulder through the frontal body, to fix child's shoulder.
10. Buckle: It is used to tighten the safety belt.
11. Crotch strap: This is a safe strap to jump over the child's hips.
12. Harness adjuster: It is used to tighten the shoulder belt, which is adjustable and generally possesses a lock device.
13. Frontal railing: It is a cushion device to protect the child from turnover and causing injuries.

3   Method to Construct the IMM Model

The construction of IMM model should include building standard child models, standard child car seat models, and connecting program to simulate the designers' designing behavior such as testing the man-machine interface, and adjusting the child model or the child car seat model to calculate the safety factors and ensure the design security. The following analyzes the algorithm of model constructing procedures.

3.1   Defining Environmental Parameters

The IMM model intends to demonstrate that a standard child model can fit for typical child car seats, as well as simulate the man-machine static vision, the effects of motion range and anthropometrical restrictions. Hence, before to construct the model system, the following man-machine environmental parameters must be defined.

Standard child models are in accordance with the anthropometrical data of children aging from one-year to three-year old, and without distinguishing gender.

Typical child car seats models conform to the children aging from one-year to three-year old and with frontal forward type.

The vertical centre of child models aim at the vertical centre of car seat models, and fit the child models to car seat models in order to make the back and the thighs of child models to contact the back-support and buttock-support of car seat models, respectively.

The initial state of child models is that the upper arms hand down lateral sides of body, and forearms and upper arms with an angle of 120 degrees, heels of both feet with vertical state, as well as lower legs and thighs stretch horizontally forward.

Child models are in accordance with normal movement ranges and anthropometrical restrictions. And designers can observe and perform the evaluation of ergonomic compatibilities of motions and activities of child models.

3.2   Building Standard Child Models

Basic skeletal frameworks of standard child models are built on the basis of body links, with the programming language of Visual Basic 6.0 and the support scripts of computer package 3DS MAX.

3.2.1   Parameter Control of Child Models

While constructing body's and limbs' dimensions and considering the characteristics of children's development, the standard child model is divided into 14 body segments and 13 joints (Huang, 1995)[12]. These body segments consist of head, body torso, left upper arm, left forearm, left hand, right upper arm, right forearm, right hand, left thigh, left shank, left foot, right thigh, right shank and right foot. The corresponding areas are shown in figure 1. The construction of overall size is in accordance with the surrounding profiles as shown in Table 1. The overall size is used for the evaluation of restrictions on the range of activities.

3.3   Building Standard Child Car Seat Model

SolidWorks is a well-developed software for constructing physical models, since it includes the function of geometric numerical data transformation and supports the program developing tools for Visual Basic and Visual C++. In order to construct an ideal seat model to conform to the dimensions of child car seat and to provide the function of spatial man-machine interference analysis, Solidworks is employed in building standard child car seat models.

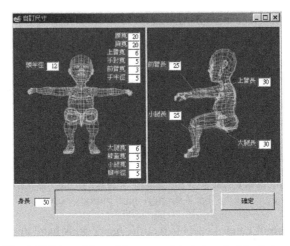

Fig. 1. Child model used for car seat designers in this study

3.3.1   Parameter Control of Seat Models

SolidWorks is a well-developed software for constructing physical models, since it includes the function of geometric numerical data transformation and supports the program developing tools for Visual Basic and Visual C++. In order to construct an ideal seat model to conform to the dimensions of child car seat and to provide the function of spatial man-machine interference analysis, Solidworks is employed in building standard child car seat models.

Table 1. Measuring items of standard child model

Class	Type of item
Basic measures	Age (1,2,3 year-old)
Linear dimensions	Head width (95th%le, 5th%le)
	Head length (95th%le, 5th%le)
	Upper arm length (95th%le, 5th%le)
	Forearm length (95th%le, 5th%le)
	Tight length (95th%le, 5th%le)
	Seat height (95th%le, 5th%le)
	Acromionheight(95th%le, 5th%le)
	Width between two elbow (95th%le, 5th%le)
	Elbow height (95th%le, 5th%le)
Thickness (surrounding length)	Upper arm thickness (95th%le, 5th%le)
	Forearm thickness (95th%le, 5th%le)
	Chest thickness (95th%le, 5th%le)
	Tight thickness (95th%le, 5th%le)
Range of joint activities	Left and right leaning of head
	Rotation of neck
	Bending of elbow
	Arm stretch, external spin and internal spin
	Elbow flection
	Shoulder raising
	Shoulder flection and stretch

3.4   Simulating Man-Machine Interface and Adjusting Models

The following infers the algorithm of this new type of simulation method to analyze the spatial interface of child model and child car seat model.

3.4.1   Method of Removing Back Face

The method of object space to identify the back of object is based on the following equation of plane.

$$Ax + By + Cz + D = 0 \tag{1}$$

Any point (x', y', z'), described at right hand coordinating sysem, if satisfied the following inequality:

$$Ax + By + Cz + D < 0 \tag{2}$$

Then this point is inside the plane. If the point (x', y', z') is an observing point, the plane satisfied the inequality (2) has to be the plane, which cannot be seen from the observing plane.

Table 2. Seat components and man-machine interference range

Name of component	Parameter	Range of man-machine interference
Seat back support	Area (length × width)	Head width, seat height, width of two elbow, acromion height, elbow height
Slot (upper, middle and lower)	Height of slot and width to the center of seat back support	Acromion height, chest thickness
Seat buttock support	Area (length × width)	Buttock width, thigh length
	Angle between seat back support and buttock support	Bending angle of waist
Lateral protective rack	Length, width and thickness	Left and right leaning of head, neck spin, acromion raising
	Angle between lateral rack and seat support	Left and right leaning of head, neck spin, arm stretch, external spin and internal spin
Frontal protective rack	Position of rotating axis	Arm stretch, seat height
	Arm length of rotating axis	Arm flections, seat height
	Length, width and height of frontal protective rack	Chest thickness, shoulder flections and stretch

3.4.2   Method of Scanning Face Line

This kind of object space method to remove the hidden plane is the extensions of scan line algorithms used by the inner part of polygon. Figure 2 demonstrates the principles of scan line method. Firstly, we define each plan a flag, which can be set as on or off, to represent the position along the scan line being faced inside or outside.

The plan with the most left margin is on, and the most right margin is off. The scan line handles from left to right. The intersecting sides of scan line 1 are AB, BC, HE and FG. Along the scan line 1 and at the position between sideline AB and BC, there is only a flag of plane S1 being on. Thus, there is no need to calculate the depth and input the numerical data of S1 to renewing buffer. Similarly, there is only a flag of S2 being on between HE and FG. The scan line 1 does not intersect with plan in other positions. Thus, intensity values of other region have to be set as background intensity. The sidelines to be past through by scan line 2 and 3 consist of DA, HE, BC and FG. Along scan line 2 and between DA and HE, there is only a flag of S1 being on. But between HE and BC, the flags of two planes are all on. That shows the depth must be calculated with the coefficient of two planes. Condensing method can be utilized from one scan line to the next scan line. There is no change between the intersection of scan line 2 and 3. These two planes must be the same directions determined by scan line 2. Any amount of overlapping polygon can be handled by this kind of scan line method. Flags of surface plan have to be set to indicate one position to be inside or outside. While calculating the depth, the mutual cover situations are reconsidered.

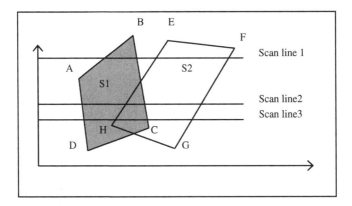

Fig. 2. Descriptions of scan line method

3.4.3   Method of Solving Spatial Intervention of Man-Machine Models

According to the extensions of the above two algorithmic concepts, to judge the mutual positions and relative relationships of two objects in the space, the coordinating system has to be defined in the space world of the objects. That is a fixed system as well as a view coordinate and a local coordinate, so as to perform transformations in comparison with relative positioning relationships among the objects themselves. The objects are constructed in sequential polygon form and have completely polygonal order as well as numbered coordinates. Employing the tool of 3D Max Studio script, component positions of each object are grouped, so as to reduce the frequencies of interferences. Depending on the established plan equations of every polygon and according to the algorithm, the judgment is proceeded with to eliminate the polygonal region, which is not interfered in the external part of a plan. In order to understand the belonging parts of objects and to become the concluding basis of ultimate interference model, before restoring the object positions, the relative object polygon and original object polygon are calculated including their intersecting points, vertical distances in accordance with the plan equations. According to the above principles, a child's head model is constructed in the current research to analyze the interferences and to understand the calculation capacity as well as the program-judgmental capacity. This will be the basis of developing the IMM model.

4   System Operation of the IMM Model

In order to have the designers more conveniently to make use of this man-machine model, a friendly user interface is provided for designers' easy operations. The picture of computer man-machine system can be divided into four views including child model view, car seat model view, man-machine model view and control parameters view. First of all, the needed parameters were set up, then the program was performed, three views appeared each model. The designers can adjust action parameters in the view of man-machine model. After each adjustment, spatial interference model is calculated. Accordingly, designers can evaluate the ergonomic effectiveness and user compatibility of new design car seat, as shown in figure 3.

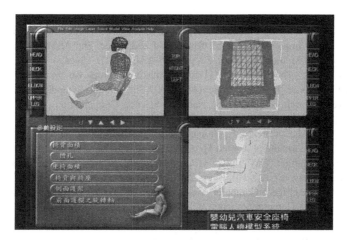

Fig. 3. System applications of the IMM model

5   Conclusion

The establishing of this IMM model will reduce the cost of making the physical model and avoid the risk hazards of child's testing as well as shorten the time of car seat model design and accurately evaluate the ergonomic compatibility and suitability of a new man-machine system. This is a new attempt in the related fields of artificial intelligence to apply the knowledge of computer simulation, spatial interference with programming analysis and ergonomic compatibility and usability to evaluate totally new product designs. Although every steps of building the IMM model system is very trivial and delicate, triviality and delicacy are the requisite for accurate evaluation for car seat design. Therefore, this new attempt of achieving the application of the related artificial intelligent knowledge and ergonomic design methodology to construct a totally new IMM model for the accurate evaluation of complicated child car seat designs has been proved to be very practical and feasible for current designers in this digital design era.

Acknowledgment. The financial support of National Science Council in R.O.C. is very appreciated (Project code: NSC98-2213-E006-029). Ms. Yu-Tian Lian also does a plenty of work to assist to build the new model and simulate the new system. Her helpings are very grateful. In addition, the children and their parents, who are invited and recruited as subjects by the doctors and nurses of pediatrics department at Medical Centre of National Cheng Kung University, enthusiastically participated in the anthropometrical measurements are also very thankful.

References

1. Chen, A., McGinnis, B., Ullman, D.G.: Design History Knowledge Representation and its basic Computer Implementation. In: Rinderle, J. (ed.) Proc. 2nd ASME Int. Conf. on Design Theory and Methodology, vol. 27, pp. 175–184. ASME, Chicago (2006)
2. Lai, H.H.: The Theory of IDP Decision-making Model on Man-Machine System Design, Conference. In: Paper Presented at 2009 Sino-Franco Symposium on Ergonomics Design & Research, sponsored by National Science Council, pp. 1–22. R.O.C, Taipei (2009)
3. Sanders, M.S., McCormick, E.I.: Human Factors in Engineering and Design, pp. 415–452. McGraw-Hill International, United States (2012)
4. Brown, D.C.: Which Way to KIC? In: Mantyla, M., Finger, S., Tomiyama, T. (eds.) Knowledge Intensive CAD, vol. II, pp. 291–294. Chapman & Hall (2007)
5. Brown, D.C.: Intelligent Computer-Aided Design. In: Williams, J.G., So-chats, K. (eds.) Encyclopaedia of Computer Science and Technology, pp. 1–23 (revision of 2009)
6. Liu, J., Brown, D.C.: Generating Design Decomposition Knowledge for Parametric Design Problems. In: Gero, J., Sudweeks, F, eds. (2009)
7. Frank, A., Marach, A.: CAD modelling of a human 3D child body. International Journal of Industrial Ergonomics 22(6), 33–41 (2008)

8. Joseph, G.: Some observations regarding the vibrational environment in child safety seats. Journal of Applied Ergonomics 32(4), 7–15 (1999)
9. Miller, T.R., Spicer, R.S., Lestina, D.C.: Who is driving when unrestrained chil-dren and teenagers are hurt. Journal of Accident Analysis and Preview 30(6), 39–49 (1998)
10. Lai, H.H., Chang, Y.M.: The Research and Development of Ergonomic Safety for Child Car Seats, Project Report of National Science Council in R.O.C. (2012)
11. Lai, H.H., Chang, Y.M.: The Research and Development of Ergonomic Safety for Child Car Seats, Project Report of National Science Council in R.O.C. (2012)
12. Huang, S.C.: Biomechanical modeling and simulations of automobile crash victims. Journal of Computer & Structures 57(3), 41–49 (1995)

How Could This Have Happened? Unintentional Injuries of Young Children at Home

Rani Lueder

Humanics Ergonomics Inc.
10202 La Costa Drive
Austin, TX 78747-1103, USA
rani@humanics-es.com

Abstract. Unintentional injuries of young children at home are preventable. The causes often relate to a range of factors that interact with inadequacies in design. Two examples of court cases involving an entrapment injuries are reviewed.

Keywords: Ergonomics for children, unintentional injuries in children, forensics, product liability, asphyxiation injuries, toddlers, ergonomic design, nursery product safety, residential elevators, LULA low volume elevators, human factors expert witness cases.

1   Overview

Unintentional injuries related to product design are more than "accidents", given their preventable nature. While participating in a variety of legal cases that followed devastating product-related injuries to children at home, this contributor saw a continuing pattern of factors that led to unnecessary tragedy. Although many manufacturers demonstrate a consistent and exemplary concern for "doing the right thing", unintentional injuries in children often result from the interaction of one particular manufacturer's defective design with other factors.

1.1   Some Manufacturers Commonly Assume That Parents Assume Primary Responsibility for Their Children's Safety

Yet caregivers cannot reasonably be expected to compensate for hazards resulting from defective products; it is unreasonable to expect parents to constantly be vigilant against the actions of their children when design solutions exist that would make such efforts unnecessary.

Parents Are Often Overworked, Under Stress and Lack Sleep. They are often distractible as they attempt to marshal competing demands from their several children while managing their other life responsibilities.

They get sick. As Garfield (1983) reminded us three decades ago, "accidents are more likely when the family routine has been upset by illness or another stress. More accidents happen just before mealtime, when parents are busiest".

V.G. Duffy (Ed.): DHM/HCII 2013, Part I, LNCS 8025, pp. 348–354, 2013.

Parents Have a Poor Understanding of Risk. Health Canada (1996) described the "optimism bias" among parents that hinders health-risk behaviors. "Perhaps the most consistent finding in research on parents' attitudes and practices related to childhood injury prevention is that parents overestimate the capabilities of their children to act in safe ways and their children's knowledge of how to handle emergency situations" (Health Canada, 1997).

Pollack-Nelson and Drago (2002) emphasized that because 95% of parents perceive that their children are at little or no risk, manufacturers must assume responsibility for ensuring their products are safe[1].

Warnings and Instructions Are Often Inadequate. The research community has long recognized that warnings and training provide inferior and far less alternatives to designing out risk through good product design.

Yet parents and other caregivers rely on such content to ensure their child is safe. Such product-related content often fails to adequately communicate safe behaviors.

1.2   In Cases Reviewed, the Manufacturer and Their Associated Industry May Display a Strong Reliance on Standards and Guidelines to Justify any Questions Regarding Their Responsibility for Good Design

Ostensibly, the aim of safety standards is often to establish guidelines for their industry to protect its users from harm. Not ironically (such as in the second case described below) these same manufacturers may undermine the effectiveness of these standards by aggressively blocking standards committees and enforcement agencies at every step to prevent the promulgation of appropriate standards. In doing so, the manufacturers sometimes establish a juggernaut subverting the appropriate development of a standard.

1.3   During Depositions, Some Manufacturers May Demonstrate an Astonishing Array of Circular Arguments

The parents are to blame because they did not use a product properly even though the manufacturer provided a complete lack of guidance regarding the associated risks. The parents are at fault because they failed to supervise the child while he/she slept during the night.

---

[1] Pollack-Nelson and Drago (2002) continued, "half of the children got out of bed in the morning always or often before a parent. Ninety-five percent of parents perceived that their child was at no risk or slight risk of injury when getting up in the morning before them."

2   Case Examples

2.1   The "Crib tent" Product for Very Young Children

One example of such a case involves a "crib tent" product that was supposedly designed to keep young children from climbing from their cribs. This manufacturer's materials described as a "safety product" that promises "peace of mind" with their "safety tested device"[2].

A 23-month old child sustained severe injuries while attempting to climb out of his crib. His efforts caused the pole supporting the frame of the crib tent to invert, trapping his neck between the rail of the crib and the reversed pole. His head was trapped inside and his torso outside the crib while his neck hung across the top side rail of the crib.

His severe chronic disability was worsened by evidence that young children under the age of three are at particular risk of asphyxiation / airway occlusion at low pressures. Stevens et al (2000) reported that young children could only sustain very low levels of force to prevent risk of strangulation (see also Garros et al, 2003; Shepherd 1990; Tarrago, 2000).

Deposition Transcripts Indicate That the Manufacturer Never Actually Performed Safety Testing on Their Product. Further, They Had No Evidence to Suggest That the Product Was Safe for a Child as Young at the Age of Three.
Court documents suggest that this manufacturer based their guidance to parents on only a single consideration. That is, the 0-36 moth age restriction for users of their products reflected the Consumer Product Safety Commission (CPSC)'s 1997 guidance that children be moved from their crib to a bed when they reach the age of three[3] reflected their conclusion that when children reach a height of 35 inches (890 mm) they become at risk of falling out of the crib.

Such circular arguments point to an Alice in Wonderland logic. The crib tent keeps children safe by preventing their climbing from their crib. On the other hand, at the age of three children should be moved to a bed because they will begin to climb out of their crib. Clearly, at least one of these arguments is false.

Deposition Transcripts Indicate That the Crib Tent Manufacturer Never Safety-tested Their Product. They Claimed Otherwise, Despite a Complete Lack of Evidence to Suggest That the Product Was Safe for a Child as Young as Three.
When asked why the executive did not take any of the prior incidents of child entrapment seriously with their product, he indicated it was because no one had died before that time.

---

[2] It might be of interest that the manufacturer provided only a 60-day warrantee from the date of purchase for a product that was intended to be used by children until they reach the age of three.

[3] Of note, the CPSC's guidance was disproved (despite remaining in place) when researchers such as Ridenour (1997, 2002) provided extensive documentation of the very young children's crib-climbing behavior (see Figure 1).

Fig. 1. Ridenour (2002) reported that 90% of the 16 to 32 month old children observed climb from cribs after moving to a corner of crib. (Source: Ridenour, 2002, p 365).

Deposition Transcripts Indicate That the Manufacturer / Executive Maintained That the Parents Were Ultimately Responsible, because It Involved the Use of a "Safety Product".
Such arguments make no sense. As Ridenour (1997) pointed out "the crib is the only infant product in which a consumer, such as a parent or caretaker, is encouraged to leave the infant unattended, usually alone in the bedroom, while the infant is sleeping or going to sleep or waking."

2.2   Entrapment Hazards in Residential Elevators

While his mother was doing the laundry on the third floor, her three-year-old boy was trapped between the outer hoistway and inner (accordion) car doors of the family's home elevator. While upstairs doing the laundry, the mother heard her son say that he wanted to come up to her. She called to him to wait for her and that she was coming down.

She pushed the elevator button and heard its motor move. The elevator started and then stopped and all was silent. She ran screaming down the stairs, broke the lock to the outer hoistway door of the elevator and saw her son's head on the floor, with his chest jammed under the bottom of the elevator car. He arrived at the hospital in a coma, immobilized and requiring ventilation. He was in critical condition, undergoing full respiratory / cardiac arrest.

Entrapment Risk in Young Children Increases When the Gap Is Greater Than the Size of Their Head. This family's tragedy resulted because the effective clearance between the outer/hoistway door and the accordion door of their elevator was excessive. The American Society of Mechanical Engineers (ASME) A17.1 Sec 5.3 standard for residential elevators that was in force at the time of installation specified that elevators could not exceed the "3 and 5 rule"[4]. In order to exclude children from the space between elevator doors, the design must prevent even the smallest child from fitting.

Young children's heads are larger than their torsos. To prevent entrapment, the maximum dimension between doors must be less than their minimum head breadth.

Research sponsored by CPSC (Schneider et al, 1986; Snyder et al., 1975a, 1975b, 1977) provided the following data for minimum and 5th percentile values for young children.		
Head Breadth measure	**Minimum value**	**5th percentile value**
Age range: 2 – 3½		
Female	11.9 cm (4.69 in)	12.5 cm (4.92 in)
Male	12.0 cm (4.72 in)	12.7 cm (5.0 in)
Male and female	11.9 cm (4.69 in)	12.5 cm (4.92 in)
Age range: 3½ - 4½		
Female	12.4 cm (4.88 in)	12.6 cm (4.96)
Male	12.8 (5.04 in)	13.0 (5.12 in)
Male and female	12.4 cm (4.88 in)	12.8 (5.04 in)

Fig. 2. Research by CPSC suggests that entrapment risk may be prevented when the gap between elevator doors are less than 4.6 inches (Source: Schneider et al, 1986; Snyder et al, 1975a, 1975b, 1977)[5]

Entrapment Risk Varies by Opening Size and Shape. The V-shape of accordion doors increases entrapment risk (Schneider et al 1986) by providing an area that supports the shape of young children's head.

Similar Entrapment Hazards for Young Children Are Evident with Other Products as Well. Stephenson (1988, 1991) found risk in children increased when exposed to then-allowed six-inch (15.24 cm) clearances between guardrail openings, writing, "It's now quite clear that the maximum dimension of openings in guardrails at locations accessible to the public should not exceed 4 in (10.16 cm) or even a lesser dimension".

- Virtually all children less than six years of age can pass through a 6 in. (15.24 cm) wide opening.

---

[4] The clearance between the hoistway doors and hoistway edge of the landing sill could not exceed three inches. ASME also mandated that the space between the hoistway door and elevator car door may not exceed five inches.

[5] Data are presented for the head breadth of children of ages that they might be strong enough to close the hoistway door behind them, enabling the elevator door to move. The activation of standard designs of residential and low volume elevators requires that the users close both the outer/hoistway and inner/accordion doors. However it should be noted that defective elevator doors have been known to open anyway.

- Almost no child one year or older can pass completely through a 4½ in (11.53 cm) wide opening.
- Approximately 50 percent of all children 13 to 18 months old can pass completely through a 5-inch (12.7) wide opening.
- The breadth of a child's head is the key to determining if he or she can pass completely through an opening.

3   Discussion

The intent of the above discussion was to provide one writer's perspective with examples about how things go wrong with unintentional injuries in young children. Such situations often involve the interaction between inadequate design and a range of colliding factors. In such cases, the responses between manufacturers are in stark contrast. Further, these tragedies would have been prevented if the manufacturer had implemented design solutions practiced by others in the industry.

Acknowledgements: I would like to express my gratitude to Andrew Scherffius Esq. of Scherffius, Ballard, Still & Ayres, LLP and David Krugler, Esq. of Cash, Krugler & Fredericks, LLC, Atlanta, Georgia for allowing me to participate in their efforts.

References

1. Garfield, E.: So Your Children Will Not Be Victims. Child Safety. Part 1. Current Contents 486, 396–403 (1983); Stevens, R.R., Lane, G.A., Milkovich, S.M., Stool, D., Rider, G., Stool, S.E.: Prevention of accidental childhood strangulation: Where is the site of obstruction? Int. J.1 Pediatr. Otorhinolaryngol. 49(suppl. 1), S321–S322 (1983)
2. Health Canada, For the Safety of Canadian Children and Youth: From Injury Data to Preventive Measures. Health Canada, Ottawa (1997)
3. Health Canada, Parental attitudes towards unintentional childhood injuries. Prepared for the Family and Child Health Unit. Health Canada by SAGE Research Corporation, 67 pages (1996)
4. Pollack-Nelson, C., Drago, D.: Supervision of children aged two through six years. Injury Control and Safety Promotion 9(2), 121–126 (2002)
5. Stevens, R.R., Lane, G.A., Milkovich, S.M., Stool, D., Rider, G., Stool, S.E.: Prevention of accidental childhood strangulation: A clinical study. Ann. Otol. Rhinol. Laryngol. 109(9), 797–802 (2000)
6. Garros, D., King, W.J., Brady-Fryer, B., Klassen, T.P.: Strangulation with intravenous tubing: a previously undescribed adverse advent in children. Pediatrics 111(6 Pt.1), e732–e734 (2003)
7. Shepherd, R.T.: Accidental self-strangulation in a young child–a case report and review. Med. Science Law. 30(2), 119–123 (1990)
8. Tarrago, S.B.: Prevention of choking, strangulation, and suffocation in childhood. WMJ 99(9), 43–46 (2000)
9. Ridenour, M.V.: Age, side height, and spindle shape of the crib in climbing over the side. Percept. Mot. Skills. 85(2), 667–674 (1997)

10. Ridenour, M.V.: How do children climb out of cribs? Percept. Mot. Skills 95(2), 363–366 (2002)
11. Schneider, L.W., Lehman, R.J., Pflueg, M.A., Owings, C.L.: Size and shape of the head and neck from birth to four years. Final report. University of Michigan, Ann Arbor, Transportation Research Institute (UMTRI). Report Number: UMTRI-86-2. Contract Number: CPSC-C-831250. 485 ps. (1986)
12. Snyder, R.G., Spencer, N.L., Schneider, L.W., Owings, C.L.: Physical Characteristics of Children as Related to Death and Injury for Consumer Product Design and Use. Ann Arbor. Ml: Highway Safety Research Institute, University of Michigan, Prepared for the U.S. Consumer Product Safety Commission. Final Report UM-HSRI-BI-75-5. May 31, 240 ps. (1975a)
13. Snyder, R.G., Spencer, N.L., Owings, C.L., Schneider, L.W. Physical Characteristics of Children as Related to Death and Injury for Consumer Product Safety Design. Highway Safety Research Institute, University of Michigan, Ann Arbor, Ml (1975b); Prepared for the U.S. Consumer Product Safety Commission. Final Report UM-HSRI-BI-75-5 under Contract FDA-72-70 31, 56 ps. (May 1975)
14. Snyder, R.G., Schneider, L.W., Owings, C.L., Reynolds, H.M., Golomb, D.H., Schork, M.A.: Anthropometry of Infants, Children and youths to Age 18 for Product Safety Design. Highway Safety Research Institute, University of Michigan. Prepared for the U.S. Consumer Product Safety Commission. May 31. UM-HSRI-77-17 Final Report, 648 ps. (1977)
15. Stephenson, E.: The silent and inviting trap. The Building Official and Code Administrator, 28–34 (November/December 1988)
16. Stephenson, E.: Update on the silent and inviting trap. Building Standards, 4–5 (January-February 1991)

Usability of Portable Fire Extinguisher: Perspectives of Ergonomics and Intuitive Use

Maria Lucia Okimoto, Maicon Puppi, Sabrina Oliveira, and Vanessa Macedo

Federal University of Parana, Pos-Graduate Program in Design, Brazil
{binah.oliveira,vanessaddmacedo,maicon.puppi}@gmail.com,
lucia.demec@ufpr.br

Abstract. The present study aims to explore the usage of portable fire extinguisher's usability from the interaction with non-specialists in emergency context. Has been noticed an absence of Brazil's proper education regarding procedures for fires, evidencing the need for portable fire extinguishers to induce intuitive usage and to improve the usability by users. Were also explored ergonomic factors, such as effort to complete the task and user's perception of discomfort. In order to simulate the emergency context, a usability test was applied with addition stress stimuli. The study allows to conclude that the portable fire extinguisher evaluated present a low level of intuitive use induction, revealing the need to state better standards from Brazilian authorities towards the label and handles of this product. This paper presents the importance of evaluating ergonomic and intuitive factors related to products required on emergency contexts. This study conducted in Brazil is the starting point for other research that explore the theme and aim to improve these devices, assisting designers to take into account aspects of intuitive use and ergonomic principles during the configuration of industrial products.

Keywords: Fire Extinguisher, Usability, Safety.

1 Introdution

Given the absence of Brazil's proper education regarding procedures for fires and emergencies, having a fire extinguisher that allows correct and intuitive use becomes paramount. When fires occur, Brazilians tend to act on impulse in the use of fire extinguishers. As an outcome of this situation, the likelihood of misinterpretation of pictorial-verbal codes and misuse of fire extinguishers can be high. Within this context, the research question raised: is portable fire extinguishers' usability appropriated and allows intuitive use for Brazilian non-specialists in emergency settings?

This research's goal was to develop an exploratory study to test the usability of fire extinguisher in subjects without previous experience of using this product. The research involved usability tests, composed under the following approaches: investigation of intuitive use provided by fire extinguishers to non-expert users; required physical effort in usage tasks; and discomfort's perception. This research also enabled to develop another study, the learnability of fire extinguisher provided by

V.G. Duffy (Ed.): DHM/HCII 2013, Part I, LNCS 8025, pp. 355–364, 2013.
© Springer-Verlag Berlin Heidelberg 2013

instructional video, that will be presented on a further paper. In order to enable both studies from the same research the test was composed by two rounds: the first, without any kind of instruction besides the fire extinguisher's label; and second, with the instructional video presentation.

The basic method applied on the study was the usability test, composed by different metrics in order to allow the different evaluation perspectives, such as: pre and post use questionnaire; success ratings to each task; time rating to each task; efficiency (with amount of physical and cognitive effort to finish the task); think aloud sessions; effort's subjective perception with modified Borg scale; and Corlett diagram. The test was applied with five volunteers, all male, without previous usage of the fire extinguisher, with different professions and educational levels.

As research's conclusions, is possible to infer the analyzed products present a low level of intuitive use induction regarding the proper extinguisher selection, the product's transportation and the positioning towards the flames. Was noticed a positive difference between the trials with and without instructions, however, it's necessary to perform deeper studies on that matter to establish significant quantitative results. So it is aimed to present in future study the learning aspects, through the comparison of both test rounds, in order to demonstrate the significant variation regards on learnability and usability evaluation in fire extinguishers, reiterating the absence of instruction in the first trial and with instruction in the second test.

2   Emergency Context and the Brazilian Fire Extinguisher

Due to its territorial location (among other factors), Brazil it's not a frequent target to natural disasters, such as earthquakes, blizzards and tornados, allowing the citizens to have low concerns on that matter, resulting on low culture of prevention and security plan to such phenomenon. However, emergency context may arise from human action, like fires, in which the population must prevent and be aware. Differently from some countries, Brazilian schools do not provide fire training, as well as many companies on private and public initiative. As an example of the need to insert the prevention culture on Brazilian people, the national government is creating a cooperation project between Brazil and Japan, a country with professional with high expertise on natural disasters. Burning is among the most serious injuries; besides physical trauma that may lead to death, it also can cause other problems of psychological and social orders. As it's pointed by Rossi et. al. [1], statistic data on many aspects on burning cases in Brazil are sparse for various reasons.

As stated by Tullis & Albert [2] "usability can sometimes mean the difference between life and death". The authors exemplify that statement through a fatal accident involving a high-occupancy vehicle (HOV) and poorly designed signing. On emergency situations, such as fires, people tend to rely on product's intuitive use, due to hurry and low concentration on the task, increasing the importance of good usability. Essential products to the emergency situation's solution have a greater need to provide intuitive use and good usability, such as fire extinguishers. Those products are meant to be used by any kind of person that's in an emergency situation, requiring use of universal design principles on the project and development of efficient strategies to communicate to the user important information, such as: type of fire extinguishers content; appropriate material that can be in touch with the fire extinguishers content; and general procedures of use. That approach is sustained by Moura & Banzato [3] that classifies packaging functions on four purposes: containing, protecting, communicating and utility. Klohn & Pereira [4] developed a research on pictograms on packages of dangerous products, stressing the need of good usability on products related to emergency or danger situations.

In order to collect information about Brazilian fire extinguishers requirements, it was performed a research on normalized Brazilian standards, allowing to identify few indications on communicational aspects on these products. Neither both of the main standards on the field "ABNT NBR 12693 – Protection systems by fire extinguisher" [5] and "ABNT NBR 15808 – Portable Fire Extinguishers" [6] doesn't approach proper pictorial procedural sequences (PPSs). These standards refer to capacities and contents, which, though necessary approaches, are incomplete through the holistic perspectives of those products. The national standards leave room to diversity of graphic representations and code labels among manufacturers. The label's standardization brings several benefits to the user, such as content's correct identification, types of fire where it should be used and instructions of the correct procedures of use.

Naumann et. al. [7] and Hurtienne [8] discuss the increasing need of intuitive use on product design. Blackler et. al. [9] defines intuition as a type of cognitive processing that applies previous knowledge in an unconscious level on most of times [10]. Hurtienne defines intuitive use as: "the extent to which a product can be used by subconsciously applying prior knowledge, resulting in an effective and satisfying interaction using a minimum of cognitive resources" [8, p.29]. That definition is congruent to the usability definition by ISO 9241-11 [11], so if a product allows intuitive use by lay users, it can be inferred that the same product has good usability. On this sense, monitoring the intuitive use is a form to investigate the product's usability. As showed by Krippendorff [12], in products that are strictly related to utility, other user experience factors, such as emotions and pleasure of use, are placed on second plane. Fire extinguishers are an example of products that the most important factor is utility.

The ways to identify and evaluate intuitive use are still solidifying on User Experience field. However, Blackler et. al. formulate "intuitive use heuristics", in order to guide professionals to identify characteristics of intuitive use. The proposed heuristics are evidence of conscious reasoning, expectation, subjective certainty of correctness, latency, relevant past experience, and correctness of use. The authors state that the lowest the user's previous experience with the product or similar, the better intuitive use will be identified. On the experiments performed by the authors, the most important metrics used are time to complete task related to familiarity or expertise, and mistakes made during the performance.

Given the stated, intuitive use, usability and measurement of user experience during the activity of extinguishing fire, are the basic factors to be considered in studies to evaluate the usage of a portable fire extinguisher, providing improvement in product design. In this sense, from this research and the simulated tests in Brazil, it is considered that ergonomic principles applied to fire extinguishers can improve task "extinguish fire" by users and facilitate the use of the product in the context of emergency.

3   Methods

Since the research on portable fire extinguishers used in emergency is still on its beginning, this experiment did not have the intent to perform statistical comparisons, but to provide an exploratory view on the theme, investigating and detecting aspects that should be more extensive in future researches. The research demanded observation of usage by non-expert users. For that, researchers chose developing a controlled fire situation. To perform a test with an actual fire on constructed environment, such as a house, many juridical complications emerged. Given the timing to develop the research and low budget available, the researchers simulated the emergency context in the University installations. At the pilot test, the fire started in a metal barrel, outdoors, but there were complaints about the smoke emitted. Therefore, the actual tests had the fire in a barbecue grill, enabling the smoke's direction and allowing fire control.

Were added several stress stimuli to the user (e.g. smoke, restricted time and visual stimuli for the context of fire), in order to cause specific physiological factors, such as the release of adrenaline in the body, increasing heart rate and body temperature. The odor presence and visual obstruction caused by smoke from burning materials are some other aggravating factors to the task execution. The procedures of usability testing with users were not invasive, so ethical aspects were assist with the implementation of the Consent Form Free and Clarification [13].

Were applied additional tasks with the goal to stimulate mental and physical users´ aspects. Mental aspects: (1) displayed video containing fire scenes and people with burns and injuries. (2) The user was asked to perform a logic game with restricted timing. Physical aspects: (3) after the game task, the user ran a circuit to the local where the fire extinguishers were placed. (4) Another running, carrying the extinguisher, to the location of the fire, followed by the procedure of fire's extinguishment.

The experiment was performed on two trials with five users for each, all with timing. The users on the first and second trials were the same. At first, users proceed without instructions. In the second trial, oral information and a fire department's instructional video were present, teaching how to proper handle a fire extinguisher. Both trials were monitored by the researchers and video recorded. The selected users were all male without previous experience in fires, with different education levels. All users were volunteers and were willing to perform tasks that required running and lifting of weight, which added difficulties to user recruiting. Since the research was part of the Federal University of Paraná (UFPR) activities, many UFPR employees were invite to participate the experiment, but only male employees attended, justifying the users' gender of the experiment.

After each trial, users answered a semi-open structured interview. The questions addressed intuitive use, physical effort, perceived discomfort during equipment use, and learnability. Since the perspective of intuitive use address to investigate how inexperienced users proceed the tasks without any kind of instructions, the evaluation of intuitive use applied only on the first trial. The perspectives of physical effort and perceived discomforts during equipment use evaluated both trials, and the issues addressed to learnability emerged from the comparison between both trials' results. However, the results discussed on this paper present the evaluation of the intuitive use and perception of effort and discomfort on the delimited task. The evaluation of users learning ability on the same task is approached on a specific study on that matter, thorough cognitive inspection, presented in detail in a future study.

The contents of fire extinguishers used on the tests were: water (type A), indicated for extinguishing fires produced from wood, paper, rubber and fabric; and dry chemical (type BC), proper to extinguish fires from inflammable liquids and electrical equipment. Still there are also fires classified as Type D, ignited from metals and type K, ignited from kitchen oil. The choice of fire extinguishers was related to its availability. In the experiment, users were requested to distinguish and choose the correct extinguisher to extinguish the fire caused from electrical equipment, so the correct fire extinguisher was the Dry Chemical.

4   Results

Relating to the main task, "extinguish fire", on the first trial, all the users were able to conclude the task, but four of the five users had some kind of difficulty to complete the task, performing multiple triggering (Figure 1). Three users had a wrong distance towards the flame, and only one user had a correct posture towards the fire (Figure X).

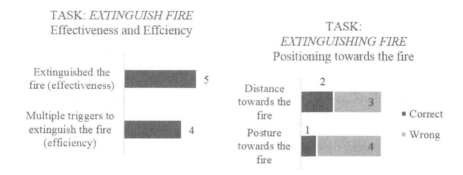

Fig. 1. Graphics regarded to the main task "Extinguishing fire"

Were evaluated the following main sub-tasks, towards the "Intuitive User" perspective on the first trial: portable fire extinguisher transporting, seal breaking, valve triggering and label checking. Four of the five users presented difficulties on removing and carrying the product to the fire's placement, the same number repeated on the valve triggering, in which four users triggered the valve several times, instead only one, as appropriate. All users showed difficulties on breaking the seal, performing that sub-task only when facing the flames, instead breaking the seal at the product's removal from original placement. Four users checked the label before the product's removal (Figure 2).

The seconds taken to choose between both fire extinguishers varied from five (5) to twenty three (23) seconds, only by the four users who checked the label before the choice. The users did not perform "think aloud", even when asked to do so. At the post-session interview, when asked about the difficulties on use, only one user stated to have some trouble, as all the others said to have no difficulties to perform portable fire extinguishers use.

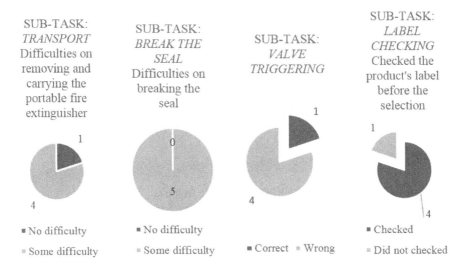

Fig. 2. Graphics regarded to the sub tasks

To measure subjective perception of discomfort was applied a questionnaire to users post-use scenario. In this survey the users identified in Diagram Corllett and Manenica [14], the perception of some kind of pain or discomfort in body parts as the Figure 3.

A protocol, illustrated by Figure 4, was also applied post-usage scenario for evaluation of subjective perception of painful areas in the upper limbs, which is commonly used for evaluation of hand tools [15]. This checklist identify any pain or discomfort in the upper right and left upper limbs.

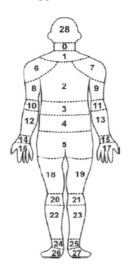

Fig. 3. Diagram of Subjective Perception of Pain or Discomfort (Source: Corlett and Manenica, 1980)

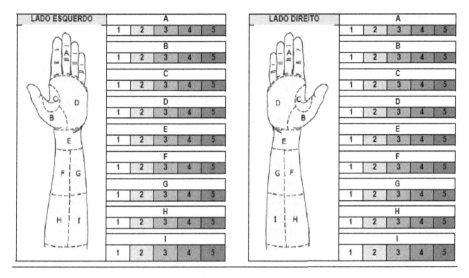

Fig. 4. Diagram of the subjective perception of pain or discomfort in the upper body (Source: Kadefords et al, 1993)

The results of the perception of pain or discomfort in the body regions demonstrate that the majority do not exhibit levels of discomfort. However, compared with the sample of five individuals, two responded that they felt some discomfort in the palmar region and during the task of carrying the extinguisher, but a moderate discomfort. At the end of the test was also applied to the Borg Scale, which is a common method used to measure the degree of effort an individual, during the performance of some activity. It is a subjective checklist, easy, but with a significant degree of efficiency compared their results with changes in heart rate. This is the estimate of the intensity of effort reported by the individual [16]. In Borg Scale, the individual assigns a score for intensity of discomfort, the scale goes from 0 (none) to 10 (maximum).

As results of perception of effort during the first round of testing, four users have given a mark of 0 on the scale, ie, no level of effort. And only one user reported having a degree of effort extremely lightweight.

Fig. 5. Examples of users during the task "Extinguish Fire"

5   Discussion

Since the users did not have prior experience with the researched product or similar, the intuitive use was perceive through the main task efficiency and the specialist observations of difficulties imposed by the product to lay users.

From the first trial, it was observed that all users were able to complete the task "extinguish fire", but most users triggered the extinguisher many times, an action not indicated by specialists. It is possible to perceive that non-expert users do not position themselves correctly towards the fire, positioning too closely and with arched posture. The positioning can be prejudicial if the flames are too high, which was not the experiment's case because the flame was controlled. It was also notice that most users did not carry the portable fire extinguisher in a proper manner; the product must be carried on a vertical positioning with only one hand at the body's side, and users tend to transport the product horizontally, with both hands. That observation may be related to the product's weight. The "seal breaking" sub-task was perform wrongly by all users, indicating a review of that attribute on the portable fire extinguisher. Most of the users checked the product's label before the choice for, at least, five seconds, evidencing the importance of a clear and self-explicative label to provide a proper product selection. The results on discomfort's perception in the hands and upper body members pointed there is a higher incidence of pains on the palm region and difficulty on breaking the extinguisher's seal. There is also occurrence of user's difficulty on pushing the valve trigger quickly.

With respect the perception of discomfort, there was a significant report by users in relation to palmar region during the task and the manipulation of the seal. There were no significant perceptions of effort by users, unless two people diagnosed with a light degree of effort performing the task.

Has been stated that the learnability analysis will be further presented on a specific study, however, it's been considered important to already present some results found, in a synthetic way. It was observe a strong performance difference between the tests with and without instructions. Without use indications, users did not read the labels to search the proper proceedings, performing the tasks intuitively, and, sometimes, wrongly. On the proper extinguisher's selection, was observe the need of better strategies to distinguish extinguisher's types, since the choice process is fast and lack of attention. The instructional video efficacy was evidence by the change of user's behavior between the two test rounds. The tasks "transporting the extinguisher" and "positioning towards the fire" were perform correctly after the video presentation.

6   Conclusions

The research had the goal to explore many perspectives addressed to portable fire extinguisher use. Since this product is required on emergency context, the study had to simulate different variables to allow the user to feel in a stressed context, approaching the actual context of product's use. The researchers faced several difficulties to simulate the emergency context, such as proper environment to execute experiments with fire, recruiting volunteers willing to participate stressful and physical activities, and collect solid background references to base the study.

From the experiment, is possible to identify that most users, although reached effectiveness, presented some kind of difficulty to perform the task without instruction. The main difficulties involved the positioning towards the flame, the seal breaking moment and the seal breaking itself, the product's transporting and the valve triggering. That indicates gaps to be studied more extensively, maybe through the label improvement or better product's shape design.

This study also show us that is required a deeper research to verify if only the label adjustment is enough for the user to perform proper use, or if it's necessary to be made larger changes in the product's design. We suggest for future works researches on developing a Brazilian technical standard for portable fire extinguishers' labels, and further study about the ergonomic aspects that influence activity with manual trigger, taking into account the ergonomics of the palm region and the upper body.

References

1. Rossi, L.A., Barruffini, R.C.P., Garcia, T.R., Chianca, T.C.M.: Queimaduras: características dos casos tratados em um Hospital Escola em Ribeirão Preto (SP). Revista Panamericana de Salud Pública 4(6), 401–404 (1998)
2. Tullis, T., Albert, B.: Measuring the User Experience: collecting, analyzing, and presenting usability metrics. Morgan Kaufmann, San Francisco (2008)
3. Moura, R.A., Banzato, J.M.: Embalagem, Unitização e Conteinerização, 2nd edn. Imam, São Paulo (1997)
4. Klohn, S.C., Pereira, P.Z.: Análise de compreensibilidade de pictogramas em embalagens de produtos perigosos. In: Proceedings of the "12° Congresso Internacional de Ergonomia e Usabilidade de Interfaces Humano-Tecnologia: Produto, Informações, Ambiente Construído e Transporte", Natal-RN, Brazil, August 12-16 (2012)
5. ABNT NBR 12693:2010 Associação Brasileira de Normas Técnicas - Sistemas de Proteção por Extintores de Incêndio (2010)
6. ABNT NBR 15808:2010 Associação Brasileira de Normas Técnicas - Extintores de Incêndio Portáteis (2010)
7. Naumann, A.B., Hurtienne, J., Israel, J.H., Mohs, C., Kindsmüller, M.C., Meyer, H.A., Hußlein, S.: Intuitive use of user interfaces: defining a vague concept. In: Harris, D. (ed.) Engin. Psychol. and Cog. Ergonomics, HCII 2007. LNCS (LNAI), vol. 4562, pp. 128–136. Springer, Heidelberg (2007)
8. Hurtienne, J.: Image schemas and Design for intuitive use. Exploring new guidance for user interface design. Tese (Doutorado em Engenharia) - Technische Universität Berlin, Germany (2011)
9. Blackler, A., Popovic, V., Mahar, D.: Investigating users' intuitive interaction with complex artefacts. Applied Ergonomics 41, 72–92 (2010)
10. Klein, G.A.: Naturalistic decision making. Human Factors – The Journal of the Human Factors and Ergonomics Society 50(3), 456–460 (2008)
11. International Organization for Standardization - ISO 9241-11:1998, Ergonomic Requirements for Office Work with Visual Display Terminals (vdts) - part 11: Guidance on usability (1998)

12. Krippendorff, K.: The Semantic Turn: A new foundation for Design. Taylor&Francis, Boca Raton (2006)
13. ABERGO. Consent Form Free and Clarification (2012),
    http://www.abergo.org.br/ (accessed on November 8, 2012)
14. Corlett, E.N., Manenica, I.: The effects and Measurement of Working Postures. Applied Ergonomics 11(1), 7–16 (1980)
15. Kadefors, R., Areskoug, A., Dahlman, S., Kilbom, A., Sperling, L., Wikström, L., Öster, J.: An approach to ergonomics evaluation of hand tools. Applied Ergonomics 24(3), 203–211 (1993)
16. Ligeiro, J.: Ferramentas de avaliação ergonômica em atividades multifuncionais: a contribuição da ergonomia para o design de ambientes de trabalho. Dissertação apresentada ao programa de Pós-graduação em Design da Universidade Estadual Paulista Julio de Mesquita Filho, Bauru, Unesp (2010)

Adaptive User-Centered Design for Safety and Comfort of Physical Human Nursing – Care Robot Interaction

Minghui Sun[1,2], Hiromichi Nakashima[2], Shinya Hirano[2], Kazuya Matsuo[2], Ming Ding[2], Chang'an Jiang[2], Toshiharu Mukai[2], and Guihe Qin[1]

[1] College of Computer Science and Technology, Jilin University,
Changchun, 130012, China
[2] RIKEN RTC, 2271-130, Nagoya, 463-0003, Japan
sunmh.cn@gmail.com

Abstract. Nowadays serving robots are more and more popular in human society. However, most of them are designed for the special people or for the special scenario. There is little robot designed to apply appropriate interface for different people that can accommodate age-related and body-related in physical interaction. We propose that user-centered design should be used in physical Human-robot interaction. In this research, we take a nursing-care robot as an example. Based on the results of the experiment, we proved that the distance between two arms of nursing-care robot, which affected the comfort and safety of patient, should be applied by different patients with different body length. We try to build the adaptive human robot interface based on the physical properties of people, such as body length. This study is an attempt to explore the adaptive human robot interaction and contributes to giving insights and implications for the future design of general serving robot.

Keywords: Physical human robot interaction, nursing-care robot, safe transferring.

1 Introduction

With the advent of an aging society, robots are popular in human society and expected to assist the human being. Many researchers explored the physical human robot interaction (PHRI) in many areas, for example, industry, medical, welfare, dancing, music, homework assistance, nursing support and so on. For example, Partner Ballroom Dance Robot (PBDR) [1] can predict the steps of the partner based on body movement and react on wheels. CB² [2] is used for safe operation and behavior learning and try to understand the human developmental process of cognitive functions through mutual feedback. Robovie-IV [3] was designed to "socially" interact with people in daily lives. However, most of these robots are designed for the special people or for the special scenario. There is little research has been targeted at adaptive user-centered design for ordinary people in public environment. Sekmen and Challa [4] built an HRI system and predicted the behaviors and preferences of the people with a Bayesian learning method. In this research, adaptive user-centered interface is explored by natural properties of the human being.

V.G. Duffy (Ed.): DHM/HCII 2013, Part I, LNCS 8025, pp. 365–372, 2013.
© Springer-Verlag Berlin Heidelberg 2013

Human being has two properties in the nature. They are physical property and social property. Physical properties include body length, thigh length, shank length, arm length, body weight, disability, and waist strength and so on. Social properties include career and aging and so on. User-centered design should be used to implement the physical Human-robot interaction (PHRI). Many PHRI happens in hospital. For example, doctor can lead a robot to a room hand by hand and then robot can lift and move the patient from one place to the other. Robot also can guide the patients' friends to the place where the patient is. During PHRI, both social and physical communications occur. Robot must adapt the interaction, such as leading, following, or lifting, based on the social properties of people, such as patient, doctor and patient's friend. At the meantime, according to the physical properties (aging, body height, body weight) of patient, different communication strategies should be applied while lifting and moving a patient. For example, when lifting an infant (shown in Figure 1a), we must hold her/his neck carefully because infant's neck is very weak. For an adult, princess lifting motion is often used (shown in Figure 1b). Moreover, robot should adjust the distance between two arms based on the different patients.

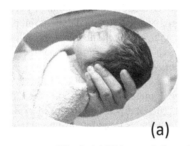 

Fig. 1. (a) lifting an infant; (b) lifting an adult

In this research, we take a nursing-care robot as an example. In RIKEN-TRI Human-Interactive Robot Research Center, we have developed a nursing-care robot named RIBA (Robot for Interactive Body Assistance) [5-8]. The entire body of RIBA (shown in Figure 2a) is covered with soft protected material. The main task of RIBA is to lift a patient from the bed and transfer her to the chair. By now, it can successfully and comfortable lift and transfer the patient whose maximum weight is 63 kg. The lifting motion (shown in Figure 2b) was designed by the results of [9]. However, like the most robots in the lab environment, the lifting motion is just considered for the special patient and hard to dynamically adjust its motion by different patients. Therefore, RIBA is a good example of adaptive physical human robot interaction based on the physical and social properties of people. In this paper, we try to let the robot detect the physical properties of patient, use the information to modify the interface or motion dynamically and finally improve the PHRI.

This paper introduced the nursing-care robot and the motivation of this research firstly. Then in section 2, a pilot study was designed to explore the relationship between different positions of RIBA arm and patient's comfort and safety. Section 3 is a presentation of equations how to calculate the most suitable positions of RIBA arms.

Section 4 is a description of the proposed system and methods. Finally we conclude with a discussion of our results, implications for adaptive human robot interaction and directions for future work.

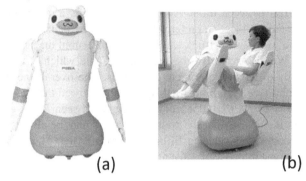

(a)   (b)

Fig. 2. (a) RIBA; (b) lifting motion

2   Pilot Study

Comfort and safety of patient are the most important factors during lifting and transferring. The objective of this experiment is to investigate the relationship between different positions of RIBA arms and patient's comfort and safety. We used two hard covers with four supporting sticks to simulate the RIBA arms (as shown in Figure 3). At the root of supporting stick, force sensor was mounted to measure the supporting force. The independent variable was the height between two arms (2, 8, 13, 18 cm). The distance between two hard covers was fixed and the number of the distance was 53cm. Therefore, inclination angle, which is the angle between the link of centers of two arms and horizontal direction, is 2.16, 8.58, 13.78, 18.76 degrees.

Fig. 3. Experiment setup

Six male volunteers participated in the experiment. All were not patient and in good health condition. Before the experiment, the task was explained to the participants. They needed to adjust their postures until they felt comfortable and painless and then they were asked to keep that posture for five seconds. Participants were allowed to have a rest between trails. After the experiment, a questionnaire should be completed to rate their subjective preferences by the participants.

To evaluate the workload of trunk and thigh, we measured the supporting forces on two hardcovers. We also recorded the waist joint angle which is the angle between trunk and thigh by different experiment conditions. The overall mean of waist joint angle is 116 degrees (see Figure 4). An ANOVA test showed that there was no significant effect ($F_{3, 15} = 2.679$, $p > 0.05$) from the height between RIBA two arms on the waist joint angle. It suggests that the waist joint angle may be always the same when user feels most comfortable during lifting and transferring. Harrison etc. [10] also explored the relationship between waist angle and user workload in sitting posture. He got the conclusion that user had the lowest dis pressures and lowest electromyography recordings from spinal muscles when the waist joint angle is around 110 to 130 degrees.

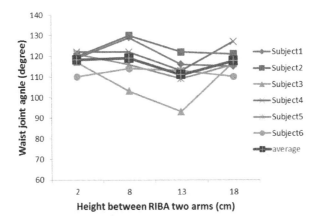

Fig. 4. Waist joint angle by different heights between RIBA arms

According to the results of the questionnaire, the majority of participants (5/6) preferred the setup in which height between RIBA two arms was 13cm. They reported that "feel comfortable with that posture likes sitting on a chair" and "compared with other conditions, the muscle of necklace is not tight and tired". Results also showed that the main effect of the height between RIBA two arms was statistically significant ($p < 0.01$) on forces of four supporting sticks. With the increase of height between RIBA two arms, the workload of trunk decreased while the one of thigh increased.

In summary, the results of pilot study and reference suggest that when waist joint angle is about 116 degrees, the inclination angle is about 13.78 degrees and lifting posture is similar to the sitting posture, user feels most safe and comfortable.

3   Setup of RIBA's Arms

Generally, the motion and trajectory of robot are set in advance. The final target of lifting robot is that, based on different subjects, custom motion and trajectory of robot can be generated dynamically. In this research, to achieve safe and comfort lifting, it is important to setup the positions of RIBA's arms.   Therefore, we analyze the relationship between several parameters of patient and RIBA. As shown in Figure 3, point A is the center of contact area between thigh and right arm of RIBA, point B is the center of contact area between trunk and left arm of RIBA, point C stands for the waist joint position, point D is the point of a horizontal line passing through A and a vertical line passing through B. *length* is the length between two contact points. *height* is the height between RIBA two arms. *distance* is the vertical distance between two contact points. *thigh* is the length between A and C and the value of thigh is approximated as half-length of patient's thigh. *trunk* is the length between B and C and the value of *trunk* is approximated as half-length of patient's trunk. In the triangle ACB, the angle between *thigh* and *trunk* is the waist joint angle. Therefore, we get this equation in the following:

$$length = \sqrt[2]{thigh^2 + trunk^2 - 2 \times thigh \times trunk \times \cos(waist)} \qquad (1)$$

In the triangle ABD, the angle between *length* and *distance* is the inclination angle. And we get these equations in the following:

$$height = \cos(inclination) \times length$$

$$= \cos(inclination) \times \sqrt[2]{thigh^2 + trunk^2 - 2 \times thigh \times trunk \times \cos(waist)}$$

$$distance = \sin(inclination) \times length$$

$$= \sin(inclination) \times \sqrt[2]{thigh^2 + trunk^2 - 2 \times thigh \times trunk \times \cos(waist)}$$

In order to life a patient stably and comfortably, *height* and *distance* are the most important input parameters of RIBA. As we proved in Section 2, when the inclination angle is 13.78 degrees and waist joint angle is around 116 degrees, patient felt most comfortable. Therefore, in equations (2) and (3), if we know the length of thigh and trunk and then RIBA can adjust the suitable arms' positions by different patients.

4   System and Methods

Human behavior analysis [12-14] has been a long focus of interest on computer vision and machine learning areas. Most of researchers used motion capture device and laser scanners to analyze the depth maps from the real world. However, these devices are very expensive and hard to be mounted on the robot. Kinect, which is a low-cost device, uses a light technique [11] to generate depth map which is made of discrete point cloud. It is a motion sensing input device [15] developed by Microsoft that enables users to naturally interact with games and other programs without the need to physically touch a game controller or object of any kind. It achieves this through a natural user interface by tracking the user's body movement and by using gestures and spoken commands. Although Microsoft Kinect can estimate different poses and detect 3D positions of body parts, it just can recognize the people skeleton in sitting and standing posture. PCL [16] is an open source and we can use this source to grab the point cloud in the real time. By considering for the task of lifting a patient from bed, our target is to recognize the patient position, the lengths of thigh and trunk. In the following, we propose an approach to achieve this target by PCL and other algorithms.

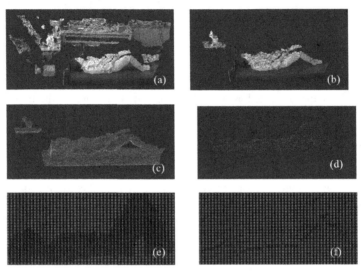

Fig. 5. Graphical illustration of the process. (a) pass filter in Y direction(a) pass filter in Z direction (c) voxel grid down sampling (d) segmented body (e) organized point cloud (f) after thinning method.

Firstly, pass filter was used to reduce the number of points in Y and Z directions (see Figure 5a, 5b). In order to do the down sampling, 3D voxel grid filter was applied and the leaf size was 1cm (see Figure 5c). Then we tried to detect the plane which was the bed plane from the rest point cloud, the patient must lie on that bed and finally we can find the patient. Similar like the way to detect the objects on the table [17], random sample consensus algorithm was used to detect the plane and the area of bed is recognized. And then, all the points above the bed from 1cm to 50cm were extracted. Finally, clustering algorithm was used to get the biggest cluster point set which was the segmentation of patient body (see Figure 5d). The patient point cloud was then transferred from 3D to 2D and we used the distance information to organize the 2D point cloud into binary array. "1" means the points belonging to the patient are in this area, "0" means the points belonging to the patient are not in this area (see Figure 5e). Simple thinning method in which calculates the center of column array was used to find the skeleton of patient (see Figure 5f). On the next step, linear least squares regression is used to model the three lines which stand for the trunk, thigh and shank. The joints of them are the knee position and waist position. Then, we can get the length of trunk and thigh.

5   Conclusion and Future Works

The concept of adaptive user-center interface for safe and comfort in PHRI was proposed. The robot can dynamically adjust its motion and trajectory based on the social and physical properties of user. In this paper, we took a nursing-care robot RIBA as an example and explored what and how the physical properties of patient affected the setup of RIBA's arms. The results of experiment showed the waist joint angle may be always the same when user feels most comfortable during lifting and transferring. After analyzing the equations between the parameters of RIBA and patient, we found that the setup of RIBA's arms should be changed by the different length of trunk and thigh of patient. Finally a method with Kinect of detecting trunk and thigh was proposed. This paper is an attempt to explore the adaptive human robot interaction and contributes to provide a more complete vocabulary in this direction that adaptive interface researcher of human robot interaction can leverage.

In the future, we plan to further investigate how incorporate the physical and social properties of people in interaction between human and robot. We are also interested in the methods how to detect the properties of people.

References

1. Aucouturier, J.J., Ikeuchi, K., Hirukawa, H., Nakaoka, S., Shiratori, T., Kudoh, S., Kanehiro, F., Ogata, T., Kozima, H., Okuno, H.G., Michalowski, M.P., Ogai, Y., Ikegami, T., Kosuge, K., Takeda, T., Hirata, Y.: Cheek to chip: dancing robots and AI's future. IEEE Intelligent Systems 23(2) (2008)
2. Minato, T., Yoshikawa, Y., Noda, T., Ikemoto, S., Ishiguro, H., Asada, M.: CB2: a child robot with biomimetic body for cognitive developmental robotics. In: Proceedings of the IEEE/RSJ International Conference on Intelligent Robots and Systems, IROS 2007 (2007)
3. Mitsunaga, N., Miyashita, T., Ishiguro, H., Kogure, K., Hagita, N.: Robovie-IV: a communication robot interacting with people daily in an office. In: Proceedings of the IEEE/RSJ International Conference on Intelligent Robots and Systems, IROS 2006 (2006)
4. Sekmen, A., Challa, P.: Assessment of Adaptive Human-Robot Interactions. Knowledge-Based Systems 42, 49–59 (2013)
5. Mukai, T., Hirano, S., Nakashima, H., Sakaida, Y., Guo, S.: Realization and Safety Measures of Patient Transfer by Nursing-Care Assistant Robot RIBA with Tactile Sensors. Journal of Robotics and Mechatronics 77(782), 116–124 (2011)
6. Mukai, T., Hirano, S., Nakashima, H., Kato, Y., Sakaida, Y., Guo, S., Hosoe, S.: Development of a Nursing-Care Assistant Robot RIBA That Can Lift a Human in Its Arms. In: 2010 IEEE/RSJ International Conference on Intelligent Robots and Systems, IROS 2010, pp. 5996–6001 (2010)
7. Mukai, T., Hirano, S., Yoshida, M., Nakashima, H., Guo, S., Hayakawa, Y.: Tactile-Based Motion Adjustment for the Nursing-Care Assistant Robot RIBA. In: 2011 IEEE International Conference on Robotics and Automation, ICRA 2011, pp. 5435–5441 (2011)
8. Mukai, T., Hirano, S., Yoshida, M., Nakashima, H., Guo, S., Hayakawa, Y.: Whole-Body Contact Manipulation Using Tactile Information for the Nursing-Care Assistant Robot RIBA. In: 2011 IEEE/RSJ International Conference on Intelligent Robots and Systems, IROS 2011, pp. 2445–2451 (2011)

9. Sakaida, Y., Masuda, H., Chugo, D., Ikeura, R.: Transfer Motion Analysis for Motion Planning of Care Giver Robot. In: ICROS-SICE International Joint Conference 2009, August 18-21, pp. 1650–1653 (2009)

10. Harrison, D., Harrison, S., Croft, A.: Sitting biomechanics, part-1: Review of the literature. J. Manipulative Physiol. Ther. 22(9), 594–609 (1999)

11. Freedman, B., Shpunt, A., Machline, M., Arieli, Y.: Depth mapping using projected patterns. Patent Application 10 (2008); WO 2008/120217 A2

12. Rodgers, J., Anguelov, D., Pang, H.-C., Koller, D.: Object pose detection in range scan data. In: Proc. of IEEE Conf. on Computer Vision and Pattern Recognition (CVPR) (2006)

13. Yang, H., Lee, S.W.: Reconstruction of 3D human body pose from stereo image sequences based on top-down learning. Pattern Recognition 40(11), 3120–3131 (2007)

14. Schwartz, W., Kembhavi, A., Harwood, D., Davis, L.: Human detection using partial least squares analysis. In: ICCV (2009)

15. Shotton, J., Fitzgibbon, A., Cook, M., Sharp, T., Finocchio, M., Moore, R., Kipman, A., Blake, A.: Real-Time Human Pose Recognition in Parts from Single Depth Images. In: CVPR (2011)

16. Point cloud library (pcl), http://pointclouds.org/

17. Rusu, R.B.: Semantic 3D Object Maps for Everyday Manipulation in Human Living Environments, PhD Thesis (2009)

Investigation of an Agent-Based Modeling on Crowd Evacuation and Its Application to Real Buildings

Fujio Yamamoto

Department of Information and Computer Sciences, Kanagawa Institute of Technology,
1030 Shimo-ogino, Atsugi-shi, Kanagawa, 243-0292 Japan
yamamoto@ic.kanagawa-it.ac.jp

Abstract. An agent-based modeling and the simulator for evacuation from multistory buildings at the time of outbreak of an earthquake and the fire are presented. The basic theory is that individual agents move in each floor and stair, unless it is filled to capacity per unit area. The simulator can reflect the situation when some destruction occurred in a passage and the stairs in the middle of refuge, because the capacity can be changed dynamically every place. Each agent moves in principle based on local information around oneself. However, as for the cases that the inside of stairs has been clogged up, wide area information equivalent to the broadcast in the hall is conveyed to agents after pre-determined time. Comparative study with the real measurement and simulation was carried out about the refuge time of the fire drill that was performed in a university building of 12 stories.

Keywords: Multi-Agent Systems, Crowd Evacuation, Behavioral Modeling.

1 Introduction

To perform evacuation smoothly when a fire or an earthquake attacked it, both construction of refuge model and the simulation are indispensable. In many cases, it is difficult to determine the most suitable refuge method and the procedure beforehand because they depend on the kind of the disaster or the situation of the place. However, useful information to help real refuge will be provided if such simulations are performed under various assumptions. In addition, knowledge to be provided by simulation can be utilized for a design of new buildings and institutions in future.

A lot of studies on such modeling and simulation were performed so far. Adopted techniques are various likewise. For example, in the case of a train fire [1], in the case of fire of the high-rise building [2], in the case of a fire of indoor stadium [3], and in the case of the earthquake [4], many studies of simulation on evacuation were performed. In addition, there are simulations based on several scenarios considering human psychological condition and group action at the time of the refuge [5,6,7]. The literature [8] presented the simulation for high-rise building designs in consideration of refuge. The comparison of simulation techniques is shown in documents [9] [10].

V.G. Duffy (Ed.): DHM/HCII 2013, Part I, LNCS 8025, pp. 373–382, 2013.
© Springer-Verlag Berlin Heidelberg 2013

Particularly, the literature [10] performs a survey on many related studies in detail. Among a variety of modeling technique, it is said that technique based on the multi agent is suitable for such a refuge modeling in particular [11]. However, the study of modeling to adapt to each building is still insufficient, due to the variety of characteristics of people there and of structures of the building including stairs, corridors and exits. Also, most studies in the past did not compare the simulation results with the data obtained from real refuge.

We made an agent-oriented general-purpose refuge model and tried to apply it to a real building. A way of thinking and the summary of the modeling are shown in the literature [12]. The first good point of our model is that every grid cell of stairs and the corridor can dynamically set the capacity that can contain refugee agents. The movement principle of an agent is simple. It facilitates an application to the structure of a variety of stairs and corridors. We developed a simulator based on this modeling, and we applied it to the evacuation of the buildings of our university. By the comparison to the actual evacuation drill that a large number of students participated in, usefulness and the problems of this simulator were evaluated.

2   Outlines of Modeling and the Simulation

2.1   Agent-Based Modeling for Crowd Evacuation

The summary of refuge modeling and the simulation used here was shown in the literature [12]. The main points are as follows:

High-rise buildings of universities or institutes where many people (about several thousand persons) exist in were targeted for this study. Those buildings are assumed to have laboratories, meeting rooms, lecture rooms, dining rooms, and so on. Most people there are assumed to know the internal structure of the buildings well. At the time of the refuge, elevators are not usable, and they escape from the building by using only plural stairs (the capacities of each stairs are different).

The modeling depends on multi agent technique. Evacuees, emergency services, and unit area of floors and stairs (patches) become agents respectively. Every each floor can set the existing number of people as a parameter. At the initial stage, each person leaves for the stairs of the place that is the nearest to oneself except a specific floor. However, after a refuge start, when agents understood that another stairs of the same floor is not crowded, they can change their target to that stairs. Also the simulator can assign specific usable stairs to evacuees of each floor.

In the middle of refuge, some kind of disorders may occur in stairs and a corridor. The passage capacity at any place can be changed dynamically to reflect it. When refugees who entered the stairs cannot move at all for a long time, such situation is conveyed to evacuees as global information, like the communications using broadcast in the hall or using the cell-phone. Each agent who received such global information can leave for another stair of nearest floor.

2.2 Movement of Agents

In a corridor or stairs, people move to their neighboring cell unless the capacity (maximum allowable number of persons) per unit area is exceeded. Otherwise, they must remain there. The speed to walk a corridor and the stairs can be set as a parameter. The default speed is set to an actual value when a person walked when stairs and a corridor are not congested at all. The default speed is set to an actual speed when a person walked in the case that stairs and a corridor are not congested at all. Due to this movement principle, a rescue crew can climb up to the target floor against the flow that a large number of people evacuate to. This is because rescue services also move according to the rule of the passage capacity mentioned above.

Fig. 1 illustrates the principle of movement mentioned above. Small grids divide stairs and the corridor. $F(C_{ij})$ denotes the maximum allowable number of people in the cell C_{ij}. About the C_{ij}, the set of the agents, which are going to move to an adjacent different cell, is $P_{exit}(C_{ij})$, and reversely the set of the agents, which are going to enter this cell, is $P_{enter}(C_{ij})$. On the other hand, the set of agents remaining in the cell C_{ij} is $P_{remain}(C_{ij})$. This figure illustrates that whether or not an agent can move to other cell is determined by $F(C_{ij})$.

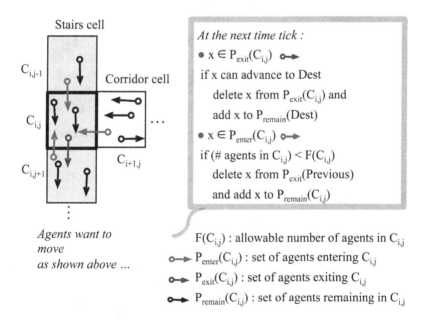

Fig. 1. Method for Agent Movement

3 Applications to University Buildings

3.1 Internal Structure of the Building

The evacuation simulation mentioned above is compared with the data provided in a real evacuation drill, so that in the first the structure of the building is shown in Fig. 2.

It is a 12-story building, in which there are laboratories, lecture rooms and an office on each floor. Usually there exist 300 to 1,800 students and staff. The existence number of people considerably changes depending whether it is an authorized class period or not. Although there are five elevators (including one for emergency), at the time of the refuge of the disaster, they are not used and two flights of stairs (north and south) are usable instead. The width of south stairs is slightly wider than north stairs. Going down the stairs, we reach the first floor, which has two exits. When a large number of people evacuate all at once, stairs and corridors may be clogged up, but also the exit of the first floor may become a bottleneck.

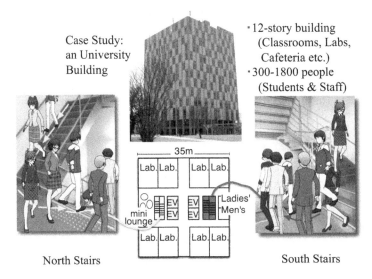

Fig. 2. Internal Structure of the Target Building

3.2   Measurement of an Evacuation Drill

At the time of a real disaster, it is difficult to measure time required for many people evacuating from a building. However, usually most universities carry out evacuation drill at least once a year. That is a good opportunity to measure real evacuation time and related data. Therefore appliances shown in Fig. 3 were prepared. First of all it is necessary to count how many people finally evacuated from a building. Both automatic counters and hand-operated counters were prepared. Using them, measurement was done in two places of exits of the lobby of the first floor. More importantly, we made a plan to record the time at which persons who were appointed as monitor passed through each floor during evacuation. Therefore, NFC (Near Field Communication) tags in which floor information was written were put on the wall of the entrance of each stair. Stairs information and the time are recorded by touching these tags at Android terminal when a monitor refugee passes through that place.

The collection method of the passage time for each stair using the NFC tag is shown in Fig. 4. In the Android terminal, which the monitor refugee has, an application program to read an NFC tag message (the floor number) and to record the time is available. In addition, the application transmits those data to Google Fusion Tables so that all data can be summarized later. The graph of the figure shows the records of five students who went down the north stairs. They were in the eighth floor, the ninth floor, and the tenth floor, and they began evacuation at different time each other. There is a record of five similar students about the south stairs, although it is not included in the figure. Although the refugees were several hundred altogether this time, the detailed action record of these ten refugees, was a valuable record as explained in the following.

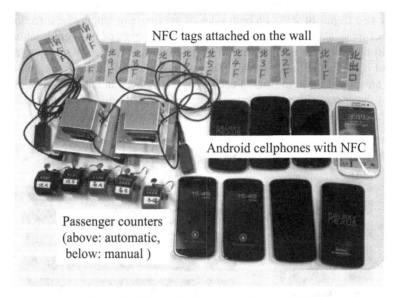

Fig. 3. Appliances for Evacuation Measurement

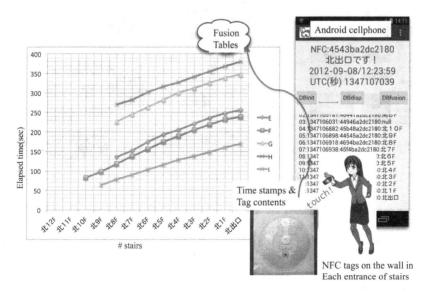

Fig. 4. Evacuation Time Recording Application

3.3   Execution of the Simulation

The typical screenshot of the refuge simulator that we developed is shown in Fig. 5. The back figure shows the situation of simulation of start time, and the front figure shows the later situation. With sliders put on the left side of the screen of the simulator, the setting of various parameters is possible. For example, existing number of people, the capacity of each floor and stairs, and also walking speed are included. There are two flights of stairs on both sides of the figure in lengthwise direction. The capacity of those stairs is set separately. In the upper part of the figure, the elapsed time from the start, the arrival time to be required to emergency services, and the number of holdovers in the building is displayed respectively. In addition, in the right side, the number of the holdovers of each floor is displayed in real time. The enlarged picture of the specific place is shown in the central small window. With this, we can observe current congestion degree near a specific entrance of stairs.

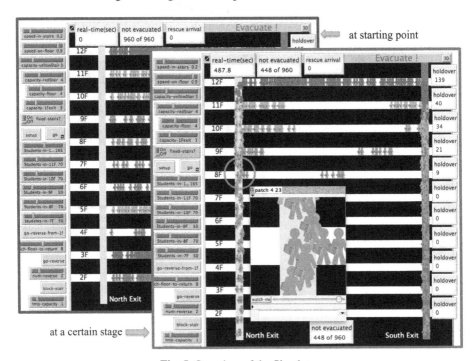

Fig. 5. Overview of the Simulator

On the other hand, Fig.6 explains other functions of this simulator. Fig.6 (1) shows the case that stairs were blocked up. In this example, the right-side stairs were damaged at the eighth floor approximately 460 seconds after a refuge start and was not able to pass. These stairs were blocked out for a while, but information on this situation was conveyed to evacuees in a manner like broadcasting in the hall after pre-determined time. By this information, the evacuees who were shut in stairs are shown to have left for another stairs of nearest floor.

Fig. 6 (2) shows such situation that one rescue crew climbs from the first floor to the eighth floor. Because a large number of evacuees go down, it is not easy for him to climb the stairs against the flow. However, according to "the movement principle of the agent" that is explained in the section 2.2, emergency services can enter the cell at the moment when the existence number of people in that cell decreases lower than the allowable number. This example illustrates such situation that a rescue crew arrives at the eighth floor somehow and then moves to the central place on the eighth floor. Two functions shown above supported a possible phenomenon by real refuge. Namely these contribute to make this simulator practical.

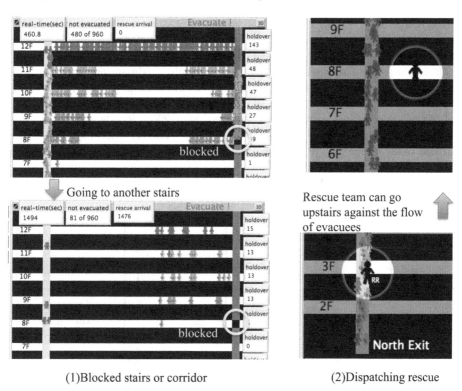

(1)Blocked stairs or corridor   (2)Dispatching rescue

Fig. 6. Additional Features of the Simulator

4   Comparisons between Simulation Result and Measurement

In this chapter, an actual value and the simulation result in the time required for the refuge from the building for university described in Chapter 3 are compared. Table 1 shows three cases, namely "No classes", "Typical case" and "Maximal case". The number of people existing in each floor from the first floor to the twelfth floor is displayed. This figure shows simulation results about the time required for overall refuge. And in addition, actual measurement result is shown about some cases.

The first case "No Classes" denotes the evacuation drill shown in Section 2.2. The normal class was not carried out on that day, and the guidance of the new school term was carried out instead. The total number of evacuees was 396 and it took 510 seconds (observed time) to finish refuge at all. With this case, a traffic jam was hardly caused in the stairs, mainly because the number of evacuees was fewer than usual. The simulation result was from 426 seconds to 547 seconds, this variation depends on the setting of parameters. With this case, it can be said that the simulation result and the actual measurement were almost equal.

The second case "Typical Case" is a typical example of the normal class period. Total number of evacuees was set as 960 people. There was not actual measurement of the refuge time, but the result of the simulation was from 920 seconds to 1,150 seconds. Judging from the result of "No classes", this simulation result would be near the observed value if measurement were performed.

In the third case "Maximal case", the approximately maximum number of people that could exist in this building was set. Total number of refugees was 1,810. About this case, at the time of the design of this building, it was estimated by a simple calculation that refuge would be completed in 1,200 seconds. However, the simulation result was from 1,684 seconds to 2,141 seconds. When they review an estimate of the refuge time from this building, these results will serve as a reference.

Table 1. Observed and Predicted Evacuation Time

No classes

	People
12F	130
11F	10
10F	10
9F	10
8F	70
7F	60
6F	10
5F	0
4F	0
3F	0
2F	110
EXIT	10
Total Exited	420
Observed Evacuees	396

Typical case

	People
12F	165
11F	70
10F	70
9F	50
8F	70
7F	50
6F	50
5F	85
4F	45
3F	135
2F	160
EXIT	10
Total Exited	960
Observed Evacuees	-

Maximal case

	People
12F	300
11F	100
10F	100
9F	100
8F	100
7F	100
6F	200
5F	200
4F	100
3F	200
2F	300
EXIT	10
Total Exited	1810
Observed Evacuees	-

Evaluation of Overall Evacuation Time

Evacuation Time (sec)

Observed	510
	426
Predicted	~547

Evacuation Time (sec)

Observed	-
	920
Predicted	~1150

Evacuation Time (sec)

Designed*	1200
	1684
Predicted	~2141

*expected value at the construction of the building

5   Conclusion

In this study, multi agent-based refuge modeling and the simulator based on it were developed. These were applied to the evacuation of a high-rise building of a real university where there were a large number of students. The simulator estimated the time required for all people to evacuate and the time required for emergency services to arrive at the target floor. In addition, other useful data such as the influence when stairs and floors were blockaded by some collapse was also provided.

About the refuge completion time, the comparison between actual observed value and the simulation results was examined. As a result, when there were relatively few refugees, it is confirmed that simulation fits well the real measurement. In the case of a large number of refugees, it was understood that real evacuation time would be longer than the value calculated by a more simple method at the time of a building design.

If these analyzed simulation results are told to general persons beforehand, dangerous panic at evacuation can be avoided. Furthermore, it can be utilized for the design of stairs and the exit in new buildings that will be constructed in future.

Acknowledgement. This work was supported by the Ministry of Education, Culture, Sports, Science and Technology Grant-in-Aid for Scientific Research (C) 23501176.

References

1. Zarboutis, N., Marmaras, N.: Design of formative evacuation plans using agent-based simulation. Safety Science 45(9), 920–940 (2007)
2. Ren, C., Yang, C., Jin, S.: Agent-Based Modeling and Simulation on Emergency Evacuation. In: Zhou, J. (ed.) Complex 2009. LNICST, vol. 5, pp. 1451–1461. Springer, Heidelberg (2009)
3. Shi, J., et al.: Agent-based evacuation model of large public buildings under fire conditions. Automation in Construction 18(3), 338–347 (2009)
4. Hori, M., et al.: Study on developing simulation method for prediction of evacuation processes after earthquake. Sociotechnica. 3, 138–145 (2005)
5. Sharma, S.: AvatarSim: A multi-agent system for emergency evacuation simulation. Journal of Computational Methods in Science and Engineering 9(suppl. 1), 13–22 (2009)
6. Pan, X., et al.: A multi-agent based framework for the simulation of human and social behaviors during emergency evacuations. Computer Science 22(2), 113–132 (2007)
7. Chen, X., Zhan, F.B.: Agent-based modeling and simulation of urban evacuation: relative effectiveness of simultaneous and staged evacuation strategies. Journal of the Operational Research Society 59(1), 25–33 (2008)
8. Pelechano, N., Malkawi, A.: Evacuation simulation models: Challenges in modeling high rise building evacuation with cellular automata approaches. Automation in Construction 17(4), 377–385 (2008)

9. Zheng, X., et al.: Modeling crowd evacuation of a building based on seven methodological approaches. Building and Environment 44(3), 437–445 (2009)
10. Kuligowski, E.D., Peacock, R.D.: A Review of Building Evacuation Models, National Institute of Standards and Technology Technical Note 1471, 156 pages (2005)
11. Ren, C., Yang, C., Jin, S.: Agent-based modeling and simulation on emergency evacuation. In: Zhou, J. (ed.) Complex 2009. LNICST, vol. 5, pp. 1451–1461. Springer, Heidelberg (2009)
12. Yamamoto, F.: Modeling and Simulation on Crowd Evacuation of a Building with Agent-Based Approaches. In: Proc. IADIS International Conference on Internet Technologies & Society, pp. 313–316 (2012)

Author Index